OPPOSITION TO LOUIS XIV

OPPOSITION TO

LOUIS XIV

THE POLITICAL
AND SOCIAL ORIGINS OF THE
FRENCH ENLIGHTENMENT

BY LIONEL ROTHKRUG

PRINCETON, NEW JERSEY

PRINCETON UNIVERSITY PRESS

1965

Publication of this book has been aided by the
Ford Foundation program to support publication,
through university presses, of works in the humani-
ties and social sciences.

Printed in the United States of America by
Princeton University Press
Princeton, New Jersey

FOR FRANÇOISE

PREFACE

THE PERSONAL government of Louis XIV, arising as
it did in 1661 out of the troubles of the *Fronde*, was
from the outset principally concerned with strengthening royal authority; it was in this spirit that Le
Tellier, Louvois, and Colbert set about to reorganize
the activities of the army, of commerce, and of industry. Their methods were entirely traditional; the
energy and thoroughness with which they carried
them out, however, did create the impression of
novelty. And, largely because of their strenuous efforts, the exercise of royal authority was extended
and made more effective. By 1683, when Colbert
passed from the scene, it appeared unlikely that the
monarchy could again be threatened by another
"time of troubles" like those following the deaths of
Henry IV and of Louis XIII.

Yet, if these first decades conclusively established
the supremacy of central government, the latter part
of the reign demonstrated both the limits of its authority and the weakness of its control. War and economic distress of course played their parts, but the
principal source of the crown's difficulties was its
own hesitancy in arriving at decisions. Problems con-
fronting government at this time were complex and
often difficult to understand. The administration
launched inquiries and, at the same time, sought
counsel from those whom it considered most competent; but the advice proved conflicting and soon public controversy grew up around matters which had

previously been of purely administrative concern. Officials, magistrates, merchants, bankers, lawyers, doctors, priests, bishops, generals—individuals from every articulate group in society, wrote their views and voiced their criticism of government in France. A powerful reform movement developed both within and without the administration.

The purpose of this study is to trace the origins of this movement, then to describe the facets of its character, and finally to consider its influence on state and society. Reformers most frequently argued about problems relating to trade, taxes, industry, finance, and agriculture. These issues were specific, and considerable space is devoted to describing the actual circumstances in which critics of Louis XIV's government wrote. In particular, we shall discuss such matters as tariffs, privateering, chartered trading companies, the effect of war on the social status, opinions, and political influence of merchants, and also the impact of war and depression, combined with unprecedented administrative growth, on rural France and ultimately on the whole of society. Ideas about state, commerce, and fiscality cannot be adequately treated, however, without first examining the wider intellectual currents with which they were intimately associated. Philosophic and religious concepts central to seventeenth century thought underlay many arguments used by reformers. Occasionally doctrines of political opposition proceeded directly from general explanations of God, man, and the universe. In this way the most abstract thoughts merged with mundane questions of duties, imposts, and cereal prices to add another dimension to economic and political controversies during the last quarter of the seventeenth century.

The intellectual backgrounds to the reform movement are intimately related to the development of

anti-mercantilist doctrines emerging in the late sixteenth and early seventeenth centuries. These views
appeared widely throughout western Europe. In
France, however, special circumstances caused anti-
mercantilist thought to become increasingly an expression of political opposition. Moreover, as dispute
about questions of trade and state grew more intense,
men began to elucidate and to extend the wide range
of implication which historically surrounded problems of political economy. By 1683 the stage was set
for the truly ideological conflicts which were to dis-
turb the second half of Louis XIV's reign. And a
principal concern of this study is to show how ideas
commonly associated with the French Enlightenment
were, in fact, widely accepted during the seventeenth
century precisely because they were then an essential
part of political dissent. Novel opinions about the
nature of man, society, and the world served as justification for criticism of government. Increasingly the
diffusion of new ideas was a mere concomitant to
resistance and to protest against royal policies. By
1700, a time when the triumph of reform seemed
imminent even to contemporaries, radical views in
religion and philosophy reached new peaks of popularity. Indeed, this date not only marks the start of
a perceptible decline of government in France, but
it also begins the period of systematic, public subversion of the fundamental values with which the
ancien régime was traditionally associated.

Part I of this work treats the disparate origins of
complaint; it discusses both the intellectual and material backgrounds to reform. Part II concerns the
appearance of mature ideology (1683-1700). Here
the fully developed reform movement is studied as
part of social change and general political decline on
one hand, and, on the other, as the result of profound
transformations affecting every area of society.

ACKNOWLEDGMENTS

FIRST written as a doctoral dissertation for the University of California at Berkeley, this book owes more than I can say to William J. Bouwsma who, giving so generously and unstintingly of his time, guided me throughout the years of graduate work. The treatise could never have been completed without his expert training and seemingly inexhaustible patience.

I am also profoundly obligated to Professor Jean Meuvret, of the *Ecole Pratique des Hautes Etudes*, who first introduced me to archival material. Monsieur Meuvret allowed me to profit from his enormous erudition in innumerable conversations over the span of several years. Needless to say, his generous and masterful aid proved invaluable on more occasions than it is possible to mention or even recall.

It is with deep gratitude that I thank John S. Bromley who, reading the manuscript in its earliest stage and under difficult circumstances, made a number of invaluable criticisms and suggestions.

To all of the people who guided me through bewildering mazes of manuscript depositories in several parts of France, I am deeply beholden. Particular acknowledgment, however, is due the staff of the *Minutier Central* at the National Archives in Paris. Madame Jurgens and Mademoiselle Fleury cheerfully provided assistance which went far beyond the bounds of professional duty. Above all it was Monsieur L.-H. Collard who, during the course of several months, patiently helped me to decipher the mysterious jargon and handwriting of seventeenth century notarial acts.

I also wish to thank especially several people in Nantes, Monsieur J. Meyer, Monsieur J. Nieuhof, and Doctor Kernéis, as well as the most friendly and helpful staff of the archives in Nantes, for communicating to me much valuable information about the merchant Descazeaux du Hallay.

Among the people who helped to prepare the manuscript, my wife's contribution has been truly monumental—to her I express heartfelt thanks. To Catherine Stodolsky and Daryl Hafter, each of whom has rendered enormous services, I owe a great obligation.

Two successive Fulbright awards for 1958-1960 and a grant in 1961 from the University of California at Berkeley, supported three consecutive years of research in France. Funds for microfilm and typing were provided by the Horace H. Rackham School of Graduate Studies at the University of Michigan in Ann Arbor.

LIONEL ROTHKRUG

Ann Arbor, Michigan
September 1964

CONTENTS

xiii

CONTENTS

PART I

PRELUDE TO REFORM
1576-1683

PRELUDE TO REFORM
1576-1683

THE DICHOTOMY between mercantilist and anti-mercantilist doctrines stands at the center of numerous,
widely disparate influences, all ultimately converging to produce movements of opposition in the second
part of Louis XIV's reign. Mercantilism, a word
coined in the eighteenth century, refers to a body of
ideas which were widely, if somewhat disjointedly,
expressed as early as the beginning of the sixteenth
century. At that time new relationships between political and material forces were suggested by an unusual combination of factors. The extension of royal
authority had, since the end of the Hundred Years
War, been accompanied by almost uninterrupted economic expansion. Most people knew, of course, how
taxes convert money from trade into political power;
a few men, however, now further recognized that
fiscal exemptions, acquired by urban centers during
the course of the Middle Ages, caused the growing
burden of state charges to fall increasingly on the
countryside. Means were sought, therefore, to divert
treasure away from towns to agricultural areas. Since
industry was predominantly rural, the crown encouraged industrial expansion in order to employ provincial populations, providing them with income to
pay their taxes and, to some extent, offsetting thereby
the rise in urban concentrations of wealth. This attempt to base future political development on rural
prosperity was moderately successful; until the 1550's
an expanding economy throughout Europe provided

markets for French manufactured goods as well as for their agricultural products.

It was during the century of general economic expansion and extending political authority, from Louis XI through the reign of François I, that there developed the concept that regions under the jurisdiction of the French crown formed a single economic unit. Many writers and officials of government were convinced that France was self-sufficient and could, in the expression of the times, "get along without the foreigner." They further insisted that, while France needed no imports, other European states were entirely dependent upon French exports. In contrast to these views, however, there were people who opposed the mercantilist program to achieve national economic autarky at the expense of neighboring countries. They said such policies were impious and "Machiavellian" in spirit. This difference between mercantilist and anti-mercantilist opinions was subsequently extended and intensified by the Wars of Religion. Theological and philosophical issues were injected into arguments used by both sides. The first chapter of this book, dealing with the intellectual backgrounds to reform, describes how rival explanations of political economy were transformed and made part of broader speculative traditions.

As mercantilist views were slowly made part of the crown's legislative program during the course of the seventeenth century, so opposition to these principles progressed gradually from mere intellectual dissent to political resistance. Moreover, the aristocracy, which was most alarmed by the crown's tendency to appeal to mercantilist theory in order to justify renewed efforts toward centralization of royal authority, early began to draft rival doctrines of political economy. Their first efforts date from the middle of the century, shortly after the *Fronde*. In Chapter II, I have tried to show how, at this time, both government and nobility began to formulate their arguments in terms of contending views about the nature of society, the structure of the cosmos, and the character of the human soul.

Novel changes in controversy, however, do not by themselves explain the nobility's increasingly militant demands for reform during Louis XIV's reign. One issue above all others intensified hostility between the monarchy and many members of its aristocracy: the fiscal problem. Questions about taxes were at first quite unrelated to mercantilist and anti-mercantilist discussion. But fiscal exemptions were most often seen as a last protection against arbitrary authority. In Chapter III, which deals with the background to reform, we shall see how the imminence of a universal direct tax drove aristocratic spokesmen to offer to surrender their fiscal privileges in exchange for wider reforms. Thus the provocative character of the fiscal issue, accelerating the evolution of radical thought among the nobility, contributed substantially to the development of ideological resistance to the policies of Louis XIV's ministers.

CHAPTER I

INTELLECTUAL BACKGROUNDS
TO REFORM

No ORGANIZED opposition movement with a program for political, institutional, and social reform existed until the personal reign of Louis XIV. The ideas of those who inveighed against his ministers' policies, however, were rooted in traditions going back to at least as early as the last quarter of the sixteenth century. At that time France was shaken by a series of political and religious struggles whose savage and destructive character transformed contemporary thought. Many Frenchmen came to regard civil war as the greatest single source of society's afflictions. The widely felt need for more effective government led men like Jean Bodin, Barthélemy Laffemas, and Antoyne de Montchrétien to examine at length means whereby monarchy could be strengthened. Elaborating on a cluster of well-known ideas, they developed among other things a fairly coherent theory of political economy, later called "mercantilist" by Adam Smith. As widely accepted as were these principles which provided the basis for Richelieu's policy, opposition to them existed from the very beginning of the seventeenth century.

Mercantilism ran directly counter to concepts lying at the heart of powerful religious and philosophical traditions. Its theories, as will be seen, were associated with new precepts declaring that Frenchmen, in their relations with foreigners, were not bound by the same ethical code governing their conduct toward each other. Moreover, mercantilist ethics very early legitimized immoral behavior if it was thought to benefit the general welfare. Such ideas aroused deep-seated hostility in early seventeenth century France, then experiencing intensely devout and widespread movements for spiritual reform. There was also a second source of opposition to the new principles of political economy: a humanist tradition. Its principal spokesmen, Guillaume Postel and Tommasio Campanella, believing in a fundamental unity behind all religious diversity, thought a universal empire would provide a framework for conversion of the world. Political authority for them was above all a means to unite mankind and to integrate human society into the harmony of the cosmos. This point of view was fundamentally opposed to mercantilist theory which, permanently dividing peoples into numerous hostile self-contained units, accepted religious and political disunity as part of man's natural condition.

These two currents of anti-mercantilist thought formed an essential part of the ideological background to criticism directed against Louis XIV's ministers. Indeed, the central purpose of this study is to explain how specific economic, social, and political grievances helped to transform these streams of purely speculative dissent first into bitter public criticism and finally into active political opposition. This chapter traces the origins of mercantilist and opposing views; it explains how, from late medieval beginnings, these rival doctrines grew increasingly elaborate as they assumed an ever more important role in French political life. In their earliest expression contrasting theories of political economy were in part an outgrowth of disputes arising in the thirteenth and fourteenth centuries. At this time conflicting views of Thomas Aquinas, William of Ockham, and Marsilius of Padua stand at the beginning of two divergent political traditions which achieve their fullest expression in the early sixteenth century. St. Thomas believed that divine principles of justice were an integral part of the human mind; they were the "natural end" toward which mankind advanced by force of reason without supernatural aid. In contrast, both William of Ockham and Marsilius of Padua denied that justice could be explained; they said it was a divine force, hidden from human understanding. Marsilius, however, did more than divorce justice from reason. He interpreted Aristotle in an extremely naturalistic sense. Perhaps encouraged by the Italian habit of projecting into the political sphere conclusions drawn from medical studies based on Aristotle, Marsilius conceived society to be a living organism regulated by biological forces called human laws, which had no ethical content. Subsequently, Italians of Machiavelli's persuasion were also convinced that society was part of the physical order; and they, too, insisted that political authority, having a purely physiological function, should not be subject to ethical precepts. But the Italians were challenged by northern humanists like Thomas More and Erasmus who asserted, as did Aquinas, that moral laws, being reflections of divine principles, were binding on governments everywhere.

Mercantilist theory emerged in France with such thinkers as Claude de Seyssel who, in 1519, expounded arguments which were similar in many respects to those of Machiavelli. The common features of both views explain why objections to mercantilist principles were often inspired by the same motives which led people to attack the author of *The Prince*.

But the nature or, more exactly, the scope of these parallel differences in outlook between More and Machiavelli, between Seyssel and anti-mercantilists, changed radically in one generation. The Wars of Religion injected philosophical and theological issues into contending explanations of political economy; both mercantilist and anti-mercantilist theories were expanded to include the most abstruse and disparate questions. These rival views became part of two comprehensive, yet diffuse, bodies of ideas. Indeed, by the middle of the seventeenth century few major intellectual themes were free from implications affecting one or the other competing doctrines of political economy.

i. MERCANTILIST AND ANTI-MERCANTILIST VIEWS IN SIXTEENTH CENTURY FRANCE

Medieval intellectual and spiritual life influenced subsequent movements not merely in the Renaissance and the Reformation, but also in the later sixteenth and early seventeenth century. The crosscurrents of thought and faith from Aquinas to Bellarmine, from Petrarch to Montaigne, from Wyclif to Calvin, were complicated by immediate political issues at hand. Increasing centralization of royal authority raised problems concerning the relation of the state to church, to religion, and to culture. Thus the concept of the state as a moral entity, for example, received new definitions as men argued about the sacred and profane elements of culture and thought. Here we can distinguish several broad stages of development, beginning with the intensive efforts of thirteenth century schoolmen to integrate Greek philosophy with theology. At that time the introduction of the complete Aristotle permitted St. Thomas finally to make philosophy an autonomous discipline, having a value independent of revealed principles, possessing unique subject matter and methods. According to St. Thomas, the theologian is distinguished from the philosopher in that the former uses logical argument to elucidate articles of faith whereas the latter applies the same method to principles apprehended by purely "natural reason." Although his purpose was to link the universe and society with the divine order, Aquinas' premise that the natural world can be studied for its own sake, without direct reference to God or to the transcendental, made logically possible the application of purely human reason to society.

In the question of church and state, for example, St. Thomas explained that, while the natural "end" of one is necessarily related to the supernatural "end" of the other, nevertheless, the state, being prior to the church, prior to society, even prior to original sin, has a value or "end" of its own. This he believed to be justice, defined as establishing the commonweal by rendering "to each his own right."[1] Also, St. Thomas thought that the state would achieve its "end" of natural justice, which is the general welfare, independently, without external aid. Adopting Aristotle's concept of "perfection" (an entity is "perfect" when it is truly self-sufficing in the sense of having fulfilled its entire potential), St. Thomas declared the state a "perfect" society, possessing within itself all the moral and material requirements necessary for the realization of its "end." Moreover, he held, society evolves toward the fulfillment of natural justice in the same manner that men reason to progressively higher levels. Human laws are the commands of "practical" reason which is a faculty identical in

---

[1] *Summa Theologica*, II, 11, Ques. 58.

operation with "speculative" reason, "for each proceeds from principle to conclusion."

> Human law is a dictate of reason, whereby hu-
> man acts are directed. Thus there may be two
> causes for the just change of human law. . . .
> The cause on the part of reason is that it seems
> natural . . . to advance gradually from the im-
> perfect to the perfect. Hence, in the speculative
> sciences, we see that the teaching of the early
> philosophers was imperfect, and that it was after-
> wards perfected by those who succeeded them. So
> also in practical matters, for those who first en-
> deavored to discover something useful for the
> human community, not being able by themselves
> to take everything into consideration, set up cer-
> tain institutions which were deficient in many
> ways; and these were changed by subsequent law-
> givers who made institutions that might prove
> less frequently deficient in relation to the com-
> mon welfare.[2]

In short, believing that human law and reason "participate" in the eternal natural law, St. Thomas, influenced by Stoic tradition, makes clear that man can
apprehend transcendental principles of justice and
to some extent approximate them on earth. But he
went on to explain that, although reason "is the measure and rule of human conduct," human behavior is
only one part of nature, and reason therefore "is not
the measure of things which are from nature."[3] In
other words, St. Thomas excluded natural reason
from areas beyond society, denying that the physical
universe reflected human "justice" in any form.

The view that reason "participates" in natural law

[2] *Ibid.*, II, 1, Ques. 97, art. 1.
[3] *Ibid.*, Ques. 91, art. 3, Reply to Obj. 2.

rested upon the epistemological assumption that the intellect assumes the very pattern of the object known—that reason is a reflection of the moral and of the physical worlds as they actually exist, both being conceived as "natural" and external to man. The extent, therefore, that transcendental justice "participates" in the natural order is the degree to which this divine principle is an integral part of the human mind: natural law "is nothing else than an imprint on us of the divine light."[4] In contrast to this position are the views of William of Ockham and his contemporary, Marsilius of Padua. Denying any necessary connection between mind and world, Ockham made the concept of an external object only a symbol for that object. Knowledge informs man about the relations between symbols which represent the world; but the world itself, the reality behind the symbols, remains hidden and inexplicable. The principles of transcendental justice are no longer perceptible in nature, which itself escapes direct apprehension; they are therefore excluded from the area of reason and restricted to the sphere of faith. Moreover, because justice has no rational foundations it is totally mysterious. Justice is done; it is not explained. God's will is just merely because it is God's will. Divine commands cannot be understood by reason nor can they be known in terms of their ethical content.

Similarly, Marsilius relegates natural law in the Thomist sense to the supernatural sphere. He defines positive law (arising out of the need to preserve "the peace") as coercive commands from the legislator, necessary to conserve "the life and health" of the state. Such laws are not dictated by right reason. Issued as medical prescriptions, the decrees of government are just merely because they express the pur-

4 *Ibid.*, art. 2.

pose of the legislator who speaks as the organic head of a body politic. Thus the contrast between Thomist and opposing ideas of human reason brings about a fundamental cleavage in conceptions of the state, important because it marks the origin of two divergent tendencies in Renaissance political theory. St. Thomas described a union between reason and transcendental justice, even though he saw no connection between these qualities and the physical universe. In contrast, Marsilius separates reason both from justice and from the cosmos. Considering society part of the physical order, Marsilius says the state is a living organism not subject to reason because, like a plant, it develops in accord with inborn impulses. Indeed, the *Defensor pacis* is the first thoroughly naturalistic interpretation of Aristotle's "perfect" society, entirely self-sufficient both politically and morally.

This view was first prominent in northern Italy. Its early civic patriotism, encouraging a tendency to subordinate moral principles to community interest, was clearly compatible with the naturalistic approach to society, perhaps inspired by the routine projection of medical principles based on Aristotle into the political sphere.[5] By the first years of the sixteenth century, Machiavelli regarded laws of society as biological principles, no more ethical than those governing the paths of planets and the rhythm of the tides. North of the Alps, however, where political units were large and patriotic loyalties weaker, human laws were not considered biological phenomena necessarily divorced from ethics; instead, as in St. Thomas, they were conceived to be emanations of natural law and natural reason, both integrally connected with moral precepts.

[5] Early Italian civic patriotism is described by Hans Baron, *The Crisis of the Early Italian Renaissance; Civic Humanism and Republican Liberty in an Age of Classicism and Tyranny*, Princeton, 1955.

Thus Thomas More, publishing his *Utopia* at about the same time as Machiavelli's *Prince*, described how a non-Christian society established a virtuous commonwealth through purely natural reason, carrying the Thomistic ideal of justice to full realization.[6] In contrast to Machiavelli's emphasis upon history, his emphasis upon the regularities in the organic development of human societies, Thomas More, subordinating love of country to the precept "love thy neighbor," emphasized the virtue of man as opposed to the fate of "republics." The *Utopia* explains how political institutions, wisely conceived, can cause men to live exemplary lives. In Machiavelli the state is raised above moral principles; in More it is bound by the same ethical rules governing the actions of its most humble resident. It is these conflicting arguments, extending from Marsilius to Machiavelli on the one side and from Aquinas to More on the other, which lie at the very heart of the gradual development of both

[6] The virtuous pagans in the *Utopia* exemplify ideals identical to those of Erasmus' *Enchiridion*: right living and simple belief are superior to correct theology. The church as an institution is merely an extension of society, helping to perfect, not to govern, mankind. *Hythlodaye*, as in the "philosophy of Christ," interprets religion predominantly as a system of ethics. Moreover, since, in this view, ethics and politics are one, religious authority is transformed into a purely secular principle. Religious life in the church is but a reflection of spirituality in society. Any deterioration in the first can be remedied, therefore, only by reform of the world, not of the church. Ecumenical councils are of no avail: spiritual aid flows only from the word of God, the Bible in the vernacular, instructing ignorant and learned alike in the "philosophy of Christ"—simple belief and the good life. This was the fundamental issue lying behind the dispute between Erasmus and Luther, separating many humanists from the Protestant cause: the former wished to improve, indeed even to sanctify man; the latter sought salvation in doctrinal and ecclesiastical reform. Erasmus saw religion as an extension of culture, interpreting it principally in terms of ethics and learned endeavor; Luther sought above all to retain the mystical purity of the Cross, reaffirming both its miraculous nature and its continuing operation in the world.

mercantilist and anti-mercantilist theories in six-teenth and seventeenth century France.

Claude de Seyssel's well-known treatise, *La grande monarchie de France*, published in 1519, illustrates how mercantilist thought was early connected with concepts which Machiavelli has made familiar. The two authors were career statesmen and diplomats speaking both from long political experience and from wide reading in the ancients. Writing perhaps independently of one another,[7] each made human law part of the physical universe, dissociating politics from both theology and morals.[8] If the radical cyni-cism in the *Prince* contrasts sharply with Seyssel's prag-matic conservatism, it is because Machiavelli, acutely conscious of Florentine political instability, stressed the purely transient and expedient factors in the acquisition and precarious retention of power. In contrast, it was the *continuity* of French monarchy through the centuries, which most impressed Seyssel; he sought above all to preserve existing institutions.[9] For Machiavelli, the Florentine humanist, political success is the achievement of an individual who, hero-ic in the possession of power, strengthens the moral character of the community. Embodying the purest expression of ancient political wisdom, the Prince is able to restore the "republic" to its original "healthy" principles. The law of the Prince transmits the cul-ture of antiquity to the living body of the community.

[7] Claude de Seyssel, *La grande monarchie de France et deux autres fragments politiques*, ed. Jacques Poujol, Paris, 1961, Introduction, p. 36.

[8] ". . . il n'est aucune chose sous le ciel perpetuelle . . . et mesmes ces corps mystiques, qui sont a la semblance des corps materiels humains . . . (pour autant qu'ils sont créés et composés de quatre éléments et humeurs contraires), jaçoit que par aucun temps se puis-sent entretenir et conserver en vie. . . . Tout ainsi advient aux corps mystiques de la société humaine" (*ibid.*, p. 108).

[9] The point is made by Poujol, *ibid.*, p. 39.

Seyssel, however, paid far less attention to individual rulers, pointing out that royal authority in France had survived the reigns of incompetent and even imbecilic kings. The monarchy, he said, is a *corps mystique*[10] whose traditional institutions, embodying the wisdom of antiquity, are sanctified by God. The living body of the state, not the Prince, transmits ancient culture and moral qualities to all subjects of the realm, who together constitute the political organism. Moreover, environmental differences between Italy and France, causing them to place different emphasis on personal and institutional concepts of government, also explain opposing economic views. Machiavelli insisted that "no opinion can be more false" than to assert that "money is the sinews of war." He thought treasure was rather a product than an instrument of military success, for soldiers—not money acquired in trade—guarantee victory. As Machiavelli put it, "Gold does not find good soldiers, but soldiers are quite capable of finding gold."[11] To Seyssel, however, the occasional booty won in battle was no more valid a foundation of state policy than military ambition; both these elements concerned only immediate ends.

[10] The term has a fascinating history which is traced by Ernst H. Kantorowicz, *"Pro patria mori* in Medieval Political Thought," *American Historical Review*, LVI (April 1951), 472-492. *Corpus mysticum,* first appearing in Carolingian times, meant the Eucharist. Toward the middle of the twelfth century the church insisted on the real presence, the *Corpus Christi,* a term hitherto used in its Pauline sense to designate the church as an institution. *Corpus mysticum* hereafter tended to supplant *Corpus Christi* when referring to the church as an organized body. The church "as one mystical body the head of which is Christ" was finally defined and dogmatized by Boniface VIII. But the influence of Roman law soon caused the phrase to lose much of its transcendental content; *corpus mysticum* became interchangeable with *persona mystica.* Meanwhile, however, the emerging secular state now embraced the expression in its most mystical sense.

[11] *The Discourses,* trans. Leslie J. Walker, 2 vols., London, 1950, I, 385.

The loss of a battle or even of a war could not radically alter French institutions, considered to be the very foundation of the state. Adhering to long-term policies, Seyssel thought that the preservation and growth of France's power, indeed to the point of predominance over her neighbors, resided ultimately in the kingdom's reserves of precious metals. In his opinion, trade and legislation would procure the most certain supply of monies.

Seyssel expounded this point at some length. Exclaiming that other states had introduced elaborate legislation "to prevent gold and silver from leaving their country and to attract [treasure] belonging to foreigners," he complained that groundless fears of foreign retaliation kept France from enforcing her own bullionist laws.[12] Morever, French retaliation would go unpunished, in Seyssel's view. He insisted that other states could take no effective economic measures against his country because France alone was capable of being entirely self-sufficient, very much a perfect community in the Aristotelian sense. Indeed, he believed, full exploitation of her vast resources would assure both peace at home and hegemony abroad.

> This kingdom can more easily do without all the others than can all the others do without it. This Monarchy is so large and weighty that it requires much to govern it. It is so powerful and so prosperous that it seems as if it can never fail, nor can anything harm it, from which most of our disorders come. Thus he who reestablishes all things in good order will achieve great merit and glory. . . . I hold it to be absolutely certain that this Monarchy shall impose its will (*donnerait la*

[12] *La grande monarchie*, p. 162.

loi) on all other Powers and Seigneuries in Christendom, and even on many others, when all things are in good order.[13]

In Seyssel's view, the power of the state resided in the prosperity of its subjects; a regular means of procuring wealth and of distributing it throughout the realm was possible if France would acquire a mighty navy. With powerful fleets

> the kingdom will be in perpetual security . . . in little time it will . . . impose its will on all the others, . . . and apart from the glory the King . . . will acquire, and the reputation he will give to the entire French nation, both will profit greatly. . . . The Prince will . . . conquer and easily retain a number of states; the people . . . will increase their wealth by means of merchandise coming in all surety by sea, thus persuading many Frenchmen to trade who do not dare at present for fear of the dangers.[14]

Moreover, insisting again that France was "so abundant in wealth that she can much more easily do without all her neighbors than they can without her," Seyssel demanded that additional regulations and tariffs be imposed on foreign ships trading in French ports.[15]

Seyssel's views were more than abstract theory; they were an expression of public policy. Thus in February 1516, Francis I ordered the towns of Rouen, Bordeaux, Paris, Toulouse, Grenoble, Dijon, Lyon, Montpellier, Tours, La Rochelle, Limoges, Orléans, Bourges, Troyes, Bayonne, Amiens, and Boulogne-

---

[13] *Ibid.*, pp. 162-163. For similar statements in the sixteenth century see C. W. Cole, *French Mercantilist Doctrines before Colbert*, New York, 1931, pp. 1-46.

[14] *Ibid.*, p. 199.　　　　[15] *Ibid.*, p. 201.

sur-Mer to send two elected deputies to Paris on 15
March 1516 to consult with royal officials "about
means to enrich the kingdom." And Chancellor Du
Prat, addressing the assembled deputies in the cham-
bers of the Paris *Parlement* on 31 March, "in the
presence of the King and several princes of the
realm,"[16] declared that "the well-being of the realm
is the well-being of the king . . . because it [the realm]
is a *"corps mistique dont le Roy est le chef."* Du Prat
also insisted that

> This kingdom . . . is so opulent and fertile in
> all things necessary to man, that it can do with-
> out all other kingdoms . . . and our neighbors
> cannot do without us. There are several doors
> by which money enters the realm . . . those by
> which it leaves must be closed in such a way that
> we draw money from our neighbors and they
> draw nothing from us.[17]

Du Prat went on to describe a substantial body of proposed legislation, covering most of French economic
life, which was designed ultimately to achieve complete economic autarky, the ideal of sixteenth and
seventeenth century mercantilist spokesmen.

Criticism appeared on two levels: intellectuals
objected to the very principles of mercantilism; merchants protested when particular laws conflicted with
their private interests. Businessmen voiced their grievances at the earliest opportunity, even to Chancellor
Du Prat,[18] but their arguments did not rise to a level
of theoretical expression until Louis XIV's reign;
they will be discussed later in that context. In con-

[16] The entire address is published in *Journal de Jean Barrillon,
secrétaire du Chancelier Duprat 1515-1521*, ed. Pierre de Vaissière,
2 vols., Paris, 1897, I, 274-302.

[17] *Ibid.*, p. 282.   [18] See editor's notes, *ibid., passim.*

trast, however, intellectual opposition developed more slowly and, enmeshed as it was with wider speculative currents, anti-mercantilist statements appeared at first as isolated pronouncements amid more general discussions. Writings prior to 1572 were mere answers to the kind of undoctrinaire views expressed by Seyssel and Du Prat. Later critics, writing after the Wars of Religion had reached their most intense phase with St. Bartholomew's Eve and Henry IV's assassination in 1610, argued with greater system against mercantilist attitudes which had themselves become progressively more militant and more comprehensive.

In the earlier period themes of universal brotherhood and universal interdependence, motivated perhaps by ethical preoccupations similar to those which inspired Thomas More, were directed against the mercantilist division of mankind into hostile self-contained political units. The issue seems to have arisen when men became aware of a growing distinction between traditional town legislation and the mercantilist re-creation of these ancient laws on a national scale. During the Middle Ages the economic activity of towns, and of the surrounding countryside under their control, was regulated by a complex and diversified body of legislation, whose avowed purpose was to increase the common wealth of the community and ensure each individual a prescribed measure suited both to his status and occupation. The crown in the course of time sporadically supplanted local authority in one area, then in another; and mercantilism gradually took form as traditional local laws, remaining substantially unchanged, were more and more frequently administered by royal officials and slowly made to serve the needs of the state rather than of the towns.[19] Meanwhile, this slow extension of govern-

[19] The classic statement on this subject is by Eli F. Heckscher,

ment control over the economy raised perplexing moral problems. During the period of purely munic- ipal control there was no apparent objection to or- ganizing all economic activity for the sole benefit of the community; this was not the case, however, when men understood that trade, industry, agriculture, and finance all took place within the much larger frame- work of the state. Could the King and his subjects sever their material ties with the rest of Christianity, reserving a vast wealth for their exclusive enjoyment?

Such a policy, requiring France to achieve complete economic autarky, was a goal which Jean Bodin thought both impossible in fact and impious in spirit. In his famous *Response aux paradoxes de M. de Males- troit* (Paris, 1568), Bodin explained that so far as

> the trade of merchandise leaving the country is
> concerned, several great personages have said . . .
> that if they had their way they would end it com-
> pletely; believing we can live happily and pros-
> perously without borrowing or receiving any-
> thing from foreigners. But in my opinion they
> are misled. We have business with foreigners,
> without whom we cannot survive . . . and when
> we can dispense with such [imported] merchan-
> dise, which is not at all possible . . . we should
> nevertheless always traffic, sell, buy, exchange,
> lend, indeed, give part of our wealth to foreign-
> ers, . . . for the purpose of maintaining friend-
> ship.[20]

Convinced that "a natural obligation" rested upon all Frenchmen to share their wealth with others,

Mercantilism, trans. Mendel Shapiro, 2 vols., London, 1935. See also G. N. Clark, *The Seventeenth Century*, 2d edn., London, 1947, pp. 22-23.

[20] Ed. Henri Hauser, Paris, 1932, pp. 32-33.

Bodin thought this duty was part of a divine plan written into the moral structure of the universe. "God in His admirable prudence has put all in right order. He has distributed His blessings in such a manner that no country is so plentiful that it does not lack many things. The Creator has done this apparently so as to maintain all subjects in His Republic in friendship, or at least to prevent them from waging war for long, [because] they are always trading with one another."[21] Divine Providence had created a kind of international division of labor and production in order to strengthen peace, the natural condition of mankind, and promote friendship through reciprocal trade.[22] Pride, driving man to draw his sword against his brother, had been curbed by the Almighty, Who willed that each should depend upon his neighbor for subsistence. Any attempt to upset the "right order" of human and material relationships could lead only to economic distress. Man could not successfully challenge the law of God.

Bodin here expressed opinions which appear to have long been familiar.[23] Yet he did not persist in

[21] *Ibid.*, pp. 33-34.

[22] "La providence de l'Eternel a voulu qu'aucune région, si riche soit-elle, ne puisse se passer des ressources d'une autre. . . . Si la nature ne cesse d'imposer à chacun lieu ces conditions déterminées et immuables, c'est pour que les peuples resserrent leurs liens réciproques et, par un commerce mutuel, affermissent entre eux la paix et l'amitié." *Méthode pour faciliter la connaissance d'Histoire*, ed. Pierre Mesnard, Paris, 1951, quoted by Théodore Ruyssen, *Les sources doctrinales de l'internationalisme*, 2 vols., Paris, 1951, 1958, I, 389.

[23] Guillaume de la Perrière, *The Mirrour of Policie: A Worke no lesse profitable than necessarie, for all Magistrates, and Gouvernours of Estates and Commonweales*, London, 1598, writes: "The conference and conversing with strangers and Aliens is oftentimes very profitable for the Commonweale for the trafficke of Merchandise. . . . Nature would not distribute all her benefites unto one place alone, but part and devide them, giving unto one climate

this point of view. Abandoning these arguments, he soon joined the ranks of his erstwhile opponents, expanding traditional mercantilist principles far beyond the statements of Seyssel and the public declarations of Du Prat. His change of mind appears to have been motivated above all by the effects of civil war. Political life in France had deteriorated seriously during the years separating the publication of the famous *Response* in 1568 and the first edition of the *Republic* eight years later. The events of St. Bartholomew's Eve revealed that an embattled and divided monarchy which, ruled one day by deceit and governed the next by crime, lay helpless before a conflagration threatening to consume the entire realm. Convinced that domestic troubles had unleashed demonic forces in France, Bodin thought no measures too extreme to avoid "the pest" of civil strife, even the waging of war abroad in order to preserve unity at home. The Romans, having learned this lesson, "found no better antidote to civil wars, no remedy more certain, than to confront their subjects with an enemy." The Senate went so far as "to create foes when there were none." And since it was "almost impossible to maintain subjects [of a realm] in peace and friendship if they are not at war," it could therefore be accepted as a general principle that "the best means to conserve a state, and to guarantee it against rebellions and seditions . . . , keeping its subjects in lasting friendship, is to

---

that which wanteth in another, recompensing the barreness of one thing with the fruitfulness of another." This is an English translation of the French edition, *Le miroir politique, contenant diverses manieres de gouverner et policier les républiques, qui sont et ont esté par cy devant*, Paris, 1567. G. Dexter, "Guillaume de la Perrière," *Bibliothèque d'humanisme et renaissance*, XVII (1955), p. 70, explains that this work probably existed in manuscript form in 1539.

have an enemy against whom they can dress themselves."[24]

Military operations against foreign powers, however cheap when compared to the ruinous cost of civil conflict, were nevertheless expensive enterprises, and the Prince should be assured of adequate resources. But recourse to domestic taxes should be avoided "unless all other methods fail." New contributions to the royal treasury should be made by France's neighbors, who were dependent upon her limitless supply of agricultural products. "Therefore in order to strengthen finances, export duties should be raised on items they cannot do without." So far as imports were concerned, tariffs should be increased on manufactured articles and raw materials in order to favor domestic industry, whose exports would provide revenue for the King and employment for his subjects.[25]

Standing in the very shadow of current anarchy, Bodin supported arguments he previously opposed and pleaded for measures to carry conflict outside of the realm. His views of man and of society had changed profoundly. Earlier, in 1568, he had described a universal "right order," where divinely ordained bonds of reciprocal interests united peoples everywhere, making prolonged conflict impossible. Peace, synonymous with submission to God's will, was a state of international harmony and repose; war, caused by defiance of divine command made manifest by natural law, was a futile attempt to prevail against

[24] *Les six livres de la république,* Paris, 1608, Bk. V, chap. 5, pp. 760-761. Montaigne expressed moral reservations against this point of view: "Indeed a foreign war is a much milder evil than a civil war. But I do not believe that God would favor so injust an enterprise as to injure and pick a quarrel with others for our own convenience" (*Essays,* trans. Donald Frame, Stanford, 1957, Bk. II, chap. 24, p. 519).

[25] *Ibid.,* Bk. VI, chap. 2, pp. 877-878.

nature and the Almighty. Economic necessity would invariably force men to come to terms with their neighbors. In the *Republic*, however, war was endemic to the human condition. Peace was no longer the mandate of God; nor was it a state of universal repose coming from submission to His will. Instead it was transformed into a purely national phenomenon, possible only *within* a country's borders. Peace was defined as order imposed by physical coercion; far from being an absence of force, it reflected the monopoly or the plenitude of power. Peace was that state of society existing when government could repress unauthorized violence in all parts of the realm, a situation Bodin thought unlikely to prevail unless the crown successfully diverted pugnacious factions or persuaded them to pursue their struggles in foreign lands.

All the same, the author of the *Republic* did not think that aggressive trade practices and a belligerent foreign policy were by themselves sufficient to guarantee peace at home. He pointed out that "of all the causes of seditions and changes in Republics, none is greater than the excessive wealth of a few subjects and the extreme poverty of the largest number."[26] The problem of unequal distribution of wealth, considered by Bodin to be virtually insoluble,[27] was further complicated by an outrageously unjust fiscal

[26] *Ibid.*, Bk. V, chap. 2, p. 702. Earlier in the century Erasmus wrote that "a great many seditions have arisen from immoderate taxation. . . . The prince should try to prevent too great an unequality of wealth" (*The Education of a Christian Prince*, trans. L. K. Born, New York, 1936, pp. 215-217). Thomas More, of course, insisted upon a communist organization of society. Interestingly, Justus Lipsius, in *Two Bookes of Constancie*, ed. Rudolf Kirk, New Brunswick, 1939, p. 96, suggested that unequal distribution of wealth is necessary to foster patriotic loyalty, the desire to defend the commonwealth; "els . . . why should the Nobility and rich men have more care for their country than the poore people."

[27] *Ibid.*, pp. 702-706.

system. The author explained that almost all existing taxes, including the *taille, taillon, aides, octrois,* and *gabelle,* were originally "extraordinary subsidies" levied in time of war as purely provisional emergency measures: the imposts came to be considered "ordinary" only because monarchs continued to demand their collection long after the causes for the imposition had vanished. Expressly rejecting the argument, apparently still heard at this time, that the King should live "on his own" and "abolish all taxes, *aides* and imposts," Bodin demanded instead that the entire fiscal system, "on which the very foundations of the state rested," be thoroughly overhauled.[28]

All members of society, especially the wealthy and the privileged, should be taxed in proportion to their personal resources. "On this matter the Romans showed themselves more just: only the rich, noble or *roturiers,* were subjected to the *tailles,* the poor were exempt." In France the roles were reversed: "the poor pay and the rich are exempt." Bodin thought the consequences of this appalling situation could very well prove fatal: "Since rich towns, nobles and the Ecclesiastical estate have discharged their load onto the poor," the latter had become like Aesop's donkey or like "the horse which would not carry anything." The feeblest and most miserable portion of society could not possibly bear the full burden of public charges.[29]

Fiscal reform was an integral part of Bodin's program for a "well-ordered state," and, careful to avoid conclusions drawn from general principles alone, he studded his arguments with numerous historical and factual references, disclosing intimate knowledge of

[28] *Ibid.,* Bk. VI, chap. 2, pp. 881-882, 885-890. See also pp. 841-843.
[29] *Ibid.,* pp. 885-886.

the subject.[30] This fastidious attention to detail above all reflected Bodin's concern to establish equity in even the most trivial cases. At bottom the author's preoccupation sprang not only from the negative fear of disorder arising from unfair taxation, but from the positive conviction that justice is the ultimate end or purpose of the state. The full import of Bodin's thought here becomes clear. Justice is inseparable from power. God, the unique source of Good, gave sovereigns the right to exercise the force necessary to impose peace and to govern according to His will. States were divinely instituted agencies consecrated for the establishment of Right Order. Legitimate rulers should not violate moral precepts, for "the purpose of law is justice. Law is the work of the Prince, the Prince is the image of God, therefore the law of the Prince ought to conform to the law of God."[31] Equating proper royal command with the Creator's will, Bodin asserted that justice is coextensive with the Prince's jurisdiction. Justice is possible only under the law of legitimate government; it cannot exist in the absence of this divinely ordained authority. Since God gave no Prince the right to impose

[30] More will be said concerning Bodin's views on taxation in Chapter IV, below, which deals with fiscal reform.

[31] *Ibid.*, Bk. I, chap. 8, p. 161. Beatrice Reynolds, *Proponents of Limited Monarchy in Sixteenth Century France: Francis Hotman and Jean Bodin*, New York, 1931, p. 177, has observed that this view of the ruler is different from the one Bodin expressed a decade earlier. And, interestingly enough, the change in outlook which she describes in Bodin is precisely analogous to his reversal of opinion with respect to mercantilist policies: "In the ten years since the publication of the *Methodus*, his [Bodin's] concept of kingship had perceptibly altered. . . . In the earlier period there had been some recognition of . . . the delegates of the nation as assistant in the business of governing—a source of information, advice and prohibition. By 1576 the prohibitory function had become inhibited, in Bodin's thought. The king was above all but God."

His will on other rulers, no law existed to govern foreign relations. Therefore states should deal with one another in the absence of justice, for outside the consecrated limits of a prince's jurisdiction, sovereignty could not exist and conflict would be inevitable.[32]

Although linked to God through divinely sanctioned institutions, Bodin's state was totally independent of other polities.[33] Almost three centuries earlier Marsilius of Padua had said that "men were assembled for the sake of the sufficient life, being able to seek out for themselves the necessaries . . . and exchanging them with one another. This assemblage, thus perfect and having the limit of self-sufficiency, is called the state."[34] Like Machiavelli, Marsilius spoke in the context of Italian city states, and, like Seyssel, Marsilius thought the Prince's power was an expression of the corporate community. In contrast, Bodin's "perfect" society was the vast realm of France; and, contrary to Seyssel, for him the source of authority was indivisible, for corporate bodies existed only by consent of the ruler. Thus the principle of self-sufficiency was extended to sovereignty itself. Understood in this new sense, self-sufficiency expressed the primacy of state in society—the ultimate union of force with transcendental justice. When, in the days of Seyssel, mercantilist principles were medieval municipal law

[32] The parallel with Machiavelli is made by G. Cardascia, "Machiavel et Jean Bodin," *Bibliothèque d'humanisme et renaissance*, III (1943), 129-167.

[33] Almost a century later Jean de Lartigue, *La politique des conquérans*, Paris, 1662, pp. 88-90, wrote: "When a state is sufficient unto itself and possesses all things necessary for its subsistence and felicity it must view the Divinity as the exterior principle of its well being, and other states as sources and authors of its evils and miseries." Lartigue is discussed below, in Chapter II, at greater length.

[34] *Defensor pacis*, trans. A. Gewirth, 2 vols., New York, 1951, 1956, I, 14.

writ large, they were part of the conservative effort to preserve existing institutions, seen as the very embodiment of ancient wisdom. Bodin, however, subordinated institutions, peoples, and culture under the sovereign state. Here mercantilist axioms became part of a radical program to change institutions, to systematize political authority at home, and to wage economic warfare abroad on a scale hitherto unknown.[35]

The idea of self-contained political units situated in a hostile world and thrown back on their own moral and material resources appeared to link the very destinies of people to the outcome of international rivalries, no longer seen as mere dynastic struggles. From Bodin to Colbert more and more writers made the policy of "getting along without the for-

[35] The revolutionary character of Bodin's writings corresponds to a period when the French monarchy was undergoing profound change. J. Russell Major, "The French Renaissance Monarchy as Seen through the Estates General," *Studies in the Renaissance*, 1962, IX, 114, no. 3, insists that a much later date, the middle third of the seventeenth century, marks the "dividing line between Renaissance monarchy and that of the old regime." According to Professor Major, "economic crisis and the Thirty Years' War" led to a dramatic transformation from weak decentralized government to a truly bureaucratic state. Perhaps Professor Major might be reminded of the vast administrative role traditionally played by the clergy. (Although concerned with a later period, E. L. Asher, *The Resistance to the Maritime Classes: the Survival of Feudalism in the France of Colbert*, Berkeley and Los Angeles, 1960, pp. 84-90, gives insight into some aspects of the clergy's administrative role.) When the Wars of Religion and conversion of entire regions to Protestantism deprived the crown of this major instrument of government, it was Bodin and the *Politiques* who, emphasizing the need for a thoroughly secular bureaucracy, heralded both the scope and character of future administrative development. Their writings and the huge army of venal office holders recruited during the civil wars (ultimately legitimized by the *droit annuel* in 1604) would appear to suggest that Professor Major's "dividing line" could be more appropriately drawn half a century prior to the time he recommends.

eigner" part of a comprehensive program aimed at undermining the economic and moral welfare of alien peoples. By reducing imports and by exporting heavily taxed agricultural surpluses, on which other states were thought to depend, France would become rich at the expense of her neighbors. Instead of buying merchandise from abroad, people would consume domestic manufactures, thereby creating employment for the idle and revenue for the King. Unable to sell their goods in France, the most populous of all kingdoms, foreign countries would suffer not only serious financial loss but also the spread of unemployment and disorder throughout their realms. In this way, distress abroad would, according to Bodin, redound necessarily to the advantage of France: "Properly speaking, the greatness of a prince is but the ruin or diminution of his neighbors and his strength consists in nothing but the feebleness of others."[36]

Men believed that subversion of domestic peace in a neighboring country was a major diplomatic goal in the perpetual conflict of states. For example, an anonymous author (ca. 1623-1624) declared that "a State cannot suffer the least disorder without its affecting the behavior of foreign powers." For proof, "one need look no further back than King Henry III," betrayed and even attacked by his friends and old allies "during the final troubled years of his feeble government." Indeed, it could be taken as a general principle that "all rulers . . . govern according to their interests and act only with respect to the good or bad fortune of others.[37]

[36] *Ibid.*, Bk. V, chap. 5, p. 793. A maxim repeated textually by François de la Mothe le Vayer, *Oeuvres*, Dresden, 1756, VII, 1e partie, p. 30.

[37] The passages are from an anonymous work entitled *Discours des Princes et Estats de la Chrétienté plus considérables à la France selon leurs diverses qualitez et conditions*, published in *Recueil de*

Throughout the first sixty years of the seventeenth century conflict and the menace of foreign interference in domestic difficulties loomed as constant threats. The persistence of this fear is explained largely by the monarchy's inability to restore order permanently within the realm. Neither Henry IV nor Richelieu was able to make the crown sufficiently strong to prevent widespread disturbances during the minorities of Louis XIII and of Louis XIV. In addition, such religious and political upheavals as the Arminian conflict in the Netherlands, the vast confused central European struggles of the Thirty Years War and civil strife in England, Catalonia, Portugal, and Naples all contributed to intensify uneasiness and apprehension in France. This is seen clearly, for example, in a confidential memoir to Mazarin, written by his librarian, Gabriel Naudé, shortly after Richelieu's death. Naudé warned that oppressive taxation could provide a fertile area for foreign machinations: "Just as we fomented the rebellions of the Dutch and of the Catalans, so can a powerful prince support those which extreme poverty will one day cause in France."[38] Fear of another "time of troubles" was not finally dispelled until the first part of the Sun King's personal reign, almost a century after St. Bartholomew and the publication of Bodin's *Republic*. During these decades hostility toward the foreigner, concern for consolidation of royal power, the ideal of the su-

---

quelques discours politiques, escrits sur diverses occurrences des affaires et Guerres Estrangeres depuis quinze ans. . . , 1632, pp. 161-162. This is the second printing of a second edition originally published in 1625; the first edition was published in 1624. For full bibliographical information see F. Meinecke, *Machiavellism*, trans. W. Stark, New Haven, 1957, p. 153, n.1.

[38] Citations are from Naudé's *Mémoire confidentiel adressé à Mazarin après la mort de Richelieu*, ed. Alfred Franklin, Paris, 1870, p. 39.

premacy of the state in society, and preoccupation with national wealth and the relation of existing fiscal practices to popular distress continued to dominate French political and economic writing.

So long as monarchy remained, as it did before 1660, a fragile institution unable to protect society adequately from danger of civil war, men continued to repeat and to elaborate familiar arguments about the need for strong government based upon a reorganized and autonomous economic structure. Questions about industry, trade, monetary problems, naval policy, taxation, and the employment of an obstreperous nobility were all brought together and considered in light of the fundamental axiom that civil war could be avoided and prosperity achieved only at the political and economic expense of other countries. Domestic problems were discussed almost exclusively in terms of foreign policy. This attitude became particularly apparent, of course, in times of crisis. The lengthy title of an anonymous pamphlet, published when the Estates General met in 1614, is by itself sufficient to illustrate a general frame of mind: *Advice to the King on means to . . . establish a great number of manufactures, prevent the export of money thus making . . . millions remain in the Kingdom, which are usually exported, thereby weakening foreigners by the same amount. To create an annual fund for naval establishments so as to be able to employ many nobles and other courageous folk. To avoid civil wars and make great progress and conquests. Finally, to render France one of the greatest Monarchies ever to have existed. All for the glory of God and the grandeur of the King without diminution or charge upon his finances and to the benefit of all his subjects with-*

out the least cost, indeed, on the contrary, to their great relief.[39]

Domestic insecurity, a stark view of international rivalry and, in the opinion of contemporaries, the possibility—indeed the positive necessity—of organizing the kingdom's affairs so as to make France economically self-sufficient were all factors leading to a division in economic thought: principles considered valid for foreign trade became inapplicable to domestic commerce. The latter, while necessary, was nevertheless thought to be of no public benefit; internal transactions, so far as the crown was concerned, were mere transfers of money from one purse to another. This opinion was clearly expressed as early as 1615 in Antoyne de Montchrétien's *Traicté de l'économie politique*:

> One man's loss is another's profit. This is true and is better known in matters of commerce than anywhere else. Yet I would say that with respect to [trade] between citizen and citizen there is no loss for the public. In this regard it is as if two vases were held and the liquor poured from one to the other. It is different, however, with foreign factors and merchants. They are among us similar to pumps drawing out . . . the pure substance of our people.[40]

Only treasure from abroad, he held, could profit the state; export should become the principal concern of those directing the kingdom's affairs. Montchrétien did not hesitate to recognize the moral implications of his position. France for him was a closed economic circuit, a completely autonomous sphere. Cut off from

[39] E. Bourgeois and L. André, *Les sources de l'histoire de France au XVIIᵉ siècle 1610-1715*, 8 vols., Paris, 1913-1935, VII, 27-28, suggest the author might be Montchrétien.

[40] Ed. Funck-Brentano, Paris, 1889, p. 161.

other men, its citizens were not bound in their relations with foreigners by the same ethical code governing their conduct toward each other: "A great difference exists between the kindness we must exercise toward a subject and that due toward a foreigner. . . . No tie of friendship links us; the citizen . . . is like our blood brother. Land and sky separate us from foreigners. . . ; [in contrast] we [Frenchmen] breathe the same air, are covered by the same sky and supported by the same land."[41]

This xenophobic element in mercantilist thought remained subdued until half a century later. At that time Louis XIV's government put mercantilist theory into practice on an unprecedented scale. Then, rightly or wrongly, men like Fénelon declared these policies to be the chief cause of war, itself in turn the major source of misery and economic distress at home and abroad. A profound Christian, outraged at the mercantilist attitude toward subjects of other realms, the Archbishop thundered: "The human race is but a single family. . . . War is the greatest of evils." And cursed were those rulers who "augment the power of their peoples" at the expense of their neighbors, seeking "a monstrous glory" in the blood of their brothers. Such individuals, "far from being demigods, are not even men; they must be an execration to all the centuries by which they thought themselves so admired. Oh ! Kings must beware of wars they undertake !"[42]

---

[41] *Ibid.*, p. 193. Elsewhere (pp. 113-114) Montchrétien explains that just as God has ordained that greater charity be exercised to members of the faith than to non-believers, so "notre affection toutesfois doit premierement embrasser l'utilité de nos citoyens, qui nous sont comme alliez par un droit de consanguinité."

[42] Quoted from *Télémaque* by P. Lorson, "Guerre et paix chez Fénelon," *Le XVIIᵉ siècle*, Numéro Spécial nos. 12-14: Fénelon et le tricentenaire de sa naissance 1651-1951, 1951-1952, p. 210.

ii. THE ORIGINS OF RELIGIOUSLY INSPIRED OPPOSITION TO MERCANTILISM

Conflicting attitudes toward foreigners, however, were often merely an expression of wider areas of controversy which concerned issues of a most disparate character. A host of seemingly unconnected questions were brought together, largely because men in the seventeenth century commonly projected their views of human nature into the political sphere; they believed that states behaved as people, that they were impelled by the same motives. This is the reason why pessimistic convictions about the innate depravity of man's soul corresponded generally to negative concepts of government. For example, spokesmen such as the more intense Augustinians, who thought political authority was a consequence of original sin,[43] conceived of the state largely in terms of its repressive functions. They placed public order above moral precepts and equated justice with defense of the peace. In contrast, writers more optimistic about the human soul argued, as did St. Thomas, that the state embodied those ethical commands which were written by nature everywhere into the hearts of men. Justice in the traditional sense of maintaining the general welfare by distributing "to each his own" would be fully realized when, as if in the *Utopia*, the golden rule became the supreme criterion for personal and political behavior. Moreover, this twofold division concerning man's ultimate destiny on one hand and his political and ethical conduct on the other was

[43] Prior to St. Thomas this view was generally accepted, and it remained influential long afterward. Claude de Seyssel, for example, wrote with the explicit assumption that "les hommes sont par nature corrompue, communément . . . ambitieux et convoiteux de dominer" (*la grande monarchie*, p. 191).

part of a further conflict about the place both of the individual and of society in nature.

This preoccupation with the role of man in the universe, becoming intensified during the course of the seventeenth century, was related partly to a division among the Augustinians and partly to dramatic changes in the scientific view of the cosmos. There were some pessimists who ennobled human reason: their opponents, however, were anti-intellectuals who disparaged the ultimate importance of rational or learned endeavor. The former tried to integrate society into a cosmos governed by the Cartesian laws of collision. They transformed both ethics and politics into a branch of physics. Social usefulness and reason of state, ideals corresponding to the proper machine-like functioning of society as a whole, were made the first criteria of ethical and of political behavior. The anti-intellectuals, however, paid little attention to science; instead, they emphasized, in the fashion of Montaigne, the feebleness of the human intellect.[43a]

[43a] Arguing against men whom he esteemed were excessively influenced by the ancients, Pierre de la Primaudaye, *Troisieme tome de l'Académie Françoise*, Lyon, 1599, criticized those who confused the laws of nature with human affairs: "Certainement je m'esmerveille de ces sages du monde, qui confessent que Dieu est tres simple et de soi mesme parfait. . . . Ils estiment que Dieu a une nécessaire liaison avecques les choses d'ici bas. . . . Mais comment est-il tres simple s'il a une nécessaire liaison avec les autres choses? Comment est-il prince de toutes, si nécessairement il est obligé au service des plus basses? . . . Brief . . . ostons toute nécessité des oeuvres du Seigneur" (p. 54).

Elsewhere, *l'Académie Françoise*, Saumur, 1613, pp. 8-9, La Primaudaye wrote: "Nous accordons bien avec les Philosophes, que l'entendement (sous lequel nous comprenons le sens et la raison) est comme le gouverneur et capitaine de l'ame; et que la volonté dépend d'icilui. Mais nous disons [que] quant . . . l'un et l'autre sont tellement corrompus et dépravez de leur nature, l'entendement est obscurci de ténebres à cause du péché du premier homme [qui] découle sur tous ses enfans par souillure héréditaire et la volonté pervertie. . . ." Peter Ramus expressed similar thoughts, see

They declared that the unrestrained exercise of power, not reason, could alone control men, all of whom are victims of an intractable nature. It was against both these pessimistic groups that the optimists continued to insist that moral precepts provide a transcendental guide for both individuals and governments;[44] but their most intense criticism was directed primarily at the anti-intellectuals, particularly against the latter's tendency to join skeptical arguments to pessimistic political views. And in the course of this polemic the more optimistic protagonists, largely members of the Counter Reformation, drew a political corollary from their tendency to exalt reason and to minimize the consequences of original sin: if man is both predominantly rational and morally educable then princes must lead him toward the good life. Governments become instruments of moral progress on earth.

The reflection of these issues can be seen in the development of mercantilist and anti-mercantilist theories. Under close examination, the unlikely routes by which mercantilism became identified with Machiavellism, with Pyrrhonian skepticism, and with the Cartesian world machine can be traced. The opposing arguments were of two kinds: religious and humanist. Religiously inspired critics up to the second decade of Louis XIV's personal reign argued largely against what was then called "Machiavellism." They attacked doctrines which justified the immoral actions of peo-

---

Léontine Zanta, *La Renaissance du stoïcisme au XVIᵉ siècle*, Paris, 1914, p. 23, n.5.

[44] Antoine Adam, in *Sur le problème religieux dans la première moitié du XVIIᵉ siècle*, Oxford, 1959, believes optimistic strains in early seventeenth century religious and philosophic thought received a great impetus from the kind of Stoicism taught by humanists in the Lowlands, particularly Justus Lipsius.

ple or polities in the name of an abstract principle, such as reason of state or the general interest. How these religious arguments became specifically anti-mercantilist is discussed in the following section. The origins of secularly inspired criticism are treated below, in the third and last part of this chapter.

Michel de Montaigne (1533-1592), a leading figure in the skeptical tradition, was convinced that the propensity to philosophize about religious mysteries was the principal cause of the Wars of Religion. Consequently, he did his best to shake the reader's confidence in the power of human intellect. And his efforts in this regard precipitated a number of controversies both in philosophy and in religion. Ruthlessly exposing weaknesses in every area of rational philosophy, while at the same time praising the intelligence and virtue of beasts and cannibals, the author suggested that man, particularly Christian man, held no special place in creation. It is difficult to know whether Montaigne was sincere or not when he justified faith by attacking reason in such a manner as to question the proposition that human beings are created in the image of God. Be that as it may, by insisting that savages were wiser than men, because "the laws of nature . . . still rule them,"[45] Montaigne removed all rational and Christian foundations from the concept of natural law, making it a purely instinctual guide to human behavior. And so controversial an idea did much to help put the problem of man's place in nature in the forefront of seventeenth century French thought. The author's disciples, known as Pyrrhonians (men like Pierre Charron and François de la Mothe le Vayer), exalted the superiority of animals and regarded the quest for knowledge as the

[45] *Essays*, Bk. I, chap. 31, p. 153.

ultimate source of misery and evil.[46] Like Montaigne, they struck out against "artificial" society whose purely local traditions, customs, and culture were said to be not only foolish but positively harmful. These conventions kept men from following "nature" or that "inner light" which guides the actions of animals and of those human beings fortunate enough to remain uncivilized.

Montaigne and his disciples so disparaged man's rational faculties that they appeared to suggest that pride rather than reason was the characteristic distinguishing human beings, at least Christians, from the rest of creation. Objections to this position were raised both by philosophers and by theologians. The former, defending the cause of reason with epistemological arguments, employed theories of knowledge to measure the distance separating men from God on one hand and from beasts on the other. Cartesians, the most extreme opponents of the Pyrrhonians, reduced all existence outside the human mind to matter and motion. In this way reason, no longer part of the phenomenal world, was made an attribute of the divine, and man's special relation to the Creator was at once reaffirmed and contrasted with that of animals, considered to be mere soulless machines.[47] The followers of Pierre Gassendi (1592-1655), unable to accept Montaigne's view of man as the lowest of creatures but unwilling to glorify mortal intelligence,

[46] Thirty-two editions of Pierre Charron's best known work, *De la Sagesse*, appeared between 1601 and 1664. François de la Mothe le Vayer's manual of skeptical thought *Quatre dialogues faits à l'imitation des Anciens* was published in 1630.

[47] Questions concerning the human or machine-like nature of beasts are elucidated in L. C. Rosenfield's *From Beast-Machine to Man-Machine*, New York, 1941. See also the more comprehensive study by Heikki Kirkinen, *Les origines de la conception moderne de l'homme-machine: le problème de l'âme en France à la fin du règne de Louis XIV (1670-1715)*, Helsinki, 1960.

tried to find a middle position between the two extremes of Pyrrhonic skepticism and the indubitability
of Cartesian intuition. Deriving all knowledge from
the five senses, Gassendi developed an epistemology
stressing both man's infinite distance from God and
his preeminence on earth. Priest and Epicurean, Gassendi tried to exalt faith by restricting reason to this
world, limiting human intellect to the function of organizing sense impressions created by the impact of
tiny atoms whirling in space. Revealed truth alone,
he felt, could penetrate the flux of external appearances.

The writings of Montaigne and his disciples also
precipitated religious controversies related to those
carried on among philosophers.[48] Spiritual life was
complex in early seventeenth century France, then
emerging from forty years of civil conflict. The Wars
of Religion had done much to impede the progress of
both Catholic reform and counterreform. Internecine
strife had sufficiently strengthened Gallicanism,
an alliance of bishops and monarchy against Rome, to
frustrate repeated efforts by the more orthodox clergy
to make the Council of Trent's decrees accepted officially as law throughout the realm.[49] Meanwhile,

[48] The following paragraphs on church and theology are based
almost entirely on the remarkable works of Jean Orcibal, especially
Les origines du Jansénisme, 5 vols., Paris, 1947-1962. See also his
pamphlet, *Le premier Port Royal: réforme ou contre-réforme?*,
Paris, 1956, which places early seventeenth century French religious
life in a larger historical and European context, and also *Louis XIV
et les protestants, la cabale des accomodeurs de religion, la caisse des
conversions, la révocation de l'Edit de Nantes*, Paris, 1951, for a
valuable discussion of the interaction of political and religious
forces in France from the Wars of Religion to the Revocation of
the Edict of Nantes.

[49] The fact that Henry IV personally strengthened France's ties
with Rome after the Edict of Nantes, favoring at the same time
the Jesuits and to some extent their ultramontane supporters (see

Gallican tendencies were further reinforced by serious disorders in French ecclesiastical organization. Conferring benefices on political favorites and converting bishoprics into part of family patrimonies were common practices which did more than encourage a secular spirit or even outright corruption among the clergy; such procedures also created strong material motivations for some churchmen to endorse theologians, like Edmond Richer, who declared the episcopacy, not the Pope, head of the Catholic Church. And writing in the same vein, the *politiques*, men like Bodin and Michel de l'Hôpital, formulated theories permitting government to subordinate religious policy to the needs of state. Thus on one side private interest and political insecurity combined to weaken spiritual endeavor; while on the other, Gallican-inspired refusals to accept the decrees of Trent deprived Catholic reform and counterreform of unity of direction in the period of their greatest expansion, the decade following the Wars of Religion. These facts do much to explain the extraordinary diversity in seventeenth century French religious life.

Peace, restored under Henry IV, introduced an unprecedented flowering of religious devotion.[50] Many faithful Christians, bypassing the corrupt secular hierarchy, infused a new spirit into the regular orders. Indeed the monastic revival reached such proportions

---

G. Pagès, *La monarchie d'ancien régime*, 5th edn., Paris, 1952, pp. 50-52) should not obscure the very substantial growth and intensification of Gallican feeling, particularly in the magistrature and to a lesser extent in the episcopacy. See the elaborate documentation in Orcibal, *Les origines*, II, 30-35.

[50] "Le début du XVIIe siècle connut une floraison monastique extraordinaire. Non seulement les ruines accumulées par les protestants furent réparées, mais les constructions nouvelles se multiplièrent tellement qu'elles changèrent complètement l'aspect des villes. . . ," Orcibal, *Les origines*, II, 21-22.

that some devout priests were alarmed lest the secular clergy, remaining uninspired by reform, continue to decline. The drive to save the traditional hierarchy from demoralization and irremediable injury led Pierre de Bérulle (1575-1629), for example, to establish the Oratorians, an order of the secular clergy but founded upon rules as severe as those in the most austere monastery. The success of these men and of others like St. François de Sales, Jean Duvergier d'Hauranne, better known as the Abbé de Saint-Cyran, and St. Vincent de Paul made priests "as venerated or at least as respected by the middle of the century as they had been despised at the beginning."[51]

Rivalry between monastic and secular reformers, however, soon led to conflict. It is these disputes which, when taken together with parallel controversies between Jesuits and Augustinians, reveal how the Augustinians divided into intellectual and anti-intellectual camps. The former transformed politics and ethics into a branch of physics, placing action and social utility above contemplative values and monastic retreat. In contrast, the anti-intellectuals were generally sympathetic to monastic ideals; indeed, the deprecation of reason was part of their contempt for the world, and both attitudes are revealed in their efforts to unite Pyrrhonian skepticism with the most pessimistic political views. But despite these fundamental differences, both groups influenced powerfully the development of mercantilist theory by their common subordination of ethical precepts to political necessity. Both groups also inspired opponents of mercantilist doctrine with religious and moral motives to attack what they believed were cynical or "Machiavellian" principles of political economy.

In the polemics between monastic and secular or-

[51] *Ibid.*, p. 27.

ders, the latter often described the monk as "belonging to himself [while] the cleric belongs to the Church"; the first seeks salvation "by fleeing," the latter "by fighting."[52] The secular priest was considered a soldier of Christ sent into this world to battle for men's souls; the monk, a religious egoist concerned merely with his own ultimate destiny. The struggle grew so heated that disagreements about the purpose of life in religious retreat appeared even among monastic reformers. The famous Abbé de Rancé, for example, founder of the order of the Trappists, insisted that contemplation and prayer rather than reason and study were the true mission of the faithful monk. Clerics like the Oratorian Bernard Lamy and the Benedictine Dom Jean Mabillon retorted that the Trappist believed one must be ignorant and lazy in order to serve God. They contended that personal retreat from the world should not absolve the individual from serving society in some way.[53]

Conflicts between clerical and monastic reformers about the proper way to serve Christ in this world were paralleled by another series of controversies between Jesuits and Augustinians on the same questions. The issue, fundamental to the character both of Catholic reform and counterreform, was bitterly fought throughout the century. Before the Council of Trent, Catholics and Protestants were separated

[52] *Ibid.*, p. 36, n.5.

[53] A brief discussion of this point may be found in Gustave Lanson, "Origines et premières manifestations de l'esprit philosophique dans la littérature française de 1675 à 1748," *Revue des cours et conférences*, XXXI (27 February 1907), 721-722. See also Henry Leclerq, *Dom Mabillon*, 2 vols., Paris, 1953-1957, II, 503-574. The intensity of the struggle between regular and secular clergy is described amply in Charles Chesneau (Julien-Eymard d'Angers), *Le Père Yves de Paris et son temps (1590-1678)*, 2 vols., Paris, 1946, I.

primarily by diametrically opposed views on the nature of the clergy and sacraments. Both groups, however, were largely in agreement about the radically sinful character of man. Ignatius Loyola was not less concerned with the agony of the human soul conscious of its depravity before God than was Luther or Calvin. Such optimistic views of human nature as those of the Spanish Jesuit Luis Molina, exaggerating one aspect of Loyola's doctrines, belong rather to Philip II's subsequent crusade to reestablish the unity of Christendom. Only during the last quarter of the sixteenth century did Molinism become the official doctrine of the Society of Jesus.[54]

Many Catholic reformers, especially Augustinians, were hostile to the theological optimism permeating the Jesuit Order at the height of the Spanish-led Counter Reformation. In France one of the earlier skirmishes between these groups occurred in 1626 when Saint-Cyran, a founder of Jansenism and a friend of Bérulle, quarreled with the Jesuit Father Garasse. The latter had firmly joined Molinism to an Erasmian love for ancient letters. Thus Saint-Cyran, imbued with love and awe before the impenetrable perfection of the Almighty, found his opponent's proposition that "theological matters are as easily allied with good letters as is the philosophy of Plato" as outrageous as the Jesuit's conviction that "it is more difficult to be desperately bad than to be perfectly virtuous."[55]

[54] The essential points of Luis Molina's doctrine, which appeared in 1588, are explained in the first chapter of Professor R. R. Palmer's *Catholics and Unbelievers in Eighteenth Century France*, Princeton, 1939. Professor Palmer, discussing Jesuit optimism at length, pointed out that eighteenth century Jansenists did not distinguish *philosophes* from Jesuits; both were thought to be imbued with similar if not identical ideas.

[55] Orcibal, *Les origines*, II, 261 and III, 90 respectively.

These struggles, with the monastics on one hand and with the Jesuits on the other, helped to split Augustinian thought into two branches. One group, resisting the intrusion of philosophy into theology, turned Montaigne's writings and those of his disciples into a formidable anti-Jesuit instrument; the other merged Augustinian theology with Cartesian science and philosophy, developing a utilitarian anti-monastic ethic. The former was anti-intellectual and discredited philosophy as a method by which man used reason to attempt either to penetrate or to deny the mysteries of faith. The latter, denying that devotion required religious retreat, considered human reason part of the divine, and placed it above prayer and contemplation.

Anti-intellectualism united skeptics and such strict Augustinians as Saint-Cyran in a common front against Jesuits. Montaigne's and Charron's eloquent humiliation of human intellect before divine omniscience appealed to Saint-Cyran, providing him, as it did Pascal at a later date, with powerful weapons to use against Molinist opponents.[56] Saint-Cyran and

[56] Orcibal highlights the persistent and crucial nature of this struggle within the Catholic Church from the late sixteenth to the early eighteenth centuries. See especially Appendix III in vol. III, and pp. 260-282 in vol. II of *Les origines*. So far as Saint-Cyran's welcome of the skeptics is concerned, Orcibal wrote, "L'ami de Jansenius voit donc en Charron un auxiliaire précieux pour l'Augustinisme et reprend contre Garasse sa critique de la raison et de la justice humaine" (II, 276).

The compatibility of the Augustinian and skeptical traditions was not peculiar to France. The following passage was written by Sir William Temple in 1652: "Going into a bookseller's shop, I asked for Montaigne's Essays; he told me he had it not. A young fellow that I took notice of for nothing but the lace upon his cloak, standing by presently said . . . 'I have it at home.' I asked him 'Sir, do you sell books?' He replied, 'No Sir, but I buy books.' 'And cry them when you have done,' said one in my company. So quick and pat a reply invited me to talk a little more with my gallant, but when he told me he loved Montaigne's Essays because

Pascal—convinced that the laws of nature provided no clues to God's will, not even to His existence—taught that God is hidden, and that man, a wretched creature torn between the nothingness of his own existence and the infinite majesty of the Creator, is incapable of reasoning about Him.[57]

Cartesian Augustinians, however, held different views: Jansenists like Antoine Arnauld, Pierre Nicole, and such eminent Oratorians as Bernard Lamy and Nicolas Malebranche thought the laws of nature did, indeed, reflect God's will. They believed man was entrusted with truth so as to serve Him in this world. Lamy, for example, thought knowledge nothing more than the product of innate ideas; knowledge comes

---

they were so like Austin's (Augustine's) confessions, I kissed his hands and made an end to the story." Quoted by Homer E. Woodbridge, *Sir William Temple: The Man and his Work*, New York and Oxford, 1940, p. 24.

Another aspect of this problem, the use of skeptical philosophy to convert Huguenots, is discussed by R. H. Popkin, "Skepticism and the Counter-Reformation in France," *Archiv für Reformationsgeschichte*, LI (1960), 58-86. According to the author, skeptical arguments proved a two-edged sword, ultimately spreading doubt even among Catholic counterreformers who used them to weaken Huguenot religious conviction. This stratagem, and its ultimately subversive consequences, is documented in greater detail in Popkin's full length study, *The History of Scepticism from Erasmus to Descartes*, Assen, the Netherlands, 1960, 2d edition; revised, 1964.

[57] Jansenist insistence on the inscrutability of God has provided the title and the point of departure for a Marxist interpretation of Pascal, Racine, and the Jansenist movement, Lucien Goldmann's *Le Dieu caché: étude sur la vision tragique dans les "Pensées" de Pascal et dans le théâtre de Racine*, Paris, 1955. The author links the idea of a "spectator God" who had abandoned the world to its own devices, "la vision tragique," to the economic and social conditions of the *noblesse de robe* from 1638 to 1677, dates corresponding respectively to the imprisonment of Saint-Cyran and to the first appearance of Racine's *Phèdre*. Despite long tendentious passages, anachronisms, oversimplifications, and the cumbersome apparatus of Marxist jargon, this book has sections of genuine interest stressing the social backgrounds of Jansenism.

from disciplined reflections about verities already im-
bedded in the hearts of all human beings. "God has
planted in men the seeds . . . of first truths from
which all others flow as streams from their sources.
The art of learning consists of nothing more than
paying particular attention to fundamental principles and subsequently remarking the consequences
which can then be drawn one after the other."[58] This
was the method used by "the great Saint Augustine."[59]
Moreover, no study could better prepare men in the
right use of reason than "Geometry and other
branches of mathematics" because they teach us
"clear and simple truths."[60] Philosophers never discover anything new; they merely "alert us" or bring
to mind that which had passed unnoticed.[61]

Knowledge, however, was not given for our pleasure. St. Augustine informs us that, while the things
of the mind may be used, they are not to be enjoyed.[62]
"A judge who studies to perform his duties more adequately can say he is learning in order better to execute God's will; but should he amuse himself with
Chinese or Indian languages he would find it diffi-

[58] "Dieu a mis dans les Hommes des semences de doctrine, c'est-
a-dire, des véritez premieres, dont les autres coulent comme les
ruisseaux de leurs sources. L'art d'apprendre ne consiste qu'a
faire une attention particuliere a ces premieres véritez, et a
remarquer ensuite les conséquences que l'on en peut tirer les unes
après les autres," *Entretiens sur les Sciences dans lesquelles outre la
méthode d'étudier on apprend comme l'on doit se servir des sciences
pour se faire l'esprit juste et le coeur droit et pour se rendre utile
à l'Eglise. . .*, Grenoble, 1683, p. 45. See François Girbal's useful
article on Bernard Lamy, with its appended chronology of his
works, both published and in manuscript, "La formation Augustinienne du P. B. Lamy, de l'Oratoire (1660-1680)," *Société des amis
de Port Royal*, VIII (1957), 48-94. More recently Girbal has expanded this article into a book: *Bernard Lamy: étude biographique et
bibliographique*, Paris, 1964.

[59] *Ibid.*, p. 47.   [60] *Ibid.*, pp. 53-54.   [61] *Ibid.*, pp. 281-282.

[62] See E. Gilson, *Introduction à l'étude de St. Augustin*, Paris,
1943.

cult . . . to say 'Oh my Lord I am doing this for you!' "[63] Prior to the Fall, "Adam knew everything,"[64] but original sin clouded our understanding, and man's duty since the Redemption has been to use intellect exclusively for the development of truth given to the world by God. The physical and moral order of the universe are the direct reflection of divine command. Science and morality are one. The supreme expression of this position can be seen in Malebranche's philosophy where "Occasionalism" identified causation in the physical world with God's will and transformed reason into His word revealed in the mind of man.[65]

Combining physical and moral precepts into a single expression of the Creator's will, Cartesian Augustinians defined obedience to God as nothing less than behavior conforming to reason. But identification of the human intellect both with the physical order and with the divine had the most pessimistic implications for Pierre Nicole. On one hand, he de-

[63] The quotation is from Nicole, *Essais de morale contenus en divers traittés sur plusieurs devoirs importans*, 13 vols., Paris, 1714-1715, II, 239. Lamy writes in a similar vein, "Un homme qui regarde comme une grande chose de scavoir quel étoit l'ordre des mois des Macédoniens est méprisable, mais celuy qui recueille cet ordre de ce qui nous reste de l'Antiquité, afin que si on a besoin de le scavoir, comme il arrive en certains points de Chronologie importans, on en trouve l'éclaircissement dans les Livres, mérite d'autant plus de louanges que son travail est pénible" (*ibid.*, p. 89).

[64] "L'ignorance est une peine du péché originel . . . Adam lorsqu'il étoit innocent scavoit toutes choses" (*ibid.*, p. 14).

[65] "Nous voyons toutes choses par cela seul que Dieu veut que ce qui est en lui qui les représente nous soit découvert, et non point parce que nous avons autant d'idées que nous pouvons voir des choses, c'est que cela met une véritable dépendence entre Dieu et les esprits créés. Car de cette sorte nous ne saurions rien voir que Dieu ne veuille bien que nous le voyions, et que Dieu ne nous fasse voir ce que nous voyons." Quoted by Henry Gouhier, *La Philosophie de Malebranche et son expérience religieuse*, Paris, 1948, p. 232.

scribed society as a lifeless system of mechanical forces; on the other, he introduced self-love and private interest as the only natural motives for human behavior. According to Nicole, reason "enlightens" self-love and directs man toward acts which, while outwardly virtuous, remain despicable in the eyes of the Lord. Praiseworthy deeds may be inspired either by grace or by self-love—the true character of our conduct remains hidden. Reason, a light leading to the noblest achievements, creates the illusion of virtue and blinds us to the deeper motives of our behavior; it is the instrument by which God drives even the damned to perform good works. Although conduct meritorious to God is impossible without grace, human activity may be socially useful if it is guided by reason; indeed, man is capable of no higher good. It is on these premises that Nicole constructed a utilitarian ethic.[66] Beginning in much the same manner as Hobbes, Nicole carefully identified the factor distinguishing his position from that of the author of the *Leviathan*:

> If he who said [man] is born in a state of war and each is naturally the enemy of all others, had wished to describe . . . only the disposition of the heart . . . without trying to justify or make such behavior legitimate, he would have said something as conformable to truth and to experience, as that which he maintains is contrary to reason and to justice.[67]

[66] So far as I know, Jansenist utilitarianism, although mentioned on several occasions, has been discussed only by Gilbert Chinard, *En lisant Pascal*, Geneva, 1948, and here quite briefly in the last chapter. Apart from the two chapters in Henri Brémond's *Histoire littéraire du sentiment religieux en France*, 12 vols., Paris, 1929-1933, IV, nothing of any consequence has, to my knowledge, been written on Nicole. The subject is certainly worth investigating.

[67] *Essais de morale*, III, 126.

Self-love drove man from intolerable anarchy into society; it is the first principle of human behavior and the foundation of the civil law. To contend that this order is just, is blasphemous. Utility is the exclusive criterion, the unique source from which the canons of human behavior are derived; and politics is merely the "art whereby cupidity is . . . [both] restrained . . . and applied to things useful to society."[68]

Social behavior, having no religious basis, is in fact nothing more than an aspect of commerce: "One has to give in order to receive. . . . We traffic not only in merchandise . . . but we also engage in commerce of works, of services, of assiduity and of civility. . . . This trade satisfies the needs of life without the aid of Charity."[69] Civilization, a perpetual exchange of deeds and goods, is, moreover, a process governed by the same laws as those regulating the course of planets and the rhythm of tides. "Nothing can better represent this spiritual world formed by concupiscence [society] than the material world formed by nature, that is to say, that assembly of bodies composing the universe."[70] The principle of linear inertia is the foundation of both orders: as a body in space moves in a straight line unless

---

[68] *Ibid.* (1713 edn.), II, 145. Pascal, *Pensées* (Brunschvicg), 451, wrote: "Tous les hommes se haïssent naturellement l'un autre. On s'est servi comme on a pu de la concupiscence pour la faire servir au bien public; mais ce n'est que feindre, et une fausse image de la charité; car au fond ce n'est que haine."

[69] *Ibid.* (1714 edn.), III, 128. Maxim LXXXIII in the *Oeuvres de la Rochefoucauld*, 3 vols., Paris, 1868, I, 66 is as follows: "Ce que les hommes ont nommé amitié n'est qu'une société, qu'un ménagement réciproque d'intérests, et qu'un échange de bons offices; ce n'est enfin qu'un commerce ou l'amour-propre se propose toujours quelque chose à gagner." Moreover the editor L. Gilbert (the volumes are part of the series *Les grands écrivains de la France*) has annotated this maxim with similar remarks from Madame de Sablé, Saint-Evremond, Claude Barbin, and J. Esprit.

[70] *Essais de morale*, III, 130.

checked or deflected by other bodies, so an individual naturally moves up the social ladder unless prevented by others. Interests conflict in society in the same manner that atoms collide in space.

> And we shall see that all other movements can be described as the consequence of this comparison. As little bodies . . . unite their forces and movements they form great masses of matter . . . called whirlpools, which are like estates and kingdoms. Since these whirlpools are themselves crowded and confined by other whirlpools, as by neighboring kingdoms, little whirlpools form in each larger one, which, while following the general movement of the larger bodies propelling them, do not cease, however, to have a movement of their own, which in turn forces smaller bodies to revolve around them. Similarly great personages of state, while following the general movement, have their own interests providing centers for quantities of people attached to them. Finally, as all little bodies propelled by whirlpools also turn around their own centers, so little people, who follow the fortunes of the great and those of the state, do not cease in all the duties and services they perform for others to think of themselves and to have their own interests continually in view.[71]

Descartes, positing linear inertia and a corpuscular plenum, constructed a universe made up of an infinite number of whirlpools whose individual motions combined perpetually with movements of smaller ones contained within themselves as well as with those of neighboring vortices. It is difficult to conceive how

[71] *Ibid.*, pp. 130-131.

Nicole could have applied this theory to society more faithfully than he did.[72]

According to Nicole, the best interests of the individual and of society are served to the extent that reason guides his conduct. It is also true, he contended, that the most reasonable behavior is so useful as to be indistinguishable from a virtuous life inspired by grace. Therefore, the first duty of a true Christian is to fight for the supremacy of reason in this world:

> From all we have said we may conclude that to reform this world entirely, that is to say, to banish all vices and all gross disorders, to make men happy in this very life, we must, in the absence of Charity, give them all an enlightened self-love which will know its true interests and will open the paths discovered by right reason. No matter how corrupt society is internally and in the eyes of God, there will be nothing outside better regulated, more civil, more just and more

[72] T. S. Kuhn, *The Copernican Revolution, Planetary Astronomy in the Development of Western Thought*, Cambridge, Mass., 1957, p. 241, reproduces a diagram of the Cartesian universe and part of his explanation is as follows: "Each of Descartes' vortices was, at least potentially, a solar system, generated and governed by the corpuscular laws of inertia and collision. For example, corpuscular impacts just balance the centrifugal tendency that inertia gives to each corpuscle in the vortex. If all others were removed, each single particle would travel straight ahead along a tangent to its normally circular path and thus leave the vortex. It does not do so only because constant collision with particles outside of it in the vortex continually drive it back towards the center. Similar impacts keep the stable corpuscular aggregates that form the planets circulating in approximately circular paths about the vortex center." Nicole clearly substituted human beings for corpuscles and conceived of legislation in terms of social physics. A similar tendency may be seen in the scientist Edme Mariotte, *Essai de Logique*, 1678, where in a section on morals the author determines the good or bad character of an act by its "conformity" or "deformity" to principles drawn from the physical world.

peaceful, more honest and more generous; and, what is most admirable, is that although animated and moved by self-love, we shall not see self-love, and, entirely empty of Charity, we shall see everywhere nothing but the signs of Charity.[73]

Cartesian Augustinians so separated morality from religion and reason from faith that they were able to reconcile corruption with happiness. They believed that human felicity, proceeding from the dominance of reason over the passions, can be attained by discovering truths latent in the human mind. In this way man acquires the illusion of virtue and is happy.

[73] *Essais de morale*, III, 165-166. Nicole's argument that reasonable behavior merely appears to conform to actions inspired by Grace is profoundly Cartesian. Descartes defined the human body as a machine. The passions are entirely physiological in character; external to man, they rule the body but have no effect on the mind. On one hand, the passions are part of the mechanical system governing the entire universe outside the human mind, and, on the other, Descartes insists that God "implanted" the laws of nature in our souls. In this way, Descartes concludes that reason may rule the passions in precisely the same manner that God governs the cosmos. To become master of himself, man need only exercise the reason by which he extends his empire over nature. Such qualities as mercy, charity, and justice are meaningless terms in this mechanical system of action and reaction, and Descartes therefore relegates them to the area of faith. Nicole's ethics are clearly derived from these premises. Charity and justice, mere terrestrial illusions of divine attributes, are not a product of reason, which alone governs both society and nature. Nicole's "self-love" inspires all human behavior. It corresponds to Descartes' "moi," described by A. J. Krailsheimer, *Studies in Self-Interest from Descartes to La Bruyère*, Oxford, 1962. Concluding a chapter on Descartes, Krailsheimer writes, "The revolution is complete; the 'moi' has become its own axis, self-sufficient, free, independent of other persons and things, contemptuously emancipated from the body spurred on by the whisper *eritis sicut dei* . . ." (p. 46).

A similar influence appears in Hobbes, whose ethics, based upon corpuscular mechanics, correspond often to the Cartesian view of man and cosmos as well as to a market society. A suggestive book in this regard is C. B. Macpherson, *The Political Theory of Possessive Individualism*, Oxford, 1962, see especially pp. 1-106.

Struggling against Pyrrhonians to maintain the supremacy of the rational intellect, Nicole equated reason with science and placed social and political behavior within the Cartesian cosmos. Acts are neither good nor evil; they are merely useful or injurious. Justice is an expression of mechanical law; the purpose of the law is to assure the proper functioning of the social machine, to protect the common interest. Although Nicole identified reason and utility in the most radical eighteenth century fashion, he stopped short of making moral progress possible by saying that reason and utility create merely the illusion of virtue: enlightened self-interest can lead man only to the outward appearance of the best of all possible worlds.

We shall also see the more politically oriented Cartesians, such as Jean Silhon, employ similar reasoning to escape the extremes of either pessimism or optimism. Explaining, in much the same way as Nicole, that human relations are a "traffic" of virtues and services, a mechanical system of ethical exchange devoid of moral content, Silhon considered the state the supreme coordinator of countless interests; government, the instrument of ultimate rationality. Thus it becomes illusory to think conflict can arise between moral precepts and the exercise of political authority because the state is reason incarnate and reason, by definition, cannot conflict with morality.

In contrast, Pyrrhonians, like Gabriel Naudé, who denied the supremacy of reason, were compelled to admit the dichotomy between politics and morality. They therefore openly embraced Machiavellian doctrine, saying that the ethically unrestrained exercise of power alone is capable of checking the irresistible passions of human nature. Despite this difference,

however, both Pyrrhonians and Augustinians subordinated moral precepts either to reason of state or to
the common utility. These principles became part of
mercantilist theory: on one hand publicists came to
legitimize immoral behavior on the grounds of general utility; on the other, Richelieu frankly joined
mercantilist doctrine to Machiavellian principles.
And, as we shall see, both these views proved anath-
ema to religiously inspired critics of mercantilist
theory.

Jean Silhon, intimate adviser to Richelieu and
friend and disciple of Descartes, published two
treatises entitled: *De la certitude des connoissances
humaines ou sont particulierement expliquez les
principes et les fondemens de la Morale et de la Politique* . . . , and a two volume work, *Le Ministre
d'Estat avec le véritable usage de la politique moderne.*[74] Silhon began by attacking the author of the
Essays. He identified Montaigne as a Pyrrhonian
whose creed he summarized thus: *"science does not
exist, we must doubt all, and knowledge, whether derived from the senses or* from understanding, is subject to illusion and mistake."[75]

After replying with a mistaken paraphrase from
the *Cogito* and a defense of the doctrine of innate
ideas,[76] Silhon went on to develop a theory of moral-

[74] The first book, *De la certitude* . . . was published in Paris
in 1661 (here the 1662 edition is used); the two volumes of the
second work, *Le Ministre d'Estat* . . . did not appear until 1665.
For more details about Silhon see the numerous references in E.
Bourgeois and L. André, *Les sources de l'histoire de France au
XVIIᵉ siècle 1610-1715*, 8 vols., Paris, 1913-1935. For Silhon's relations with Descartes see Antoine Adam, *Histoire de la littérature
française au XVIIᵉ siècle*, 5 vols., Paris, 1949-1956, I, 297, 320, 327,
n.4.

[75] *De la certitude*, p. 9, italics in the original. Chapter VIII, p. 40
et seq. is devoted to a more lengthy refutation of the Pyrrhonians.

[76] For discussion of Silhon's misunderstanding of Descartes see
R. H. Popkin, *The History of Scepticism*, p. 170.

ity and politics. Positing two basic premises, he asserted, first, that one person's behavior describes "an abbreviated portrait of the government of states."[77] Second, the key to man's moral character may be found in the dichotomy between his machine-like body and his mind. Internally man experiences a perpetual struggle of reason and passion; externally he lives in society and is restrained by that part of ethics pertaining to social relations, called justice. The two areas are closely related. When passions gain the upper hand men draw their swords against their neighbors. To avoid this, states everywhere have abolished the private natural right to exact vengeance in a just cause, establishing in its place law based on reason. Laws have no trace of passion, and their disinterested character assists men in combating the "lower regions." Princes, being subject to no earthly authority, alone retain the natural right to exact vengeance in a just cause. As legislators, however, they are bound by the principle upon which all law is based, the primacy of reason. The state is to the body politic what mind is to our physical beings.[78]

[77] *Min. d'Estat*, I, 15.

[78] *Ibid.*, II, 1-12, and *De la certitude*, p. 84. Richelieu appears to have had ideas similar to those of his adviser: "La lumière naturelle fait connoître à un chacun, que l'homme ayant été fait Raisonnable, il ne doit rien faire que par Raison, puis qu'autrement il seroit contre sa Nature, et par conséquent contre celui même qui en est l'Auteur. . . . Il doit souverainement faire régner la Raison; ce qui ne requiert pas seulement qu'il ne fasse rien sans elle, mais l'oblige de plus à faire que tous ceux qui sont sous son Autorité la révèrent et la suivent religieusement. . . . La pratique de cette Règle est d'autant plus aisée que l'Amour est le plus puissant motif qui oblige à obéir, et qu'il est impossible que des Sujets n'aiment pas un Prince s'ils connoissent que la Raison soit le Guide de toutes ses Actions." *Testament politique*, Amsterdam, 1688, Part II, pp. 8-9. Louis André published a critical edition in 1947. Professor Edmond Esmonin then demonstrated serious errors in André's edition. Since that time the authenticity of the

The first rule of justice or the government of social relations is derived from self-love and from man's dependence on "countless external supports." Loving themselves and unable to live without others, men love those who contribute to the preservation of their existence, the intensity of affection varying directly with the importance of the aid received. Thus men are most thankful to God, next, to their fatherland, and finally to their parents. "Almost all actions . . . are motivated by one kind of interest or another. We traffic perpetually for virtues in this world and for merits in the next." Interest provides the "springs" and "form" for human activity; it is "the soul of civil harmony."[79] Only princes, dependent upon no earthly superior, remain unmoved by forces impelling common mortals. "Their virtue, derived from Reason, is purer . . . than that of their subjects who frequently are *gens de bien* only because they are afraid . . . to be bad."[80] The natural purity of rulers and the objective character of law are the best proof that God has provided man with means to subdue passion. As a result, universal obedience and support of the state will usher in the Age of Reason.

Since Pyrrhonians did not share the Cartesian faith in reason, nothing could logically prevent their more pessimistic spokesmen from open espousal of Machiavellian principles. Gabriel Naudé, for example, li-

---

Testament has been much discussed, see, for example, Ruyssen, *Les sources doctrinales*, II, 137-138. More recently, however, R. Pithon, "A propos du testament politique de Richelieu," *Revue Suisse d'histoire*, VI (1956), 177-214 (reviewed at length by Edmond Esmonin in *Revue d'histoire moderne et contemporaine*, V [1958], 74-77) demonstrates that while sections of the *Testament* were undoubtedly written by Richelieu, other parts are from sources outside the Cardinal's immediate entourage. Indeed some elements even conflict with Richelieu's other writings. In short, the *Testament*, although far from spurious, must be used with caution.

[79] *De la certitude*, p. 78.   [80] *Ibid.*, p. 116.

brarian successively to Cardinals Bagni, Richelieu, and Mazarin, admirer of Charron and La Mothe le Vayer, thought "human malice and depravity so great" that it is naive in the extreme to believe government can be at once effective and moral.[81] Naudé, regarding critics of Machiavelli as either fools or hypocrites, stated that the Florentine's writings were "everywhere prohibited but his doctrines are practiced by the very people who authorize their censure."[82] Moral considerations should always give way to political expedience. Princes were "masters of the laws in order to lengthen or shorten or to confirm or abolish them."[83]

The illusion of certain knowledge and the chimera of external laws blinded ministers to the best interests of state. Everything, both material and spiritual, according to Naudé, was unstable and variable. "Monarchies, religions, sects, towns, men, beasts, trees, stones and generally all that enclosed within this great Machine," the very heavens beyond the moon—all were subject to generation and corruption. States succumbed to revolutions and civil wars, justice was slowly strangled and dismembered by venality and the sale of offices, churches shattered under the impact of schisms and heresies, and, finally, belief in God was destroyed by the drive for knowledge:

> The surfeit of colleges, seminaries and students along with the facility of printing and of transporting books, has already shaken sects and religion. It is certain that more new systems in

[81] *Considérations politiques sur les coups d'Estat*, Rome, 1639, p. 11. On Naudé himself see the monumental thesis of René Pintard, *Le libertinage érudit dans la première moitié du XVIIᵉ siècle*, 2 vols., Paris, 1943, I, 156-178, 206-208, 209-214, 245-270, 304-311, 442-476, 540-551. See also R. H. Popkin, *op.cit.*, pp. 90-92.

[82] *Considérations*, p. 71.   [83] *Ibid.*, pp. 77-78.

Astronomy, more novelties in Philosophy, Medicine and Theology and more atheists have appeared since 1452 . . . than in the preceding thousand years. For myself, I defy those most versed in French history to show me someone accused of atheism prior to the reign of Francis I, surnamed the Restorer of Letters.[84]

A wise minister aware of the mutability of man and nature would know that no law would impede the creation or destruction of states; success might very well attend a skillful plan to "ruin some Republic or Empire." Interest of state, without regard to changeable values of religion or opinion, alone should guide "all actions of Princes."[85]

Cartesians and Pyrrhonians discussed political theory in the light of their respective philosophies. Silhon divided existence into mind and extension, reason and passion. Classifying the state in the first category, Descartes' friend transformed government into reason incarnate. In contrast, Naudé's political thinking was founded on the denigration of the rational intellect. Viewing philosophy more as a curse than a benefit and believing man inferior in some respects to beasts, Richelieu's librarian thought the state existed primarily to protect men from the consequences of unbridled reason. Government alone, he believed, could contain the centrifugal forces set loose in society by intellectual pride. Moral values and religious opinions, different in one part of the world from another and always subject to change, should not interfere with reason of state, the only source of order in a chaotic universe. The opinions of Nicole, Silhon, and Naudé, who each in his own way raised the common utility or reason of state

[84] *Ibid.*, pp. 143-145.   [85] *Ibid.*, pp. 142, 77-78.

above moral precepts, were first anticipated and later merged with mercantilist theory.

In Montchrétien's day (1615) the concept of social usefulness was advanced by mercantilist spokesmen above all in opposition to the monastic ideal of withdrawal and contemplation, which received great impetus during the spiritual revival. Later, when monastic values were no longer a major issue, it was Richelieu who established mercantilist doctrine explicitly on Machiavellian principles. In the earlier period, Montchrétien was aware that his views of political economy, emphasizing action and utility at the expense of religious contemplation and asceticism, placed the general secular welfare above the Christian ideal of individual salvation. He could scarcely have been more clear: "The welfare of the people is the supreme law." All other considerations depended upon "policies of government [which] differ . . . according to necessity."[86] Indeed, nature herself had directed that human conduct be guided away from contemplation and toward socially useful activity.

> Nature, giving man understanding, raising him not only above the level of beasts but above . . . the elements and even the heavens, willed that he be like *une table raze* where all kinds of spiritual images can be imprinted without confusion . . . so that from his knowledge, as from a well stocked storehouse, he can draw all the arts necessary for the upkeep and commodity of life. . . . Man is born to live in continual activity and occupation. . . . Contemplative life is in truth the highest and nearest to God; but without action it remains imperfect and . . . more prejudicial than useful to Republics. . . . Also

[86] *L'économie politique*, p. 120.

action combined with contemplation sometimes does great good for human society. . . . If civil occupations are as if asleep in the breast of contemplation, the Republic will necessarily fall in ruin. Action alone is the most profitable. . . . If love of truth requires contemplation, the union and profit of our society seeks and demands action.[87]

Montchrétien wrote during the height of the monastic revival and his treatise was published in the year after fear of civil war had driven Marie de Medici to convoke the Estates General. In these circumstances he, like Bodin before him, openly chose a philosophy and religion which saw God's will being executed through the ruler of a "well-ordered state." Civic virtue was transformed into the ultimate good and retreat from this world was regarded as a kind of politico-religious treason.[87a] Religion should be subordinated to the general interest. Labor rather than meditation pointed the way toward the good life, and man's first duty was to help produce the wealth necessary for establishing the permanent supremacy of the state in society.

These principles, central to the mercantilist ethic, were entirely compatible with Louis Machon's rehabilitation of Machiavelli, written under Richelieu's personal direction.[88] Machon, like Naudé, wrote that

[87] *Ibid.*, pp. 20-21.

[87a] Guillaume Du Vair's "Exhortation à la vie civile," *Oeuvres*, Paris, 1625, pp. 332ff. (written during the Wars of Religion) is a most eloquent and forceful patriotic appeal for the active as opposed to the contemplative life.

[88] The full title is "Apologie pour Machiavelle en faveur des princes et les ministres d'Estat," B.N., Fds. fr., MSS 1946-1947. Richelieu's direction of Machon's work has been explained and documented by Raymond Céleste, *Louis Machon apologiste de Machiavel et de la politique du cardinal de Richelieu: Recherches sur sa vie et ses oeuvres*, Bordeaux, 1882; and also in a supplementary

"human brutality is so great and widespread, malice and perfidy so irrepressible that violence alone can keep [man] in the path of duty."[89] For him, as for Bodin, justice was inseparable from power; the coercive force of the state, man's sole protection against anarchy. Moral precepts should not interfere with the effective exercise of government. "Religion can be made to adapt to the state . . . ; both are intimately connected. One is but the interior police and the other exterior." Princes, divinely appointed agents, were "masters of the life and possessions of their subjects as God alone is of their persons and conscience." The crown was the depository of the general interest, and there existed "no other goal nor rule of conduct than the welfare of the people, public utility and the conservation of the state."[90]

These doctrines aroused the most determined opposition from religious quarters during Richelieu's ministry. Saint-Cyran's and, indeed, much of *Port Royal's* resistance to the Cardinal-Minister was in fact a direct attack against the principle *Salus populi suprema lex est*.[91] Indeed, the evidence suggests strongly that Richelieu imprisoned Saint-Cyran because *Port Royal* was becoming the center of profound resistance to the regime.[92] Much of the same

---

study by the same author, *Louis Machon apologiste de Machiavel . . . nouvelles recherches sur sa vie et ses oeuvres 1600-1672*, Bordeaux, 1883. More recently, K. T. Butler, "Louis Machon's 'Apologie pour Machiavelle'—1643 and 1668," *Journal of the Warburg and Courtauld Institutes*, III (1939-1940), 208-227, contributes further information about Machon's life and ably discusses both the original and a subsequently expanded version of Machon's work.

[89] *Ibid.*, p. 55.

[90] *Apologie pour Machiavelle*, B.N. Fds. fr. 1946-1947, MS 1946, p. 138 and preface respectively. See also Albert Cherel, *La pensée de Machiavel en France*, Paris, 1935, pp. 81-82.

[91] Orcibal, *Les origines*, II, 490.   [92] *Ibid.*, pp. 535-551.

spirit seems to have also inspired Michel de Marillac's earlier opposition to Richelieu. It is well established that the Keeper of the Seals, close friend to
Bérulle and to St. François de Sales was the spokesman for the *parti des dévots* in government.[93] Marillac's bitter criticism of Richelieu's expansionist policies, leading to his disgrace and imprisonment in
1630, was based squarely on the principle that it is
evil for the state to seek to become strong at the expense of its subjects. Marillac's insistence on "the
great and unbelievable miseries of the French people" and his demands for a "general reform of the
interior of the kingdom" reflected in part the *dévot*
conviction that the crown is bound by the same moral
laws as those governing the conduct of its most humble subjects.[94]

The same conviction, several decades later, also
persuaded Fénelon and his friend and teacher, the
Abbé Claude Fleury, to organize resistance to Louis
XIV's policies. These men were leaders of a later generation of *dévots*. Fénelon's uncle, for example, Antoine
de Salignac, Marquis de la Motte Fénelon, who was
early instrumental in directing his young nephew
into the priesthood,[95] was a member of the Company
of the Holy Sacrament of Paris,[96] an organization
which replaced the *parti des dévots* after the deaths
of Bérulle and Marillac.[97] Antoine de Salignac was
also a close friend to St. Vincent de Paul,[98] and he

[93] Georges Pagès, "Autour du grand orage, Richelieu et Marillac:
deux politiques," *Revue historique*, CLXXIX (1937), 63-97.

[94] *Ibid.* In this connection see also the unpublished doctoral dis-
sertation by Emanuel Stanley Chill, "The Company of the Holy
Sacrament (1630-1666): Social Aspects of the French Counter
Reformation," Columbia University, 1960, particularly pp. 184-200.

[95] Jeanne-Lydie Goré, *L'itinéraire de Fénelon: Humanisme et
spiritualité*, Paris, 1957, p. 53.

[96] E. S. Chill, *op.cit.*, App. A, p. 362.   [97] *Ibid.*, pp. 66-73.

[98] J. L. Goré, *op.cit.*, p. 53.

certainly knew St. Vincent's chief assistant, *Sainte*
Louise de Marillac, niece of the devout Keeper of
the Seals.[99] The theology of the *dévots*, a theology
which inspired an enormous effort to establish a system of national charity, earning for St. Vincent the
title of *père de la patrie*, was permeated with religious
optimism. In contrast to the solitaries of *Port Royal*,
St. Vincent literally sought the person of Christ in
this world; he looked for Jesus among the poor and
the suffering. He believed God existed *both* in the
church and in society; worship in one area was identical with service in the other.[100] This unique concept
of charity is also reflected in Fénelon's writings. The
difference, however, is explained by the rise of political views in the period separating the two figures:
political controversy drove further apart those who
sought salvation in the service of society from men
who denied that Redemption is even remotely connected to the general secular welfare.[100a] The latter
were religious pessimists, and many of them used Pyrrhonian skepticism to justify mercantilist doctrine

[99] *Sainte* Louise de Marillac was St. Vincent de Paul's chief
assistant in establishing and directing the first secular order of
women in the history of Christianity.

[100] This sentiment emerges clearly from even a desultory reading
among the fourteen volumes of St. Vincent de Paul's letters and
papers. On one page, for example (I have unfortunately mislaid the
precise reference), St. Vincent wrote that the faithful should interrupt attendance at mass, even prior to partaking of the Eucharist, in
order to assist someone in need. To quit the mass in these circumstances, said St. Vincent, "is to leave God only to find Him again."

[100a] Early in the century, even so strict an Augustinian as Bérulle
was friendly with confirmed Molinists (see Louis Cognet, *Le Jansénisme*, Paris, 1964, p. 18). After St. Cyran's imprisonment, however,
hostility between the two groups, becoming intense, grew out of the
fact that the crown, and finally the Papacy, declared war on the
Augustinians. See, for example, the radical change in the attitude
of St. Vincent of Paul toward his old friend St. Cyran, described by
Orcibal, *Les Origines*, III, 28-33.

and Machiavellian principles. Conversely, by opposing skeptical contempt for the intellect and by denying the soul's innate depravity, Fleury and Fénelon
were led to assert that man, being predominantly
rational and morally educable, will achieve the good
life when he is guided by a virtuous exercise of political authority. In this way government was transformed into an instrument of moral progress on
earth.

Another and equally disturbing irritant to religious
sensibilities was the ethical and political issues raised
by mercantilist policies concerning production and
consumption of luxury goods.[101] So long as merchandise designed to encourage extravagance or vice was
manufactured abroad, forbidding its import was both
morally and politically sound, because money otherwise spent for such items was kept in the kingdom.
The case was different, however, with luxury goods
manufactured in France. One of Barthélemy de Laffemas's first pamphlets, for example, *Les trésors et
richesses pour mettre l'estat en splendeur* (1598), bitterly attacked those employing moral arguments
against the widespread use of French silks. Declaring
the ethical consequences of such matters a purely
private affair, Henry IV's economic adviser insisted
that consumption of home-manufactured luxury
goods provided employment for the poor and rendered valuable service to the state. Indeed, universal
abstinence would cause economic distress and under-

[101] A small but intensely interesting book discusses this question
as largely an eighteenth century problem, André Morize, *L'Apologie
du luxe au XVIIIᵉ siècle et "Le Mondain" de Voltaire: étude
critique sur le mondain et ses sources*, Paris, 1909. Heckscher notes
that the problem is important in France at the turn of the sixteenth
and seventeenth centuries; his brief discussion in *Mercantilism*, II,
289-291, merely states, however, that there was "a great revolution
from the ethical point of view."

mine the power of the sovereign. Montchrétien, discussing the same subject, said that "times have changed" and luxury is to be encouraged "as long as we retain the profit, otherwise it is too expensive." A country's customs "are formed in the mould of its prince."[102]

More extreme statements, legitimizing private vice because it was socially and politically useful, did not appear until mercantilism and the luxury trade reached their apogee under Colbert and his successors.[102a] At this time the most radical skeptic of the century, Pierre Bayle, demonstrates how all the amoral implications in his philosophy combined with those of Epicureanism (made popular in different ways by the priest, Gassendi, and by the libertine, Saint-Evremond)[103] could be woven into a statement of mercantilist principles:

[102] *L'économie politique*, see pp. 80 and 74 respectively.

[102a] Although not specifically concerned with the luxury issue, an amazing essay, written in 1598 by Antoine Hotman, brother of the famous François Hotman, advocates the unbridled pursuit of private profit in the name of social utility. The document, discussed at length in Chapter VI, is written entirely in the following spirit: "Pourquoy . . . quel qu'un ne voudroit pas avoir de grands biens, . . . et quel inconvénient il trouve d'estre grandement riche, . . . nous essayerons de monstrer que le meilleur est d'estre le plus riche que l'on peut." Elsewhere Hotman exclaimed: "Je soutiens que quiconque rejette les richesses qui nous apportent les commoditez de nostre vie est desnaturé, et ne scait que c'est de vivre" (*Opuscules françoises des Hotmans*, Paris, 1616, pp. 176 and 169 respectively).

[103] Were Gassendi's views religious or irreligious? Bernard Rochot's "Pierre Gassendi: la vie, le caractère et la formation intellectuelle," *Pierre Gassendi, sa vie et son oeuvre 1592-1655* in *Centre international de Synthèse*, Paris, 1955, pp. 48-54, appears very convincing when he maintains that Gassendi was sincerely devout. He takes issue with René Pintard, *Le libertinage érudit*. . . . In contrast, Saint-Evremond established an irreligious Epicurean ethic and an idea of progress on the sensational theory of knowledge. Men seek pleasure and avoid pain; reason, however, guides them to enjoy those pleasures leading to a happy life. Intellect makes us aware of our best interests, and reason directs our voluptuous

The more we study this and preceding centuries, the more we recognize that any society exposed to foreign wars would soon succumb if it conformed to Evangelical spirit. If you wish a nation to be sufficiently strong to resist its neighbors, leave Christian maxims for preachers' themes and conserve them for theory. Bring practice under nature's laws which permit us to return blow for blow, and excite us to raise ourselves above our state and become richer and of better condition than our fathers. Conserve avarice and ambition in all their force . . . , promise pensions to those inventing new manufactures or new means of increasing commerce. Send expeditions for the discovery of gold everywhere; make your fleets pass through the two tropics so that neither cold nor heat nor anything can halt the passion to grow rich and you will accumulate the wealth of several other countries in your own. The finances of state will support a great fleet and a powerful army. . . . True, the love of gold is the source of a thousand corrupt passions. . . . This was the cause of the most pernicious disorders in the Roman Republic. . . . Avarice spoils everything. But don't be embarrassed; the same things do not necessarily occur in all centuries and in all climates. . . . A moderate luxury is very useful in a Republic, it causes money to circulate and supports the little people. . . . Think of the opulence of today, it

---

natures toward socially useful behavior. History, the record of man's search for the intelligent experience of pleasure, demonstrates that progress toward an ethic derived from social rather than religious principles is the only sure foundation for a happy society. For further light on Saint-Evremond see H. T. Barnwell, *Les idées morales et critiques de Saint-Evremond*, Paris, 1957.

will lead you to a hundred resources to satisfy the exigencies of public welfare.[104]

This passage reflects mercantilist spirit at its height during the administrations of Controllers General Le Pelletier and Pontchartrain. Under their direction French luxury industry was given a tremendous impetus. The splendor of Versailles symbolized the ideal of authority and power based on cynical principles and on the immoral worldliness of money. This regime was a sacrilege in the eyes of those imbued with the teachings of Bérulle, St. François de Sales, St. Vincent de Paul, and a host of other profoundly devout seventeenth century French Christians. It is this deeply rooted hostility which was to inspire Fénelon's relentless attacks against luxury and against all the fundamental principles of mercantilism.

iii. HUMANIST SOURCES OF OPPOSITION
TO MERCANTILISM

Several writers early in the seventeenth century opposed the grim mercantilist view of international relations because they believed the world to be inhabited by a single family of peoples united by bonds of Providence and living according to the divinely regulated harmony of the cosmos. This view was not a mere vestige of the ideal of a united Christendom expanded to include peoples of every religion. On the contrary, it was part of an intensely vigorous later Christian humanist tradition. Its chief spokesmen, Guillaume Postel and Tommasio Campanella, Emeric Crucé, Hugo Grotius, and the Duc de Sully, laid the foundations for philosophical, political, and

[104] *Continuation des Pensées diverses*, 4 vols., Rotterdam, 1721, IV, 362-364. Morize in *L'Apologie* discusses Bayle as if he were at the beginning rather than at the end, or at least the middle, of a tradition.

economic theories totally opposed to those of Bodin and Montchrétien. And their writings strongly influenced a secular current of French mercantilist opposition which also reached its height during Louis XIV's reign.

For some writers, in contrast to Bodin, the Wars of Religion only confirmed their conviction that armed conflict severs the material bonds of economic interdependence uniting mankind. They were outraged by theories declaring peace at home obtainable only at the economic and political expense of France's neighbors. Profoundly shocked by the inhumanity of war and of mercantilist thought, they combined a kind of pacifist economics with a program to "reform morals." Ethics, they taught, were a matter of natural reason rather than a topic for theological controversy. One Emeric Crucé, for example, in a book entitled *Le Nouveau Cynée ou Discours d'Estat représentant les occasions et moyens d'establir une paix générale et la liberté du commerce par tout le monde* (Paris, 1623), explained the purpose of his book in the following manner:

> Religion can be maintained only by moral virtue, to which we must exhort great and small, kings and peoples, without remaining long on scholastic disputes which produce more noise than fruit. I know that it is necessary to refute heresies, but I find none greater than the error of those who make a sovereign glory of injustice and recognize nothing more praiseworthy than the force of arms. Can we hope for progress in religion or for tranquility in the state so long as this damnable opinion is received? . . . We pursue peace . . . only half-heartedly. Some exhort Christian princes to unite against their common

enemy and a famous personage has even described a means to exterminate the Turk in four
years or thereabouts. . . . [105] Others are more
limited in their style: they invent means to enrich their country and care so little about foreigners that they esteem it prudent politics to
sow divisions among them so as to enjoy a more
certain repose. But I am emphatically of another
opinion. To me it seems that when we see our
neighbor's house burning or about to fall we
have reason to be both afraid and compassionate.
. . . Human society is a single body whose members have a sympathy of such a nature that it is
impossible that the ailments of one are not communicated to the others.[106] Now this little book
contains a universal guide, useful alike to all
nations, and agreeable to those having a few
lights of reason and some sentiments of humanity.[107]

Crucé's "universal guide" envisioned an international organization composed of representatives from
nations in Europe, Africa, and Asia. Its principal

[105] Crucé could be referring here either to Father Joseph, the
Grey Eminence, or perhaps to Sully, who may already have spoken
about the ideas he wrote down a decade later. In François de La
Noue's *Discours politiques et militaires*, Basle, 1587, the XXVIth
Discours is entitled: "Que les Princes Chrestiens estans bien unis
ensemble, peuvent en quatre ans chasser les Turcs de l'Europe."

[106] The famous lines of John Donne, a contemporary of Crucé,
might here be recalled: "No man is an *Iland*, intire of it selfe;
every man is a peece of the *Continent*, a part of the *maine*; if a
Clod bee washed away by the *Sea*, *Europe* is the lesse, as well as if
a *Promontorie* were, as well as if a *Mannor* of thy *friends* or of *thine*
owne were; any mans *death* diminishes *me*, because I am involved
in *Mankinde*," *Meditations from "Devotions Upon Emergent Occasions*," no. XVII.

[107] Preface, 1624 edn. Théodore Ruyssen, *Les sources doctrinales*,
pp. 277-289, 482-485 discusses Crucé and gives ample bibliographical
information in the notes.

function was to arbitrate differences between sovereign powers, decisions in particular cases being made
and enforced by the combined strength of members
not directly involved in the dispute. Of special interest, however, is the author's conviction that the
relativity of morals reflected a natural harmony of
diverse, mutually interdependent interests. Turks,
Mohammedans, and Chinese did not follow the true
religion; yet they were "men like us, formed in the
same mould and by the same artisan, capable of reason and moral virtue and deserving of friendship and
admiration." Their peculiar customs are explained
by the fact that "the harmony of the world is composed of diverse humors and what is praiseworthy in
one place is not found so everywhere else."[108] Customs in all parts of the earth formed a living structure which embody the moral laws of nature; moreover, these eternal decrees were communicated to
mankind through international trade which, arising
out of universal interdependence, caused people to
become acquainted with customs everywhere. Trade
was part of a divine plan guiding humanity toward
universal concord and well-being under the salubri-
ous direction of natural law. "Commerce is the most
beautiful fruit of universal peace. Monarchs must

[108] *Le Nouveau Cynée*, pp. 51-54. Elsewhere, on page 48, the author
writes: "Comment est-il possible, dira quelqu'un, d'accorder des
peuples qui sont si separez de volonté et d'affection, comme le
Turc et le Persan, le François et l'Espagnol, le Chinois et le Tartare,
le Crestien et le Juif ou Mahometain. Je dis que telles inimités
ne sont que politiques, et ne peuvent oster la conjunction qui est et
doibt estre entre les hommes. La distance, la séparation des
domiciles n'amoindrit point la proximité du sang. Elle ne peut
non plus oster la similitude du naturel, vray fondement d'amitié
et société humaine. Pourquoy moy qui suis François voudray-je
du mal à un Anglois, Hespagnol, et Indien? Je ne le puis, quand
je considere qu'ils sont hommes come moy, que je suis subjet
comme eux à erreur et péché, et que toutes les nations sont
associées par un lien naturel. . . ."

permit their subjects to traffic without fear by sea and land."[109] Sovereigns should make "no distinction between native and foreign merchants as several Princes do today because conditions of trade must be equal everywhere, especially during universal peace when we must live in good intelligence with the entire world."[110] Continuing, Crucé exclaimed: "What a pleasure it would be to see men going freely from one place to another, communicating together without thought of country, ceremonies or other similar diversities, as if the world was as it truly is, a common city for all."[111]

Crucé thought sovereign states were bound to one another as the several regions of a single kingdom. He was not alone in his views. Hugo Grotius, for example, said men, finding it impossible to live in isolation, organized into groups called states; and states, also unable to divorce themselves from the rest of humanity, were tied to their neighbors in the same manner as their subjects were bound to one another. The mutual obligations of each formed respectively the substance of domestic and international law. This was the eternal order of society. Moreover, the bonds of natural instinct and of contract uniting mankind were strengthened by the material ties of trade:

> God did not bestow all products upon all parts of the earth, but distributed His gifts over different regions, to the end that men might culti-

[109] *Ibid.*, p. 32.   [110] *Ibid.*, p. 172.
[111] *Ibid.*, p. 36.

In 1577 Louis LeRoy, *De la vicissitude ou variété des choses en l'univers* (here using London edn., 1594) wrote: ". . . We may truely affirm that the world is wholly manifested, at this day, and all mankind entierly knowen: for now all men may communicate one to another their commodities, and supply their mutual wants; as inhabiting all the selfe same citie and common wealth of the world" (f. 123).

vate a social relationship because one would need
the help of another. And so He called commerce
into being, that all might have common enjoyment of the fruits of the earth. . . . If you destroy commerce, you sunder the alliance binding together the human race.[112]

The idea that trade was created to unify rather
than to separate mankind was also endorsed by Maxi-
milien de Béthune, Duc de Sully, who wrote his
Mémoires in 1638. He restricted the operation of
natural laws of trade to Christendom, but even within this reduced framework, his anti-mercantilism is
apparent. The creation of new industry, especially
luxury manufacture, said Sully, would be out of
place in France. Moreover, "God has created divers
climates, regions and countries so as to make them
abound in certain properties, commodities, produce,
raw materials, arts and special trades which are not
common or at least of such good quality in other
places. By commerce of things plentiful with some
and rare with others, human society between nations
will be conserved and maintained."[113] This was
neither a passing thought nor mere rhetoric. Sully's
well-known plan for international peace, which he
ascribed to Henry IV, contains the following clause:
"There will be an entire liberty of commerce between
all the associates . . . on land and by sea."[114]

Crucé and Grotius, more than Sully, reflected a

[112] *Three Books on the Law of War and Peace*, Amsterdam,
1625, cited from James Brown Scott's edn., *The Classics of International Law*, Publ. of the Carnegie Endowment for International
Peace, Oxford, 1925, III, 199-200.

[113] "Mémoires des sages et royales oeconomies d'estat . . . ," cited
from Michaud and Poujoulat's edn., *Nouvelle collection des
mémoires relatifs à l'histoire de France, depuis le XIIIe siècle jusqu'à
la fin du XVIIIe*, II, III, Paris, 1837; II, 515.

[114] *Ibid.*, III, 329.

powerful later Christian humanist tradition, frequently associated with Guillaume Postel (1510-1581) and Tommasio Campanella (1568-1639). In a recent study,[115] William J. Bouwsma describes how Postel, following the tradition of Joachim of Flora and the radical Franciscans, had secularized St. Augustine's thought. The terms "peace" and "justice" had much the same meaning for the Bishop of Hippo; that is, the arrangement of all elements in creation, both within and without the human soul, into a harmonious cosmic union subordinated to the will of God. Since the Fall, however, man continually sought to substitute his will for that of the Lord, thus destroying divinely established relationships. Man's hopelessly corrupt nature precludes any possibility of ultimate peace on earth; Augustine believed therefore that the millennium was a purely spiritual phenomenon.[116] In contrast, Postel, although profoundly influenced by Augustine, paid little attention to the problem of evil. Indeed, he thought, as Bernard Lamy and the Cartesian Augustinians did later, that sin or disharmony of the soul was mere ignorance, implying that mistake rather than corruption was the source of evil and that knowledge was the key to moral progress and to salvation.[117]

Prior to its material creation, Postel maintained, the universe was a structure of ideas. The Fall, however, shattered the divine system of correspondences and symbols, scattering them to all parts of the earth. The task of the humanist movement, he felt, was to gather together and restore the original body of learning in preparation for a Golden Age, when the union of peoples would become part of a culminating con-

---

[115] *Concordia Mundi: the Career and Thought of Guillaume Postel, 1510-1581*, Cambridge, Mass., 1957.
[116] *Ibid.*, pp. 67-68.   [117] *Ibid.*, p. 118.

cord of all Creation under God's law, made manifest by the reestablished harmony of natural and revealed knowledge. This great enterprise was to be made possible by philology on one hand and world empire under French leadership on the other. By studying ancient tongues, man could learn the names and essences which God had originally assigned to all things material and spiritual. The organization of the earth into a single political unit, a task for which Postel thought the French divinely destined, would provide the framework for a vast missionary movement designed to bring mankind under the rule of true and original religious principles, preparing the world for the final hour, the Last Judgment.

Postel merely associated reason with political authority; Campanella fused the two and developed a theory of a perfect society conforming in every respect to the laws of nature. His *City of the Sun* describes a society where egoism was impossible and personal interests never valued more highly than those of the public. Marriage and private property, the two institutions causing men to place family or fortune above the general welfare, did not exist. Astrologers regulated sexual relations and people were mated so as to breed superior progeny. So far as wealth was concerned "all individuals are at once rich and poor; rich because they possess everything, poor because they personally own nothing. In the community every man enjoys all as would a private owner without being a slave to property."[118] There was, however, a general obligation to work; although necessities were refused to no one, "each is paid according to his labor" and occupations were allocated according to natural abil-

[118] Trans. Villegardelle, *Abonnement Germinal*, vol. 7, no. 10, Gand, 1911, p. 47. A lengthy and intelligent study of all aspects of Campanella's thought has been written by Léon Blanchet, *Campanella*, Paris, 1920.

ity. "Neither birth nor wealth" could protect the citizen; he was "delivered from egoism and nothing remains but love of the community."[119]

Campanella thought the solar republic a replica of cosmic government, an integral part of God's plan revealed by natural law. The universe was an immense chain of sentient bodies, each receiving motion from the Sun—considered the World Soul—and consciousness from God. Space was infinite extension, and every point revealed phenomena whose individual movements and degrees of sensitivity were determined by position in the transcendental hierarchy. Man's place, however, was unique in that he possessed reason as well as sense perception. Sense experience arose from mere contact between two or more bodies; reason was the ability to assimilate the essence of the thing sensed. It was the total identification of the perceiver with the object known. Becoming what we know, we could know only ourselves; no distinction could exist between knowing and Being. And the Supreme Being, God, knows all simply by knowing Himself. He also loves all from mere love of Himself and, going down the scale of Being, love descended by degrees to even tiny particles, there taking the form of instinctual self-preservation. Reason, however, informed man that self-love was a finite expression of infinite love and, alone having the power to know God, he was destined ultimately for union with the divine.

This glorious event, however, would take place only after society had been integrated into the life of the cosmos. The purpose of political authority was to make human activity conform to nature's operations. The exercise of government was merely philosophy or reason in action. And a truly philosophic state like

[119] *Ibid.*, pp. 30, 33.

the City of the Sun would eventually lead peoples everywhere into union with the spiritual orders of Creation, inaugurating a Golden Age and announcing the Last Judgment. To establish such a society on earth, some prince must extend his dominion over the entire world. In 1602 Campanella thought Spain the logical candidate. Toward the end of his life, however, the author drew the Dauphin's horoscope and forecast that this "wonder child," later Louis XIV, would rule the Sun State.

Standing in the tradition of Postel, Campanella was diametrically opposed to Bodin and to the principles of political economy expounded by Laffemas and Montchrétien. No one understood the full implications of mercantilism better than Campanella. First, he confined himself merely to ridiculing the idea of a favorable balance of trade:

> Merchants come from different parts of the world to buy surplus [products] from the inhabitants of the Sun City; but the Solarians will accept in exchange only those goods which they need. They refuse therefore to sell for money, while on the other hand they often use money to buy. The children of the City . . . cannot help laughing when they see foreigners deliver a great quantity of merchandise in exchange for a feeble quantity of metal.[120]

In the last pages of his utopia, however, Campanella reveals the fundamental reasons for his opposition: all men were responsible for their brothers' welfare, and those who did not know that the golden rule is the first principle of government had not "studied and understood the heart of God" as revealed in nature.

120 *La Cité du Soleil*, p. 57.

In our age states are overwhelmed with trouble; and what is deplorable is that we give the name of peace and of happiness to this disorder because we have never known the good and we imagine that chance rules the world. But he who has contemplated the structure of the universe and who has studied the anatomy of plants, of animals and of man (because we [the Solarians] dissect the bodies of executed criminals) is forced to confess aloud the wisdom and the providence of God. Man must devote himself entirely to religion and adore his Creator. . . . But this is possible only for him who has studied and understood the heart of God; for him who has observed His laws and has philosophically put to practice this precept: "Never do unto others what you would not have them do unto you, and act toward them according to their desire, which is what you would wish them to do toward you." And if we demand that our sons and other men respect us and do good unto us in exchange for the little we do for them, what do we not owe to God from whom we hold everything, by whom we are what we are and in whom we live always![121]

The anatomy of the universe, of plants, and of humans, containing the secrets of the macrocosm and the microcosm, revealed the natural principles ruling man and all Creation: ultimately they would unite the peoples of the earth. Mercantilism, permanently dividing humanity into numerous hostile self-contained political units each with its own religious policy, struck at the very heart of this later humanist tradition. The new principles of political economy

[121] *Ibid.*, p. 78.

accepted disunity as part of mankind's natural condition. Men like Postel and Campanella, on the contrary, thought the source of all evil lay in human failure to recognize the fundamental oneness behind all apparent diversity. Two world views could not have been more opposed.

*

Two distinct intellectual currents, therefore, were hostile to mercantilist theory in early seventeenth century France: on one hand, religious thinkers were antagonistic to the mercantilist ethic and to the Machiavellian principles with which it was so compatible; on the other, men, influenced by a humanist drive to unite peoples everywhere, were appalled by the prospect of international political and religious anarchy. The former associated politics and the public welfare in some way with individual salvation and the transcendental; the latter identified the general interest with nature and the order of the cosmos. The first resisted to some extent the humanist tendency to make knowledge the key to salvation, whereas the second, reflecting precisely the opposite movement, sought to transform faith into reason and subordinate religion to culture. Nevertheless, both subordinated political authority to God and to moral law. The humanists, however, expanding Christianity to include all mankind, transformed God into abstract universal principles. They were, therefore, inclined to criticize purely local institutions or policies in the name of nature and of all mankind, a tendency which became more general during the latter part of the century.

A most important development, however, concerning both mercantilist and anti-mercantilist doctrine, is the progressive encroachment of politics into successive areas of speculative thought. Montaigne attempted seriously to subordinate religion to culture, but Bodin, his almost exact contemporary, took a further step: he subsumed institutions, religion, and culture under the sovereign state. And the immense success of the Republic throughout the seventeenth century[122] reflects above all the fact that centralizing policies in the reigns of Louis XIII and Louis XIV include for the first time large-scale efforts to place all branches of culture directly under the coercive power of the state. This is the principal reason why, as the century progressed, political issues were injected increasingly into discussions about the most recondite and obscure matters. Moreover, the growing influence of politics distorted traditional arguments. This may be seen, for example, in changing concepts of natural and positive law. St. Thomas believed positive law was an expression of universal reason or natural law; the decrees of rulers therefore "participated" in transcendental principles of justice. In contrast, Marsilius of Padua dissociated positive law from reason. Integrating society into the cosmos, contrary to St. Thomas who said the rules of civilization could not be derived from the physical order, Marsilius transformed human justice into a biological principle, an inborn impulse; the laws of society no longer participated in the transcendental because Marsilius transposed justice to the realm of God, relegating it to the sphere of faith. Later, during the Wars of Religion, sixteenth century skeptics, particularly Montaigne, transformed the concept of natural law from the Thomist expression of universal reason to an instinctive principle, an "inner light," especially luminous among savages and beasts. Here the first

[122] The remarkable popularity of the *Republic* is discussed by Roger Chauviré, *Jean Bodin, auteur de la "République,"* Paris, 1914, pp. 42-43.

"natural" principle of behavior is the instinct for self-preservation.[123] And considering the seventeenth century propensity to deduce political theory from psychological principles, it is not surprising to discover "reason of state" subsequently discussed in terms of self-defense, the natural law of necessity common to all creatures—animal, human, or political. In this way positive law becomes susceptible to a truly revolutionary interpretation: although it had neither reasonable nor ethical bases, positive law from Marsilius to Machiavelli, being part of the cosmic order, was at least an expression of unchanging principles; with Montaigne, however, it was an individual and exclusively instinctual expression: all that remained was the possibility that insight into our own personal natures would provide merely local and empirical guides to ethical and political conduct. Moral and political laws, based on no general principles, varied from region to region according to tradition, circumstances, and physical environment.

Words like expedience, necessity, utility, self-interest, and the general welfare appear with increasing frequency in early seventeenth century tracts. And in a period when royal authority appeared to offer only fragile protection against anarchic forces, the new concept of natural law seemed to correspond with actual experience, thereby strengthening Augustinian belief in the radically corrupt nature of man's soul. Moreover the establishment of an instinctual rather than a rational foundation for natural law was a doctrine diffused by Charron and François de La Mothe le Vayer at the time when Descartes and Gas-

[123] Ulpian, a third century glossator of Justinian's *Digest*, said natural law was an instinctive attribute governing both animals and men. The rival view regarded natural law as essentially rational, therefore peculiarly human. See John B. Morrall, *Political Thought in Medieval Times*, London, 1958, chap. 4.

sendi administered the *coup de grâce* to Aristotelian cosmology. This confluence of the new cosmology with skepticism also strengthened political and religious Augustinianism. Finality was destroyed. The universe was no longer held to be an animate finite interlocking system, every part of which was created for a determinate cause. Instead man lived in an infinite corpuscular cosmos, a lifeless system of atoms and mechanical forces. Pyrrhonians like Gabriel Naudé thought the universe incomprehensible, "the very heavens beyond the moon are subject to generation and corruption." Moreover, Naudé believed our inability to understand the deeper meaning behind the flux of appearances corresponded to the feebleness of human reason before the fierce passions of depraved nature. Force alone was capable of governing man. In this context, Machiavelli's denial that government could be at once effective and moral appeared axiomatic. Equally obvious was the compatibility of Machiavellism with mercantilist doctrine and royal centralizing efforts. Thus Cardinal Richelieu thought it necessary to rehabilitate the hitherto notorious author of the *Prince*, whose work aroused immense controversy in France.[124]

Cartesian Augustinians, men like Pierre Nicole, attacked Pyrrhonians while trying at the same time to reconcile their faith in reason with the Bishop of Hippo's teachings. Here the new science and the new cosmos appeared to provide an answer to the intellectual dilemma. Descartes was the first thinker to ap-

[124] During the seventeenth century Machiavelli was probably the most intensely debated figure among political philosophers: "D'Henri IV au déclin de Louis XIV, il n'est guère d'années où la mémoire de Machiavel et de ses avis ne vienne exiter le ressentiment ou la reconnaissance de quelqu'un de nos théoriciens politiques." Albert Cherel, *La pensée de Machiavel*, p. 71. Cf., also Meinecke, *Machiavellism*, pp. 146-204, 244-256.

ply systematically a revived ancient atomism to the Copernican model of the universe; the result was his infinite system of vortices. Pierre Gassendi, although Descartes' opponent on many issues, provided a psychological and social dimension to the new philosophy. He rehabilitated the ancient atomist Epicurus and interpreted his writings to mean that outside the sphere of faith and revelation man is governed by his senses, that is, by a desire to avoid pain and seek pleasure. Subsequently, the pleasure-pain principle was easily represented as linear inertia in a system where each individual is an upwardly moving atom impelled by self-love. There was also the additional implication that a machine-like society was entirely consistent with the market-society. Social behavior, a continuous "exchange of services, of assiduity and of civility," is a process governed by physical law. The mercantilist state is an exact reflection of the cosmic order. In this way Nicole tried to remain faithful to Augustine by showing how men are naturally motivated by self-love alone, that political institutions are a consequence of original sin. Charity can come only from God. Yet despite his conviction that without grace man is radically corrupt, Nicole's desire to establish the supremacy of the human intellect caused him, as did Postel and Campanella earlier, to identify sin with ignorance and reason with the divine. He, too, thought knowledge was a key to the divine and nature the mirror of God's will. Thus Nicole could say that a kingdom organized according to Cartesian physics glorified God because these principles, being the laws of nature, caused an inwardly corrupt society to conform outwardly in every respect to the first rules of charity and justice. In contrast to Nicole's conviction that ultimate knowledge, true charity, and justice were inaccessible to man without grace, Postel and

Campanella sought to reestablish the Golden Age on earth. Both Campanella and Nicole thought nature would guide men to better government, but Nicole alone interpreted this to mean that private advantage, when well understood, conformed perfectly with civic virtue.[125] Moreover, just as social usefulness, defined by Nicole as "enlightened self-interest," replaced virtue in the realm of ethics, so the Cartesian Jean Silhon, close adviser to Richelieu, substituted the "general interest" for traditional views of justice. In other words, "self-interest" in one area became "reason of state" in the other. Thus, despite clear crosscurrents, we can say generally that the immoral implications of mercantilism came to be associated by the middle of the century with one or another form of revived Augustinianism. It is no surprise to discover, therefore, that in Louis XIV's personal reign, religious leaders of more optimistic persuasion, the men around Archbishop Fénelon, were to be in the anti-mercantilist camp. The enemies of *Port Royal* were to be among the most bitter critics of the Sun King's regime.

[125] "Quelle charité seroit-ce que de bâtire une maison toute entiere pour un autre, de la meubler, de la tapisser, de la lui rendre la clef à la main? La cupidité le fera gaiement. Quelle charité d'aller querir des remedes aux Indes; de s'abaisser aux plus vils ministeres, & de rendre aux autres les services les plus bas & les plus pénibles? La cupidité fait tout cela sans s'en plaindre." P. Nicole, *Essais de morale* . . . (1713 edn.), II, 144-145.

CHAPTER II

MERCANTILIST THEORY AND EXPRESSIONS OF EARLY ARISTOCRATIC PROTEST

THEORETICAL opposition to the principles of political economy laid down by Bodin, Laffemas, and Mont-chrétien existed, as we have seen, as early as the end of the sixteenth century. Later, under Richelieu and Mazarin, mercantilist ideas appeared in the form of legislation, and the theory behind these laws became increasingly elaborate. Toward the middle of the century, especially after the *Fronde*, a few members of the aristocracy protested that mercantilist policies directly threatened their traditional position in society. Although such writings are rare prior to Colbert's ministry (1661-1683), a forgotten treatise, standing in relative isolation, is of particular importance: on one hand the work reflects the well-known criticism by Postel, Campanella, Crucé, and Grotius; on the other, it points directly toward later opposition theory, anticipating the aristocratic resistance of the future.

Jean de Lartigue, the author of this work, scholar, priest, and noble of ancient lineage, is a transition figure who distorted familiar themes in such a way as to illustrate the increasingly political and aristocratic character of anti-mercantilist protest. Mercantilism was developing more and more into a comprehensive system. Its doctrines not only stressed the permanent political and religious division of mankind, but also became associated with a view of man as isolated in an impersonal universe made up of particles and lifeless mechanical forces. In this context Lartigue's insistence on themes of world and cosmic unity can be seen to reflect the tension between a growing central administration and the aristocracy of the sword. With the struggle between the crown and the nobility in the forefront of his thought, Lartigue, in his writing, transformed the speculative ideas of Postel and Campanella into the beginnings of political doctrine. The following chapter begins with the development of mercantilist theory and practice to 1661; a second section discusses Lartigue and early aristocratic dissent.

i. MERCANTILISM: ECONOMIC THEORY, STATE ORGANIZATION, AND POLITICAL PHILOSOPHY

Perhaps the most important and least discussed aspect of traditional principles of political economy, from Laffemas to Colbert and his successors, is the unremitting campaign to bring relief to depressed rural areas. French industry throughout the seventeenth century was overwhelmingly rural.[1] In spurring it to greater production for export the government also helped to provide employment for the countryside whose inhabitants rarely devoted full time to agriculture during the entire year. Moreover, increased economic activity would bring additional

[1] This point is firmly established by economic and social historians. See, for example, Jean Meuvret, "Circulation monétaire et utilisation économique de la monnaie dans la France du XVIe et du XVIIe siècles," *Etudes d'histoire moderne et contemporaine*, I (1947), 17-18. An extended discussion may be found in Pierre Goubert's valuable thesis, *Beauvais et le Beauvaisis de 1600 à 1730: contribution à l'histoire sociale de la France du XVIIe siècle*, Paris, 1960, pp. 126-132.

revenue from indirect taxes, permitting the crown to lighten the burden of direct taxes which fell almost entirely on the most indigent members of provincial society. The program rested above all on one unquestioned premise: the circulatory theory of money.[2] Trade with other countries brought treasure into the kingdom, while rural industry and domestic commerce were said to put money into movement, causing it to circulate among the people, contributing to their well-being and, most important, permitting them to support the charges of state without hardship. Colbert, for example, thought political power varied directly with the speed and flow of foreign treasure circulating in all parts of France. "When money is in the kingdom," he wrote, "the universal desire to profit therefrom causes men to put it into movement and it is in this movement that the public treasure finds its share."[3] The minister never tired of repeating to intendants that their first duty was to bring prosperity to rural populations by increasing production in provincial industry, commerce, and agriculture: "I have written you frequently that com-

[2] Eli F. Heckscher, *Mercantilism*, trans. Mendel Shapiro, 2 vols., London, 1935, II, 217, writes: "One cannot possibly overrate the importance of the circulation of money in the ideology of the mercantilists." Heckscher did not realize, however, that the idea, at least in France, was an integral part of the program to relieve depressed rural areas. The same observation may be made of Paul Harsin's discussion of this problem in *Les doctrines monétaires et financières en France du XVIe au XVIIIe siècle*, Paris, 1928, pp. 97-98.

[3] "Mémoire au roi sur les finances," pub. by Pierre Clément, *Lettres, instructions et mémoires de Colbert*, 7 vols., Paris, 1861-1882, VII, 235.

In 1697 Vaubourg Desmarets, intendant in Lorraine, wrote the Controller General: "Or, la grande dépense que le roi a faite et fait tous les jours met les paysans en état de payer assez facilement ce que sa Majesté tire d'eux . . ." (*Recueil de documents sur l'histoire de Lorraine,* ed. Abbé Laurent Marchal, Nancy, 1859, IV, 75).

merce, manufactures and the raising of livestock are the only means to attract money to the provinces. His Majesty wishes . . . that you remain always informed on these three points and that you employ all your industry and every expedient . . . to excite the people to increase these [activities]."[4] Domestic peace would be assured and royal revenues would increase when money became plentiful among *all* Frenchmen. "The obedience owed to His Majesty by the people is so well established that he must work only to attract money to the interior of his kingdom by every possible means, being well assured that when the people have money they will easily pay the expenses of state."[5] A prosperous countryside, producing industrial and agricultural products for export and consuming manufactures of domestic provenance, would supply the crown with unlimited revenues from tariffs and other indirect taxes, without undue demands on the population and consequently without danger of rebellion. The subordination of all economic activity to the requirements of foreign trade[6] was not, as was frequently said, conceived as a sacrifice of domestic well-being in order to augment state power. On the contrary, such a policy was considered essential to create the rural prosperity on which political strength alone could rest.[7]

4 Circular letter to intendants, 6 January 1679, P. Clément, *Lettres*, II, Part I, p. 89. See also pp. 97, 129, 255 for similar remarks.

5 Circular letters to intendants, 24 April 1676, *ibid.*, p. 375.

6 This idea, Henri Hauser writes, is "L'essence même de la conception mercantiliste." *La Pensée et l'action économique du Cardinal de Richelieu*, Paris, 1944, pp. 146-147.

7 On 21 November 1670, Colbert wrote Marin de la Chataigneraie, intendant at Orleans, the following: "Ne croyez pas que la manufacture des bas de Dourdan nuise au labourage; au contraire, faites tout ce qui dépendra de vous pour la fortifier, n'y ayant rien qui serve tant à augmenter les peuples dans un pays que les différants moyens de gagner leur vie, et reposez-vous sur moy que le Roy et

The circulatory theory, lying at the heart of mid-seventeenth century French economic thought, was one of those powerful unconscious assumptions which only rarely reach the level of explicit formulation. Occasionally men of learning did clearly state the principle. Jean de Lartigue, for example, explained in 1664 that government must spend its revenues as rapidly as possible lest the money, remaining idle, stagnate:

> The Prince's affairs must be put in order, his debts paid, . . . his treasury filled . . . and employed immediately for outlays and the needs of state, in fear that it [money] will languish and fail; if we do not keep the existing [stock] of money in circulation it is put in reserve and produces nothing. Instead, by passing from hand to hand it gives vigor to commerce of which it is the soul.[8]

Even among intellectuals, however, general statements of this type are rare during the period stretching from Richelieu to Colbert.[9] The extent to which the circulatory theory colored contemporary think-

---

les peuples s'en trouveront bien." Clément, *Lettres*, II, Part II, p. 584. For an account of mercantilist preoccupation with poverty in England see C. H. Wilson, "The Other Face of Mercantilism," *Transactions of the Royal Historical Society*, 5th series, 9, 1959, pp. 81-101.

[8] B.N., Fds. fr., MS 4164, f. 40.

[9] They do, however, exist. Consider, for example, the following passage from a fascinating treatise written by Sully's brother, Philippe de Béthune, entitled *Le Conseiller d'Estat ou recueil des plus générales considérations servant au maniement des affaires publiques,* first published in 1632: "L'autre considération est de ne mettre pas tant d'argent en réserve, que cela incommode le commerce et le trafic des sujets, car ce seroit tarir la source des Finances [comme] si la mer retenoit toutes les eaux des rivières qui s'y deschargent, sans les rendre à leurs sources par les conduits sous-terrains, elle sécheroit les rivières et enfin se sécheroit après." Cited from 1645 edn., p. 285.

ing is more often revealed in its frequent connection with wider issues. Richelieu, for example, explained that indirect taxes must be adjusted to the volume of commerce, i.e. to the rate of monetary circulation, in such a way as to maintain price levels at a point which would assure maximum spending by the population and consequently maximum revenues for the crown:

> Increases in royal revenues can come only from taxes imposed on all sorts of provisions, yet it is clear that if we increase receipts by this method we also raise expenses because we will be compelled to pay more dearly for what was previously purchased at cheaper prices.
>
> If meat is dearer, if the price of textiles and of all things increase, the soldier will have more difficulty in eating and maintaining himself properly, his pay therefore will have to be raised; the salaries of all artisans will be greater . . . all of which will cause added expenses to approach the rise in receipts while bringing great loss to individuals for a very mediocre gain made by the Prince.
>
> . . . The poor noble whose wealth consists only in landed estates will not increase his revenue by such taxes; the fruits of the earth will remain always around the same price, particularly so far as he is concerned, and even if in time they become more expensive, the excessive price will cause sales to diminish so that at the end of a year the poor noble will find no additional income but instead greater expenses. . . . He may yet be able to remain on his estate and support his family, though with difficulty, but he will no longer send his children into the

armies to serve the King and his country in accordance with the obligations of his birth.

If it is true, and it appears certain, that the sale of what is in commerce among the subjects diminishes to the extent that taxes are increased, it is possible that such increases can reduce rather than raise revenue from duties in the realm.

So far as consumption inside the realm is concerned, it is certain that more is bought when merchandise is at a reasonable price and thus more [money] is spent.[10]

Richelieu's idea of circulating wealth is implicit in his description of how indirect taxes must be adjusted to the volume of domestic commerce. Colbert had precisely the same thought when he said that royal revenues varied directly with the "movement" of money in the realm. Other men elaborated further on the need to maintain an uninterrupted flow of precious metals in all parts of France. In 1646, for example, Jean Eon, Carmelite prior at Nantes and secretary to the Duke of Meilleraye, Governor of Brittany,[11] argued that internal circulation of foreign treasure contributed toward national unity; it linked the destinies of the state to all levels of society, making them everywhere increasingly dependent on one another. Eon declared that "as several persons form a family, several families a bourg, several bourgs a town and several towns a kingdom, so . . . the good of the kingdom depends upon the well-being of the towns, that of the towns upon the happy condition of the bourgs and [that] of the bourgs on the ease

[10] *Testament politique d'Armand du Plessis, Cardinal duc de Richelieu*, Amsterdam, 1688, Part II, pp. 145-150.

[11] For further information about this author and his work see Henri Sée's "Le commerce des étrangers et notamment des Hollandais à Nantes pendant la minorité de Louis XIV," *Tijdschrift Voor Geschiedenis* (1926).

and facility of individual persons. Thus by relating
the first to the last we find the happiness and complete felicity of the state depend upon the prosperity
and good fortune of individual people." Commerce,
he held, is of "perfect utility": men in all ranks of
society have an interest in its proper functioning.
Landowning nobles profit from the sale of agricultural products. Magistrates would find income
from "judicial offices . . . very modest" without trade
which creates more business and "brings money into
the hands of the people, all of whom have recourse to
the courts for judgment." Similarly, artisans and the
entire populations of maritime towns were supported
directly or indirectly from trade. The chain of prosperity did not end there, however, for it continued
and branched out in every direction:

> As for the rest it must be said that although the
> above mentioned towns . . . where commerce is
> practiced . . . enjoy the first and principal ad-
> vantage from trade, the fruit is communicated
> to other towns and to neighboring provinces
> who also become enriched. Maritime towns are
> like general depots where adjoining cities and
> bourgs bring their fruits, produce and manufac-
> tures to obtain a good price. They are the centers
> where divers peoples and artisans bring their
> work to completion, and earn their subsistence
> by the salaries given them. To others [cities]
> maritime centers are like the sea with respect to
> streams and rivers who find their source in the
> ocean, borrowing the water and then, return-
> ing in a perpetual flow, support one another by
> continual communication.
>   . . . Commerce puts everyone to work, [all
> people] need fruits, provisions and manufactures.

Trade brings general utility to all communities and to all kinds of persons in the realm. Great and small, rich and poor are universally obliged to devote themselves to commerce according to their condition and to their faculties.[12]

Finally, it is explained that the flow of foreign treasure in France supported rural life, the principal source of state power. An anonymous Norman noble, writing some time after 9 September 1656 and before 3 September 1658, said with respect to the advantages of trade with Spain:

It is . . . this commerce which pays the cloths of Normandy, the "free gift" of Brittany and the impositions of Poitou and Guienne. This commerce permits the *éclat* of the King's house, pays pensions, and nourishes and supports the armies. All money coming back finally to the King by the ebb and flow of trade which makes it pass from one hand to the other, to return ultimately to the Prince, *because at the very time money arrives from Spain merchants distribute it in the countryside to buy wheat and cloth and the villagers no sooner receive it than they carry it to the Receivers of the* tailles *and of other impositions, and from there to the treasury which pays all necessary expenses.*[13]

[12] Jean Eon, *Le Commerce honorable*, Nantes, 1646, pp. 175-184.
[13] Cahiers du plan véritable de l'estat présent des affaires de l'Europe, *B.N., Cinq cents Colbert*, MS 497, ff. 195-196, italics added. Another copy is catalogued in the same collection as MS 203. As far as the date of the document is concerned, the author (fol. 188) refers to Admiral Blake's capture of Spanish galleons in the Mediterranean (9 September 1656) and he frequently speaks of Cromwell, who died on 3 September 1658, as still alive.
Some fifteen years previously, in 1643, the Estates of Normandy explained: "La manufacture des toilles qui se font en ceste Province donne au peuple du plat pays de quoy payer ses tailles et son

In sum, the circulatory theory of money was a corollary to the more general theory of seventeenth century French mercantilism. The rate and quantity of treasure in domestic circulation, varying directly with the volume of industrial production—for the most part rural, determined both the amount of royal revenues and the degree to which taxes prove onerous to individual payers of the *taille*. If production were high, indirect revenues would increase and direct taxes might be reduced; but a fall in production, slowing the movement of money, would curtail individual income and diminish the proceeds from indirect taxes, thereby compelling government to depend more and more on direct impositions at a time when people could least afford to pay them.

The money from abroad was to be obtained, of course, at the expense of other countries. Although Colbert emphasized more than had people before him the concept of an international struggle for the greatest share of a fixed quantity of money existing in the world, the idea had been formulated much earlier. In 1615, for example, Montchrétien declared: "We lose as much as the foreigner earns . . . one hand becomes empty and the other is filled, it is like a transfer from one full jar to a dry one."[14] Colbert's particular stress on a "war of money" appears to have been motivated above all by universally depressed economic conditions and the scarcity of specie. But the difference is only one of emphasis. More important is the fact that this long-established concept was

sel. . . ." (*Cahier des Etats de Normandie sous les règnes de Louis XIII et Louis XIV*, ed. Ch. de Robillard de Beaurepaire, 3 vols., Paris, 1876-1878, III, 127).

14 Antoyne de Montchrétien, *L'économie politique*, ed. and pub. Funck-Brentano, Paris, 1889, p. 111. Oddly enough Hauser, *La pensée*, p. 189, appears mistakenly to have thought this idea, which he calls "quasi enfantine," peculiar to Colbert.

connected with a growing conviction that France was naturally or divinely destined to become the leader of Christendom and, indeed, the arbiter of all states on earth.

Men of mercantilist persuasion, seemingly without exception, were convinced, as were Seyssel and Du Prat in the previous century, that France alone was capable of getting along without foreign trade, while the rest of Europe was dependent upon her products.[15] Moreover, they thought failure to organize the kingdom's immense resources so as to produce the greatest possible export would cause unemployment and widespread misery. In other words, full exploitation of France's economic superiority was required for national survival; and such a policy would also draw the largest portion of world treasure to French shores, transforming the kingdom into the most powerful state on earth. A clear statement of this position,

[15] The texts abound with statements to this effect. In 1570 Loys le Roy expressed this conviction as part of a veritable paean of patriotism. This extraordinarily eloquent passage is quoted at length in A. Henri Becker, *Un humaniste au XVIe siècle: Loys Le Roy de Coutances*, Paris, 1896, pp. 230-231. Montchrétien, *ibid.*, p. 23, wrote "la France seule se peut passer de tout ce qu'elle a de terres voisines, et toutes les terres voisines nullement d'elle." Richelieu, *Testament*, Part II, pp. 127-128, despite hesitations about high taxes on agricultural exports (Part II, p. 148), declared: "Et pourvu que nous sachions nous bien aider des Avantages que la Nature nous a procurés, nous tirerons l'argent de ceux qui voudront avoir nos marchandises qui leur sont si nécessaires et nous ne nous chargerons pas beaucoup de leurs Denrées, qui nous sont si peu utiles." Jean Eon, *Commerce honorable*, p. 203, announced: "Il suffit de dire qu'elle [France] possède tout ce qui est nécessaire et utile à la vie, sans qu'elle ait besoin de recourir aux autres pais pour sa subsistance. Mais bien au contraire il y a grand nombre de fruits et de manufactures, dont les voisins et étrangers sont dépourveuz, qu'ils doivent par nécessité venir prendre en France." In 1651, Colbert himself wrote Mazarin (Clément, *Lettres*, II, Part II, p. 405), "God was pleased to endow the provinces of this kingdom so that it could be prepared to suffice unto itself." For more examples see Harsin, *Les Doctrines*, p. 13, n.3.

for example, was made in 1634 by the Marquis de la Gomberdière, in a small pamphlet entitled *Nouveau Règlement Général sur toutes sortes de marchandises et manufactures qui sont utiles et nécessaires dans ce Royaume, représenté au Roy pour le grand bien et profit des villes et autres lieux de la France.*[16] Addressing Louis XIII, the author explained how the incomparable wealth of France, the only state capable of remaining sufficient unto herself, was clear proof that the Creator had intended her to lead all nations on earth:

> Sire, God has so abundantly strewn his sacred blessings on your Kingdom that it appears He has designated it to have authority and command over all others in the universe. He has so well constituted it and provisioned it with all things necessary and useful to the life of your peoples and with such abundance that we can truly say that this Monarchy is the only one which can do without all her neighbors and no single one can get along without her.[17]

After making a rapid inventory of national wealth, La Gomberdière cautioned His Majesty: "But Sire, it will be in vain that your Kingdom is the most beautiful, the most opulent in the universe (as she truly is), if the French (your subjects) do not reestablish their work in manufacture and apply themselves to the gifts God has bestowed on them." By doing without imported goods, "we will employ poor people and the profit from their labor will save them from

---

[16] Hauser, *La pensée*, pp. 156-159, discusses this pamphlet at length; nothing, however, appears to be known about the author.

[17] *Nouveau Règlement général*, pp. 3-4. La Gomberdière's statement is identical with that of the Assembly of Notables in 1583; see *Des Etats Généraux et Autres Assemblées Nationales*, ed. Charles Joseph Mayer, 18 Vols., La Haye, 1789, XIV, 233.

their present misery, providing the means necessary for their subsistence." Toward this end, the writer suggested the "creation of Bureaus in all the principal towns and other places in your Kingdom to keep manufactures constantly at work." Products exported from every point in France would "attract foreign treasures to French shores; money, flowing throughout the realm, will become common everywhere."[18] In short France's economic advantages over other states were thought to be of such a character that their full exploitation, a policy necessary to avoid widespread distress, would lead inevitably to French world political hegemony.

A number of interesting ideas were advanced to support the view of France's necessarily preeminent role among nations. The most well-known theme was a theory of geographical determinism. Writers declared that the character, genius, disposition, and inborn talents of every people corresponded to the peculiar climatic, topographical, and other natural conditions of its country. Bodin, for example, insisted "there are almost as many varieties of men as there are countries";[19] for national character, molded by physical conditions, was the product of such factors as humidity, heat, wind, cold, marshes, deserts, plains, and mountains. Moreover, terrestrial patterns formed by the psycho-geographical traits of nations conformed in every detail to the image of the universe as revealed by the course of celestial bodies and the signs of the Zodiac. "The proportions of the planets" correspond to the natural divisions of humanity and to the divers characters of nations. In general, northern peoples, under the signs of Mars and Diana, the

[18] *Ibid.*, pp. 12-14.
[19] *Les six livres de la république*, Paris, 1608, Bk. V, chap. 1, p. 663.

moon, were proper for war and the hunt. Physically large and deliberate in gesture, they were heavy in spirit and slow to understand. Southern populations, living under the influence of Venus and Saturn, bathed in the warmth of meridian regions, were slight of build, rapid and vivacious of nature, and endowed with surpassing intellectual talents. It was in the middle region, however, where the two sets of qualities mingle under the planets Jupiter and Mercury, that great states were born and people are imbued with political wisdom. Such men were destined to "establish Republics and to compose laws and ordinances for other peoples."[20] And, according to Bodin, of all nations inhabiting the intermediate zone none were "quicker of mind and more fitted for all things in arms, in letters, in commerce . . . , than the French."[21]

Some mercantilist polemicists adopted and modified Bodin's theories. Jean Eon, the Carmelite prior at Nantes, for example, was especially concerned with trade in the Far East and in the New World. He wanted to see French rather than Dutch ships entering harbors in the Orient and in the West Indies. Supporting his views with an unusual combination of familiar arguments, the author explained that "each climate receives particular influences, these influences communicate divers qualities, these qualities form different talents and consequently varied kinds of sciences and industries." The Creator had "by this method distributed His gifts and talents unequally, making men dependent upon one another and obliging them to communicate" their particular arts and knowledge. Were it not for commerce "each science would remain imprisoned in one country, the arts would be unknown." Similarly, with respect to the

[20] *Ibid.*, p. 690.   [21] *Ibid.*, p. 698.

terrestrial distribution of material wealth, God invented trade "to maintain human society so that if love and the desire to ornament the spirit are not bonds sufficiently strong to keep men in union and communication, material needs will compel them to visit and to deal with one another." It was for this reason that "the influence of celestial bodies, . . . so necessary for the production of the fruits of the earth, are unequally communicated to divers parts of the world, making some abound in things that others need; each possessing something useful and necessary to other areas of the world." Every country was destined to carry both its products and its talents to other states. And, according to Eon, France's mission was to free helpless natives of the New World and of the Orient from the tyranny of other nations, especially the Dutch, and to extend the beneficent influences of French culture and trade to uncivilized peoples everywhere:

> Some nation must visit and instruct these barbarous peoples. It is France which inherently possesses the glory of letters, of arms, the honor of the arts and the politeness of morals, a nation free, liberal and debonaire, sensitive to the necessities of men and most charitable in her aid to them. Also we know that all peoples of barbarous nations love the French by natural inclination as much as they abhor the domination of our neighbors whose rigors they have experienced. So powerful is this motive that, even though purely natural, it alone will inspire the French to reestablish sea commerce, and contribute in this way to the instruction and to the courtesy of uncivilized nations.[22]

22 *Commerce honorable*, pp. 135-138. Belief in France's "civiliz-

For Bodin, and to some extent for Eon, the cosmos was not only reflected in the natural psycho-geographical divisons of peoples, but it was also mirrored in the ordering of the human soul and in the social and political structure of societies. An absolute sovereign would bring unity to conflicting interests in the state in the same manner that God reconciled contrary elements in both the soul and in the rest of creation:

> Vices and virtues, different qualities, elements, opposing forces and sympathies and antipathies are linked and reconciled in the harmony of the world and of its parts; just as in the Republic good and bad, poor and rich, wise and foolish, strong and weak are allied by those [qualities] in between linking one to the other. . . . And all this is like the three parts of the soul. . . . We can say that the great Eternal King, unique, pure, simple, indivisible, lifted above the world of elements, celestial and intelligible, unites [all] together . . . in divine harmony, an example to which the wise sovereign must conform in governing his realm.[23]

Eon, accepting Bodin's transcendental hierarchy, changed the emphasis from a political to a material harmony of status and fortune. Just as national character was shaped by physical conditions and natural resources, so the position of each subject within the state was determined by the Providential and unequal distribution of wealth:

---

ing" mission appears in a more literary form among humanists during Francis I's reign. See Roland Mousnier "Etudes sur la France de 1494 à 1559," *Les cours de Sorbonne*, Paris, 1957, I, 59-63.

23 *République*, Bk. VI, p. 1060.

> Divine Providence has ordered that in the midst of the equality of our natures, the conditions of men and their fortunes will be unequal; composing in this way an harmonious economy among universal inequalities found in the conditions of men.[24]

Montchrétien appears to have expressed a similar thought when he declared "everything here below and above is regulated by the infinite wisdom of God. . . . We hold it certain that we do come to our profession by fortune; each receives his task in the public work of this life from a superior providence, to whom all without exception are born and destined."[25] But it is only with Richelieu that we see clearly expressed the idea that France's economy would not flourish unless her class structure continued to conform to the pattern of the universe. Descartes at this time had not yet constructed his world machine and most literate people were still imbued with Aristotelian-Ptolemaic concepts. The earth was thought to be located at the precise center of a universe composed of a series of invisible crystalline homocentric spheres, each propelling a planet. The elements contained within this system were assigned ascending positions of rank. Matter, whose nature was base, sought its appropriate location at the center while the nobler elements, water, air, and fire respectively sought their superior places in the cosmic order. The distance an element was separated from its natural location was the measure that its essence remained potential and unrealized. With the final attainment of its natural location, the complete fulfillment of essence, a body lost all weight and per-

[24] *Commerce honorable*, pp. 176-177.
[25] *L'économie politique*, p. 14.

formed best its natural functions in the divine scheme of things. And Richelieu thought no political and social principles more important than those revealed by the sacred order of the physical universe:

> After having spoken separately about the divers orders composing a state . . . , I must say in general that the whole subsists only by the union of its parts in their order and in their natural place. A great kingdom can never flourish if Your Majesty does not make the bodies composing it subsist in their order: the Church holding first place, the nobility second and the officers marching at the head of the people, third.
>
> As it is very certain that the elements, all capable of weight, have no weight when they are in their place, so is it equally sure that no order of your state will be a charge on another when each is constrained to remain in the place designated by his birth.
>
> And as neither fire nor air nor water can support a terrestrial body, because it is heavy outside its place, it is certain that neither the Church nor the nobility will be able to support the burden of the officers when they wish to leave their place.[26]

A traditional view of this kind was still possible under Richelieu. After the *Fronde*, however, the social implications of mercantilist principles conformed more and more to the Cartesian cosmos. Atoms and vortices were rapidly displacing crystalline spheres and a natural physical or social place was a meaning-

[26] *Testament*, pp. 182-184. For a more complete description of the Ptolemaic and Aristotelian universe, see T. S. Kuhn, *The Copernican Revolution, Planetary Astronomy in the Development of Western Thought*, Cambridge, Mass., 1957.

less concept. Corpuscular and human behavior, it was held, conformed to laws of linear inertia operating in a plenum of undifferentiated bodies. Physical and social weight was explained as mere pressure from colliding particles and from conflicting interests. Hence government was to society what God was to the universe: the supreme organizer coordinating perpetually moving parts of a vast machine. The position of one or another unit was determined only by its momentary function. Status, moral values, and political relations were matters to be judged according to purely utilitarian standards. This position, so strongly suggestive of Pierre Nicole's Cartesian utilitarianism, is revealed with all the mercantilist trappings by Jean Pottier de la Hestroye who, writing in 1698, considered Colbert one of "France's greatest ministers":

> I admit that fashions cause unnecessary spending, that they serve to diminish the wealth of some families; but if the rich and those who enter most into luxury reduce their wealth in this way, it is certain that they also support at the same time an infinity of poor families, who, without work would die from starvation, become rich by their industry. Thus if some lose others profit, and it is our subjects and not the foreigners who earn from the loss in this perpetual circulation. Also the state profits from the loss of one and the gain of others. The grandeur of a state is not to have individuals distinguished by their wealth, all subjects must be rich. . . . The gold and silver which a state must possess should be in the hands of every subject without distinction. It is not even wise politics for a state to have subjects who think only of accu-

mulating great savings; it distinguishes individuals too greatly and renders them idle and idleness is almost always accompanied by vices pernicious to the state and to the authority of the sovereign. . . . *All subjects must work in the state; everyone must be occupied. The state is properly speaking a machine, the movements of which although different must be regulated without interruption; we cannot interfere with the movements without running the risk of destroying the state.* Similarly subjects must act and work in a state to support it and to render it flourishing. The poor by hand, the rich by their purse, [spending] so as to make others work. The Rule, Charity and even Religion demand that the rich share . . . with the poor. Of what matter that the rich share their money gratuitously or by . . . spending uselessly for superfluities . . . *it is a vice of their spirit which does no harm to the state. Far from losing, the state profits, everyone is able to find work and no one is useless,* not even those who impoverished themselves with unnecessary spending.[27]

Pottier did not live in the animistic universe of Richelieu's day when justice concerned the elements as much as it did men. Now atoms replaced noble and

[27] Bibliothèque municipale de Poitiers, MS 548, pp. 178-184, italics added. Almost a century previously, Turquet de la Mayerne wrote a blueprint to reform society according to his understanding of the laws of nature, *La monarchie aristodémocratique*, Paris, 1611. Like Pottier, Turquet said that any idle member of society endangered the entire social mechanism: "[C'est] bien certain que s'il advenoit en ceste machine mondaine tant bien mesurée et proportionée, perte, défaut ou diminution, cessation ou oisiveté quelconque, elle ruineroit tout" (p. 6). What is most revealing here is that although Turquet and Pottier had in mind different models of the cosmos, *both men argued in favor of luxury and against the aristocracy.* (Turquet's treatise is discussed briefly in Chapter Six.)

base elements, previously thought to correspond to the inequality of human conditions in an all-embracing transcendental hierarchy. Mercantilists like Pottier compared state and society to a cosmos devoid of hierarchy and personality: an inanimate system of corpuscles and mechanical forces. Cosmic and human government became increasingly a task of adjusting anonymous atoms and nameless interests indifferently here or there for the proper functioning of the system as a whole. Law for Pottier, as for Nicole, was less concerned with justice than with narrowing the area of human activity to manageable proportions. And money, dissolving traditional values and social structures, was said to enable the state to shape human beings into more easily combinable parts of a total pattern.

The tendency among administrators to think of men as interchangeable units of a machine was intimately related to belief in the predestined superiority of France over all other states. The connection is made clear by considering the mercantilist program for kingdom-wide royal inquiries. It will be remembered that Richelieu and Colbert sought to adjust indirect taxes to the rate of monetary circulation measured by the volume of domestic trade and of export. Only a vast machinery of inquiry, however, could furnish the data necessary to determine the volume of internal trade. Large-scale royal investigations had also long been considered necessary for a general reform of France's fiscal system, both direct and indirect. Bodin and Montchrétien, the latter alternatively plagiarizing and paraphrasing from the *Republic* on this matter,[28] argued that the astonish-

---

[28] Plato, it may be remembered, wrote: "As concerns payment to the public treasury, every man must have his estate valued . . . members of every tribe shall also furnish the rural commission with a

ing number and variety of imposts made fiscal reform difficult. They insisted that government-directed surveys, designed to ascertain the wealth of every subject, alone could provide the information necessary for efficient and equitable tax legislation.[29]

The idea of such systematic inquiry was certainly not new, for precedents go back all the way to William the Conqueror.[30] In seventeenth century France, however, the concept had special significance. It was not only related to the circulatory theory of money and to an unprecedented concern with fiscal reforms,

---

written record of each year's produce that the exchequer may be free to choose at its pleasure, between the two means of raising revenue. . . ." *The Collected Dialogues*, ed. E. Hamilton and H. Cairns, New York, 1961, *Laws*, chap. xii, p. 1500.

[29] Bodin's ideas on this matter have been described in Chapter I; Montchrétien's thoughts are discussed in *L'économie politique*, pp. 342-353.

[30] James E. King, *Science and Rationalism in the Government of Louis XIV 1661-1683*, Series LXVI of *The Johns Hopkins University Studies in Historical and Political Science*, Baltimore, 1949, II, argues that the "administrators of France from 1661 to 1663 were convinced that they were engineers of a successful revolution by bringing science into government" (p. 29). Moreover, says this author, the "spirit of rationalism and science" is particularly reflected by the launching of large-scale inquiries and the issuance of subsequent administrative rulings based on statistical data thus obtained. Apart from pointing to Bodin, Montchrétien, Laffemas, and La Gomberdière, all of whom insisted on large-scale royal investigations, one need only consider the far-flung inquiries *actually* carried out by Richelieu to appreciate the thoroughly traditional character of Colbert's efforts in this regard. Examples of only *a few* of Richelieu's inquiries may be found in Hauser, *La pensée*, pp. 43-47. The Cardinal's *Instruction que le roi a commandé être mise entre les mains des commissaires envoyés aux provinces pour l'exécution de ses lettres de déclaration en forme d'édit . . .* , pub. in Lazare Du Crot, *Traité des aides, tailles et gabelles*, Paris, 1636, pp. 476-488, appears to have been used as a model by Colbert for his fiscal inquiries. See E. Bourgeois and L. André, *Les sources de l'histoire de France au XVIIe siècle 1610-1715*, 8 vols., Paris, 1913-1935, VII, 185, art. 6175. It is difficult to understand in precisely what respect Colbert thought himself a revolutionary.

but the demand for kingdom-wide royal economic surveys reflected above all a growing tendency to idealize the state. Montchrétien, for example, drives this point home with particular force: *"Une seule chose te manque, o grand Estat: la connoissance de toy-mesme et l'usage de ta force."*[31] Royal fact-finding commissions provided information necessary to transform disparate interests and scattered populations into a monolithic social and political structure:

> In short that all parts of this great body of the state link themselves together more easily, let there be nothing foreign in between . . . , not more nor less than the iron soldered at the forge. This is surely the clearest and most certain sign of a police reduced to good order under the government of justice and of reason.[32]

Finally, precise knowledge of France's strength would guide rulers infallibly toward new heights of national achievement: "Here Sire is all I have to say concerning the census . . . it alone can disclose what you can and ought to do with this rich and populous kingdom which God has put in your hands as a perfect instrument of power and of glory."[33]

No trait was more fundamental to seventeenth century French mercantilism than this interest in a census. The drive to inventory national wealth, a major factor in the origin of the intendancy, was as much a part of the program to unify France under an all-powerful monarch as was the continual and largely unsuccessful effort to abolish interior tariff barriers and create a truly national market. Moreover, the relation between the ideals of national economic unity and of foreign conquest was clear to contemporaries like Jean de Lartigue:

[31] *L'économie politique*, p. 34.   [32] *Ibid.*, p. 353.
[33] *Loc.cit.*

Tolls and tributes in too great number on rivers and at the gates of towns not only injure commerce, but they occupy and divide the minds of subjects, preventing them from devoting themselves to the great things of outside. And in this way they cause great and deplorable damage to the Sovereign, cutting and dividing his state in several parts, making peoples different and creating opposition among them, among the towns and the provinces and severing in this way the union and conformity which renders subjects prompt for external enterprises and expeditions. And since these inventions have been introduced into Rome and into Italy they have no longer dreamed of conquest.[34]

The rise of mercantilism in France was intimately related to the idealization of state and an increasing tendency to identify political expansion with national self-realization. The connection between foreign policy and the principles of political economy is clear. Richelieu's and Louis XIV's persistent efforts to impose French preponderance in European affairs reflect, at least in part, a conviction that only the full exploitation of France's God-given economic superiority at the expense of other countries would assure prosperity and create an enduring union of people and state. The effort to make the crown permanently supreme in society was indistinguishable from an attempt to extend its jurisdiction over other peoples. Indeed, the symbol of this attitude may be read even today on the face of the Sun King's palace at Versailles: *A toutes les gloires de la France!*

The nationalism which developed as an integral part of the mercantilist program was highly intellec-

[34] B.N., Fds. fr., MS 4164, f. 37.

tual. Yet, for the first time the French people were cast in a special role. Acceptance of Bodin's propositions that there are "as many varieties of men as there are countries" and that the French, more than any other nation, are destined to "establish Republics and to compose laws . . . for other peoples" made the mercantilist effort to impose French preponderance in Europe more than a mere affair of government. Foreign policy became a means by which the French people, as distinguished from the state, fulfilled their manifest destiny. Now that the ideal of an indissoluble union between people and state had gained acceptance, diplomatic defeat or victory could be viewed as a matter concerning all subjects without distinction.

Another aspect of this complex stream of nationalist and mercantilist thought was its social implications. The aristocracy was profoundly hostile to mercantilism which, after Richelieu, and particularly after Colbert, became more and more a comprehensive philosophy of state that seriously undermined existing theoretical bases for inequality among men. Resistance was slow in forming. But there did rapidly appear the outline of a rival political philosophy, very broad in scope, which struck at the heart of mercantilist doctrine. Moreover, its aristocratic spokesman, Jean de Lartigue, was imbued with a kind of nationalism which, dissociated from the general context of centralization, drew its inspiration, as the following section shows, from the traditional humanist and crusading drive for world and cosmic unity.[35]

[35] Association between arguments hostile to centralization and universalist tendencies seems to have existed, at least in embryo, as early as the sixteenth century. Guillaume de la Perrière, *Mirrour of Policie* . . . , speaking of Louis XI, writes: "This King immedi-

ii. JEAN DE LARTIGUE AND ARISTOCRATIC DISSENT

Early examples of aristocratic attacks on mercantilist theory are connected with contemporary views about relations between town and country. Eli Heckscher has shown how seventeenth century regulation of the national economy was an outgrowth of earlier policies whereby medieval municipal government directed city affairs for the benefit of the town as a whole.[36] A specific consequence of this policy for France was progressive liberation of rural areas from direct exploitation by urban centers. The mercantilist drive to enrich the countryside, to aid poor people from *les plats pays* was all part of a program to end

---

ately after his coronation (upon what humour, is unknoune) did as it were banish from the court, as well the Princes of blood, as the other Lords, and determined to serve himselfe with men of meane estate, and almost of no account, but base companions, imagining (as some presume) he should draw better service from them, and be better obeied by them, then men extracted of noble parentage. . . . The Princes and Lords of France seeing themselves to be contemned in such sort, they gathered an army together, encamped themselves heere to Paris, and offered the King battle . . . the battle was given at a place called Monthery the 27 of Julie 1465, the place giving name to this day. This contempt put the king in hazard to loose both his Estate and his life, if by great prudence and policy he had not appeased the fury and wrath of the said Prince and Nobility. This notable example ought to be imprinted in the memory of all Princes and politicke Governors, that they may thereby learne to keepe themselves from despising their subjects, lest they incure the like danger which king Lewis did, who after the said sedition became more wise and prudent than before: for the remainder of his life, he was a Lyon in Force, and a Foxe in counsell" (folios 40-41). Moreover, in another breath, La Perrière also states that "the conference and conversing with strangers and Aliens is oftentimes very profitable for the Commonweale for the trafficke of Merchandise . . . Nature would not distribute all her benefites unto one place alone, but part and devide them, giving unto one climate that which wanteth in another, recompensing the barrenes of one thing with the fruitfulness of another."

[36] *Mercantilism*, I, especially 128-137.

municipal monopolization of capital and to disperse gold and silver throughout the kingdom.

Town domination of the countryside, however, had existed for centuries. Most people accepted the situation as part of the natural or proper order of things. So deeply rooted was this view that, toward the end of the seventeenth century, intellectuals based their idea of progress squarely on the concept of urban superiority and town exploitation of dependent—indeed, enslaved—rural areas. Fontenelle, for example, in his *Digression on the Ancients and Moderns* (Paris, 1688) explained that pastoral poetry, "the most ancient of all verse," became highly developed in antiquity because at this early date rural folk enjoyed much leisure and "lived . . . in great opulence." Times changed, however, and

> societies became perfected, or maybe more corrupt, at any rate men turned to occupations which appeared more important. Acting from greater interests they built cities on every side, and in time great states were formed. Then inhabitants of the country became the slaves of those in cities and pastoral life, being the most unhappy lot of man, no longer inspired anything agreeable.

> Culture requires minds which are in a position to raise themselves above the more urgent needs of life, and which have been polished by prolonged intercourse with society; shepherds have always lacked one or the other of these conditions. The first ones . . . lived in sufficient abundance, but in their day the world had not yet time to become polished . . . during the following centuries the shepherds were too miserable.[37]

37 *Digression*, pp. 142-146.

The urban conviction that the unprivileged among rural populations were generally destined to be exploited is also suggested by contemporary dictionaries. Antoine Furetière's *Dictionnaire Universel* (La Haye, 1727), for example, describes peasants as "those people who support the charges of State, who pay the *taille*, who labor in the *corvées, etc.* Peasants who are rich are ordinarily clever and insolent." Another dictionary explained that peasants in the area surrounding Paris were particularly "sly and wicked."[38] Finally, the very structure of the fiscal system, weighing almost exclusively on rural populations, reinforced the profoundly engrained notion that the collective wealth and power of the state rested upon rural enslavement.

Toward the middle of the century, particularly after the *Fronde,* some nobles, misunderstanding the true aim of the mercantilists, protested that mercantilist policy was directed at subjecting them also to urban domination, threatening to destroy their traditional status in society.[38a] They alleged that the inflow of large quantities of foreign treasure into the kingdom dispossessed the aristocracy from their lands, and ultimately drove them into the hands of townsmen:

[38] Pierre Richelet, *Dictionnaire de la langue françoise ancienne et moderne*, Paris, 1728. Professor Meuvret called attention to this fact in his seminar at the Sorbonne during the academic year 1959-1960.

[38a] Discussing a new tax on wine, the Intendant de Heer, for example, wrote: "Je scay Monsieur que cette ferme est de grande conséquence, mais . . . les ecclésiastiques et les gentilhommes disent que c'est les mettre à la taille" (Boris Porchnev, *Les soulèvements populaires en France de 1623 à 1648*, Paris, 1963, app. 41, p. 625). In this regard see also the very interesting article by Pierre Deyon, "A propos des rapports entre la noblesse française et la monarchie absolue pendant la première moitié du XVIIe siècle," *Revue historique*, Avril-Juin 1964, pp. 341-356.

All order has been perverted since this great abundance of money has introduced tax-farmers,[39] who were unknown in France before Henry III. . . . Another kind of person has also risen among us, in truth less dangerous, protected by royal authority but nevertheless born to bring about the ruin of others. . . . The rentiers,[40] ignorant and unlettered individuals who amass great wealth without trouble, without labor and without risk: great good-for-nothings who commerce only with notaries in order to receive back-payments. It is they who have chased the two pillars of the state, the gentry and the *laboureurs*,[41] from their ancient holdings. . . . Three things have ruined the nobility: facility in finding money, luxury and war. In peace they are consumed by luxury; in war, since they have no money in reserve, the most comfortable gentlemen can go only by mortgaging his field and his mill. So true is this that it can be proved that since 1492, when money became more common, men from the towns have acquired more than 6,000,000 gold livres of revenues from noble lands possessed by gentlemen rendering service

[39] Financiers paid a certain sum to the government in exchange for the right to collect a tax or group of taxes or duties for private profit, and often exercised their right ruthlessly and with such avarice as to become an object of widespread hatred. The functions of the *gens d'affaires*, those groups of financiers who borrowed money from the bourgeoisie and then lent it to the government in return for various kinds of financial concessions or special privileges are discussed in George T. Matthews, *The Royal General Farms in Eighteenth Century France*, New York, 1958; see particularly chap. 7 and also p. 37.

[40] A holder of a government annuity or *rente*, called a *rentier*, is one who owns an interest-bearing government obligation.

[41] "Rien de clair comme la définition du laboureur: celui qui possède au moins deux chevaux qui, attelés à une charrue, lui permettent de labourer" (Goubert, *Le Beauvais*, p. 170).

in war according to the nature and quality of their fiefs. . . . It must be confessed that men from the towns lend money and the back-payments and costs consume them [the nobles] in such a way that [the land] passes insensibly from an industrious hand to one which is good-for-nothing and inexorable. All the proprietors are chased from the countryside, there not being one who retains an inch of land, principally in Normandy when he has a *greffier* or a *procureur* for a neighbor.[42]

These complaints, written by an anonymous noble sometime between 1656 and 1658, that a "great abundance of money has perverted all order," that luxury "consumes" the nobility, driving aristocrats from "ancient holdings" and delivering their lands into the worthless depraved hands of those "men from the towns . . . protected by royal authority," are more than particular grievances against government policy. They are also a condemnation of the mercantilist principle that a continual flow of increasing quantities of foreign treasure throughout the realm is necessary for developing both the power of the state and the prosperity of its subjects.[43]

[42] Cahiers du plan véritable, B.N., Cinq cents Colbert, MS 497, ff. 192-193.

[43] Interestingly enough, this author thought that international rivalry for foreign treasure had grown so intense and had become so deeply rooted that it would be impossible to return to less corrupting practices and also remain a great power; France had no alternative but to continue in the trade regardless of cost (see ff. 193 *et seq.*). Belief that government encouragement of the luxury trade would lead both to the strengthening of the state and to the eventual subjugation of the aristocrats to the merchants was perhaps reinforced by the Italian experience, particularly that of Florence; and also by later sixteenth century Italian writers like Giovanni Botero who gave industry far higher priority than agriculture. In Botero's words, "Nothing is of greater importance for

The writer was certainly not alone in his opinions. A forgotten treatise by Jean de Lartigue provides a link between future aristocratic opposition and the complex currents of thought going back to the sixteenth century. In some respects it is difficult to assess the man's importance. A few of his works are listed in L. Moreri's great *Dictionnaire*, where Lartigue is described as "known and esteemed by scholars." Moreri found corroboration for his statement in the subtlety of Lartigue's "spirit" and in the fact that he was appointed royal historian during the Sun King's personal reign.[44] The one published work

---

increasing the power of a state and gaining for it more inhabitants and wealth of every kind than the industry of its people and the number of crafts they exercise. . . . Since art is the rival of nature I must consider which is of more importance to make a state great and populous, the fertility of the soil or the industry of man. Without hesitation I shall say industry. . . . Moreover a far greater number of people live by industry than by rents, as the many cities of Italy bear witness—in particular Venice, Florence, Genoa and Milan, whose greatness and magnificence are manifest, and almost two-thirds of whose inhabitants live by the silk and woollen industries. Leaving the cities for the provinces, those who are informed as to the resources of France say that the produce of that kingdom amounts to fifteen million crowns a year, and affirm that it numbers more than fifteen million souls; supposing that it has only fifteen million, this allows one crown of revenue per head: the remainder of its wealth, therefore, must come from industry." Cited from *The Reason of State*, trans. P. J. and D. P. Waley, New Haven, Conn., 1956, Bk. VIII, no. 3, pp. 150-152.

[44] *Le grand dictionnaire historique*, Paris, 1759: "Jean de Lartigue, seigneur de Caplice, prêtre, docteur en Théologie et religieux Prémontré; il fut ensuite reçu docteur de Sorbonne à Paris, où son mérite et ses ouvrages l'avoient attiré. Il fut connu et estimé des savants. Son esprit était aussi profond que fin et subtil: parmi un nombre d'écrits qu'il a fait, on distingue ceux de *L'immortalité de l'âme*, *La politique des conquérans*, *Le flux et le reflux de la mer et autres*. Il fut ensuite historiographe de France et mourut après 1680." I know of no other secondary work which even mentions the author's name. Apart from the treatise studied here, the Bibliothèque Nationale possesses three other works, two religious and one concerning Aristotle's rhetoric.

considered here, *La politique des conquérans* (Paris, 1661), went into two editions and one reprinting by 1664.[45] Although a gentleman of ancient lineage, doctor at the Sorbonne, author of some repute and royal historian, Jean de Lartigue apparently is not mentioned by any primary or secondary source other than Moreri. In any event his political writings are part of a current of thought extending from Postel, Campanella, Crucé, and Grotius[46] to important leaders of opposition in Louis XIV's reign. Lartigue is a spokesman for this tradition, contributing both to its continuity and to its further elaboration. His peculiar anti-statist nationalism, his positive view of government based upon an optimistic concept of man—all became an important part of the theories expounded by later aristocratic reformers.

La politique des conquérans is a treatise, one part of which is published; the other is in manuscript. The printed half concerning political theory in general, attempts to formulate "a science of politics" wherein the role of the aristocracy is reexamined in the light of wider speculative considerations. The manuscript section, written in 1664, entitled "La seconde partie de la politique des conquérans . . . ," deals with the application of general theory to French policy at that time. Clearly not meant for public consumption, this part was presented in manuscript form to the King, copies being made for his principal ministers, Le Tellier and Colbert.[47] The two sections are treated

---

[45] The second edition appeared in 1663 and was reprinted in the following year.

[46] Loys le Roy de Coutances, a contemporary of Postel, is essentially within the same tradition. See Becker's *Un humaniste*, esp. pp. 212-281.

[47] A copy belonging to the Le Tellier–Louvois family may be found at the B.N., Fds. fr., MS 4165; the copy destined for Colbert and bound with his arms is also at the B.N., Mélanges Colbert, MS 66.

as a unit, belonging to the pre-Colbert period because, although written during the very first years of his administration, the text reveals that the author was not yet clear about the Controller General's policies.[48]

Lartigue believed he had "discovered" a method "to reduce politics to one general view"; a comprehensive theory able to "serve in practical affairs and the more excellent because by one same light" it made clear a multitude of details. The principles were derived from nature which provided "a model for policies to be followed." Indeed, cosmic regularities, the "movements of this admirable machine," represented "nothing but the command and authority governing the actions of . . . men." And one trait above all others revealed nature's intentions: "The dependence and subordination linking all things one to the other."[49] The science of politics, therefore, is the study of "the proper means to preserve this subordination and dependence among men" according to "nature's works and operations," independent of "private opinion and imagination."[50]

Taking a page from Hobbes, Lartigue at first appears to agree with mercantilist and pessimistic doc-

---

[48] Referring to the Dutch, for example, Lartigue speaks approvingly of the "traitté d'amitié, d'alliance, de commerce et navigation qu'elle leur a accordé depuis deux ans" (f. 142). This passage dates the document sometime during 1664; the treaty in question was concluded on 27 April 1662. I am using a copy presented to the King, B.N., Fds. fr., MS. 4164.

[49] Guillaume de la Perrière, *Mirrour of Policie* . . . , writes in the sixteenth century: "Do not we see one Sunne beare rule and principality over the rest of the starres? Do not we see that unity is the beginning of number and that after we have made a long reckoning, and cast up our account, we returne to one totall summe? What might this signifie, that amongst all things created, we shal alwaies find someone to have preheminence above the rest of the same kind, . . ." (f. 8).

[50] *La politique des conquérans* (hereafter designated as *Politique*), pp. 5-7.

trines: Man was born free, but to preserve his natural liberty he was driven by original sin to seek always to dominate rather than accept subordination. It is therefore a natural law that conquerors command the vanquished and the feeble obey the strong. Force was the universal arbiter, but when used in the public interest or in a just cause, force destroyed "injustice, causing law and equity to reign." Moreover, war made men virtuous, creating a genuine aristocracy.[51] The austere life of campaigning cut "at the root of vice"; inurement to physical danger led to contempt for this life, driving the warrior's thoughts toward eternal principles of divine justice. Heroism in conflict was "the most elevated of deeds." Such sacrifices were for public rather than for private interest.[52] The state therefore owed these men a special obligation and "the people knowing well their incomparable debt to those who expose their lives in the service of the Republic . . . distinguish them with the highest possible recompense . . . and continue this honor into posterity because having sacrificed their lives for *la Patrie* by an extraordinary act of virtue, they [the people] wish to see their merit . . . born again in the children. And this is what we call the nobility."[53]

The nature of the state system (which Lartigue subsequently replaced with "world empire,") required an aristocracy in order to conduct international relations. The stronger and more self-sufficient a state, the closer were its ties to God and the worse its relations with other powers: "When a state is sufficient unto itself and possessing all things necessary for its subsistence and felicity, it must view the Divinity as the exterior principle of its well-being and other states as the source and authors of its evils and miseries."

[51] *Seconde partie,* ff. 68-69.
[52] *Ibid.,* ff. 9-10. [53] *Politique,* p. 90.

The designs of men, by nature "vague and indefinite," ultimately converged on the same objects; conflict arose "and this is the true reason why one state . . . is enemy to another. . . . " No state existed whose neighbor was not suspect . . . and against whom defenses must not be prepared. From which it followed that armed force was "a necessary and essential part" of society and "persons destined for the defense of the state" were worthy of special recognition.[54]

The legal exercise of force so essential for political survival was also a unique instrument designed to lead mankind toward the good life. Nature was by definition perfect and government "a natural human action for the aid and betterment of man": total conformity of one to the other would therefore render political authority "good and perfect."[55] Thus a prince who was aware that force was the source "from which all other virtues draw their excellence and even their essence" could, by compelling his people to obey the laws of nature, lead them toward the ultimate purpose of civilization: the reestablishment of the Golden Age when humanity would once again rejoice under the sway of universal justice. Opposing mercantilist principles with a secularized version of the familiar program for a union of mankind under the predestined rule of the French crown, Lartigue insisted that it was "necessary and advantageous for the well-being of all [men] that they have one leader whose unity links and attaches all parts together, keeping away discord and diversity." Just as one man naturally sought to dominate another, so did a state seek to conquer its neighbor. Under the Roman Empire, the word of the Bible spread to peoples everywhere; but this happy situation was destroyed when each country separated from the Empire and "wished to govern itself." Clear-

[54] *Ibid.*, pp. 88-90.   [55] *Ibid.*, p. 7.

ly it was necessary for humanity to adopt once again "a common *patrie* under one Prince."[56]

The eschatological themes so apparent in Postel and Campanella are absent in Lartigue. Realization of universal virtue on earth, he maintained, no longer announced the end of the world. Instead, the Golden Age had become the ultimate goal toward which mankind was advancing by way of French national expansion. Moreover, if Lartigue, like Campanella, believed that Louis XIV, the Sun King, was the divinely appointed agent destined to bring all peoples together under a beneficent rule, he further insisted that ac-

[56] *Seconde partie*, ff. 161-162. The treatise is permeated with this odd combination of national feeling and a traditional desire to unite the world in peace and plenty. Postel and Campanella subordinated politics to philosophy; Lartigue does the contrary: "Il n'est point d'amour plus excellent que celuy de la patrie qui comprend le Prince et toutes les choses que la nature nous rend chères, et il n'est point aussi de fin, qu'un philosophe se puisse proposer plus glorieuse, que d'augmenter la puissance et la prospérité de son pays" (*Seconde partie*, préface). This transition suggests a fundamental distinction between what is called medieval patriotism and modern nationalism: the latter appears only when central government is developed sufficiently to make possible the ideal of an enduring union of state and people. Postel and Campanella viewed universal monarchy as a framework permitting the *religious* union of mankind; Lartigue's writings point toward a permanent *political* union.

Some idea of the factors contributing to the transition from the ideal of religious unity to political unity is suggested in the curious folio volume written in 1643 by the Jesuit Father George Fournier: *Hydrographe contenant la théorie et la practique de toutes les parties de la navigation.* Speaking of how the sea and navigation provide a means for converting peoples in the remotest regions of the earth, Fournier observed that the task is so great that it is folly to declare that "le grand et final Jugement est si proche, comme quelques uns veulent faire croire" (p. 199). The true function of navigation is to unite all humanity: "La nature humaine estant sociable, tous les hommes estant descendus d'une commune tige, il faut que dans la nature il se trouve quelque moyen d'entretenir cette Société, et admirable communication, ce qui est tout a faict impossible entre les pays fort esloignez, sans la Navigation et usage de la Mer" (p. 200).

complishment of this glorious mission depended not upon philosophy, but above all on anti-mercantilist policies. It was foolish to believe that money and finance were "the nerves of war," as was vulgarly said: "This is an error emanating from the flattery of favorites wishing to give the King occasion to levy exactions on the people." Elsewhere Lartigue repeats: "It is also a mistake to imagine that treasures protect a state and render it safe against enemies from outside": experience had shown that great quantities of gold and silver only ruined and corrupted the nobility on one hand and tempted foreign powers on the other to try to capture the kingdom's reserves of precious metals. History had demonstrated that "demoralization and decadence arrive when Princes have given themselves to amassing excessive wealth, this is the most certain sign of their approaching ruin."[57]

Strength resided in virtue, union, the proper harmony of the parts, and above all in the subject's love for his Prince and for the state. In France, an hereditary monarchy where women were excluded from the throne and government rested upon the military prowess of the aristocracy, a just balance should be struck between the forces of union and those of love and devotion. Unity required that "arms and conquest" must be "the rule, the measure" and "the principal object" of domestic policy. But if "such a maxim might appear to encourage . . . an entire union and conformity among all citizens, thereby inspiring greater love among them," it must be remembered that a certain point existed beyond which unifying or centralizing policies would be injurious, indeed positively divisive, forces:

> For this reason [unity and love] some great statesmen have tried to introduce the same cus-

[57] *Politique*, pp. 145-147.

toms and the same laws into the realm: some have even descended so far as language, weights and measures, the manner of dress and other such particularities. But this was passing to the extreme. We do not seek total unity in families . . . nor even among the parts of a natural body. Political wisdom cannot always change nature, she must make use of the material in the form left by her [nature]. . . . Diversity is founded on the natural inclinations of the people, most varied in the state of France where . . . a vast expanse composed of quantities of provinces which, having been under other domination, have retained their laws and customs . . . confirmed for the most part by stipulation. . . . To want to bring total conformity in all this would be to violate their natural inclinations . . . the peoples would imagine their liberties and privileges threatened. An advantage would be gained at the expense of directing their love toward neighboring rulers and thus, by similarities in mores and customs, opening the door to conquest.[58]

Lartigue distinguished between natural and artificial factors separating subjects. Local ways and traditions, being natural, he contended, were stabilizing forces; to attack them would invite rebellion and disaster. In contrast, luxury, "not an effect of nature but of vice," divided and distracted "the people, preventing them from thinking of things important for the glory of the state."[59] Another divisive force was the "tolls and tributes in too great number on rivers and at the gates of towns. . . . They cause great and deplorable damage to the sovereign, cutting and dividing his state . . . making people different and creating

[58] *Seconde partie,* ff. 35-36. [59] *Loc.cit.*

opposition among them, . . . severing in this way the
union and conformity which renders subjects prompt
for external enterprises." And most important was the
fiscal question. Condemning what he called "modern"
political theory which ignored the "happiness" of the
mass of people, Lartigue insisted that foreign conquest and the ultimate establishment of a Universal
Monarchy depended upon equitable and humane
tax policies:

> Excessive impositions are opposed . . . to the
> goodness of government. I know very well there
> is a modern political doctrine contemptuous of
> the desires and affection of the people, believing
> it necessary to be sure only of the [loyalty of] the
> most important subjects by [giving them] offices,
> favors and hope, and, having citadels and other
> keys and nerves of the state in hand, there is
> nothing to fear from the multitude no matter
> how they cry or threaten.

Such thinking was absurd. "What kings can get along
without the affection and the force of their subjects?
. . . Princes rule imperfectly . . . when they do not
have the hearts [of their people]." It could be held as
indubitable . . . that "nothing is so contrary to him
who would extend his domination as to have it weigh
heavy on his own subjects." Furthermore, this "maxim" must be extended to newly conquered peoples
so that they also could *"jouir . . . des douceurs de
la vie."* The "true Conqueror" must aspire to be a
source "of happiness and of felicity among men and
not [one] of sadness, affliction and misery." It could
be taken as a general principle that "civil society is a
society of free men which common utility has assembled and reduced into a body not only to live, but to

live content and happy."[60] And if the conqueror would establish happiness throughout the earth, he must begin in his own country in such a way as "to attract the love and the hope of foreign peoples."[61]

Lartigue goes on to list other reforms necessary to prepare France for the glorious mission of sending armies over the face of the earth to spread happiness and virtue to all human kind: abolition of venality, repurchase of alienated royal domains, payment of the crown's debts, and several measures calculated to increase the effectiveness of the army and navy.[62] Beyond these policies, however, conquest of the world required also "a particular effect of Providence, which . . . has reserved this high destiny for France and for her kings." Previous attempts by other countries to establish permanent world dominion failed because nature reserved this great task for France. Geographically, she stood toward the world as Corinth stood to Greece: just as the city "dominated the two seas enclosing the entire archipelago," France controlled the two bodies of water surrounding Europe, "the Mediterranean and the ocean," and was destined to "rule the earth" in the same manner that Corinth extended "her empire over Greece."[63] Spain, it could

---

[60] *Seconde partie*, p. 25. His opinion was shared on this point by an early reforming aristocrat, Paul Hay du Chastelet, whose book, *Traité de la politique de la France*, Paris, 1669, incurred Louis XIV's displeasure and brought exile to the author. See J. B. Maurice Vignes, *Histoire des doctrines sur l'impôt en France: les origines et les destinées de la Dixme Royale de Vauban*, Paris, 1909, p. 42. Chastelet writes, for example, "l'intention de la politique est de faire en sorte que les hommes vivent heureusement, comme je l'ay remarqué dans le précédent chapitre. Il est donc certain qu'elle veut qu'ils soient actuellement vertueux" (p. 22, edn. 1677). The chapters containing general thoughts such as these are not in the edition of 1669; they may be found, however, in a manuscript copy of this work, dated 1667, Archives Aff. Et. mém. et doc., MS 93.

[61] *Ibid.*, ff. 37-39.

[62] *Ibid.*, ff. 39-60, for the navy see ff. 29-34.

[63] *Ibid.*, ff. 165-170.

be argued, was in a similar position, located at "the head of Europe"; but France occupied the "middle region." And Lartigue, like Bodin, made much of this location. Characteristics like heat, cold, dryness, and humidity, called "elemental qualities," were dispersed to the extremities of the planet where they resided in such quantity as to be unfavorable to vegetable, animal, and human fecundity. A central position accounted for France's "fertility in wheat, wine and other things necessary for nourishment," making it possible for a "multitude of men" to live on her soil. And for this reason she had become "an inexhaustible source of warriors whose arms are sufficiently numerous to inundate the most distant parts of the earth."

The disposition of elemental qualities explained more than mere numbers. Climate also determined the natural character of men and France's happy middle situation rendered her peoples particularly disposed for large-scale military operations. Such activities required organization and discipline, and in the middle regions elemental qualities were "so balanced in men" as to leave them "indifferent" and ready "to receive any impression given to them from outside." Without firm discipline such people were subject to influence by even the most fleeting stimuli. Indeed, this was the origin of their reputation for frivolity and inconstancy. Yet, having no natural predispositions, they were admirably suited for foreign conquest: "France has been more advantageously endowed by heaven than other regions where men are inclined, limited, and determined for certain functions, for certain vices and for certain virtues and qualities." French impressionableness made it easy for her occupying armies "to receive the manners, customs and ways of life of neighboring peoples," a quality rendering Frenchmen "more welcome . . . to foreign nations" which would readily "accept domination" . . . and would not "combat those who adopt their ways of life."[64]

Receptivity to discipline not only made Frenchmen particularly apt for foreign conquest, it also permitted the crown to impose a perfectly virtuous life on all subjects. Indeed, the good or evil character of every Frenchman was determined by the quality of government:

> Those advantages France has received from Nature with respect to Conquests are thus to be numerous, populous, fertile in men, . . . capable and disposed to receive all movements and the most beautiful impressions of generosity and glory and any others which we would wish to light in their hearts. And it is no doubt a great satisfaction for a Prince to find himself at the head of a nation gifted with so many natural advantages for conquest. But with respect to that disquieting changeable and frivolous humour about which we have spoken, coming from the same principles, the Prince must realize that they [Frenchmen] have . . . as much facility to receive these as well as opposite virtues and qualities. *Thus all depends on the will and on the conduct of the sovereign: it will be his glory or his fault, because his peoples receive [their character] according to the occupations to which we wish to accustom them.*[65]

Force in the form of political authority based on natural law had been, since the Fall, the mother of

64 *Loc.cit.*

65 *Loc.cit.* In a fascinating study, for which he employed only literary sources, Paul Bénichou, *Les morales du grand siècle*, Paris, 1948 (see especially pages 1-87), explains the strong aristocratic roots of seventeenth century French theological and religious optimism.

virtue; a wise government in France, the most populous and powerful state on earth, would bring her peoples to the summit of moral perfection, preparing them for their predetermined mission of uniting mankind under one supremely beneficent rule, and delivering humanity from discord, evil, and misery.

Lartigue devoted at least half the manuscript section of his treatise to detailed considerations about the interests, forces, resources, character, and disposition of all European states with a view to guiding France toward leadership of a European alliance against the Turk,[66] a policy he thought necessary for establishing a Universal Monarchy under the French crown. This curious vestige of the crusading spirit helps to tie the author more firmly to the tradition which sought to unite peoples everywhere into an expanded Christianity. But most unusual is Lartigue's view of nature. His emphasis on subordination, dependence, affection, love, and virtue seems clearly directed against the social and mercantilist implications of a lifeless cosmic system made up of atoms and mechanical forces devoid of personality. The issue was fundamental. Postel, Campanella, Bodin, Montchrétien, even Richelieu, thought justice concerned the elements as much as it did man. These men lived in an animistic universe and were still imbued with some form of the Augustinian idea of an all-inclusive cosmic order where everything and everybody obeyed or was supposed to obey God's will. Perfect order was synonymous with perfect justice. During the mid-seventeenth century the universe lost its animistic character, but men could not rid themselves of the deeply rooted conviction that the laws of nature were part of a sys-

[66] Indeed, Lartigue wrote a substantial memoire entitled "Conduite politique pour les Chrétiens contre le Turc," B.N. Mélanges Colbert, MS 64.

tem of perfect justice. The heirs of Postel and Campanella, people like Lartigue, no longer able to place
man in the center of an animistic universe stretching
up to the Godhead, now insisted that the pattern of
divine justice is revealed by the way lifeless elements
shape the moral character of human beings. Lartigue
could not be more clear: "Remember . . . virtues and
vices come from ways of life. . . , ways of life from
temperament, temperament from Climate and elemental qualities, and all is reduced to heaven or more
precisely to Nature, where one must search as if in
the source, the origin of all our movements and our
. . . knowledge as well as our good and bad qualities."[67]

The heirs of Bodin, Montchrétien, and Richelieu—
people like Colbert and his disciple Pottier de la
Hestroye—also thought society part of nature, but
their view of nature, and therefore of society, was
that of the Cartesian world machine. Vast quantities
of foreign treasure would permit the mercantilist
state to sweep away local government, traditional
social structures, established moral precepts, and all
obstructions to political centralization. Society, they
thought, should be transformed into a clockwork
mechanism lubricated by streams of foreign treasure.
Moreover, people holding these views were encouraged by the widely accepted idea that divine law concerned man's soul, not his behavior, which, coming
under the jurisdiction of fallible human justice, was
governed according to principles of order and utility.

To govern society as if it were a machine made up
of purely functional, undifferentiated atoms was a
point of view admirably suited to administrators like
Pottier and Colbert. But such a position was understandably resisted by aristocrats of ancient lineage
like Lartigue, who refused to associate public utility

[67] *Seconde partie*, f. 171. The parallel with Montesquieu is striking.

with political centralization. Lartigue thought public utility inseparable from what he called virtue,
justice, and happiness; in this context public utility
was "the unique purpose of a legitimate sovereign."
And, most important, he joined these concepts
to a peculiar kind of nationalism which was also dissociated from the general context of centralization.
Believing in the predestined superiority of Frenchmen, Lartigue called upon the crown to carry out
those reforms necessary to raise the people to that
level of happiness and virtue which would permit
French warriors to communicate the good life to all
humanity.[67a] Virtue, to him, was a product of environmental factors and of proper government. However
unwittingly, Lartigue is very close to defining good
and evil as purely social phenomena. He exhibits the
first signs of a movement to which aristocrats became
receptive during the second half of Louis XIV's reign:
the merger of an optimistic ultilitarianism with a
messianic political spirit which, while opposing centralization of government, nevertheless identifies
national expansion with the spread of truth, justice,
and virtue.

[67a] In 1553 an anonymous author wrote:
"Entre toutes les créatures de Dieu, la plus noble est l'homme,
entre tous les hommes le Chrestien, entre tous les Chrestiens le
François. Ce n'est point une flaterie générale indulgente à la
nation: c'est une vérité notoire, par évidence de faicts permanens.
. . . En somme le pays de France se peult glorifier qu'il n'y a . . .
de pays sur la face de la terre qui en l'enclave de circonférence et
diametre égal, ait produict plus de vertu, plus de justice, plus de
Noblesse, plus de Saincteté, plus de louange et gloire à Dieu" (*De
la vertu de Noblesse*, an essay contained in a volume without a
title page. Its call number at the Bibliothèque Nationale is: Inv.
G 18022).

CHAPTER III

ADMINISTRATIVE GROWTH AND
RURAL GOVERNMENT:
FISCAL REFORM 1648-1684*

IN THE generation extending from the *Fronde* to Colbert's death far-reaching political centralization, coinciding with widespread economic depression, caused government expenses to multiply at a time when money grew increasingly scarce. The resultant strain upon royal finances gave a new urgency to fiscal problems. No issue aroused more hostility: persistent and bitter concern about taxes worsened the monarchy's relations with the nobility who, contrary to established opinion, did by 1683 generally recognize the need for some form of universal imposition. Many aristocrats, however, believed fiscal exemptions were a bulwark against arbitrary rule. The nobility, unwilling to surrender these privileges without receiving something in exchange, demanded protection of their social position *and* a role in government.[1] These

---

* Conclusions drawn from the material presented in the following pages alter considerably the viewpoint expressed by my article, "Critiques de la politique commerciale et projets de réforme de la fiscalité au temps de Colbert," *Revue d'histoire moderne et contemporaine*, VIII (April-June 1961), 83-102, which deals largely with the subject discussed in this chapter.

[1] The nobility addressed the following lines to the government in 1617, at the Assembly of Notables in Rouen:

"Il y a au maniement de l'état des affaires secrètes, et qui ne

revindications, which later inspired the most radical political programs, were not elaborated, however, until after 1683 when projects for fiscal reform became part of the more general categories of resistance and opposition described earlier. This chapter, dealing with the period prior to Colbert's death, seeks to describe only a stage preparatory to the evolution of radical thought within the aristocracy.

The following pages explain how in the course of a single generation many among the nobility came to accept the principle of paying some kind of direct tax. Indeed, thinking the imposition inevitable, it was aristocrats who proposed the most efficient legislation in this regard. Their attitude was in part the result of a process of education, the consequence of an increased knowledge about the resources and population of France. This information, providing the nobility with greater insight into the general problem of government finance, was acquired largely after 1660 in a manner best revealed through study of aristocratic plans to reform the fiscal structure. These writings were, in Mazarin's day, naive and unrealistic to an extreme; by Colbert's death, however, such projects were drafted with considerably greater sophistication. Moreover, the documents of the two periods explain something beyond mere im-

---

peuvent être divulgées, qu'au grand préjudice d'icelui.

"Bien que le roi en sa majorité, peut, comme ses prédécesseurs, en commettre le maniement à qui bon lui semble, toutefois son désir a été d'y donner le plus de part qu'il sera possible aux princes et grands de son royaume" (Charles J. Mayer, *Des Etats Généraux*, XVIII, pp. 54-55).

These lines were by no means idle rhetoric: Roland Mousnier, "Sully et le conseil d'état et des finances: la lutte entre Bellièvre et Sully," *Revue historique*, 1941, CXCII, 68-86, demonstrates that the role of the nobility in government was a burning issue at the turn of the century, profoundly dividing men in the highest councils of state.

proved technical proficiency: the history of projects for fiscal reform shows that after 1660, the crown's efforts to inventory national wealth, its repeated use of large-scale public inquiries, educated men to believe it was possible to assemble and organize the vast amount of data necessary to execute efficiently a graduated universal direct tax. Once convinced of the program's feasibility, many aristocrats were also persuaded that depressed economic conditions and mounting charges of state would sooner or later compel government to levy a charge on all Frenchmen without distinction. It was this prospect, posing an urgent threat to their traditional position in society, which prepared the aristocracy for the radical role they subsequently assumed during the second part of the Sun King's reign.

i. THE PROBLEM OF FISCAL REFORM

Alexis de Tocqueville, discussing the Great Revolution, declared that when Charles VII imposed a tax in the fifteenth century without the consent of the estates, "the seeds were sown of almost all the vices and abuses which led to the violent downfall of the old regime."[2] Although the statement requires considerable qualification, there is clearly a direct relation between fiscal policy and the increasingly deplorable state of royal finances on one hand and the decline of the monarchy on the other. The aristocracy and numerous groups, professions, towns, and communities enjoying fiscal privileges resisted the crown's efforts to infringe on their "liberties" without prior consultation. But by Richelieu's time, more than economic interest was at issue: in the absence of an Estates General after 1614, defense of

[2] *The Old Regime and the French Revolution*, trans. Stuart Gilbert, Anchor Book edn., New York, 1955, p. 99.

local or particular privileges provided the only protection against the incursions of an increasingly powerful central government. As the century advanced, fiscal exemptions appeared, especially to the nobility, as one of the few remaining defenses against despotism. Time and again the aristocracy insisted that the King had no right to raise "extraordinary" levies without the consent of the Estates.[3]

On the other hand the crown, intensely insecure, could not view the prospect of an Estates General with equanimity. Louis XIV, for example, was certain that such an event would be "the worst possible calamity."[4] Refusal to consult with the privileged classes, however, obliged the King's ministers to impose the growing burden of government almost entirely on the mass of the rural population. The increasing exactions of royal tax officials drove many country folk to seek the protection of their *seigneur* who, during the seventeenth century, was frequently seen at the head of a local uprising or revolt.[5] Thus

[3] See for example Fénelon's "Plans de gouvernement concertés avec le duc de Chevreuse pour être proposés au duc de Bourgogne," *Ecrits et lettres politiques de Fénelon*, published by Charles Urbain, Paris, 1920; these "Tables de Chaulnes" (the title given to the project by Fénelon) also represented the views of aristocrats as different as the duke of Beauvillier and the duke of Saint-Simon. Most striking, however, is an exclamation made by an insubordinate noble, La Tréaumont, "Quand la noblesse sera à cheval il faudra venir faire révolter Paris et demander les Etats généraux" (quoted from the judicial records by Pierre Clément, *La police sous Louis XIV*, Paris, 1866, p. 161).

[4] Quoted from Louis XIV's memoirs by M. Marion, *Dictionnaire des Institutions de la France*, Paris, 1923, p. 217. J. R. Major, *Representative Institutions in Renaissance France 1421-1559*, Madison, 1960, shows that royal distrust of the Estates General did not exist prior to the Wars of Religion.

[5] Professor Roland Mousnier has written a brief note on precisely this point: "Monarchie contre Aristocratie dans la France du XVIIᵉ siècle," *Le XVIIᵉ siècle*, no. 31 (April 1956), pp. 377-381; and at greater length in "Recherches sur les soulèvements populaires

from an early date it was easy to confuse purely selfish defense of private interest with the nobler desire to stand firm against the intrusions of a despotic power.

Political considerations, however, did not obscure the fact that the peasantry was economically incapable of assuming a larger burden of public charges. Even as early as the late sixteenth century Jean Bodin, for example, had warned that an outrageously unjust fiscal policy could lead only "to seditions and changes in Republics." He regarded fiscal reform as an essential part of a wider program to establish strong government and to dispel permanently all fear of civil war. Bodin, it is worth repeating, thought that every citizen in a "well-ordered state," including the wealthy and the privileged, should be taxed in proportion to his personal resources. "On this matter the Romans showed themselves more just: only the rich, noble or *Roturier*, were subjected to the *tailles*, the poor were exempt." In France the roles were reversed: "The poor pay and the rich are exempt." The consequences of so absurd a policy was rural misery: "Since rich towns, nobles and the ecclesiastical estate have discharged their load onto the poor," the latter had become like Aesop's donkey or like "the horse which would not carry anything." The most

---

en France avant la Fronde," *Revue d'histoire moderne et contemporaine*, V (1958), 81-113.

It should be remembered, however, that aristocratic-peasant relations varied widely, and facts in particular cases lend themselves to different interpretations. Indeed, Mousnier's articles are directed expressly against the views of Boris Porchnev, *Les soulèvements populaires en France 1623 à 1648*, Paris, 1963. This book is a French translation appearing fifteen years after the original version in Russian and nine years after the German translation: *Die Volkaufstände in Frankreich, 1623-1648*, Berlin, 1954.

indigent members of society could not possibly contribute the greatest portion of royal revenue.[6]

The author of the *Republic* proposed several remedies. First, direct taxes should "be real rather than personal, as is practiced in Languedoc and . . . in Provence . . . so that rich and poor, noble and *roturier*, priest and *laboureur* pay imposts on land subject to the *taille*. The law exempts neither pontiff nor noble . . . and should extraordinary levies be required each will bear his share as is the case with duties on salt, wine and other similar products."[7] Concerning indirect taxes, Bodin suggested that, to avoid the exactions of *Gabelleurs* and other rapacious fiscal agents, some duties, especially those falling most heavily on the poor, ought to be abolished and the others converted into fixed annual payments. In this regard, however, the author observed that "the honor of God and the profit of the Republic" would be

[6] *Les six livres de la république*, Paris, 1608, Bk. VI, chap. II, pp. 885-886.

[7] *Ibid.*, pp. 887-888. It might be observed that if the *taille réelle* were universalized, as Bodin suggests, the aristocracy would nevertheless have continued to enjoy fiscal exemption: the *taille réelle* affected non-noble lands even if the owner was a member of the privileged classes, but noble lands remained totally exempt from this imposition. Here, however, Bodin's reference to the fact that indirect duties fell on all Frenchmen without distinction is most significant. Reformers throughout the seventeenth century urged that the nobility would benefit from a universal direct tax which would replace the multitude of indirect duties so burdensome to the privileged and the unprivileged alike. Du Noyer de Saint-Martin (1639) suggested that tax-farming be replaced by a "production" duty levied on goods "at their source"; in this, Du Noyer sought no doubt to combine the advantages of indirect duties, which raised no difficult political issues, with the efficiency of a universalized and simplified schedule of impositions. L. A. Boiteux, "Un économiste méconnu: Du Noyer de Saint-Martin 1608-1639," *Revue d'histoire des colonies*, XLIV (1957), 5-68, has called attention to this interesting figure.

equally served if luxury items alone were taxed; heavy duties on these products would not diminish consumption because the wealthy could afford the added charges.[8]

Another aspect of Bodin's fiscal reforms concerned the methods of acquiring sufficient information so that "we know the tax which every person ought to bear." In some areas, where relevant data were inadequate, "each subject must declare his possessions and his income"; elsewhere, in provinces which conducted periodic land surveys, records should be brought up to date with information furnished by large-scale royal inquiries. In this way, the "extreme poverty of some and the excessive riches of others" would be discovered. "When the wealth of each person is known . . . seditions common to all Republics because of the inequality of charges will cease." No one would be exempt from the "distribution of true justice"; and the people would once again prosper in the quiet repose of peace.[9]

Bodin said little about consent of the Estates, and it is principally in this regard that his views clearly foreshadow the modern principle of a regular public contribution, permitting the proper and continuous function of state services. In comparison, Jehan Combes, a more traditional thinker, published his unexceptional *Traicté des tailles et aultres charges . . .* in 1576, the same year that Bodin's *Republic* appeared. Like Bodin, Combes thought "all persons of whatever quality and without regard to privilege must aid their sovereign in times of necessity," but he further insisted that no ruler could "raise ex-

8 *République*, Bk. VI, chap. II, pp. 884-888. On this point see also Erasmus, *The Education of a Christian Prince*, trans. L. K. Born, New York, 1936, pp. 217-218.

9 *Ibid.*, pp. 841-842.

traordinary levies without consent of the Estates."[10] Although even Bodin appears to have restricted his discussion to purely provisional subsidies required in periods of special need, he nevertheless gave government the sole right to decide the time, duration, and manner in which these exceptional duties would be imposed. And elsewhere, expressly rejecting the argument that the King should normally "live on his own" and, except when revenue needs were urgent, should "abolish all taxes, aides and imposts," Bodin declared that permanent revenues provided "the very foundations of the state."[11] In sum, the *Republic* clearly envisaged a society where privilege could offer no protection against demands made by government in the name of the general interest.

Those who feared the extension of royal authority, however, were keenly aware of the desperate cir-

[10] *Traicté des tailles et aultres charges et subsides tant ordinaires qu'extraordinaires*, Paris, 1576, f. 6, cited by J. B. Maurice Vignes, *Histoire des Doctrines sur l'impôt en France: les origines et les destinées de la Dixme Royale de Vauban*, Paris, 1909, pp. 227-228.

[11] *République*, Bk. VI, chap. II, pp. 881-885. Bodin here seems somewhat ill at ease. He begins by citing Philippe de Commines who said "qu'il n'y avoit Prince qui eust puissance de lever d'impost sur les subjects, n'y prescrire ce droit sinon de leur consentement" (p. 880). He goes on to say, however, that the King can no longer "live on his own" because the larger part of his domain has been alienated and, even more important, "l'argent est venu en si grande abondance des terres neuves . . . que toutes choses sont enchéries dix fois plus qu'elles n'estoyent, comme j'ay montré contre le paradox du seigneur de Malestroit" (p. 882). In these circumstances, to wish "d'abolir tous les imposts, aides et tailles comme plusieurs se sont efforcés de faire. . . , c'est oster les fondements principaux sur lesquels elle [the *Republic*] est appuyée" (p. 882). By saying that, however regrettable, the clock cannot be turned back, Bodin goes on to talk of extraordinary revenues as if they were regular taxes. Moreover, he also continues to outline his projects for fiscal reform without another word about the consent of the Estates. In this case, as in many others, Bodin places necessity before principle; indeed, the one maxim to which he held steadfast is the "nothing is more just than that which is necessary" (p. 878).

cumstances of growing numbers of unprivileged. Indeed, when conditions were particularly bad the landlord was obliged to pay the *taille* for his share-croppers and advance them seed and livestock in order to continue the exploitation of his estates.[12] And fiscal charges of course weighed even more heavily on rural populations, both privileged and unprivileged, in times of depressed cereal prices.[13] The situation became next to intolerable during the first half of Louis XIV's reign, not only because this was largely a period

[12] "Aujourd'hui il n'y a plus que de pauvres métayers qui n'ont rien, il faut que les maitres leur fournissent les bestiaux, qu'ils leur avancent de quoi se nourrir, qu'ils payent leurs tailles, et qu'ils prennent en paiement toute leur portion de la récolte, laquelle même, quelque fois ne suffit pas" (from a report submitted by Henri d'Aguesseau and Antoine-François de Paule Le Fèvre d'Ormesson in 1687 concerning conditions in the generalities of Orléans and Maine, published by A. de Boislisle, "Mémoire de l'intendant de Paris," *Mémoire de la généralité de Paris*. Paris, 1881, pp. 781-786). See also B. Porchnev, *Les Soulèvements*, pp. 78-79.

The fact that unjust fiscal charges on the peasantry often proved financially onerous to a landlord, who was not always an aristocrat, may also explain why the crown on several occasions held the *parlements* responsible for uprisings in their jurisdiction. See Jean Meuvret, "Comment les Français voyaient l'impôt au XVIIe siècle?" *Le XVIIe siècle*, nos. 25-26 (1955), p. 77.

Another aspect to this problem is that in the seventeenth century aristocratic exemptions from the *taille* did not extend to people exploiting lands where the noble was not residing. Thus in 1638 an anonymous author of a project for fiscal reform wrote: "Cette suppression et abolition desdictes tailles et imposts . . . ne délivrera pas seulement les pauvres et les chétives de misère et d'oppression, mais aussi soulagera grandement les Ecclésiastiques, les nobles, et les principaux du tiers Estat . . . des tailles, taillons, aydes, péages et autres imposts qu'ils payent eux mesmes és noms et personnes de leurs fermiers et rentiers, qui font nécessairement de la terre le fossé, . . ." (B.N., Fds. fr., MS 17461, ff. 295-296).

[13] "Enfin on voit dans tous les ordres et dans tous les états une diminution sensible et une chute presque universelle qui a besoin d'un prompt remède, . . . il est fort à craindre que, même sans aucune nouvelle surcharge, les choses ne tombent dans un point d'où il sera très difficile de les relever," *loc.cit.*

of abundant harvests and low cereal prices,[14] but also because rapid administrative growth and large-scale military expansion caused government to make unprecedented fiscal demands at a time when money was most scarce. This situation caused Colbert particular concern, and his correspondence reveals that he did his utmost to reduce "all the expenses and vexations which are imposed on the people."[15] Under his direction, improved accounting procedures and more severe methods of inspection and verification did in fact increase fiscal administrative efficiency; but while the royal treasury benefited from these measures, the effect on the population was to increase the burden of taxation. Prior to improvement of the fiscal machine, for example, it was comparatively easy to purchase relief from the *taille* in the form of deferments from the receiver. This official, using government funds, often assumed the role of a local banker and extended credit throughout the region. When conditions were poor, it was to his interest to protect his jurisdiction from ruinous taxation. Such practices were less feasible under Colbert, however, whose success in substantially reducing the amount of the *taille* was more than offset by the efficiency which he introduced into its collection and imposition.[16]

[14] J. Meuvret, "Les mouvements des prix de 1661 à 1715 et leurs répercussions," *Journal de la Société de Statistique de Paris* (May 1944).

[15] Letter of Colbert to Le Blanc, intendant in Normandy, 19 September 1679, pub. by Pierre Clément, *Lettres, instructions et mémoires de Colbert*, 7 vols., Paris, 1861-1882, II, 116. See Edmond Esmonin, *La taille en Normandie au temps de Colbert 1661-1683*, Paris, 1913, *passim*. Richelieu had similar preoccupations. See Orest Ranum, *Richelieu and the Councillors of Louis XIII*, Oxford, 1963, pp. 145-147.

[16] "Le retranchement des remises et des non-valeurs [those too poor to pay anything at all], et la sévérité avec laquelle on obligea

But the *taille* was by no means the exclusive object of attention. Seventeenth century France was entangled in a confused maze of indirect taxes which varied widely from region to region. They had long been the chief source of local uprisings and rebellions.[17] After 1660, however, these imposts became even more oppressive. Duties on beverages, for example, rose from 5 million livres in 1661 to 22 million livres in 1682.[18] During the same period new

---

les Partisans de payer ponctuellement les deniers de leurs réceptes, leur ayant osté le crédit, les a mis aussi dans la nécessité de presser les peuples de la campagne sans leur donner aucun quartier, de sorte qu'on leur a fait payer jusques au dernier sol, non seulement du courant des impositions, mais aussi tout ce qu'ils devoient du reste des années précédentes. Adjoutez à cela qu'une rigueur si extraordinaire commance de se pratiquer dans le tems d'une extrême disette, ce qui fut un surcroit de malheur pour les pauvres Peuples, qui avoient à souffrir par ce moyen plusieurs sortes de maux" (*Mémoires pour servir à l'histoire de D.M.R. avec quelques réflexions politiques sur les mémoires*, n.p., 1668, pp. 230-231; hereafter cited as *D.M.R.*). Esmonin discusses the adverse effects of increased efficiency in fiscal administration in *La taille en Normandie*, pp. 529-531.

[17] See for example, J. H. Mariéjol, "Henri IV et Louis XIII," *Histoire de France. . .*, VI, Part II, pp. 431-434. For the Colbertian period see VII, Part I, pp. 345-358, written by E. Lavisse. Numerous sources and works concerning this point are cited, in addition, by E. Bourgeois and L. André, *Les sources de l'histoire de France au XVIIe siècle 1610-1715*, 8 vols., Paris, 1913-1935, VII, 420-449.

[18] Charles Woolsey Cole, *Colbert and a Century of French Mercantilism*, 2 vols., New York, 1939, I, 305. It might also be observed that the tendency to resort to indirect taxation for additional revenue appears to have been reinforced by the traditional idea that products circulating in domestic or foreign trade were the surplus remaining after people had consumed the fruits of their own labor. Duties on such merchandise were considered the most equitable form of taxation because only the wealthier members of the community could afford to engage in the purchase and sale of surplus products. Lazare du Crot, *Le nouveau traité des aides, tailles et gabelles*, Paris, 1636, f. 2 *et seq.*, wrote: "C'est que le roi Louis XII disoit que l'ayde ne se paye que par les plus riches et aysez de ses sujets, qui ont toujours de l'argent à la main, en vendant ou achetant; et que les tailles se payent au contraire par les plus

charges were imposed on paper, tinware, and tobacco; and the salt tax, the *gabelle*, proved more onerous as traditional imposts were increased and new ones established on other items. The collection of all these duties was farmed out to private contractors whose agents swarmed over the countryside. And the violent, often passionate, protests about fiscal abuses were directed above all against this system of indirect taxation.

The landed aristocracy, having a direct interest in reducing taxes, was most active in proposing measures for fiscal reform. Some of their early projects were concerned only with cutting the expense of tax administration by replacing the multitude of imposts with a single graduated tax on the non-privileged members of society.[18a] Others, suggesting reforms

---

pauvres qui n'ont et ne manient argent que celuy qui procède de leur labour en grattant la terre. Et de faict, nous voyons que la moitié ou environ de ceux qui sont mis à la taille la payent de leur labeur, sans avoir un poulce d'héritage et nul ne paye l'ayde en France que comme une demie dixme de l'argent qu'il reçoit en vendant, trafiquant ou acheptant." Twenty years later François des Maisons, *Traité des aydes, tailles et gabelles*, Paris, 1666, p. 434, suggested that in order to relieve the poor one ought to establish the *taille* "sur les marchandises." See also the treatise of Jesuit Father Le Moyne, *L'Art de Régner*, Paris, 1665, p. 615.

[18a] A precedent for these projects may be suggested by merchant proposals to consolidate indirected taxes. Merchants at the Assembly of St. Germain, Nov. 1583, for example, explained: "Et d'autant que l'on fait plusieurs plaintes de l'incommodité que reçoivent les marchands trafiquans, au payement des droits que sa Majesté fait lever sur les denrées et marchandises, au moyen de la diversité des fermes ci-dessus, et des bureaux qui sont pour ce establis en divers lieux. Et ayant lesdits sieurs considéré la proposition qui a esté faite, de joindre et incorporer ensemble tous et chacuns les droits qui se prennent ainsi diversement sur chacune sorte de marchandise en un seul, comme l'on dit qu'il se peut faire sans aucune diminution pour sa Majesté, et iceux faire recevoir par un seul receveur ou baillé à un seul fermier en chacune province; sont d'avis que sa Majesté se doive . . . commettre quelques personnages de qualité et d'intelligence en telles affaires pour le pénétrer davantage. . . .

in the administration of the *taille* also demanded that the *gabelle* be transformed into a direct graduated tax on all Frenchmen without regard to class or privilege. The proposal was somewhat less radical than might appear at first sight. In principle no one in the old regime was exempt from the *gabelle*;[19] its transformation into a universal graduated income tax could be made to look like a purely technical reform, creating no dangerous precedent with respect to class privileges. Therefore, all projects to transform the *gabelle* into a graduated universal direct tax also demanded that the *taille*, however reduced, be retained in order "to distinguish the nobility from the populace."

In fact, however, it proved difficult to recommend universal taxation without at the same time undermining the case for fiscal exemption. In a later chapter, we shall see that toward the last decade of the century, when it became clear that further increases in state revenues might very well have to come from hitherto privileged areas of society, the aristocracy did not question the principle of universal taxation; instead, it tried to obtain protection against a hostile

---

Pour réduire toutes les susdites impositions soubs une seule loi, s'il est possible, dont lesdits marchands recevront une extreme commodité, et y a apparence qu'elle ne seroit pas moindre pour sadite Majesté" (C. J. Mayer, *Les Etats Généraux*, XIV, 217-218).

19 At the Estates General in 1614, "la Noblesse se plaint amèrement des officiers de gabelle que l'on voit effrontément entrer dans les maisons avec armes, voir jusques aux lieux les plus secrets, sans considération ni respect de la qualité" (Pierre Blet, *Le clergé de France et la monarchie*, 2 vols., Rome, 1959, I, 28). E. Coornaert, in the introduction to his edition of Vauban's *Dixme Royale*, Paris, 1933, p. xxxi, observed: "Vauban la conserve [the gabelle] parce que tout le monde y est soumis." George T. Matthews, *The Royal General Farms in Eighteenth Century France*, New York, 1958, pp. 88-117, gives a good general description of the administration of the *gabelle*.

administration by insisting that fiscal changes be made part of a wider program of reform. The nobility was willing on the whole to pay some form of imposition if, in return, it could obtain an important role in government and be sure that abolition of its fiscal privileges would not undermine its already threatened social position. This was precisely the reason why the Duke of Saint-Simon, for example, had nothing but praise for Vauban's *Dixme Royale* and contempt for the *Capitation*: the latter was "arbitrary" and could be used by the crown as a weapon against his class. Faced with progressive weakening of the principle of tax privilege on one hand, and with impending fiscal charges on the other, the nobility felt intensely threatened. Aristocrats became the most radical group among all those who clamored for change during the second part of the reign.

ii. PROJECTS FOR FISCAL REFORM 1648-1684

Many contemporaries, seeing that administrative growth was accompanied by economic stagnation, thought the first was the cause of the second. In their eyes both crown and people were left without adequate resources because hordes of pestilential officials consumed the tribute which they exacted from the countryside. Since the officers in question were part of the tax-farming administration, concerned only with indirect taxes, some reformers declared that all Frenchmen from Prince to beggar would benefit if these innumerable duties were replaced by a single direct tax levied on the wealthier unprivileged members of society. Such was the argument in a tract appearing during the disorders of the *Fronde*. Written by Isaac Loppin 1648, it went through at least four editions[20] and directly influenced later reformers. Speaking of the anarchy of impositions, Loppin explained how all members of society, privileged and unprivileged, suffered from the exactions of armies of fiscal officials:

[20] See J. B. Maurice Vignes, *Histoire des doctrines*, p. 128, n.1. The author apparently first published the text in 1638 under the title *Les mines gallicanes ou le trésor du royaume de France* according to Bourgeois and André, *Les sources*, VII, 304. At that time the work was dedicated to Richelieu. When it later appeared as a pamphlet during the *Fronde*, it was entitled *Advis tres juste et légitime au Roy tres Chrestien pour le repos et soulagement des trois ordres de son estat et le moyen de dresser une milice de cinquante mil hommes . . . pour la descharge de toutes Tailles, Taillons, Aydes, Gabelles, et générallement tous subsides et impots tant Anciens que Nouveaux.*

I have come upon an interesting manuscript version of this text (B.N., Fds. fr., MS 17461, ff. 277-309), unfortunately too late to permit extended discussion in these pages. In general, however, the manuscript reveals that the project was directed above all against venality. Moreover, it formed part of the *dévot* resistance to Richelieu. An immense number of venal office-holders were little people who sought to rise socially through purchase of minor posts in the fiscal administration. Thus, for example, Georges Pagès, "La Vénalité des offices dans l'ancienne France," *Revue historique*, 1932, CLXIX, 492, explained that one should not think of venality only in terms of rich offices in the judiciary, "mais il faut penser aussi à tous les menus offices de finances, qui sont à tout moment jetés sur le marché et dont le prix modique est à la portée des petites bourses. . . . Des qu'ils s'y sont un peu mieux garnis les mains, ils les revendent, pour en acheter d'autres, qui pourront leur procurer de plus gros profits." (See also Roland Mousnier, *La Vénalité des offices sous Henri IV et Louis XIII*, Rouen, 1949, pp. 58-62.) It was against the *roturier* invasion of aristocratic ranks via the purchase of offices in *les finances* that the aristocratic *dévots* were drafting projects for fiscal reform. They were also outraged by the fact that someone with even the most modest savings would avoid taxation through purchase of an office, thereby throwing the fiscal burden first on the poor and ultimately on the landlord. In fact, the manuscript reveals that the *dévots*, associating venality with simony, did not distinguish between purification of the church and reform of the state. This was probably the issue which separated Richelieu from Marillac in the early part of the century. Later, during Louis XIV's reign, Bossuet and Fénelon would wage a similar struggle.

By the usage of the *tailles* and the diversity and multiplicity of subsidies and imposts on all sorts of merchandise and entries, and by the pernicious custom of contracting their collection out to an unbridled number of partisans, farmers, sub-farmers, exacters, who have no other goal but their avarice and private profit, not only are the *roturiers* and *taillables* subjected to these subsidies and imposts, but also . . . so are the King, the Queen, the Regent, all the Royal Household, the Princes, Prelates, Gentlemen, Ecclesiastics, Officers of the Sovereign Courts . . . and generally all His Majesty's subjects of every quality and condition. Because without excepting even the sacred person of His Majesty, there is not a single inhabitant in his Kingdom who, from the top of his head to the soles of his feet, does not carry some vestment or eat some food which is not burdened by the said subsidies and imposts.[21]

Since both rich and poor suffered from one or another type of tribute, Loppin saw no reason why the wealthiest unprivileged members of the community, whom he estimated to number six million out of an imagined total population of sixty million, would object to paying the negligible sum of 12 deniers a day in exchange for the abolition of all other existing taxes. At this rate royal revenues would total 9 million livres a month, not counting the income from the King's personal domain. In addition, His Majesty would be able to sell the offices necessary for collecting this new impost, and the proceeds could be used to reimburse office-holders employed in the prior fiscal administration. Thus, "by means of a small tribute, God will be glorified, the King mightily

21 *Ibid.*, p. 10.

honored, . . . his peoples . . . relieved and rendered very happy, and the poor, who are the brothers and members of the body of Jesus Christ our Savior and Redeemer, assisted in their misery and necessity."[22]

Loppin's arguments, however unrealistic, were the immediate source of an early project to establish fiscal reform upon truly statistical foundations. Around 1675, one Sieur de Bresson, sometime assistant to the Secretary of State for Foreign Affairs, elaborated Loppin's arguments in a handsomely decorated text addressed directly to Louis XIV.[23] The very title of this small treatise testifies to Bresson's desire to uproot and scrap the entire fiscal regime: *Propositions au Roy en faveur de tous ses peuples pour la décharge générale des impôts.* Repeating some of Loppin's arguments, the author insisted that

> by the great diversity and multiplicity of . . . imposts, the perception of which we abandon to legions of officials and exacters who have no goal other than their private interests, not only are the *Roturiers* and *Taillables* subject to them but, Sire, even Your Majesty, the Queen, the Princes and Princesses of Royal Blood and all the subjects of Your Majesty of every rank, dig-

[22] *Ibid.*, p. 9.
[23] The memoir is at the Bibliothèque municipale de Rouen, Collection Leber, MS 5804; the manuscript gives the name of the author without any further details. An anonymous manuscript at the Bibliothèque Sainte-Geneviève, MS 2012, which describes Bresson's memoir tells us that about 1670 he "étoit un vieillard d'assez bonne mine, d'environ 62 à 63 ans qui avoit été un des principaux commis de Monsieur de Brienne." Here it is difficult to ascertain whether Bresson had been in the employ of the father or son or both; Henri-Auguste de Loménie de Brienne, seigneur de la Ville-aux-Clercs, was Secretary of State for Foreign Affairs from 1643 to 1663. After 1651, however, his office was left to his son Henri-Louis de Loménie de Brienne who retained this charge until 1663 when Hugues de Lionne, Marquis de Fresnes became Secretary for Foreign Affairs.

nity and condition. Because, Sire, without excepting your sacred person, there is no one in
all the realm who does not carry some vestment
or partake of some food which is not subjected
daily to all of these taxes.

This truth, Sire, has already been made public to the people of Paris at the beginning of
the Regency of the Queen Mother by the late
Sieur Loppin who said there was not a person
whose expenses were not increased . . . more
than twenty-five percent because of the said imposts. And of the said twenty-five percent, which
amounts to a monstrous and unbelievable sum,
Your Majesty does not receive the twentieth
part. In such a way, he [Loppin] continues, that
the nineteen other parts remain in the hands of
the Partisans and Exacters; thus rendering great
and small more tributaries to them than to Your
Majesty.[24]

Although directly inspired by Loppin, Bresson
approached the problem with more detail and system. He wished to replace all existing levies with
a single graduated direct tax, called a *Droit Royal*,
on the non-privileged members of society. Consulting ecclesiastical records, the author counted fifteen
archdioceses, one hundred dioceses, one hundred and
twenty thousand parishes; but, unlike Loppin, Bresson prudently avoided any estimate of the total population. He did conclude, however, that in all France
there were a minimum of four million non-privileged families who, if freed from all other taxes,
would "voluntarily pay" the *Droit Royal*. Bresson
divided the four million families into nineteen classes
or income groups; the wealthiest, which he estimated

[24] Bib. mun. de Rouen, MS 5804, ff. 12, 26.

to comprise four thousand families, would pay 150 livres annually. The poorest, estimated at four hundred thousand families, would contribute only five sous a year. In this way the King would receive an annual revenue of 365 million livres from the *Droit Royal*, which, "like a single tree of life planted in a new Terrestrial Paradise," would replace "the accumulation of imposts upon imposts" created in the past by "the necessity of Affairs of State."[25]

Bresson also had precise ideas about the way to establish the new tax. A royal edict, to be published and distributed throughout the realm, would inform Frenchmen that all existing taxes were to be immediately suppressed. In their place a single *Droit Royal* would be imposed in a manner proportional to each person's ability to pay. The mayors and aldermen of every locality, along with five or six duly elected notables from each parish, would be convoked by royal commissioners. After examining the rolls of the *taille* for the preceding three years, these personages would draw the first draft of a graduated tax list, to be posted publicly in every parish for all to see. Anyone discovering that he was scheduled to pay more than another who was wealthier could appeal directly to the royal commissioners, who would decide his case on the spot and without cost. After all appeals were heard and decided, the graduated tax list would be signed by the royal commissioners, by the mayor, by the aldermen, and by the duly elected deputies from each parish. It would then be placed in the hands of the mayor or one of the aldermen elected to receive all payments of the *Droit Royal*, and this individual was bound to deposit the returns of every collection within a prescribed period with the nearest local or general receiver.[26]

25 *Ibid.*, ff. 22, 27-28.   26 *Ibid.*, ff. 17-18.

Bresson's plan was a conscientious and, in comparison with Loppin's project, a fairly realistic effort to tap the resources of the non-privileged members of society with the maximum of equity and efficiency. His reasoning, however, also opened the way for an attack against the exemptions of the privileged. If all Frenchmen, privileged and unprivileged, would benefit from the reform of a universally despised fiscal system, it would not be unreasonable to oblige everyone to contribute something, each according to his capacity, in exchange or payment for this benefit. Bresson was quite clear on this matter:

> These truths, Sire, are so palpable and solid that no one, whatever his birth and dignity . . . , can reasonably take offense if he were to be charged with the *Droit Royal* . . . , especially since it will be so moderate that he will not even notice it in comparison to the tribute which he pays insensibly for all his necessities.[27]

No doubt aware of the wider political implications surrounding the question of privilege, Bresson elaborated no further on the idea of unrestricted universal imposition, suggested by the logic of his own argument. But the problem was acute and everywhere it was a subject of discussion. George Ascoli has explained how Frenchmen during the 1660's were keenly interested in the system of taxation existing in England where, allegedly "the great of the realm bear their part in proportion to their wealth and station."[28] The archives at Nantes contain a fragment of "a Dutch writing" which, while the date of translation is unknown, was originally written in 1667.

[27] *Ibid.*, f. 14.
[28] *La Grande-Bretagne devant l'opinion Française au XVII⁰ siècle*, 2 vols., Paris, 1930, I, 390-391.

It describes "a kind of capitation to be paid by everyone . . . without distinction."[29] In 1668 Géraud de Cordemoy dedicated his curious "Letter Concerning the Reform of State" to the Abbé Claude Fleury.[30] Cordemoy dreamed that he encountered visitors from an ideal state, called *l'Etat Réformé*. In that happy land all taxes were replaced with "capitations" paid "by each person" for the "charges and necessities of state." No coercion would be needed for their collection because everyone

> knows from the experience of his ancestors and of neighboring peoples that when levies are not raised by head, so great a quantity of duties are imposed on so many different things, so unequally, both with regard to persons and to goods, by so many . . . hands and consequently with so little order, that the people are always oppressed, profiteers always rich and the Prince always so hampered that, unable to undertake anything at all, the state becomes a prey for everyone.[31]

[29] Arch. dép. de la Loire-Atlantique, C. 694.

[30] The letter was published posthumously in 1691 in a book entitled *Divers traitez de métaphysique, d'histoire et de politique par feu M. de Cordemoy. . .* , Paris. For details about the circumstances and the time in which it was written, see François Gaquère, *La vie et les Oeuvres de Claude Fleury 1640-1723*, Paris, 1925, p. 51.

[31] "De la réformation d'un Etat. . .," *op.cit.*, pp. 141, 146. The term *capitation* was familiar not only from writings of publicists, but also from the use which towns made of this type of imposition in order to collect sufficient funds to liquidate their debts. The tax frequently proved most objectionable to the nobility. The intendant at Moulins, M. de Bercy, for example, wrote the Controller General on 15 March 1684: "L'inconvénient de la capitation est de porter sur les gentilshommes comme sur les classes non privilégiées, et de les pousser à quitter la ville plutot que de renoncer à leurs privileges" (A. de Boislisle, *Correspondance des contrôleurs-généraux des finances avec les intendants des provinces 1683-1715*, 3 vols., Paris, 1874-1897, I, no. 56, p. 16).

151

One project for fiscal reform dating from the 1660's appears to have exercised a particular influence over later writers. Although the first edition of Paul Hay Marquis du Chastelet's *Traité de la politique de la France* did not appear until 1669, numerous manuscript copies had been circulating in Paris and in the provinces since 1667.[32] Devoting one chapter to finance Chastelet observed that although the *tailles* "are considerably diminished today, the people are barely able to pay them because the countryside is in distress." After describing several abuses in the administration of the *taille*, favoritism of assessors, gentlemen extending their fiscal exemption to overseers working their estates, dishonest practices by receivers and their staffs, etc., Chastelet, like Bodin, demanded that "all *tailles* be real as in Languedoc, so that everyone will pay."[33] By "everyone" Chastelet obviously meant any person, even an aristocrat, holding non-noble land. It was common knowledge that noble estates were exempt from all impositions in Languedoc and Provence where, as the phrase *taille réelle* indicates, taxes were imposed on property as distinguished from persons holding it. Finally, in order to make matters easier for the peasantry who had so little money, Chastelet declared that collectors should accept a portion of the harvest or some other

[32] See J. B. Maurice Vignes, *L'Histoire des doctrines*, pp. 27-39. The popularity of this work was immense. In addition to the numerous copies mentioned by Vignes, manuscripts may be found at the Archives des Affaires Etrangères, mém. et doc. (France), MS 94 and at the Bibliothèque Sainte-Geneviève, MS 3085. And, more interesting, a half-century later a certain Garnison, long in the service of Madame de Maintenon, dedicated a lengthy abridged version of the text to Louis XIV's morganatic wife (B.N., Fds. fr., MS 13585). He of course refrained from mentioning the author's identity; Hay had been exiled by the King, who was violently displeased by the treatise.

[33] *Traité*, 1669 edn., pp. 90-91.

form of payment in kind as a legal substitute for specie.

J. B. Maurice Vignes has shown how Chastelet's idea of payment in kind exercised a direct influence on Vauban, whose *Project for a Royal Tithe* was above all a plan to relieve rural penury by allowing farmers to pay the tax collector with part of their crop.[34] Another aspect of Chastelet's plan for fiscal reform was his wish to transform the *gabelle* into a direct universal tax falling on all Frenchmen without distinction. As we have seen, no one theoretically was exempt from the *gabelle*; hence Chastelet's proposal was not particularly radical. But it is significant that the first known full-length plan calling for a universal *graduated* income tax to be imposed on all Frenchmen without distinction, written in January 1684,[35] took its departure from a much earlier and more conservative project to transform the *gabelle* into a direct graduated tax on the unprivileged.

The plan of January 1684 is a revised and extended version of the earlier text which, although dated 1679, is a summary by an unknown author of a project conceived by Abraham Fabert sometime between 1656 and 1662.[36] Written in all likelihood by the same author,[37] the two documents reveal an important and complex evolution in fiscal thought which cannot be appreciated merely by comparing the

[34] A century earlier, as Vignes pointed out, Bodin wrote: "Pour tenir un estat certain des impositions, il faudroit qu'elles se fissent en espèce, comme en grains, vins, huiles . . . c'est la forme de laquelle ont tousjours usé et usent encores les Rois de Pologne et mesme le Roy d'Ethiopie" (*République*, Bk. VI, chap. II, p. 885).

[35] B.N., Fds. fr. 7732. A copy among Vauban's papers in the Fonds Rosambo, on microfilm at the Archives Nationales, is dated January 1684.

[36] The memoir was published by Jules Bourelly, *Le Maréchal de Fabert 1599-1662*, 2 vols., Paris, 1880-1881, II, App. IV, 396-414.

[37] This question is discussed below at length.

earlier writing with the later one. Both projects can be understood only in reference to the outside factors that affected them. The circumstances surrounding the plan of 1656-1662, for example, reveal that concern for reliable statistics, necessary for drafting realistic fiscal schedules, was intimately related to inquests preceding certain army reforms in 1655. Prior to that date, winter quarters for troops were located in walled towns where fortifications protected them from surprise attack. Little attention was paid to the town's financial ability to support this burden, and the expense of large numbers of soldiers often caused considerable hardship. The troops, sufficiently numerous to make themselves masters of the town, frequently resorted to open violence in order to assert their authority over the hostile inhabitants. In 1655 Michel Le Tellier, Minister of War, decided to remedy the situation by dispersing the troops throughout the generalities. Some soldiers would be assigned to each parish, but the precise number could not be determined without an exact knowledge of the material resources of every community. This information was not available, and could be supplied only by systematic investigation. A precedent for such a procedure had recently been established by Abraham de Fabert, Marshal of France, in the principality of Sedan where he was Governor. The results were encouraging, but a larger-scale experiment was needed. Consequently Le Tellier chose the province of Champagne and entrusted the direction of the inquest to an officer of Fabert's choice, le Sieur Terwel.[38]

Terwel, who began preparing for the great inquiry

[38] This development is described at greater length in Louis André, *Michel Le Tellier et l'organisation de l'armée monarchique*, Paris, 1906, pp. 383-396. For Fabert's role see Bourelly, *Le Maréchal*, II, 120-162.

in 1655, was in constant communication with Fabert. By 9 December 1656, the Marshal wrote Mazarin that a reform of the *taille* was necessary "for the more perfect establishment of the winter quarters." In particular, the dishonest and extortionate practices of local officers responsible for assessments, the *élus*, had put "the elections of Reims, Rethel and Saint-Menehould in danger of not being able to pay their imposts for the winter quarters." Indeed, quartering troops in those areas would ruin the local economy and consequently reduce the King's revenues. To avoid this evil Fabert thought it necessary to reform the assessment of the *taille* so that it would correspond to the resources of each locality. And "for the execution of this project I know of no person more capable than Monsieur Terwel, who will show Your Eminence the map of Champagne which he made. . . . *Since we can not put on paper all our thoughts for a much greater project . . . I have communicated my visions to Monsieur Terwel who will explain them to Your Eminence.*"[39]

The only surviving record of Fabert's ideas for a more general reform is in the form of a brief analysis of his writings, presented in 1679 to Michel Le Tellier, then Chancellor of France. Fabert died in 1662, but the content of this second-hand report conforms so well with what we know about Fabert's thinking that it may be regarded as a reliable testimony of the Marshal's thought some twenty years previously.[40] Fabert wished to transform the *gabelle* into a graduated direct tax upon the non-privileged members of society. He thought income from this reform would permit the King to abolish "all new taxes" and re-

[39] The letter is published *in extenso* by Bourelly, *Le Maréchal*, II, 120-124, italics added.

[40] This is brought out clearly in the second volume of Bourelly's work.

duce traditional imposts to their allegedly original tariffs.

Fabert's method of levying the tax recalls some aspects of Bresson's plan. Counting 40,000 parishes, each containing an average of 500 inhabitants, including 75 non-noble families, the Marshal calculated that the number of taxable subjects in the realm amounted to three million heads of families out of an estimated total population of about twenty million persons. His plan provided for three income groups (low, middle, and high), each containing a million families subdivided into ten classes of 100,000. The tariffs ranged from an annual payment of 20 sous to one of 200 livres; their total provided a yearly revenue of 216 million livres. Out of this sum Fabert thought 16 million livres was sufficient to pay for the purchase, transport, storage, and distribution of the salt, as well as providing a fund for payment of all government obligations, *rentes*, previously issued against the revenues from the *gabelles*. Expenses for collection would be kept to a minimum and the King and his subjects would be liberated from "one hundred thousand" blood-sucking tax officials. Four traveling receivers, assigned by turn to each diocese or archdiocese, would collect receipts from both the *taille* and the newly reformed *gabelle*; they would then deposit the proceeds with "sedentary" receivers, their number remaining unspecified, who in turn would be responsible for deposits with the royal treasury. Fabert believed the total expenses for the "general receipt" would not amount to even three million livres a year.

Whatever Fabert's intentions concerning statistical procedures, his calculations were as primitive and unrefined as those of Bresson, who, content to make use of existing records, said nothing about fact-finding surveys. This is not the case, however, with the extended version of the text written in 1684. The manuscript, entitled *Mémoire concernant le droit d'amortissement des gabelles*, makes no mention of the Marshal's name. Written four months after Colbert's death and apparently addressed to Louvois, the writing has been mistakenly attributed by some to Henri de Boulainvillier and by others to Vauban. The author remains unknown, but the memoir is unquestionably an elaboration of the one presented to the Chancellor in 1679; and the two texts were most probably written by the same man.[41]

41 That the first part of the second memoir—the section devoted to the *gabelle*—is largely a paraphrase of the first is documented in L. Rothkrug, "Politique commerciale et fiscalité," p. 99. So far as common authorship is concerned, a close reading of the two texts gives the distinct, indeed almost inescapable, impression of an individual's reworking and elaborating ideas he had previously set down. Moreover, the section in the later version which is not contained in the first is so similar in style to the earlier sections that the presumption of common authorship is very strong.

An interesting literature has grown up around the "Mémoire concernant le droit d'amortissement des gabelles." It is found among the memoirs presented to the Regent by Henri de Boulainvillier in 1715. At the end of the last century, one Th. Ducroq demonstrated by internal evidence that the memoir must have been written toward the middle of Louis XIV's reign: see "Le mémoire de Boulainvillier sur le droit d'amortissement des gabelles et la conversion du revenu des aides, antérieurs au Détail de Boisguilbert et à *la Dîme Royale de Vauban*," *Etudes d'histoire financière et monétaire*, Poitiers, 1887, pp. 3-32. Since then Paul Harsin, "Vauban ou Boulainvillier?" *Bulletin de la société d'histoire moderne* (October 1936), p. 183, has pointed out that the work is listed in the catalogue of Vauban's manuscripts, which at that time were not yet open to the public, with the date 1684. He argues that Boulainvillier, born in 1658, would have been too young to write a document requiring such detailed knowledge; Professor Harsin suggested that Vauban was the author. Renée Simon, *Henri de Boulainvillier 1658-1722*, Paris, 1951, pp. 241-242, continued to insist that Boulainvillier was the author. The copies of the manuscript in Vauban's papers bear annotations in the Marshal's hand which are of such a character as to eliminate any possibility of his authorship. But the manuscript could not have been written by Boulainvillier. In

The manuscript of 1684 is replete with tables and calculations, much more elaborate and refined than previous treatments of the same subject. This is exemplified by the question of population and assessment. In 1679 the author disposed of the problem rapidly, giving no explanation for the figures of 40,000 parishes, each containing an average of 500 people and 75 non-noble families. In 1684, however, he drew tables describing precisely how the number of parishes in each diocese was counted. A brief footnote explained that the 39,116 parishes in the 125 dioceses and archdioceses of France made an average of 313 parishes per diocese. For purposes of convenience, however, the author said that all calculations would be made on the bases of 40,000 parishes, 300 to each diocese. With respect to assessment, the familiar plan of three income groups (low, middle, and high), each subdivided into ten classes of 100,000 families was again presented; this time, however, the author explained that in the absence "of an exact count made in detail parish by parish" he was obliged to use arbitrary figures.

Another important development revealed by the document of 1684 is the demand for the suppression of fiscal privilege. Here the author did his best to limit the political implications of this reform. First,

---

1684 the author was advanced in years; indeed, he even tells us of his age by reminiscing about ministers during Mazarin's administration: "Ceux qui se souviennent des manieres dont on gouvernoit les finances du temps de M. d'Hemery, de Servien et Fouquet, et qui feront réflection sur le changement notable que M. Colbert y apporta. . ." (f. 13). These do not appear to be the words of a man who was twenty-six years old in 1684. Furthermore, if we accept the common authorship of the two texts, we are dealing with someone who knew Fabert personally and who was in possession of his papers, manifestly not Boulainvillier. The question of authorship still remains open.

like Bresson, he argued that payment of a single tax in lieu of a host of indirect duties would benefit nobility as much as anyone else: "A duke and peer, whose household consumes five *minots* of salt per year and fifty *muids* of wine, the taxes on which cost him twelve hundred livres, will pay only seven livres for five *minots* of salt and a hundred francs for his *droit d'amortissement.*"[42] Second, care should be taken to avoid threatening the aristocracy; therefore the *taille*, although reduced by two-thirds, should be retained "in order to distinguish the nobility from the populace." Thus by having "everyone pay the *droit d'amortissement*, each according to his faculties, . . . without regard to quality," the noble as well as the *roturier* would be freed from the burden of a multitude of indirect duties, and payment of a direct tax in exchange for this benefit would constitute no danger to the aristocrat's political or social position: he would continue to be exempt from the *taille*, the one impost traditionally separating the privileged from the unprivileged.[43]

The project for a *Droit d'amortissement* had a wide circulation; copies may even be found among Vauban's papers with the Marshal's annotations in the

[42] The author refers to a duty on wine because this expanded version of Fabert's plan also provides for a *droit de bouchon*.

[43] Although he wished to abolish the *taille*, Vauban also took care to write a list entitled "Privilèges qu'on peut accorder à la noblesse en faveur de la *Dixme Royale*." The table, containing ten articles, is prefaced by the following remarks: "Il faut distinguer deux sortes de Nobles, les uns qui le sont par le mérite et les services que leurs Ancestres ont rendus à l'Estat, ou qu'ils ont rendus et rendent encore eux-mêmes; les autres pour avoir acheté la Noblesse par l'argent. Les premiers sont utiles à l'Estat, parce qu'ils le soutiennent et lui font honneur; au lieu que les autres lui sont à charge. . . . Ainsi ce qui va estre dit regarde la véritable Noblesse, dont il seroit bon de faire un Catalogue dans chaque Province pour ne s'y pas méprendre" (*Dixme Royale*, ed. Coornaert, p. 181).

margin.[44] Despite the author's precautions, this document, saying nothing about any form of consent prior to imposing a direct tax on the nobility, strikes at the very heart of the principle of privilege. It is the first known project demonstrating a serious concern with the statistical procedures necessary for any practicable plan to establish a graduated universal income tax. The full significance of the idea cannot be made clear, however, by merely tracing its development from a comparison of texts. Outside influences which drove men to reconsider problems of fiscal reform during Colbert's ministry must also be examined.

iii. EXTERNAL INFLUENCES ON THE DEVELOPMENT OF FISCAL THOUGHT 1660-1684

Two factors contributed powerfully to the development of fiscal thought during the first half of the reign. On one hand, numerous state-directed inquiries launched by Colbert during the early years of his ministry appear to have incited or encouraged proposals for reform based upon precise statistical information; on the other, financial crisis, widespread revolt, and sedition made clear to both government and reformers the urgent need for fundamental changes in the tax structure. The influence of fact-finding surveys is particularly apparent in Colbert's large-scale investigations into the state of the kingdom in 1664; the detailed plans for this famous census, incidentally, may well have been drawn up under Nicolas Foucquet, Colbert's predecessor.[45] Among

44 Vauban's papers in the Rosambo Collection have been microfilmed by the Archives Nationales. At least five other copies of the manuscripts exist: see Simon, *Boulainvillier*, p. 242, n.68. A lengthy extract may also be found at the Bibliothèque Sainte-Geneviève, MS 2012.

45 Among the papers of Abbé de St. Pierre, in the Archives at

the reports of the answering intendants there is the memoir from the Controller General's brother, Colbert de Croissy. Proposing extensive reforms in the assessment of the *taille,* Croissy admitted that the intendant "could not by himself know the resources of each parish." But, like Bodin a century before, he remained content to recommend a system of open

---

Neuchâtel, is a copy, in a seventeenth century hand, of instructions for a national inquest substantially identical to the one issued by Colbert in 1664. In the margin of the first page, in an eighteenth century hand, is written: "imprimé à Amsterdam dans un écrit atribué au Cardinal de Richelieu en 1689. On croit qu'il a été fait vers 1655. Sanson qui y est cité Etoit déja géographe ordinaire du Roi." Although Sanson remained royal geographer until 1667 and no other internal evidence confirms the dating given by the marginal notation (I was unable to find any trace of the printed version), external evidence does support the view that the circular letter was in fact drawn up by Pierre Chanut during Foucquet's administration. Jacques Savary, in a memoir on the history of French commerce (B.N., Joly de Fleury, MS 2510, ff. 105-116), writes:

Monsieur fouquet surintendant des finances avoit les mesmes inclinations que Mr Son père pour le commerce. Il s'y estoit beaucoup Instruit par les mémoires et pieces qu'il avoit trouvées sur ce sujet apres son déceds, il s'estoit encore fait donner plusieurs autres mémoires par les plus habiles négociants du Royaume, et des pays Estrangers. Sur tous lesquels mémoires il faisoit actuellement travailler monsieur Chanut qui avoit esté du Conl de la marine avec Mr Son pere du vivant de Monsieur le Cardinal de Richelieu. Et cela dans le dessein de restablir le commerce tant en France que sur la mer par des voyages de long cours, et de suivre en cela les intentions de monseigneur le Cardinal de Richelieu ce qu'il auroit exécuté sans sa disgrace . . . le 5e Septembre 1661. . . .

Des que Mr fouquet fut arresté l'on opposa le Scellé dans touttes ses maisons. L'on dit que Mr Colbert ayant trouvé parmy ses papiers lors de la levée desdites Scellés quantité de mémoires concernants le commerce qu'il les lu d'abord par curiosité, mais qu'ayant bien gousté les propositions qui estoit mentionés dans lesdites mémoires et les moyens qu'il y avoit pour parvenir a l'exécution du projet qu'en avoit fait MonSieur fouquet que cela luy fist naistre dans l'esprit le desir d'Executer seul sous les ordres de Sa Ma'té, ce que n'avoient

declarations.[46] In December 1666, however, Dorieu, the intendant at Soissons, proposed a model plan for gathering and recording information from each parish.[47] A more impressive effort was conducted in Burgundy from 1665 to 1670 by the intendant Bouchu, with the cooperation of the provincial estates. A detailed questionnaire reveals the care with which this ambitious enterprise was undertaken.[48]

---

pu faire les ministres qui avoient esté sous francois premier, henry quatre et Louis treize . . . (f. 111).

The reference to Pierre Chanut, who worked "sur tous les . . . mémoires," is of special interest because in April 1654 Chanut drafted a plan for a permanent national Council of Commerce in order to "understand commerce perfectly" at all times (see Chapter IV below). It does seem probable that plans for a kingdom-wide inquiry would accompany a project for the establishment of a permanent Council of Commerce as was subsequently done in 1697 and 1700. The date 1655 in the margin of the Neuchâtel copy, so near April 1654, the date of Chanut's draft, would suggest such a view. Certainly in the light of Chanut's insistence on the need to observe the smallest details of all French economic life some qualifications must be placed on Professor Esmonin's statement that "personne avant 1661 n'avait conçu et entrepris une enquête générale, portant sur l'ensemble des institutions de la France." (See his introduction to *Voysin de la Noiraye: Mémoire sur la généralité de Rouen, 1665*, Paris, 1913, p. vi.) It is Foucquet who in 1659 promulgated the fifty sous per ton tariff on all foreign ships entering French ports. Foucquet, following Chanut's advice, also established a Council of Commerce on 10 April 1661. Although it was dissolved with his arrest, Colbert reestablished the Council in 1664, the very year that he issued the instructions for a national inquest. They, too, may well have been drafted originally by Pierre Chanut.

[46] The Croissy report was published by Charles Du Gast-Matifeux, *Etat du Poitou sous Louis XIV. Rapport au roi et mémoire sur le clergé, la noblesse, la justice et les finances par Charles Colbert de Croissy*, Fontenay-le Comte, 1865. Bodin insisted "qu'un chacun apporte par déclaration les biens et les revenus qu'il a" (*République*, Bk. VI, chap. 2, p. 841).

[47] B.N., Mélanges Colbert, MS 142 bis, f. 803. I am indebted to Professor J. Meuvret who brought this document to my attention.

[48] The questionnaire was published by A. Challe, "Documents statistiques," *Annuaire historique du département de l'Yonne*, Auxerre, 1853. Was the author of the *Droit d'amortissement* re-

Another indication of the influence of state-directed inquiries on the development of fiscal thought may be found in a curious manuscript at the Bibliothèque Sainte-Geneviève in Paris.[49] Several years after Bresson wrote his *Droit Royal,* an anonymous author claimed to have heard Bresson, in the company of several friends, read his project aloud "from beginning to end." In a brief, unreliable account, the author imputes to Bresson an accurate estimate of France's population, and he further suggests that Bresson intended the *Droit Royal* to be imposed on all Frenchmen without distinction. The author said Bresson counted sixty thousand parishes in all of France, each containing an average of a hundred hearths. Since every household was said to number an average of three persons, it was estimated that the entire population totaled eighteen million. If all people were divided into three categories, rich, comfortable, and poor, and each category in turn subdivided into three classes, "it would be very easy to apply the present tariff when we know, for sure, the wealth . . . of the inhabitants of each parish." And to this end, His Majesty ought to order "all bishops to enjoin priests in their dioceses to draw up memoirs in search of the exact number, the revenue and comfort of all the inhabitants in their parishes in order that each one pay the *Droit Royal* in proportion to his wealth."[50] This brief, distorted version of Bresson's project was bound and placed as a kind of preface to a lengthy extract written in the same hand from the *Droit d'amortissement!* Such an arrangement indicates that the author, although saying nothing

---

ferring to this inquest when he complained that in the absence "of an exact count made in detail parish by parish," he was obliged to use arbitrary figures?

[49] MS 2012.   [50] *Ibid.,* p. 3.

about privilege in his version of Bresson's plan, probably had the suppression of fiscal exemption in mind when he demanded that eighteen million Frenchmen be obliged to make some contribution to the royal treasury. And his project, to be based on statistical data obtained by careful inquiries conducted parish by parish into the resources of every person in the realm, strongly suggests that the long-established practice of state-directed surveys contributed powerfully to make people believe it was possible to gather the immense quantity of information necessary for any intelligent program to tax all subjects directly and in proportion to their personal wealth.

If increasing numbers of royal inquests and growing confidence in the power of statistics explain why some men thought it possible to establish a graduated universal imposition, they tell us nothing about why so radical a reform was considered either necessary or desirable. The answer is clear: increasing numbers of Frenchmen were unable to pay their taxes. Rural poverty was already acute in 1670, because of repeated abundant harvests and very low prices. It reached crisis proportions during the Dutch War (1672-1679) when additional revenue demands provoked entire provinces to rise in rebellion. Revolt and sedition were not confined entirely to the peasantry, for many *seigneurs* participated in provincial revolts, and elements of the aristocracy actually negotiated agreements with enemy powers to coordinate local uprisings with the landing of invasion forces.[51] Meanwhile the treasury was desperately in need of funds. Apart

[51] Clément emphasizes this fact in *La police sous Louis XIV*, pp. 150-166. Most important is the plot of the Chevalier de Rohan and his accomplices who sought foreign aid in their attempt to transform the province of Normandy into an independent aristocratic republic; their trial and execution in 1674 was an affair

from a more thorough exploitation of existing fiscal resources and the establishment of new taxes on paper and tin, the crown resorted to numerous expedients calculated to furnish immediate supplies of money.

---

of state, occupying the highest ranking officials in the realm.

Alfred Maury, "Une conspiration républicaine sous Louis XIV," *Revue des Deux Mondes*, LXXVI (July-August 1886), 376-406, 756-784, published a copy of one of the placards by which the conspirators planned to call at least the literate population to arms. Some passages are worth quoting here:

> La noblesse et le peuple de Normandie assemblés pour le bien de l'état et le service du roi, voyant la misere publique et le pitoyable état ou la cruauté et l'avarice des partisans [word substituted for "Colbert" which was erased] ont réduit le royaume au dedans et le grand nombre d'ennemis que la témérité et l'insuffisance des mauvais conseillers nous ont attirés au dehors, se sont promis réciproquement . . . de ne séparer jamais leurs intérets et de sacrifier leurs biens et leurs vies pour le bien commun et général et pour obtenir *une assemblée libre des états-généraux du royaume dans laquelle on puisse avec sécurité délibérer et résoudre la réformation du gouvernement présent* et établir, dans ladite assemblée et par ladite assemblée des lois justes qu'on ne puisse changer a l'avenir, et par moyen desquelles les peuples vivent exempts de tyrannie et de vexation. . . .
>
> . . . Ladite noblesse et ledit peuple assemblés se sont encore promis et ont encore juré solonellement, les uns aux autres, de ne point mettre les armes bas qu'ils n'aient obtenu l'effet de leurs justes demandes, ... Tous les habitans de ladite province . . . seront réunis en deux corps, a savoir: la noblesse et le peuple, ordonnant a tous ecclésiastiques et gens de judicature de se réduire dans l'un de ces deux corps. . . .
>
> . . . On declare que tous ceux de la religion prétendue réformée y sont compris sans aucune différence, la liberté et le pouvoir d'entrer dans toutes les assemblées générales et particulieres pour y donner leurs voix, avoir les emplois et même présider.
>
> . . . Ladite noblesse et ledit peuple assemblés, ont ordonné et ordonnent qu'il ne se levera à l'avenir aucuns deniers des impositions établies, déclarant tous les habitans des villes ou de la campagne exemptes de taille, de sel, des entrées et généralement de tous les autres subsides dont le nombre est infini. . . .
>
> (Italics added.)

In the absence of any really adequate study of the Rohan affair, it is difficult to evaluate this document. The subject is certainly

Farming out the exclusive right to sell tobacco and stamp pewter brought in between 5 and 6 million livres per annum. Creation of new offices and disguised taxes on old ones, called *augmentation des gages*, increased the receipt of the *parties casuelles*. Artisans and merchants were subjected to a new direct imposition.[52] All this was not enough, however, and the crown turned to more questionable, even downright fraudulent, procedures.

The Treasurers of France, for example, were venal officeholders. Colbert suppressed about one-third of those dignitaries, reimbursing them with part of the money obtained from a "supplement" imposed on the remaining two-thirds of their colleagues.[53] More serious was the scandal of the *affaire des quatre sols*.[54] The monarchy did not follow a consistent policy with respect to coinage: sometimes the privilege was farmed out to private contractors and on other occasions the state itself undertook the task of minting.[55] In 1662 Colbert negotiated a lease with Denis Gomisseau, bourgeois of Paris, whereby the latter paid 200,000 livres in exchange for the exclusive right of coinage in the six towns of Paris, Rouen, Lyon, Bayonne, Aix, and Rennes. Compare this sum with the amount specified in the lease negotiated with a syn-

---

worth investigating and there is no lack of source material; oddly enough, a substantial bibliography may be found in a book written more for the public than for the historian: Claude Derblay, *Un drame sous Louis XIV: l'affaire du Chevalier Rohan*, Paris, 1945.

[52] These and other details are described by Germain Martin and Marcel Bezançon, *L'Histoire du crédit en France sous le règne de Louis XIV*, Paris, 1913, pp. 115-120.

[53] *Ibid.*, pp. 117-118.

[54] An excellent, detailed account of the *affaire des quatre sols* is given by Saint-Simon, *Mémoires*, ed. A. de Boislisle, 41 vols., Paris, 1879-1928, VII, App. XI, 521-591.

[55] On this point see Frank C. Spooner, *L'économie mondiale et les frappes monétaires en France 1493-1680*, Paris, 1956, p. 100.

dicate of capitalists in 1674: 630,000 livres! Among other things the contract gave these men the right to mint a new coin of four sous in order to replace an existing five-sous piece. The syndicate reduced the intrinsic value of the new coin, however, to a value slightly below the amount indicated by the sum marked on its face, and they struck off these depreciated pieces in numbers far exceeding the existing circulation of five-sous coins. The illicit profits were enormous. Public indignation over this outrageous maneuver was so intense that Colbert abrogated the contract. As might be expected the depreciated currency drove good money out of circulation, and the Controller General was obliged to issue decrees limiting the proportion of four-sous pieces which could be used to pay obligations over certain specified amounts. In short, the affair was not only scandalous but also economically injurious. The members of the syndicate, hailed before a *Chambre de Justice* immediately after Colbert's death, were forced to make restitutions totaling over a million livres; Desmaretz, Colbert's nephew, was fined and exiled and the Controller General's agent and most trusted official, Bellinzani, was fined and imprisoned.

All of this led one wag to remark that Colbert's ministry, which had begun with bankruptcy, ended with counterfeiting. Certainly public confidence had been undermined. More important, however, is the fact that these events caused men both within and without the government to recognize an urgent need for fundamental changes in the direction of finance. The spirit of reform grew mightily between 1670 and 1675, years when rebellion, sedition, and protest were at their height. Colbert in his well-known memoir on finances, written in 1670, after saying that "abundance has been great for the past nine years," explained how "during the course of the present year. . . , the farmers and general receivers" had complained that "the prodigious necessity which they find in the provinces makes them fear for their ruin."[56]

It is no surprise to discover that, as receivers and tax officials found it increasingly difficult to exact money from the provinces, talk about fiscal reform became both more persistent and more widespread. For example, a letter from William Perwich, English agent in Paris, dated 15 August 1671, declared:

> A new proposition has been made to the King by certain Undertakers who will give him a million *livres* every day and pretend to ease the people of much oppression as the paying of taxes and wine duties. The foundation is a certain Poll Tax or head money, without excepting the nobility, and a general Chimney money, and a new invention for the distribution of salt, which will bring in twice as much as the *Gabelles* have formerly done. The land will not be taxed, but every man according to the number of his children and servants shall be rated at so much, it may be two shillings a head. This, everybody looks on as most feaseable, and has been many years digesting, but the nobility will be much troubled if it take effect, as in all probability it will.[57]

---

[56] "Mémoire au roi sur les finances," *Lettres,* ed. Clément, VII, 234.

[57] *The Despatches of William Perwich, English Agent in Paris 1669-1677,* ed. Beryl Curren, London, 1903, p. 162. In another letter, written on the same day, Perwich makes clear that the new taxes will replace all existing imposts: "They pretend, hereby, to ease the people of much oppression, as particularly they shall pay no Land Tax, only each *Paterfamilias* shall pay according to the number of children and servants, it may be 20 sous a head, besides a chimney

If there was reason to believe in August 1671 that the time had come for major fiscal reforms, the need became clearly more apparent and more urgent during the first years of the Dutch War when increased revenue demands caused widespread revolt and sedition.

Although not directly concerned with finances, the preamble to an edict of March 1673, regulating charges called *épices* which judge and counsel exacted from parties in litigation, reveals an early sign of the new spirit of reform:

> Although justice should be rendered without cost, the usage of preceding centuries has nevertheless introduced some remunerations in favor of judges in addition to the stipends which we have accorded them. *We have the intention of assuming these charges in the future, however, as soon as our affairs permit us.*[58]

No doubt the government was also promising fiscal reform as soon as practicable, that is, when peace would be concluded. Disorder was widespread, however, and the specter of civil war, looming increasingly large on the political horizon,[59] persuaded

---

money and a new invention for the distribution of salt, whereby the *Gabelles* will amount unto twice as much as formerly and no burthen to the people. It seems the many thousand officers employed for the *Tailles, Gabelles*, etc., will be thus retrenched and consequently so much saved" (p. 160).

[58] Isambert, Jourdan *et al., Recueil général des anciennes lois françaises . . . jusqu'à la révolution de 1789,* 29 vols., Paris, 1821-1833, XIX, 86-87 (italics added).

[59] The authorities grew noticeably more insecure and apprehensive between 1672 and 1675. Consider, for example, the following letter from the intendant at Bordeaux, written on 22 August 1675:

Le parlement commença hier à donner des exemples en public, en faisant pendre dans la place St. Michel deux des séditieux. Il y en aura cette apres-disnée un 3e qui court la mesme fortune, et ce ne sera pas apparemment le dernier; car les com-

Jacques Bénigne Bossuet, Bishop of Meaux, that further delay was impossible. Writing a personal letter
to Louis XIV, Bossuet explained on 10 July 1675:

> I understand, Sire, how difficult it is to give
> them [the people] this relief in the middle of a
> great war. . . . But the war which causes Your
> Majesty such great expenditures compels him at
> the same time not to overburden the people who
> make it possible for him to afford [these spend-
> ings]. Thus their alleviation is as necessary for

---

missaires travaillent avec toute la diligence possible à l'instruction du procez des autres prisonniers. Pour assurer les exécutions
pendant qu'elles se sont faictes, on a mis en battaille, dans la
place, 10 compagnies du régiment de Navailles, dont les officiers,
pendant la sédition, avoient tesmoigné beaucoup de bravoure
et beaucoup de prudence.

La peuple est icy dans une grande consternation; mais la
crainte de la potence n'a pas desraciné de leur coeur l'esprit
de sédition et de révolte, et la pluspart des bourgeois ne sont
gueres mieux disposez, quoy qu'ils n'aient pas osé faire parois-
tre leur mauvaise volonté, pour ne pas exposer leurs vies et leurs
biens. *C'est, Monsieur, le plus grand bonheur du monde que la
nouvelle de la défaite de M. le mareschal de Créquy* ne soit pas
arrivée a Bordeaux quelques jours plus tost, elle auroit redoublé
l'insolence du peuple, et peut-estre que M. le mareschal d'Albret
auroit eu peine à le réduire comme il a faict . . . (Depping,
Correspondance Administrative sous le règne de Louis XIV, 4
vols., Paris, 1850-1855, II, 201-202, italics added).

Royal officials were perhaps rereading Bodin's words: since it is "almost impossible to maintain subjects [of a realm] in peace and friendship if they are not at war," it may therefore be accepted as a general
principle that "the best means to conserve a state, and to guarantee
it against rebellions and seditions . . . , and to keep its subjects in
lasting friendship, is to have an enemy against whom they can dress
themselves" (*République*, Bk. V, chap. 5, pp. 760-761). In this connection, it might be further observed that Colbert's well-known
phrase, "tous les grands Etats, et particulierement ce royaume, ne
se soutiennent que par la guerre," was written on 8 June 1674 (see
Pierre Clément, *Histoire de Colbert*, 2 vols., Paris, 1874, II, 46), a
date when popular agitation had recently exploded in the Bordeaux
region and when suspicion about events leading to the *Affaire Rohan*
were already aroused.

your service as it is for their rest. Your Majesty knows all this; and, with this understanding, . . . I think there is a precise and immediate obligation for him above all other things to investigate thoroughly the misery in the provinces. . . .

It is not possible that evils so great, capable of ruining the State, are without remedy; otherwise all would be lost. . . .

I know that peace is the true time to accomplish perfectly all these things; but since the necessity of waging a great war requires that we work for the conservation of the peoples' resources, I do not doubt, Sire, that Your Majesty will apply himself even more [assiduously].[60]

Bossuet did not here express his thoughts on the precise character which fiscal reform ought to take; in fact, he protested "it is not for me to discourse on such matters."[61] It should occasion no surprise, however, to read in *La politique tirée des propres paroles de l'Ecriture Sainte* that "reason demonstrates that everyone in the state must contribute to public necessities which face the Prince."[62] The proposition that all Frenchmen without exception should pay some form of direct imposition, far from being a thought restricted to a few isolated thinkers, became a widely accepted principle during the last years of Colbert's ministry. And the new concern for reliable statistical procedures revealed by the *Droit d'amortissement* was partially the result of a widespread and persistent demand for more effective and more realistic projects for fiscal reform. The pres-

[60] *Correspondance de Bossuet*, ed. Ch. Urbain and E. Levesque, 15 vols., Paris, 1909-1925, I, 368-375.

[61] *Ibid.*, p. 370.

[62] Bossuet, *Oeuvres complètes*, ed. F. Lachat, 31 vols., Paris, 1864, XXIV, Bk. VI, art. II, prop. III, 11.

sure for fundamental changes in the tax system is explained by increasingly heavy impositions levied on the peasants who, bearing almost the entire weight of rapid administrative growth and large-scale military expansion, were frequently reduced to a state where they became even a burden on the privileged landlords for whom they labored. The aristocracy, however, was determined not to surrender its fiscal privileges without obtaining in exchange both an important role in government and protection against any threat to its social position. This fact above all others explains why the nobility played so prominent a role in the movement for political, social, and economic reform during the second part of Louis XIV's personal reign.

PART II

THE MOVEMENT FOR REFORM
1684-1700

THE MOVEMENT FOR REFORM
1684-1700

Two DISTINCT philosophies of political opposition, one spiritual in origin, the other entirely secular, were developed by aristocratic spokesmen between 1684 and 1700. Moreover, reformers in this period went beyond the limits of theory and drew up plans for political action. Indeed, in one instance a conspiratorial shadow government, organized in preparation for far-reaching reforms to be enacted after Louis XIV's death, was established in the entourage of the Duke of Burgundy, heir apparent to the throne. Resistance to mercantilism, however, was by no means confined to the nobility. Criticism flowed as an undercurrent through the world of affairs where businessmen, hesitant in expression and working in the shadow of ministerial surveillance, could not make known their views with either the sophistication or the boldness traditionally displayed by the aristocracy. If protest rose occasionally to the surface, particularly in periods of crisis, it only rarely attained the level of theoretical expression. And lack of confidence continued to inspire timorous speech so long as government dominated the business community. But after 1694-1695, with their influence in purely state affairs reaching unprecedented heights, merchants expounded opposition views with both eloquence and surprising audacity. The dramatic reversal of roles was brought about by the power and wealth acquired at the expense of royal authority during the war (1688-1697), when government depended increasingly upon the unique services of the merchant. It was at this time, with the approach of peace, a period when administrative conflict with the aristocracy was at its height, that the business community demanded an end to mercantilist restrictions and a voice in the direction of economic affairs.

Confronted with a new magnitude of resistance and placed on the defensive for the first time, the crown was thrown into confusion. On the one hand, it reacted violently against what appeared to be the most powerful groups of aristocratic reformers, those led by Fénelon; on the other, the administration, failing either to placate or to control the merchants, established a Council of Commerce in 1700, providing them unwittingly with a public forum from which they violently criticized official policies. At the same time there was a division of authority and the task of economic regulation was parceled out among several different agencies. No longer able to exercise effective control, the monarchy entered into a precipitous and ultimately fatal period of decline. Merchant protest not only strengthened the aristocratic cause, it also accelerated the diffusion of new ideas associated with secularly inspired theories of opposition. Some merchants, perhaps largely for reasons of social emulation, espoused the wider speculative principles expounded by more militant aristocratic reformers. Conflict between mercantilist and opposing forces assumed ideological proportions as established principles of political economy were increasingly attacked by arguments, later called "enlightened," which denied many of the values traditionally associated with the *ancien régime*. It is principally the task of this section to explain how, as resistance to the crown grew stronger, new ideas, spreading as political doctrine, gained ever wider acceptance. Indeed, the French Enlightenment is in several respects a direct outgrowth of movements, led by the aristocracy and joined belatedly by merchants, which opposed the centralizing programs and economic philosophy of the King and his ministers during the second half of the seventeenth century.

CHAPTER IV

FROM
REMONSTRANCE TO PROTEST:
THE RISE OF OPPOSITION
1642-1689

MERCHANTS began to criticize mercantilist principles about the time of Richelieu's death in 1642. At first only occasional complaints were heard, but after Colbert's appointment in 1661 criticism reflected widespread and intense hostility to the new government. The more intelligent critics among both the merchants and aristocracy realized, perhaps at first only dimly, that to make France a maritime power would work changes of an alarming magnitude in domestic and in external affairs. The experience of Portugal, Spain, England, and the Lowlands since the early years of the Atlantic trade showed that heavy state investment or participation in overseas commerce tended to transform every sailing ship, every company agent abroad into a potential diplomatic incident. Colbert's critics were, in varying degrees, aware that commercial expansion, extending the area of diplomatic vulnerability, complicating and making more unpredictable the direction of foreign affairs, impelled governments to exercise greater control over merchant activities, a policy leading logically toward administrative regulation in all spheres of economic life. Among the European powers the smaller states were the most intensely maritime, and this circumstance worked both to limit their foreign adventure and to restrain their administrative development. But to transform the most formidable of all European countries, France, into a colossal maritime state would not only revolutionize international relations, but it would spur administrative growth at home to unmanageable proportions. So general a view was implicit in only a few writings. Most critics were concerned with specific and more immediate issues. For example, merchants were especially disturbed by Colbert's arrogation of power. He assumed the direction of finances by causing the disgrace, trial, and imprisonment of his predecessor Nicolas Foucquet. Pursuing an implacable and at times almost hysterical prosecution of the disgraced Superintendent of Finance, accused of corruption, Colbert became the ardent leader of a campaign for honest financial administration. In November 1661, he caused the establishment of a special tribunal, the *Chambre de Justice*. This extraordinary body, concerned with more than Foucquet's trial, was also empowered to investigate and prosecute all instances of financial abuse and profiteering during the previous twenty-five years. In addition, the *Chambre* helped to carry out the Controller General's complicated plan for gradually repudiating substantial portions of government obligations (the *rentes*).

Hostility engendered by the *Affaire Foucquet* in the very beginning of Colbert's ministry was soon directed toward other areas of his administration. As depression deepened, so the tendency to hold his policies responsible for France's economic distress became more and more apparent.[1] In 1667 tariffs

[1] The energy and ruthlessness of Colbert's administration may to

rose to new heights, and criticism of Colbert's "detestable principles," now intensified, extended beyond the merchant communities to the aristocracy. After three years of futile negotiation, the Dutch, aware of Colbert's unpopularity, sent a new Ambassador, De Groot, to Versailles to present to the King and his ministers a memoir pleading, in a manner reminiscent of Hugo Grotius and Emeric Crucé, the cause of free trade. At about the same time, in 1670, perhaps in reply to De Groot and certainly in answer to his critics, Colbert wrote the well-known *Mémoire au Roi sur les finances.* Here the Controller General formulated what has since become a classic statement of mercantilist theory. His principles of political economy were thus transformed by pronunciamento into the declared tenets of official policy: after this date criticism of mercantilist theory, considered nothing less than opposition of Louis XIV's government, was silenced, only to burst forth again with greater fury at Colbert's death.

At this time, 1684-1689, economic conditions deteriorated even more seriously than before. Aristocrats and merchants from every part of France lashed out bitterly against mercantilist policies. Meanwhile, in the midst of a storm of criticism, the government

---

some extent be explained by the fact that a European-wide depression especially severe after 1660 (see, for example, Jean Meuvret, "Les mouvements des prix de 1661 à 1715 et leurs répercussions," *Journal de la Société de Statistique de Paris* [May 1944] *passim*; the numerous references in Pierre Goubert, *Beauvais et le Beauvaisis de 1600 à 1730: contribution à l'histoire sociale de la France du XVIIe siècle*, Paris, 1960; and Roland Mousnier, *Les XVIe et XVIIe siècles* in *Histoire générale des civilisations*, Paris, 1956, IV, 146-150), made the Controller General's vast program for industrial and commercial expansion more difficult to carry out. Economic distress alone, however, cannot account for the profound antagonism aroused among merchants and aristocrats throughout France during the first years of Colbert's ministry.

organized a series of inquests with the expressed determination to make a break with the past. Although these investigations were launched largely as instruments of rivalry between the Le Tellier and Colbert families for control of ministerial posts, we shall see that no action could have been better calculated to incite demands for reform. The crown gave the impression that it was about to take important steps to remedy France's economic distress: in this context the inquests, suggesting that the government was inadequately informed, incited people everywhere to offer information and advice. "Liberty of commerce," an expression frequently used by Colbert, was transformed by merchants, publicists, and aristocrats into a slogan—indeed, a battle cry—directed against the continuation of that minister's program to control all aspects of France's economic activity.

i. MERCHANT COMPLAINTS ABOUT MERCANTILIST POLICIES PRIOR TO COLBERT

The mercantilist ideal of national economic autarky had been challenged as far back as 1623 on the grounds that it was impossible for France to subsist entirely on her own resources.[2] The question then seems to have been purely academic. Later, however, after Richelieu's death, an unfavorable balance of trade with the Dutch made the issue more concrete and more urgent. Declining French exports combined with Dutch commercial ascendancy to create alarm in the port towns along the Atlantic and

[2] "L'on objectera que . . . si nous refusions a nos voisins de recevoir leurs marchandises, que pour mesmes considérations ils refuseront les nostres, feront divorse avec nous, et que les douanes et Impositions du Royaume en diminueront . . . ("Advis au Roy a Nosseigneurs de son Conseil . . . ," 1623, B.N., Joly de Fleury, MS 2510, f. 30).

Channel coasts, especially in Bordeaux and Nantes. Jean Eon, for example, consulting merchants and records in both cities, complained in 1646 that the United Provinces were "draining away" France's reserves of gold and silver. He further alleged that with help from their own information centers in several French towns, the Dutch were gradually gaining control of French domestic markets, exploiting local economies as they would colonies. Furthermore, warned Eon, England was beginning to follow the Dutch example.[3] Government concern about the situation led finally to legislation aimed at excluding Dutch and English textiles, in the hope both of reducing imports and of reviving domestic industry. These laws proved important in the development of a national mercantilist policy on one hand and the crystallization of conflicting attitudes toward it on the other. In 1648, prior to the *Fronde*, the sovereign courts of France, the *parlements*, the *chambre des comptes*, the *Grand Conseil* and the *cours des monnaies*, assembled in the hall of St. Louis and made the following petition, granted and issued as a decree in the same year:

> Seeing that woolen and silk textiles and all kinds of fabrications are no longer manufactured in the kingdom . . . because of those brought by Dutch and English merchants, thus reducing an infinite number of little people previously employed . . . to mendicity, obliging them to

[3] Jean Eon's arguments are ably discussed by Henri Sée, "Le commerce des étrangers et notamment des Hollandais à Nantes pendant la minorité de Louis XIV," *Tidschrift Voor Geschiedenis* (1926), pp. 246-260. The practices of Dutch merchants in France, especially before 1660, are also ably described by Violet Barbour, *Capitalism in Amsterdam in the Seventeenth Century, The Johns Hopkins University Studies in Historical and Political Science*, Series LXVII, no. I, Baltimore, 1950; see particularly pp. 96-97.

transfer their domiciles to foreign countries, . . .
His Majesty is humbly supplicated to prohibit
all merchants from bringing or engaging others
to bring [into France] the said woolen and silk
textiles manufactured in the said countries of
England and Holland.[4]

The resulting edict envenomed Anglo-French relations. A fierce tariff war, beginning in 1649, was
accompanied by unremitting hostilities at sea; privateering, even downright piracy, reached alarming
proportions on both sides. The English Navigation
Act of 1651 was answered in 1654 by a general em-
bargo on English ships and goods in France.[5] Meanwhile textiles from the maritime powers had been
entering the country via Italy and Switzerland, obliging Nicolas Foucquet, appointed Superintendent of
Finance in 1653, to extend the law of 1648 by imposing prohibitive duties on textiles from all foreign
countries. Complaints arose from every quarter. Some
people objected to the tariff increases in themselves,
although others, insisting that undeclared war against
the English was disastrous for trade, were content to
demand better relations with Cromwell.

Merchants in Paris, for example, were indignant
over Foucquet's legislation. Presenting a formal remonstrance to the King on 26 January 1654, the *six
grands corps*[6] denounced the new duties. Excessive

[4] Isambert, Jourdan *et al.*, *Recueil général des anciennes lois
françaises . . . jusqu'à la révolution de 1789*, 29 vols., Paris, 1821-
1833, XVII, 72-85.

[5] Anglo-French relations in this period are skillfully discussed by
Maurice P. Ashley, *Financial and Commercial Policy under the
Cromwellian Protectorate*, London, 1934, pp. 138 *et seq.*

[6] Since 1625 the drapers, grocers, mercers, hatters, furriers, and
goldsmiths constituted the *six grands corps* of Paris, see Marcel Marion, *Dictionnaire des institutions de la France aux XVIIe et XVIIIe
siècles*, Paris, 1923.

impositions, they explained, "never increase Your Majesty's revenues, . . . greater trade is more profitable than any tariff rise . . . because private abundance grows with commerce and in time flows through many channels into the coffers of Your Majesty." Experience had demonstrated that liberty of commerce was the cause of prosperity: "abundance exists where all is exempt from imposition . . . and where everyone, indiscriminately, is permitted to trade." The crown, declared the Paris merchants, "would forbid us all commerce with our neighbors." So misguided a policy could only lead to ruin: other powers would "forbid entry of our merchandise or impose new duties on it; in either event the consequence is only loss of revenue for his Majesty and lack of employment for his subjects." In the past, for example, France exported most of her wines to England; now, however, "in revenge for the prohibition of 1648," they were excluded or "confiscated and thrown into the sea." As for textiles, foreign imports "furnish us with all our fine wool, ourselves having only thick [wool] which supplies barely a fourth of that needed for industry." Indeed, it could be taken as a general principle that reciprocal trade was necessary for the well-being of mankind as a whole: "common necessity" caused men "to export surplus and import what they need; the ebb and flow of mutual aid produces the abundance in which consists the repose and the felicity of peoples."[7] Although these statements were directly contrary to mercantilist principles, they were not yet part of an established movement of merchant opposition. But their level of generalization, being well above mere complaint,

[7] B.N., Cinq cents Colbert, MS 203, "Très-humbles Remonstrances Au Roy par les six corps des Marchands de la Ville de Paris . . . ," ff. 373-378.

does suggest that the basic doctrines, upon which such a movement was soon to be founded, were being defined. The continued elaboration of these ideas along with the growth of merchant political opposition during the next three decades is explained largely by profound hostility toward the increasingly severe mercantilist measures imposed year after year in a vain effort to combat deepening depression.

Protests similar to those of the Paris merchants may also be read in an anonymous pamphlet published about the same time, entitled: *Plainte publique sur l'interruption du commerce.* The author objected to the "multiplicity and diversity" of duties. Considering "the interdiction" of English textiles responsible "for the exclusions of our wines," he complained that this measure had caused Guyenne and the entire Loire valley to "suffer an intolerable loss." Moreover, by needlessly provoking the English, France had created a "state of undeclared war" between the two countries. Also indemnification for the unlawful actions of French "pirates" must be paid; otherwise England would join the Spanish, destroying sea traffic on one side and encouraging continued warfare on the other.[8]

The author's view of Anglo-French relations conformed in some respects with Mazarin's attitude. At war with Spain since 1635 and weakened seriously by the *Fronde*, France appeared in no position to enter into hostilities with England; the Cardinal, therefore, brought about a major shift in foreign policy by opening negotiations and concluding a commercial treaty with England in 1655. Anglo-Spanish relations, already strained, deteriorated rapidly. When Cromwell launched an expedition against the Spanish Indies in 1654, capturing the island of Ja-

[8] B.N., Fonds français, MS 4826, ff. 42-52.

maica, Philip IV probably refrained from declaring war only because France, Spain's archenemy, appeared on the verge of armed conflict with England. The Anglo-French treaty of 1655, however, removed all reason for Spanish hesitation: the two countries, England and Spain, immediately entered into war.

Mazarin's shift in foreign policy, and the resultant opening of Anglo-Spanish hostilities, however, proved disastrous for a number of French merchants. In the past many of them habitually delivered merchandise, especially textiles, to agents in Spain who shipped them under fraudulent papers to Spanish America. War did not seriously hamper these operations and proceeds from the sale of goods in America continued to reach French merchants at Cadiz or Seville in returning galleons and flotas.[9] But in 1656-1657, Anglo-Spanish conflict led to the capture and destruction of these treasure fleets by Admirals Penn, Stayner, and Blake, causing immense financial loss to the French merchants awaiting their return. According to one spokesman, "Rouen alone was committed to the sum of four millions, Saint-Malo for about the same. . . . At present no traffic exists with Spain; all the textiles sent last year remain there yet. No one among us is able to sell, neither in Normandy nor in Brittany."[10] There was a general fear "of great

[9] The activities of French merchants in Spain have been studied by Albert Girard, *Le commerce français à Séville et Cadix au temps des Habsbourgs*, Paris, 1932. So far as the question of war and trade prior to the Treaty of the Pyrenees is concerned, Girard writes that merchants sent their goods under neutral rather than French flags. The volume of traffic does not appear to have diminished; indeed Girard says that French merchants remembered this period as a kind of "golden age" (pp. 86-87).

[10] This passage and the others quoted throughout the paragraph are from the anonymous Norman noble, writing sometime between 9 September 1656 and 3 September 1658, who was discussed above in Chapter II.

bankruptcies." The author insisted that if ministers thought more clearly about France's economic interests they would view England as an enemy, not an ally. "Spain . . . needs grain to live and textiles to supply the Indies." France "nourishes her" with this trade; and in return gold and silver flowed into the kingdom from the Indies in such quantities that "the great Henry IV had a habit of saying there were more Spanish pistoles in France than in Spain." In this way France would extend a measure of control over the Indies and "shares the vast booty with Spain." Both countries were bound by necessity: war only causes the French to "use neutral ships" and go through "unimportant ceremonies." Alliance with the English, who desired nothing more than the riches of the Indies, would be in these circumstances unwise and most dangerous. Having come to power by illegitimate means, the Lord Protector "needs money to avoid rebellion." Determined to make England master of all commerce, Cromwell defeated the Dutch "in three or four combats," compelling them to accept "shameful terms." This was only one step toward the ultimate goal of gaining a foothold in the Indies, from which he would subsequently force the Spaniards to share their colonial wealth. The capture of Jamaica, the blockade of the Spanish coast, and France's alliance with England put intolerable pressure on Spain. Furthermore, Cromwell's offers to purchase French textiles certainly were made with a view toward capturing part of France's American trade. Friendship with the Lord Protector could bring nothing but disaster. In general, therefore, the crown was caught between conflicting interests and contradictory advice. In 1654 Paris merchants and wine interests from Guyenne and the Loire valley complained bitterly about the injurious effects of

Anglo-French hostilities; three years later powerful merchants in Rouen, Saint-Malo, and the Atlantic ports insisted that an alliance with England was economically ruinous.

The difficult task of formulating a foreign policy consistent with opposing economic interests was simplified, however, by Cromwell's death in 1658 and by extremely favorable economic concessions obtained at the Peace of the Pyrenees in 1659. On one side an advantageous position with respect to Spanish trade and West Indian market were assured by treaty;[11] on the other, England, preoccupied by the Restoration, appeared to withdraw from the international scene, permitting France to turn her full attention to reducing the commercial ascendancy of the maritime powers. Thus in 1659 Nicolas Foucquet promulgated the law which laid the basis for French trade legislation during the next four decades: a tax of 50 sous per ton was imposed on all foreign ships entering French ports. This second major foreign policy shift, in contrast to the one of 1655, reflected confidence in France's growing strength. She had vanquished her enemies both internal and external: Spain was defeated, the *Fronde* had been crushed, and England was embroiled in domestic difficulties. It seemed as if no force could interfere with either the consolidation of royal power at home or the extension of French hegemony abroad.

The glory of France did not look so bright, however, to people seriously affected by prohibitive tariffs. Fine wools from Peru, Poland, England, and Spain were "needed to make hats" and certain types of cloth, and in 1659 France was still importing dyes, spices, sugar, soap, and leather products. In addition,

11 The economic aspects of the Treaty of the Pyrenees are discussed by Girard, *Le commerce français*, pp. 89-130.

special paper made in England and Ireland was required to manufacture playing cards—an industry which alone employed "seven or eight thousand people" in the Rouen area.[12] This region appears to have been particularly hard hit by the new tariff legislation. Indeed, the *Parlement* of Rouen itself addressed a formal remonstrance to Louis XIV in January 1661. Begging "the King to reflect on the cessation of trade and industry, notorious and constant in the town of Rouen and in the province of Normandy," the *Parlement* insisted that the deteriorating economic situation was caused principally by "great duties imposed on merchandise destined for the manufactures of France." High tariffs, far from reducing imports from abroad, only increased production costs and allowed foreign competitors to sell their goods more cheaply than the French. And for this reason "the manufacture of cloth, linen, leather, hats, cards, paper and sugar refining, previously creating a considerable trade and employing infinite numbers of people, have entirely ceased in the said province."[13]

It is difficult to judge the assertion that the crown failed to distinguish adequately between imported raw materials essential for production and foreign manufactured articles competitive with French merchandise. One thing, however, is certain: conditions were depressed and all signs suggested they were getting worse. The formal petitions from Paris merchants in January 1654 and from the Rouen *Parlement* in January 1661, holding tariffs responsible

[12] "Très-humbles Remonstrances au Roy par les six corps," f.7. On the importance of the playing card industry at Rouen, see W. C. Scoville, *The Persecution of Huguenots*, pp. 232-233, 381.

[13] B.N., Fds. fr., MS 18591, "Mémoire des choses sur lesquelles les Deputez du parlement de Rouen ont à faire très humbles remonstrances," ff. 75-76.

for economic decline, seriously perplexed Foucquet and his advisers. No one really knew whether or not existing tariffs were aggravating France's ailing affairs. Fresh information alone could throw light on the subject. Foucquet's intimate adviser, Pierre Chanut,[14] for example, discussed this problem in April 1654, three months after the Paris merchants had remonstrated. His memoir proposed the establishment of a "perpetual Commission for Commerce" to hear advice and complaints from merchants throughout the realm. Although organizations of this kind had been established previously[15] they had existed for only brief periods. Insisting that a permanent body was needed to "observe continually the state of trade inside and outside the realm," Chanut said the future Council of Commerce should examine proposals, "concerning the increase and commodity of trade, navigation, fishing and manufactures, putting them in form of *Cahiers* to be presented to the King." It would hear "all grievances of merchants" and attempt to remove every "interference and disturbance of their traffic." Moreover, "this institution" would make it possible for

> commerce to be understood perfectly, which it has not been and cannot be without communication from every part of the kingdom in one as-

[14] A close friend of Descartes, Chanut (1601-1662) was reputed to be a man of wide culture and considerable linguistic ability. He also proved loyal to those he served: he defended Foucquet after the Superintendent's arrest; see *Dictionnaire de biographie française*, eds. M. Prévost and Roman d'Amat, Paris, 1939-1960.

[15] A short account of the several Councils of Commerce in seventeenth century France is given in P. Bonnassieux and E. Lelong, *Conseil de commerce et bureau de commerce, 1700-1791, inventaire analytique des procès-verbaux*, Paris, 1900, introduction. See also Saint-Simon, "Conseils sous Louis XIV," *Mémoires*, ed. A. de Boislisle, 41 vols., Paris, 1879-1928, VII, 405-443.

sembled body, because all kinds of traffic are related one with the other.

And in this general view of trade merchants will discover by themselves and among themselves how to do what they are now leaving to foreigners because they do not understand. . . .

We will know the strength and weakness of all transactions made by foreigners and among other things this will serve to regulate royal duties and tariffs which we believe have not yet been precisely proportioned.

Manufactures will go from one province to the other. . . .

Finally, the true price of all things will be known by the Commissioners and when the King will wish to construct ships, forge artillery, provision his fortresses and build magazines, establish public graineries and other similar expenses he will find in the Commission . . . all advice necessary to avoid unpleasant surprises in contract negotiations.[16]

Made in the spring of 1654, Chanut's proposal was poorly timed. Official attention was wholly occupied with consolidation of royal authority at home, after the *Fronde,* and more vigorous prosecution of the war against Spain, tasks calling for immediate attention. But the depression continued to deepen. Finally on 10 April 1661, three months after the powerful Rouen *Parlement* added its remonstrance to the growing chorus of discontent, a Royal Edict was issued

[16] This document is published by M. C. Dareste de la Chavanne, *Histoire de l'administration en France,* 2 vols., Paris, 1848, II, 370-373. His source cited, however, is mistakenly indicated as vol. 204 instead of 203, in the collection Cinq cents Colbert. E. Lelong in his introduction to Bonnassieux's *Conseil de Commerce* cites Chavanne and makes the same error. Another copy of Chanut's memoirs may be found in the B.N., Joly de Fleury, MS 2510, ff. 56-57.

establishing a Council of Commerce. A long preamble explained both the functions of this body and the reasons for its creation. Meeting "every week" the Council, headed by Foucquet and staffed by Colbert, Chanut, d'Aligre (future Chancellor) and Arnoul, Intendant of Finance,[17] would examine the causes for "the diminution of commerce both foreign and domestic and the cessation of manufactures in areas where they were most firmly established." Admitting that merchants were pointing particularly to the "inequality and disproportion in import and export duties paid" in the region of the Five Great Farms, the crown further conceded that it was not prepared to legislate in this area "until the members of the Council discuss and enter into the detail of all kinds of traffic in every province . . . and in the entire state of navigation." They would hear individual businessmen from every part of the realm and from a study of all particular interests where "each sees merely his private utility" valid conclusions concerning "the general good of the kingdom" would be drawn. In brief, the aim of the new council was identical with the goal expressed by Chanut seven years earlier: "To understand perfectly" every aspect of trade in preparation for truly effective legislation in economic affairs.

ii. THE AFFAIRE FOUCQUET: THE SPREAD OF CRITICISM AND THE JOINING OF ISSUES

The Council's existence was suddenly cut short, however, on 5 September 1661 by Foucquet's arrest.

17 The phrase "every week" appears in Foucquet's *Les oeuvres de M. Foucquet ministre d'Estat contenant son accusation, son proces et ses défenses, contre Louis XIV Roy de France*, 16 vols., Paris, 1693, V, 339-340. A reference is made by Jules Lair, *Nicolas Foucquet*, 2 vols., Paris, 1890, I, 562.

Three years later, in September 1664, Colbert created another Council of Commerce, similar in most respects to the organization founded in 1661.[18] But the new body could no longer rely on the merchants' cooperation in its efforts to investigate the causes of France's economic distress, for Colbert had alienated them in the interval. The new minister had established the *Chambre de Justice* on 15 November 1661: not wanting the Foucquet affair to be an isolated case, the trial of the former Superintendent was made part of the tribunal's more general duty to investigate and prosecute "all abuses and malversations . . . committed since 1635."[19] Thousands of businessmen were fined or compelled to make restitutions for financial misdeeds allegedly committed ten to twenty years previously. Many others found their holdings of *rentes* reduced arbitrarily to a fraction of their face value.[20] Antagonism toward the new administration was further intensified by deepening depression and by Colbert's determined efforts to force merchants to invest heavily in newly organized royal trading companies. People began to say that the minister's policies were the cause of France's economic plight. Specific grievances no longer gave rise to mere passing expressions of general criticism. Rather, discontent gradually assumed the character of steady political opposition.

An historian has recently observed that Louis XIV, intending above all to exercise personal power after

[18] Although Boislisle (Saint-Simon, *Mémoires*, VII, 415-421) does not mention the Council of 1661, he does describe the one of 1664 in considerable detail.

[19] Quoted from the Royal Edict of 15 November 1661, creating the *Chambre*, by George Mongrédien, *L'Affaire Foucquet*, Paris, 1956, p. 95.

[20] Charles Woolsey Cole, *Colbert and a Century of French Mercantilism*, 2 vols., New York, 1939, I, 302.

Mazarin's death, wanted to break both with the tradition of "first ministers" and with an entire history of political and financial disorders. "Foucquet was the man who, by his immense fortune and his strong personal position in the state, best symbolized this odious past in the eyes of a sovereign who cherished authority." His trial was a *procès politique,* a condemnation of Mazarin's administration, a "spectacular rupture" with the errors of the past. With the exception of the Dreyfus case, no trial in French history had so profound an effect on public opinion as did the *Affaire Foucquet.*[21]

Louis XIV's opinion of Foucquet, while not entirely false, was in fact grossly distorted; the man who did most to create this misconception was Jean Baptiste Colbert. First with Mazarin, then with Louis XIV, Colbert worked tenaciously toward the Superintendent's ruin. Not content with accomplishing his predecessor's disgrace, Colbert also was determined to obtain Foucquet's execution, thereby rendering impossible personal vengeance or a return to power. The Controller General directed all preparations for the trial. As an isolated case, prosecution of Foucquet alone would make Colbert's attitude embarrassingly clear. For this reason the proceedings were made part of a general investigation leading to punishment of persons convicted of corrupt practices and profiteering during Mazarin's administration. It is not surprising therefore that businessmen who paid fines or restitutions, or who suffered financial loss from the partial repudiation of government obligations, early identified themselves with Foucquet's cause. Thus Olivier LeFèvre d'Ormesson, a major judicial officer in the trial, wrote: "Never have there been so many prayers as for this affair; the con-

21 Mongrédien, *L'Affaire Foucquet, Avant Propos.*

juncture of *rentes etc.*, where everyone believes himself injured, makes it such that there is no one who does not wish for the salvation of M. Foucquet."[22]

The trial lasted for three years. Defending himself with consummate skill, Foucquet, on more than one occasion seriously embarrassed his accusers and judges. Every victory, every compromising disclosure, every clever turn of phrase was clandestinely circulated in the form of pamphlets, rhymes, and memoirs. Even the many volumes of Foucquet's brilliant *Défenses* circulated throughout the realm. Although Colbert staffed the *Chambre de Justice* with men hostile to Foucquet, the Superintendent showed signs of gaining the sympathy of several magistrates. Colbert was thoroughly alarmed. He resorted to flagrantly irregular procedures: subornation of witnesses, suppression of evidence, intimidation of judges, and other similar practices.[23] D'Ormesson, however, a man of monumental integrity, braved Colbert's wrath and opposed the Controller General's maneuvers. In the end, d'Ormesson's sincerity and eloquence persuaded thirteen out of twenty-two judges to vote for exile, rather than for the death penalty demanded by the crown. The magistrate's honesty cost him his career, but his popularity was immense. And d'Ormesson's reaction to public acclaim is most revealing:

> All Paris awaited this news with impatience and it was carried immediately everywhere and received with extreme joy, even by the smallest shopkeepers, each expressing a thousand blessings for my name without knowing me. Thus

[22] Olivier LeFèvre d'Ormesson, *Journal*, ed. Albert Chéruel, 2 vols., Paris, 1860, II, 270.

[23] All this is clearly described by Mongrédien, *L'Affaire Foucquet*, *passim*.

M. Foucquet . . . has become the subject of public pain and commiseration by the hate which everyone carries in his heart against the present government, and this is the true cause for the applause.[24]

Hostility toward the new administration clearly made it difficult for Colbert to persuade businessmen to invest in his newly organized state trading companies; and deepening depression, intensifying discontent and diminishing the available stock of investment capital, made the task appear almost hopeless.[25] To be sure antagonism toward trading companies appears to have existed before Colbert, among at least some French merchants,[26] but during his

[24] LeFèvre d'Ormesson, *Journal*, II, 283-284.

[25] Colbert's difficulties in raising capital among merchants for trading companies have been described in an excellent study by P. Boissonade and P. Charliat, *Colbert et la compagnie de commerce du Nord 1661-1689*, Paris, 1930. The Controller General, however, did not restrict his efforts to merchants. LeFèvre d'Ormesson, for example, in August 1664, writes: "J'ay oublié à escrire que le jeudy, après midy, il y eut conseil de grande direction [Finances], durant lequel le Roy envoya quérir M. le chancelier, qui revint peu après et dit que le Roy l'avoit mandé pour lui dire qu'il affectionnoit fort la compagnie pour le commerce des Indes Orientales et qu'il désiroit que tous Messieurs du Conseil y entrassent. . . . Je fus heureux de ne m'y pas trouver; car je suis persuadé que le commerce des Indes Orientales ne réussira pas" (*Journal*, II, 196). Indeed, Colbert's desperate fund-seeking campaign created such widespread resistance that E. Lavisse, "Louis XIV de 1643 à 1685," *Histoire de France*, VII, Part I, Paris, 1911, 241, observed that "un peu partout, la souscription fut considérée comme un impôt déguisé. On accusa le fisc d'avoir inventé un nouveau tour."

[26] Sometime near 1647 the merchants of Rouen, trying to avoid entrance into a royal trading company for whaling, complained: "Ce n'est pas que les compagnies ne soient un moyen propre pour l'accroissement de la navigation, mais elles doivent estre libres et non pas forcées, comme ladite prétendue Compagnie du Nord [not to be confused with Colbert's later organization of 1664, see Boissonade and Charliat, *Colbert et la compagnie*, p. 29], en laquelle on permet à tous Marchands d'entrer, faisant les soubmissions requises,

ministry the antipathy was particularly intense. In 1664, for example, the engineer Chevalier de Clerville, was despatched to maritime ports in Picardy and Normandy to investigate "all things regarding the revival of commerce." He reported that merchant aversion for trading companies was profound.[27] Colbert, concerned only with commercial and industrial expansion, would have welcomed private initiative in this regard. He explained that "commerce must be left free, unless there is an indispensable necessity to commit it into the hands of a company of a few contractors."[28] Capital was scarce, however, and the trading company, among its other presumed virtues, appeared as the only means to drive unwilling merchants into the service of the state. For this reason, although acting less from principle than from force of circumstances, Colbert, intent upon commercial and industrial expansion, did more to establish trading companies in France than any other man in history. Criticism of these institutions became an in-

---

sans considérer que cette permission est une rude contrainte, puis qu'il faut nécessairement ou quitter le traffic qu'on avoit accoustumé de faire, ou s'engager avec des personnes qu'on ne connoit point, avec lesquelles on n'est pas asseuré de compatir, et sous des conditions sur lesquelles on n'a point concerté: ce qui est directement contraire à la nature du contract de société, qui veut que le choix des associez soit libre et que les loix d'association soient arrestées par tous les interessez" (B.N., Fds. fr., MS 18592, ff. 124-125). As early as 1632 merchant aversion to state-chartered trading companies caused Philippe de Béthune, Sully's brother, to write that it is necessary "de contraindre les marchands . . . de s'associer les uns avec les autres, et non de faire leur traffic à part" (*Le conseiller d'Estat ou recueil des plus générales considérations* . . . , Paris, 1645, p. 240).

[27] "Rapport que faict le chevallier de Clerville . . . ," pub. by M. C. Dareste de la Chavanne, *Histoire de l'administration*, II, 373-384.

[28] Pierre Clément, *Lettres, instructions et mémoires de Colbert*, 7 vols., Paris, 1861-1882, III, Part II, 477. In this letter Colbert demonstrates clearly his dislike for monopolies and his preference for a free market.

tegral part of the growing opposition to both the Controller General and to mercantilist theory.

The most controversial issue, however, was tariffs. We have seen how protests and debate about import duties played a central role in the founding of the Council of Commerce in 1661. After its collapse and Foucquet's arrest, Colbert moved cautiously. His first important tariff legislation, that of 1664 was moderate and designed largely to give a single set of import and export duties to the Five Big Farms, a customs bloc embracing most of the northern half of France. Not until 1667 did Colbert's policy finally become clear. Tariffs established in that year applied to all France and were frankly prohibitive.[29] The legislation caused violent reactions not only in the merchant community but also among aristocrats throughout France.

The years 1668 to 1670 saw an outburst of criticism which expressed the views of both merchants and aristocracy. The nobility, however, seemed most alarmed by the legislation of 1667. Many of them believed the new tariffs were part of a determined government effort to undermine their traditional position in society. With the personal rule of Louis XIV, the formerly powerful provincial office of governor, held by the upper nobility, was reduced to an almost honorary function. Meanwhile the petty nobility was taught to obey royal authority by the famous *Grands Jours* held in Auvergne and elsewhere. To these measures Colbert added investigations, called *recherches de la noblesse*. In theory their sole purpose was to verify the titles of those claiming fiscal exemptions on grounds of birth; in practice, however,

29 Cole, *Colbert*, I, 428, writes: "While the tariff of 1664 had been an internal reform, that of 1667 was aimed to injure drastically the trade of other countries. That of 1667 was a fighting tariff, while that of 1664 had been a peaceful one. That of 1667 was vigorously protectionist, while that of 1664 had been mildly so."

some officials were abusive and frequently exacted money from poorer nobles who failed to meet what were, under the particular circumstances, unfair criteria of evidence.[30] These political difficulties occurred in the midst of depressed agricultural conditions when good harvests caused low cereal prices to prevail by and large throughout continental Europe. The tariff of 1667 aggravated the situation by discouraging foreign ships from sailing into French ports and selling their cargoes in order to buy agricultural products with the proceeds. Attributing reduced foreign demand for French grain to Colbert's protectionist measures,[31] some nobles said these decrees, together with *"la recherche de la noblesse,* the establishment of companies for commerce . . . and for various manufactures,"* were a general attack by Colbert on the aristocracy and on agriculture.[32]

Almost all of these criticisms from merchants and from nobles were brought together and expounded at length in a treatise, *Mémoires pour servir à l'histoire D.M.R. avec quelques réflexions politiques sur les mémoires,* published anonymously in 1668.[33] It

[30] "La Noblesse fut ruinée sous prétexte de la recherche des faux Nobles." Anonymous, *Histoire de la décadence de la France procurée par sa conduite,* Cologne, 1687, p. 233.

[31] "M. Colbert dont la conduite n'est jamais égale, si ce n'est pour faire du mal, et de qui les différentes pensées et les divers desseins s'entrechoquent et s'entredestruisent ordinairement s'estant mis dans l'Esprit qu'une augmentation de droits sur les cinq grosses fermes seroit une chose fort avantageuse au Roy, il chargea si extraordinairement toutes sortes de marchandises, qu'on peut dire que c'est une des causes qui ont empesché la sortie de nos denrées et qui ont par conséquent rendu inutiles et infructueuses aux sujets de S.M. des années aussi abondantes en toutes sortes de grains qu'estoient celles que nous avons veues." *Mémoires pour servir à l'histoire D.M.R. avec quelques réflexions politiques sur les mémoires,* n.p., 1668, pp. 231-232. Henceforth cited as *D.M.R.*

[32] *Ibid.,* pp. 180 *et seq.*

[33] *Loc.cit.* This highly informed book with no indication of its

is the first extended polemic against Colbert. Although impassioned in character, the work is eloquent and highly informed, containing a wealth of detail. After a more than two-hundred page diatribe against the injustices of the *Chambre de Justice* and the "shameful" proceeding against Foucquet, the author turned to matters of trade. Merchants, he explained, were suspicious of trading companies because "they doubted very strongly that he [Colbert] who has demonstrated such bad faith . . . could occupy the sovereign direction of commerce with moderation and probity." Indeed, what was to prevent "monsieur Colbert, to whom nothing is sacred or inviolable . . . from putting his hands on the assets of a company" upon pretext of some public necessity?[34] Furthermore, the absurd tariff policies upon which these organizations were based had caused considerable damage:

> Monsieur Colbert should beware that by wanting to put France in a position to dispense [with the trade] of all other peoples, that, on their side, they do not think of doing the same. It is certain they have taken another route and have gone elsewhere to obtain most of the things

---

place of publication is a shrewdly and ably written work of immense interest. Perhaps one reason for the neglect of this published source is that it is not mentioned in E. Bourgeois and L. André, *Les sources de l'histoire de France au XVII⁰ siècle*, 8 vols., Paris, 1913-1935. A brief reference may be found in J. B. Maurice Vignes, *L'Histoire des doctrines sur l'impôt en France: les origines et les destinées de la Dixme Royale de Vauban*, Paris, 1909, p. 257, n. 1. Pierre Clément, *Histoire du système protectioniste en France, depuis le ministère de Colbert jusqu'à la révolution de 1848-1854*, Paris, 1854, pp. 37-49, quotes several paragraphs from this document. A more complete analysis may be found in Jacques Lelong, *Bibliothèque historique de la France*, nouvelle edn., 5 vols., Paris, 1769, II, 574.

[34] *D.M.R.*, pp. 309-311.

> with which they used to furnish themselves in
> our Provinces. One of the principal causes of
> the scarcity of money which we see in France
> in the midst of so great an abundance of grain
> and wine proceeds from [the fact] that the Dutch
> no longer come and discharge [France of her
> surpluses] as they did previously, because our
> conduct towards them in matters of commerce
> makes them see clearly that we will take noth-
> ing from them in exchange. . . . We propose
> to oblige them to pay us entirely in cash.[35]

Indeed, continued the author, to try to capture
Dutch trade would reveal Colbert's profound ignorance of the true interests of both countries. "Everyone agrees that the [Dutch] nation was born for commerce." Their country, "almost entirely surrounded
by sea," had little arable land, and they must resort
to international trade for sustenance and for revenues
necessary to support the state. Economic need drove
them to establish trading posts in the East Indies at
the end of the last century when they were at war
with Spain. In the course of time more than two-
thirds of their men became employed on the sea; and,
for this reason, the Dutch now controlled most of
Europe's carrying trade. It was the source of their
wealth. But the French should not conclude they
could do the same. "It is . . . highly ridiculous to . . .
think" France could become a serious rival of the
United Provinces. For this to be possible Louis XIV
would have to change the customs and occupations
of most of his subjects and send them to sea. It would
be necessary to abandon the cultivation of large areas
of fertile lands, to reduce the size of France's great
armies, and abolish most of the offices in finance and

[35] *Ibid.*, pp. 325-326.

judicature. "In sum we must risk ruin and lose all the solid and real assets we enjoy, so as to capture the ten or twelve percent which the Dutch earn from the merchandise they furnish us. . . . It is true, however, that monsieur Colbert has resolved . . . that if we are so unfortunate as to enjoy peace, he will abolish the remaining officeholders and complete the task of reducing the nobility to mendicity, so that commerce may flourish in a hundred years."[36] Finally, the author declared the ideal of national economic autarky contrary to natural law: "divine providence" had created a huge diversity of natural wealth in different regions of the earth for the purpose of uniting mankind through the bonds of mutual interdependence. The need for trade was "a link in Civil Society no less ancient than the world itself."[37]

The author considered Colbert an innovator. He accused him of substituting "new and pernicious maxims" for the "sacred laws which have sustained this monarchy during the space of so many centuries." His detestable principles had "overturned" the ancient practices and customs of the realm. Colbert, in short, launched France on a wild adventure, and in the midst of novelty, no one could "depend on anything," the future was "uncertain."[38] Although Colbert's economic policies were in fact thoroughly traditional,[39] this criticism had a long life. Reformers and

[36] *Ibid.*, pp. 302-304.   [37] *Ibid.*, p. 327.   [38] *Ibid.*, pp. 214-215.
[39] After outlining a program for commercial and industrial expansion similar to that later laid down by Colbert, an anonymous author, writing in March 1663, declared, "Pour y parvenir a cette bonne fin il n'est pas besoins d'aucuns Edits nouveaux. . . . Il suffit de donner le pouvoir et l'autorité nécessaire [to enforce] les articles négligez des ordonnances des Rois Henry IV et Louis XIII concernans le commerce . . . et qui n'ont point esté révoqués et auxquels il ne manque sinon que de les effectuer, moyennant quoy il est infaillible que toutes les manufactures seront attirées et restablies en France que les bons ouvriers y retourneront et que plusieurs

critics during the second half of Louis XIV's reign insisted they were seeking only to reestablish the traditional or "natural" order said to have existed prior to the Controller General's "revolutionary" administration.

Meanwhile Colbert debated the tariff issue with the Dutch, who, seriously concerned about the legislation of 1667, threatened retaliatory measures, especially on French wines. The Controller General, however, argued that such action could only profit, not harm, French interests. Explaining his position to Arnauld de Pomponne, French Ambassador to The Hague,[40] Colbert observed, in March 1669, that the

---

millions de personnes et de familles y trouveront le moyen de gaigner leur vie et de sortir de mendicité" (B.N., Joly de Fleury, MS 2510, ff. 79-81). Indeed, even the legislation for the great inquests of 1664, reputed to be among the most revolutionary acts of Colbert's ministry, may well have been drafted, as we have seen, during Foucquet's term of office. See Chapter III, n.45, above.

Learned opinion on the extent to which Colbert may be seen as an innovator has undergone considerable revision since the days of Lavisse, who viewed the Controller General as a revolutionary ("Louis XIV de 1643 à 1685," *Histoire de France*, VII, Part I, 172). Henri Sée in an excellent article, "Que faut-il penser de l'oeuvre économique de Colbert?" *Revue historique*, CLII (May-August 1926), 181-194, corrects Lavisse and demonstrates both the traditional and conservative character of Colbert's work. This point has been greatly elaborated and documented in the first volume of Cole's work on Colbert. Henri Hauser, *La pensée et l'action économiques du Cardinal de Richelieu*, Paris, 1944, concludes that, apart from Colbert's own intellectual shortcomings, no important difference can be found in the economic thought and policies of the two ministers. It should be remembered, nevertheless, that however traditional the content of Colbert's program, the determination and force he showed in its execution were in fact novel—indeed, revolutionary.

[40] Pomponne's diplomatic mission to the United Provinces has been described by Herbert H. Rowen, *The Ambassador Prepares for War, the Dutch Embassy of Arnauld de Pomponne, 1669-1671*, The Hague, 1957. Professor Rowen has also published an edition of Pomponne's *Relation de mon ambassade en Hollande*, Utrecht, 1955.

Dutch sailed "three or four thousand ships every year during the months of October, November and December into the rivers Garonne and Charente to pick up wines." One-third was consumed in the United Provinces; the rest was stored and sent to the Baltic and "northern countries" in March and April "when the seas open." These ships then returned "charged with wood, hemp, iron, and other merchandise of large volume." If duties on French wines were raised uniformly, the Dutch would "risk having the English or even the French, who don't pay these taxes," transport wines more cheaply. On the other hand, if the Dutch increased tariffs only on wine they themselves consumed, they would reduce the number of ships sent to France by "one vessel for every hundred or two hundred barrels," no longer purchased because of higher prices, thereby causing unemployment among seamen who would emigrate in order to find work. Thus Dutch retaliatory measures could serve only to advance "His Majesty's design to augment manufactures and commerce." Indeed, the general laws of trade made any other result impossible:

> The world's sea commerce is carried by twenty thousand ships, or thereabout. According to the natural order, each nation should have a share proportional to her power, her population and [the length] of her sea coasts. Of this number the Dutch possess fifteen or sixteen thousand, the French perhaps five or six hundred at the most. The King is employing every method he thinks useful to approach the natural number his subjects ought to have. *If the Dutch employ the same methods there is every reason to expect they will [produce] the same effect, namely, they also will approach the natural number of [ships] they*

ought to have. And in doing this they greatly advance His Majesty's plans.[41]

Unable to change Colbert's attitude about tariffs, the Dutch, fully aware of his unpopularity, tried to intensify pressure against the Controller General. On 10 October 1670 they drew up a memoir pleading the cause of free trade. Although officially destined for the King and his ministers, the contents of the document were quickly made public in France and in England.[42] This brief memoir transformed the question of tariffs into more than a mere administrative matter: free trade, ordained by nature, was an essential element in the moral structure of the universe. Legislation contrary to this inviolate principle, severing the providential ties of friendship which unite mankind, would destroy natural harmony and amity among peoples, everywhere spreading discord, economic distress, and misery:

> God by His Divine Providence, wanting not only to bestow everything which may serve to bring about the felicity of His creatures, but also desiring to create amity and a universal society. . . , has diversified lands and climates so each country produces something . . . not common elsewhere. And wishing to exchange surplus for [products] more rare, a country must have recourse to that universal correspondence and mutual exchange which we call commerce. It is simple to understand that by blocking entry [of goods] with impositions so excessive as to prohibit their sale, a country prevents its subjects

[41] Clément, *Letters*, II, Part II, 461-464.

[42] See the remarks of William Perwich from October 1670 through January 1671, *The Despatches of William Perwich, English Agent in Paris 1669 to 1677*, ed. Beryl Curran, London, 1903.

from easily enjoying that which is grown elsewhere and also stops them from exchanging or
selling their own products, in this way compelling
people to remain encumbered with things they
have in overabundance while rendering them at
the same time incapable of procuring that which
they need.[43]

De Groot's insistence that trade was being "smoth-
ered under the weight of impositions," fell on receptive ears, intensifying hostility throughout a broad
spectrum of society.[44] Plunged in depression, France
was starving in the midst of abundance. Many people
thought, as did the anonymous author of *D.M.R.* that
Colbert's tariff policies were either absurd or part of
some nefarious plan. Protest was widespread. Sir William Perwich, English agent in Paris, observed on 5
March 1670, for example, "how pleasant it is to see
the proposalls made by criticks" of government policy
"about ruining Dutch trade." On 29 November he
declared "the French merchants do as generally complain as the forreigners." Finally, on 24 January the
English agent wrote:

> We hear great complaints of poverty and misery
> for want of trade, and certainly the next year
> will convince these Ministers that more damage
> will arise to France by its late inhibitions than
> to any of its neighbours. As to this place, the

[43] "Mémoire de M. de Groot Ambassadeur d'Hollande," Archives
Aff. Et., Correspondance Hollande, vol. 90, ff. 351-352.

[44] "Almost every step taken by Louis XIV's ministers to break the
long commercial intercourse between the two peoples [Dutch and
French], evoked cries of protest from Frenchmen, especially from
wine merchants of Bordeaux and the exporters of crude sugars of
Nantes, but also from a wide variety of interests ranging from
makers of petty haberdashery, to landowners" (Barbour, *Capitalism
in Amsterdam*, p. 99). The author fully documents the dependence
of wide areas of the French economy on Dutch trade and finance.

ablest merchants cannot find ready money upon any account of trading as formerly.[45]

Colbert could not question the deteriorating economic situation. The treasures he had hoped to capture from abroad proved always more elusive; and, despite heroic efforts to conserve domestic reserves of gold and silver, the Controller General admitted these precious metals were becoming increasingly rare.[46] The ailing affairs of France failed to respond to the minister's remedies. Fearing "a general collapse" and harassed by growing opposition to his tariff and commercial policies, Colbert addressed a memoir to the King in 1670,[47] perhaps in answer to the Dutch document presented to Louis XIV in the same year. The minister now insisted that, far from liberalizing commercial policies, it was necessary to increase the activities of trading companies and intensify trade war against other powers, particularly the United Provinces. Indeed, taking up a most extreme position, Colbert wrote what has since become an almost classical statement of mercantilist theory.

The Controller General thought France's distress was caused by Louis XIV's failure to observe the "natural and legitimate order" of monetary distribution. No province, not even the state itself, ought to possess a disproportionate share of the total stock of money available in the realm. If Limousin, for example, could not pay its taxes for want of funds, no increase could be made in assessments on those provinces profiting from Limousin's loss, because it would be impossible to discover precisely where the money went. Thus the royal treasury suffered when a

---

[45] *Despatches of William Perwich*, pp. 72, 120, 135.
[46] Clément, *Letters*, VII, 254.
[47] "Mémoire au Roy sur les Finances," *ibid.*, pp. 233-256.

province was deprived of its fair share of the common wealth. Sometimes, however, all provinces found it difficult to pay their taxes. This situation, which, according to Colbert, was the source of France's financial difficulties in 1670, occurred when state revenues were disproportionately high in relation to the amount of money in circulation.

Two remedies were possible: "either reduce taxes and expenses or increase the amount of money in commerce." Since the greatness of the King and the power of the state reposed upon "all the spendings occasioned by great revenues," it was necessary to examine how to increase the flow of treasure from abroad. Once "attracted from other countries," money must be "conserved . . . and prevented from leaving" the realm. And because there was

> only one same quantity of money circulating in all Europe, increased from time to time by that coming from the West Indies, it is certain and demonstrable that if there is only 150 millions . . . circulating in the public, an increase of 20, 30 or 50 millions is possible only if, at the same time, we take the identical quantity away from neighboring states. Thus arises a two-fold increase, which has been so clearly discernible for several years past: on the one hand the greatness of Your Majesty increases, on the other, that of your enemies and ill-wishers falls.

Colbert observed, however, that foreign trade had suffered from years of neglect; indeed, when he took office it was almost entirely in the hands of the English and the Dutch. While high tariffs and the establishment of native industries had encouraged exports and also reduced imports, much still remained to be done. A large navy and merchant fleet would be needed to supplant the carrying trade of other nations. Colonies must be transformed into both the sole source of raw materials and into exclusive markets for domestic industry. The ultimate point in France's power thus corresponded in Colbert's mind, to total economic autarky, complete national self-sufficiency. And in 1670 this goal appeared distant; the Controller General himself admitted that its attainment would require "obstinate work and application." In the interim France should consider herself in a perpetual state of conflict: "Since [Your Majesty] has undertaken the administration of finances he has entered into a war of money with all the states of Europe."

The struggle, not one of armed force, was a war "consisting only of spirit and industry." According to Colbert, France since 1660 had defeated Spain, Italy, Germany, and England; their populations were "thrown into great misery" and Louis XIV was enriched by the spoils. The Dutch alone remained a serious rival. Their ultimate defeat "should be one of Your Majesty's principal objects of application throughout his life." Indeed, final victory would be assured only if the vessels of the Northern Company were increased to four hundred; the eighty ships plying the routes to the West Indies, to one hundred and fifty; the six of the Guinea Company, to thirty or forty; the twenty of the Orient to a hundred; the twelve of the Levant, to sixty or eighty, "and all other enterprises expand in proportion." Such a program might appear extraordinarily difficult; but, "I dare say to Your Majesty he will have less trouble than he had in creating and bringing the existing establishments to their present state." Much time would be needed, but "every year [Your Majesty] will see by certain and indubitable proofs Dutch power diminish

. . . and within twelve or thirteen years they shall be reduced to a great extremity." The final triumph over the Dutch would "attract a very great quantity of money into [Your Majesty's] kingdom." It would reestablish "that necessary proportion between the [amount] of money circulating in trade and the [amount] of taxes paid by the people." The treasury would benefit from new riches, and the people would be "in a position to assist [Your Majesty] more substantially in the event of war or other necessity."

Colbert had answered his critics. Never had mercantilist doctrine been so coherently expressed. Attacked from all directions in the years 1668 to 1670, Colbert transformed principles of political economy into the ideological foundations of government policy. Dissent could no longer be tolerated. Colbert imposed silence on his detractors for the remainder of his ministry, and the torrent of criticism unleashed at his death marked the irrevocable passage from protest to genuine political opposition.

iii. COLBERT'S DEATH: THE RISE OF OPPOSITION AND THE DEMAND FOR REFORM 1684-1689

News of Colbert's death on 6 September 1683 caused intense popular emotion. In Paris the event was hailed with joy. Indeed, only armed force prevented the minister's body from being dragged through the streets. Many among the common people thought France was entering a new era: "Taxes would cease and the Golden Age would return."[48] But experience

---

[48] "M. Colbert mourut en 1683. Le peuple, qui n'est qu'une bête féroce crut avoir tout gagné par sa mort, que les impôts allaient cesser et que l'âge d'or allait revenir. . . . La haine publique alla jusqu'à vouloir traîner son corps par les rues. Il fallut, pour le porter en terre, envoyer des gens de guerre." Robert de Challes, *Mémoires*, ed. A. Augustin-Thierry, Paris, 1931, pp. 134-135.

proved otherwise. Alarming numbers of Frenchmen were reduced to truly desperate circumstances during the years between Colbert's death and the crowning disaster in 1693-1694 when a great famine swept the entire realm.[49] The post left vacant by the deceased Controller General amidst so many difficulties might well have been filled by Nicolas Desmaretz, his nephew who, trained in finance since the early years of his uncle's ministry, was Colbert's logical successor.[50] Yet, despite his eminent qualifications, Desmaretz did not receive the appointment. Instead, the office went to Claude Le Pelletier, protégé of Chancellor Michel Le Tellier. The unexpected choice, made one day after the minister's death, pointed toward the declining fortunes of the Colbert family. By December their disfavor was clear to everyone. Desmaretz was disgraced and exiled to his estates at Maillebois on partially trumped up or at least grossly exaggerated charges of corruption. This event caused many eyes to turn toward the long-time rivals of the Colberts, the three Le Telliers who now faced one Colbert (de Croissy) in the all-powerful *Conseil d'en Haut.*

Only moderately qualified for the post and faced with a formidable series of problems caused by deepening depression, Le Pelletier's task was further complicated by the incomplete state of Colbert's records[51] and by Desmaretz' retention of papers belong-

49 An able and fully documented analysis of France's economic distress in this period was written by Warren C. Scoville, *The Persecution of the Huguenots and French Economic Development 1680-1720*, Berkeley, 1960, pp. 156-209.

50 The only published work on Desmaretz is a very mediocre law thesis, René Dumas, *La politique financière de Nicolas Desmaretz*, Paris, 1927. Source material is plentiful and the subject certainly merits scholarly attention.

51 In the "Mémoire présenté au Roi par M. Le Pelletier, après avoir quitter les finances, par lequel il rend compte de son ad-

ing to the late minister.[52] Frightened by lack of information and determined to get at the causes of economic distress, Le Pelletier set out to gather data from every possible source. Never before had government made so extensive and varied use of the technique of inquiry. The increased tempo of investigation indicates, at first glance, no apparent break with the past. Superficially the growth of fact-finding activity seems like a mere extension of policies carried out earlier by Richelieu and then by Colbert. In fact, however, Le Pelletier organized a series of important inquests with the expressed determination to make a radical break with the past.

People everywhere thought royal investigating commissions were a prelude to reform. Chancellor d'Aguesseau, for example, writing a biography of his

---

ministration," *Correspondance des contrôleurs-généraux des finances avec les intendants des provinces 1683-1715*, ed. A. de Boislisle, 3 vols., Paris, 1874-1897, I, 554, Le Pelletier wrote: "Je reconnus que M. Colbert avoit renfermé en luy-mesme toute la direction des finances, et qu'il n'y avoit personne qui fust dans la suite des affaires et en estat de m'en instruire."

52 On 28 February 1686 Le Pelletier wrote Desmaretz the following letter: "Le Roy a resolu de finir présentement le reglement général auquel feu M. Colbert avoit commencé de travailler pour les cinq grosses fermes, et comme il y a dessus plusieurs mémoires apostiller de sa main je vous prie monsieur de me faire donner s'ils sont encore entre vos mains, ou de me mander qui les peut avoir. Je vous prie aussy de me mander un peu amplement ce que vous scaver des veues géneralles que feu M. Colbert avoit eues sur ce sujet, affin que j'en puisse rendre compte à Sa Majesté" (A.N. G⁷ 2). Previously, on 2 March 1684, Colbert's brother, Edouard-Philippe Colbert de Maulevrier, wrote his nephew Desmaretz: "Quand ils [Le Pelletier and the Louvois family] vous demanderont en particulier quelque éclaircissement sur quelque nature d'affaire particuliere, l'avis de M. de Croissy et le mien est que vous leur donniez de bonne grace. Mais, pour des instructions générales sur les finances, nous croyons que vous vous en pouvez dispenser" (Saint-Simon, *Mémoires*, VII, 557).

father, a member of two investigating commissions, was very clear on this point:

> In 1687 his [my father's] rest was interrupted by the new ideas which M. Pelletier, then Controller General, conceived for reforming finance. He caused the King to appoint a certain number of Councillors of State to visit the provinces . . . to receive complaints . . . and proposals for everything that can be done to render it [the *taille*] more useful to the state and less burdensome for the people, *in order to work subsequently toward a general reform.*[53]

Enormous publicity surrounded the inquest of 1687. The Marquis de Sourches, for example, wrote in early May:

> We heard some news which has caused a great stir. The King has chosen six Councillors of State and six Masters of Requests under them to go into the provinces and examine everything which can be done for the relief of the people.[54]

The Marquis de Dangeau, writing several paragraphs concerning the Commission, even invoked the glory of Charlemagne: "All this strongly resembles the *Missi Dominici*. The departments are not well governed, they require change."[55] The spirit of reform was not confined to Paris; fact-finding teams carried it into the most distant parts of the realm. Thus on 7 July 1688, De Ribyère, a member of the commission

[53] *Discours sur la vie et la mort, le caractère et les moeurs de M. d'Aguesseau, conseiller d'état,* Paris, 1812, p. 110 (italics added).

[54] *Mémoires secrets et inédits de la cour de France sur la fin du règne de Louis XIV,* ed. de Cosnac, Bertrand and Pontal, 13 vols., Paris, 1882-1883, II, 44-45.

[55] *Mémoires,* ed. E. Soulié, Dussieux *et al.,* 19 vols., Paris, 1854-1860, II, 40-41.

investigating tariffs and indirect taxes in the Five Great Farms area, received a letter from one Dorinville, a retired petty official living in the Breton town of Guingamp. Concerned with the "good of the state," Dorinville offered to write "several memoirs dealing with quantities of unknown abuses . . . which began in 1688 and have continued down to the present day."[56]

While Le Pelletier was establishing royal inquests in order to "reform finance," similar programs in another branch of government were being carried out by Colbert's son, Seignelay, Minister of Marine. His vast organization for inquiry, motivated by reasons of family-faction rivalry, was above all a determined attempt to keep the direction of trade in the hands of the Colbert family. Whatever the intentions, however, the political impact of countless royal investigating commissions was enormous: people everywhere seemed convinced that the crown, publicly concerned with their plight, would soon enact measures to alleviate popular distress. Moreover, the merchants not only thought public inquests presaged formulation of new economic policies, they further believed commissions of inquiry, being associated with Desmaretz' disgrace, were an official condemnation of the past regime they so despised. Thus Seignelay unwittingly helped both to provoke attacks against his father's ministry and to encourage criticism of the mercantilist principles which Colbert's name had now come to symbolize.

When Le Pelletier took office, he, like Colbert before him, established a *Chambre de Justice* whose

[56] A.N., G⁷1143. This carton contains some of the Commission's reports; other reports may also be found in the Archives du Château de Saint-Aignan, Fonds Beauvillier, MSS 278, 282-283, 304. I am here indebted to the kindness of M. le duc de la Roche Aymont who granted me access to his private archives.

principal function was to eliminate rivals. The Colbert family was not long in preparing a counterattack, which ultimately drove Le Pelletier to resign in 1689. Accusing the new Controller General of ruining the King's credit, the Colbert family insisted that reestablishment of the confidence of the business community was essential to economic recovery.[57] And in 1685 Seignelay took a significant step in this direction: he created the office of Director General of Commerce, placing merchants under a new department headed by Marius Basile Morel de Boistiroux, successor to Bellinzani, Colbert's intendant general for industry disgraced and imprisoned by the recently established *Chambre de Justice*. Morel immediately set out to entice with special favor and privilege the most powerful merchants in the chief maritime towns to work as government information agents.[58] Although he died soon after taking office, his policy was continued by his successor, a tax farmer, Jean Baptiste de Lagny, appointed in March 1686. De Lagny's recruiting methods and the object of his efforts were clearly ex-

[57] On this point see Saint-Simon, *Mémoires*, VII, 574-576.

[58] Morel's circular letter to a number of prospective merchant correspondents, written on 21 March 1685, is as follows:

J'ay besoin d'avoir un correspondant exact et fidel dans le lieu ou vous estes pour estre informé de tout ce qui regarde le commerce, de la quantité et qualité des vaisseaux qui sortiront de votre port, et de ceux qui y arriveront, et de ce qui peut contribuer à la satisfaction des négotients; il seroit pareillement nécessaire que je sois bien averti des disgraces et des faillites dans lesquelles tombent les marchands, de ce qu'il y a donné lieu, des remedes et des secours qu'on pourroit donner à ceux à qui pareil malheur arrive; et comme je scay, Monsieur, que je ne scaurois prendre confiance en un plus honnete homme que vous, je m'y addresse pour vous supplier que nous ayions une correspondance réglée sur toutes ces choses, vous asseurant de ma part de reconnoitre autant qu'il dépendra de moy les peines que vous voudrez bien prendre dans cette occasion (A.N., Archives de la Marine, B⁷58, f. 21).

plained in a circular letter to merchants considered
most qualified for the post of correspondent. Dated
19 April 1686, the letter is worth quoting at length:

> Among the things which Monseigneur le Mar-
> quis de Seignelay has particularly recommended
> for the commerce of——in the instructions he
> gave me . . . for the functions of Director Gen-
> eral of Commerce for France . . . he above all
> recommended that I maintain an exact corre-
> spondence with you, *Monsieur*, and he assured
> me that I should have respect for your advice, as
> it comes from a well informed person of broad
> experience who is particularly sensitive to the
> public interest. . . . That is why, *Monsieur*, your
> reputation, about which I had already heard
> much, disposed me to follow with pleasure the
> orders which he . . . gave me, and to beg you,
> *Monsieur*, to be convinced that I shall ardently
> devote myself to your service at every occasion.
> Let me also ask, *Monsieur*, the grace of having
> you tell your clients that when they will give me
> the honor of addressing me concerning difficul-
> ties they might have in trade . . . both within and
> without the kingdom, I will devote all the care
> and affection possible in order to . . . procure
> promptly the relief and satisfaction which they
> can reasonably expect. I will follow in this way
> the intentions of the King . . . for the reestablish-
> ment of trade and the express orders of Mon-
> seigneur le Marquis de Seignelay. It is for this
> reason, *Monsieur*, that he has ordered me to beg
> you to alert me regularly to everything concern-
> ing matters of trade in your town, so that on the
> basis of your advice he can explain to the King
> the measures necessary for the protection of

trade. Towards this end, *Monsieur*, I beg you to inform me of the names of foreign ships and their masters, the ports from which they sailed and the quality and approximate quantity of the merchandise with which they are charged. I need to be informed about all the difficulties and obstacles which the French encounter in foreign countries. . . . In addition, . . . please alert me to ships, both French and foreign, preparing to depart . . . and their destination and cargoes. I also need, *Monsieur*, for my personal instruction so that I will be in a better position to serve *Messieurs les negotians*, that you take the trouble to send me a separate memoir accounting for the merchandise and manufactures brought to you by the foreigners, and the quality and quantity of French products and merchandise which make up the usual trade in your area, along with an account of the defects in our manufactures destined for export. . . .

I also beg you, *Monsieur*, to send me the rate of exchange in your locality, both for inside and outside the kingdom, and finally, anything which can put me in a position to better serve the merchants and the public. *Monseigneur* the Marquis has told me that any trouble you might take in our correspondence will not be without reward, and as for myself, I will do everything possible to demonstrate my personal gratitude.[59]

Government favor was no small matter. La Lande Magon, a well-known merchant *armateur* in Saint-Malo, for example, discovered the advantages of his new position when, on 8 May 1686, De Lagny wrote: "I received your private bill for the manufactures

[59] A.N., Archives de la Marine, B⁷ 58, ff. 4-5.

charged in 1683 on the fleet for New Spain, as well as those for the Sieurs Du Fresne, André Marion and . . . Estienne Picot; I will show them to Monseigneur le Marquis de Seignelay, assuring him of the justice of their contents."[60] Profits and prestige soon led some of the most powerful merchants in the realm to become agents of the crown.[61]

In their dealings with the Director General, the correspondents may have acted also as delegates representing the business communities in their particular region. So much is suggested by the fact that the local business community paid the correspondent's traveling and incidental expenses when he was ordered to Versailles for deliberations with the minister or with the Director General. Indeed, one letter in the correspondence surrounding a dispute about the sum due Pierre Le Gendre, who accompanied his brother Thomas, summoned to Versailles on 1 March 1686, explicitly states that Pierre Le Gendre's expenses were incurred "while in the service of the said community [of merchants in Rouen]."[62]

[60] *Ibid.*, f. 18.

[61] A document in the Marine Archives (B7 60, f. 37), dated 9 February 1689, for example, contains the following list of the Director's correspondents:

Rouen	Thomas Le Gendre
Havre	Messieurs Houssay (brothers)
Honfleur	Pallier
Dieppe	Chauvel
Bayonne	Marion
Bordeaux	Boutoise
Nantes	Grilleau (f. 78 also indicates Messieurs Danguay père et fils)
St. Malo	La Lande Magon
Dunkirk	Denis Fauconnier
Calais	Molien
La Rochelle	Héron (f. 78 also indicates Théodore Pagez).

[62] The letter summoning some merchant correspondents to Versailles is at the A.N., Archives de la Marine, B2 57, f. 142.

Correspondents were only one source of information. Determined to keep the direction of commerce in the Colbert family, Seignelay did his utmost on the one hand to gain the goodwill and cooperation of merchants and on the other to discover the causes for the decline of trade. He launched inquiries in all directions. On 3 July 1686 De Lagny confided to De la Place, general agent at Nantes of the syndicate farming the King's colonial ventures, "between you and me, let me tell you that the plan is to make a general table for the King of what we receive from foreigners and what we give, classified by nations, by quality, type and price."[63] Most impressive, however, was the mission entrusted to Anne-Louis Jules de Malon de Bercy, intendant at Lyon. On 14 February 1686 Seignelay wrote Bercy the following letter:

> Monsieur,
>
> . . . I have proposed your name to the King for a . . . position where you will be able to demonstrate your abilities and your diligence. It is to visit all seaports in the realm in order to enter into the detail of everything concerning trade, hear merchants and other business people, examine their grievances . . . and begin to apply His Majesty's great plans for the increase of trade. His Majesty . . . has promised me to write you so that you may prepare to leave immediately after your vacation. . . . I can tell you in advance that this is a position of great distinction, seeing that you will have occasion every week to pay court to His Majesty and to demonstrate your wit and your ability.[64]

[63] A.N., Archives de la Marine, B7 58, f. 47.
[64] *Ibid.*, B2 57, ff. 111-112.

A draft of Bercy's instructions, running to more than twenty folios, may be found in the Archives for Foreign Affairs;[65] here the full scope of the inquiry becomes clear.

The document begins by explaining that war,

[65] Aff. Et., mém. et doc., France, 302. A short and interesting summary of these instructions may be found in the A.N., Archives de la Marine, G[40], pp. 246-249. Bercy's inquiry seems to have been co-ordinated with that of Sr Patoulet, whose instructions, dated 11 December 1685, are in part as follows:

> Le Roy voulant connoitre à fonds le commerce des Espagnols aux Indes, et celuy qui se fait à Cadix par toutes les nations de l'Europe, et trouver les moyens d'y rétablir celuy de France altéré par les vexations et la mauvaise foy du ministre Espagnol, le Sr Patoulet Commissaire de la Marine eut ordre de se rendre d'abord a St. Malo, d'y voir tous les Marchands intéressés a ce Commerce afin de connoitre la qualité et quantité des marchandises qu'ils envoyoient à Cadix, de quelles manufactures ils les tiroient, qu'elles étoient les plus Estimées et qui avoient le plus de débit en Espagne, et quel étoit le profit que l'on y pouvoit faire. D'aprofondir si la décadence de ce commerce ne viendroit pas de la mauvaise qualité de ces marchandises et si la facilité que celuy des Anglois, Hollandois et Genois trouvoit en Espagne ne venoit pas de la supériorité de leur marchandises sur celles de France. De scavoir en quoy y consistoit leur commerce, quel nombre de vaisseaux ils envoyent, et quelle somme chacune de ces nations retiroit ordinairement des retours des Gallions.
>
> De chercher les moyens de conserver l'argent que ce commerce attire dans le Royaume, et que les marchands envoyent en barres et en réaux en Angleterre et en Hollande ou il est plus cher qu'en France, et de voir si en augmentant sa valeur, on pourroit les engager à le porter dans les monnoyes [French mints].
>
> Apres y avoir pris toutes ces connoissances a Saint-Malo, il luy étoit ordonné de se rendre a Cadix, d'y voir tous les marchands françois qui y sont habitués et qui seront en Etat de luy donner des connoissances certaines du Commerce des Indes, de l'autorité des Gouverneurs et des officiers qui y sont envoyés d'Espagne, de l'Etat du pays, des lieux où se fait le plus grand commerce, et où l'or et l'argent des mines a coutume d'aborder (*ibid.*, pp. 236-238).

The memoir which Patoulet drew up is discussed frequently in Girard, *Le commerce français, passim.*

emigration of Protestants, and the flight of capital and industrial techniques had caused trade to decline despite all measures taken for its protection. Since Europe was at peace, His Majesty, "thinking nothing could so contribute towards increasing commerce both within and without the realm than a certain and precise knowledge of the state of commerce in all maritime towns and regions . . . has chosen the Sieur de Bercy . . . who is informed of His Majesty's intentions by the present instruction which will serve him as a guide throughout his mission." In the execution of his task, Bercy should keep "three principal goals" in mind: first, see to the enforcement of existing ordinances and regulations concerning trade; second, discover "the true causes of the diminution of trade . . . and the means to reestablish it"; third, enter "into an exact knowledge of all which concerns the continual complaints of merchants about vexations caused them by [tax] farmers and their clerks."

His Majesty "wishes the Sieur de Bercy to begin . . . in the town of Dunkirk; he will [subsequently] follow the coast of Picardy, Normandy, Brittany, Poitou, the region of Aunis, Saintonge, Guyenne, Bayonne . . . and, by the canal connecting the two oceans, the coast of Roussillon and Languedoc." In each area the intendant or other representative of central authority was instructed to give Bercy and his staff "every possible assistance." There follows a lengthy account of the prodigious detail into which Bercy was to inquire.

The spate of investigating activities, beginning with Le Pelletier's administration, connected as they were with the establishment of a *Chambre de Justice*. Desmaretz' disgrace and Bellinzani's imprisonment appeared above all as a condemnation of the past. Understandably bitter about what seems to have been systematic attacks against almost everyone who had stood in some relation of trust with his deceased uncle, Desmaretz wrote:

> The memory of Monsieur Colbert was attacked with great animosity after his death. At that time all authority was in the hands of his enemies, and they had the pleasure of exercising their hatred by violent persecution against all those whom he employed or to whom he had in some fashion revealed his confidence. And [they] destroyed every trace in the King's mind of the important services which he [Colbert] had rendered to His Majesty and to the state.[66]

The widespread and continued public activities of official inquiry, appeared not only to condemn the past, but to further encourage an outpouring of criticism against mercantilist doctrine. In May 1684, for example, an unidentified noble held Colbert responsible for the "ruin of finance and trade." The founding of "manufactures . . . [presumably the *manufactures royales*] has deprived commerce of liberty . . . and denied merchants the means to attract money from abroad." Believing that high tariffs reduced foreign demand for French farm products, the noble declared: "Poverty will be banished . . . when Frenchmen are permitted to sell their agricultural products abroad."[67] A more extended statement of this position appeared in print during the next year. In 1685 Gatien de Courtilz de Sandras, Sieur du Verger,[68]

---

66 "Justification de Mr Colbert," B.N., Fds. fr., n. a., MS 9505, ff. 1-26.

67 A.N., G7 694, "Advis sur l'état présent des finances."

68 Considerable biographical information may be found in **B. M.** Woodbridge, *Gatien de Courtilz sieur du Verger: étude sur un précurseur de roman réaliste en France, The Johns Hopkins University Studies in Romance Literature and Languages,* V, Paris and Baltimore, 1925.

published a book concerning the "interests" of European states. Speaking of France, Gatien wrote:

> It seems to us, that ministers have committed a great error when, under pretext of doing without quantities of things customarily imported from foreign countries, they deprived the realm of income from the sale of wines and other products. . . . We are the more astonished that two or three provinces have not been thrown into despair, which seeing no more money, have the distress of watching their wines and spirits perish by the false policies of a Minister who, with the idea of making the Kingdom flourish by his manufactures, found precisely the means to make it perish.

Gatien also observed that "if Monsieur Colbert, the author of these counsels, was so obstinate about his manufactures, nothing prevented him from establishing these enterprises for better or for worse," but international trade should not be made to suffer. Each state should be "free" to trade with another. Gatien warned that continued observance of Colbert's policies would lead to war with England and Holland which, allied together, were sufficiently powerful to make France "lose her commerce."[69] The book in which these passages are written was widely circulated. By 1689 it had gone into four editions and even called forth admiring remarks from Pierre Bayle.[70] Here

---

[69] *Nouveaux intérests des princes de l'Europe, où l'on traite des maximes qu'ils doivent observer pour se maintenir dans leurs états et pour empecher qu'il ne se forme une monarchie universelle,* La Haye, 1685, pp. 183-186. An excellent chapter on Courtilz and the idea of *raison d'état* may be found in F. Meinecke, *Machiavellism,* trans. W. Stark, New Haven, 1957, pp. 244-256.

[70] Three other editions "reveues et augmentées selon l'état actuel des affaires" appeared in 1686, 1688, 1689 (2 vols.): see E. Bour-

probably is one source for the lines found in the first pamphlet of that famous collection of tracts entitled, *Les soupirs de la France esclave qui aspire après la liberté*:

> Commerce provides the riches of towns and of the state. The present government has made it a great affair of honor to improve French trade. The deceased Monsieur Colbert took considerable pains in this regard. In this spirit he established the East India Company, . . . erected manufactures . . . so that we could find all we need in France without passing our money to the foreigner. All this, however, has not caused misery to diminish; moreover, commerce, instead of increasing, is totally crushed. . . . Prohibition of foreign merchandise, far from encouraging trade, has . . . ruined it.[71]

---

geois and L. André, *Les sources*, IV, 335. In November 1685 Pierre Bayle concluded his discussion of Courtilz's book with a comment that probably caught Meinecke's attention: "Enfin on doit reconnoitre qu'il parle en homme d'esprit des intérets de chaque nation en particulier, et qu'il donne l'agrément à ses réflexions par quantité de faits curieux. Mais ce qu'il y a de bien étrange, c'est qu'il paroit évidemment que les maximes sur quoi l'on fonde les intérets politiques des Etats sont presque toujours destituées de bonne foi" (*Nouvelles de la République des lettres*, November 1685, p. 1299).

[71] Amsterdam, 1689, p. 14. This criticism found an echo in Court circles during the same year. In January 1689 the Marquis de Sourches, *Mémoires*, III, 29, n.2, wrote: "On sut aussi que les vaisseaux françois qui étoit allés charger à Cadix ce qui appartenoit aux marchands françois sur la flotte du roi d'Espagne, qui venoit des Indes occidentales, étoient arrivées heureusement à Marseilles, chargés de lingots d'argent ou de piastres pour douze ou quinze millions.

Cela étoit bon, car l'espece commencoit à manquer en France tant parce qu'on avoit envoyé beaucoup d'argent dans les pays étrangers que parce que leur politique avoit été d'en tirer de France le plus qu'ils pouvoient et de n'y en apporter presque point; à *quoi les manufactures nouvelles de France avoient aussi beaucoup*

Political pamphleteers and irate aristocrats were not the only people who wrote in this vein; merchants expressed similar views. In 1686 one unidentified businessman, protesting against proposed tariff increases, said they

> would infallibly cause an interruption in commerce, which is already only too diminished, by the establishment of manufactures in the kingdom; on the pretext of getting along without foreigners, sufficient weight is not given to the fact that when foreigners used to supply numerous goods to the kingdom, they carried away, in exchange, our products, which they bought at a good price, so that they always left behind some of their money, stimulating commerce, which since that time has ceased because we have attempted to do without them, they have done the same thing with regard to us.[72]

Other statements, dating from the same year, may be found among the papers of the East India Com-

---

contribué, car les Hollandois et les Anglois, voyant que la France ne vouloit plus tirer leurs étoffes, ne vinrent plus y prendre de vin, d'eau-de-vie et de toiles" (italics added).

Marcel Langlois, "Le journal du ministre Chamillard ou les mémoires attribués au marquis de Sourches," *Extrait des compte rendus de l'Académie des Sciences Morales et Politiques*, Paris, 1925, has attempted to show that Sourches' memoirs were actually written by Michel Chamillart who became Controller General in 1698. This reasoning has caused at least one later historian, M. R. Schmittlein, *L'aspect politique du différend Bossuet-Fénelon*, Baden, 1954, to treat Sourches' memoirs as if they were written by Chamillart. Edmond Esmonin, however, in an article "A propos des mémoires Sourches," *Bulletin Revue d'histoire moderne* (1926), 121-124, has established conclusively that the Marquis de Sourches was the author.

[72] Charles Woolsey Cole, *French Mercantilism 1683-1700*, New York, 1943, p. 10, quoted this passage from the papers of the Controller General.

pany. During the early 1680's, when Dutch naval forces had practically excluded France from the Spice Islands, the company became heavily dependent upon the import of cottons, especially printed or painted calicoes, from the Indian mainland. The rapidly growing market for *indiennes* adversely affected long-established domestic industries. People whose interests were injured could argue not only that Indian fabrics were "the ruin" of French manufactures, but, having been exchanged for gold and silver, their import also drained the kingdom of "infinite sums of money." The government was placed in a difficult position: satisfaction of what, by all traditional standards, were the legitimate demands of the textile industry, would seriously endanger the future of Colbert's renowned East India Company. The situation became still more critical in 1685 when the revocation of the Edict of Nantes and the subsequent flight of capital and of skilled artisans further disrupted French industry. The tide of protest mounted. Deeply concerned, the directors of the company in 1686 answered the attacks of their opponents in a memoir entitled: *Responses aux mémoires qui se répandent dans Paris contre la Compagnie des Indes Orientales de France*. Denying all responsibility, the directors announced that the government was to blame for the distress of home industries:

> Experience has shown that trade cannot be conducted without a total liberty and without a mutual correspondence with foreign countries. The moment we wanted to take another attitude and violated [trade], for reasons we are unable to penetrate, the foreigners withdrew. They attracted French workers and established our manufactures in their country, . . . and have dispensed

with ours. This is the cause of the great diminution of the manufactures of France, and it is the righteous subject of complaints from merchants and from manufacturers.[73]

Also accused of exporting specie to pay for their imports, the directors of the East India Company did not deny the charge. Instead, they answered that in general such practices were not without merit and might very well be encouraged:

> As to the second [argument attacking the Company] which concerns transporting specie out of the kingdom, we reply that in general in England and in Holland the ports are always open for the entry and exit of specie with every possible liberty, . . . moreover, in Holland the same liberty is accorded for the export of money in the coin of the country. It is this great freedom which attracts abundance to the point where it is [in the United Provinces] and renders them masters of all trade.[74]

No argument could be more contrary to mercantilist principles than one advocating the unrestricted export of gold and silver. If widespread support for this position can be shown to have existed in the merchant community, a source of serious opposition to government policy would then be revealed. No further direct testimony from businessmen during the 1680's has yet been uncovered, however, and little weight can be given to remarks from refugee political critics.[75] Evidence does exist, nevertheless, which strongly

[73] A.N., Archives des Colonies, C² 5, f. 214.

[74] *Ibid.*, ff. 216-217. An excellent study of the East India Company in this period has been written by Paul Kaeppelin, *La Compagnie des Indes Orientales et François Martin*, Paris, 1908, pp. 193-205.

[75] In 1688 *Les soupirs de la France esclave* . . . , p. 14, declared:

suggests that merchants had been demanding the right of unrestricted export and import of precious metals since at least 1661-1662. At this time Saint-Evremond wrote a satirical play entitled, *Sir Politick Would-be*.[76] Appearing among the list of characters, we find *Monsieur de Riche-Source, Homme d'affaires François, Chimériques en Projets*. The personage could not possibly have had comic appeal unless merchant arguments about the free traffic of precious metals were common political coin. Merchant *Riche-Source* believed free international circulation of treasure would enrich and unite all of mankind:

> My plan is to establish circulation; it is the purpose of my entire project. Gold must flow unimpeded through canals, communicating its price to all men; following a movement which is never interrupted . . . it will enrich every country through which it passes. Nothing will be sterile or without reward. . . . Present [difficulties] exist because gold, so necessary to the world, no longer has free passage.

Riche-Source explained that his ideas, as indicated by the title of his project, *The Science of Circulation and the Doctrine of Canals*, were suggested to him "by the recent discovery of the circulation of the blood." In the most general terms, his plan was to establish an international commission composed of merchants from Paris and London and representatives from Venice. Its task would be to convince all states that

---

"On ne pense pas que l'ame du Commerce c'est l'argent et que la vie de l'argent est dans le mouvement. Le Commerce s'entretient que par le mouvement qui se fait de l'argent d'un Pais à l'autre."

[76] *Oeuvres de Monsieur de Saint-Evremond, avec la vie de l'auteur*, ed. Monsieur Des Maizeaux, Membre de la Société Royale, 5 vols., Paris, 1740, II. The quotations which follow are taken from pp. 223-229.

"circulation is a human right, interference would encourage Nations to violate the natural liberty of all peoples." Finally, *Riche-Source's* description of the geographical route taken by the world's treasure, once all obstacles were removed, is a transparent attack against France's efforts to reduce the commercial ascendancy of the maritime powers:

> All the money from Marseille which goes into the coffers of the Great *Seigneur* [the Sultan] will go into those of the King of Persia, from Persia to those of the Great Mogol, where it will no longer stop as has been the custom, it will return to Europe by means of the English and the Dutch who traffic in the Indies. From England and the United Provinces it will pass into France, where after a small isolated circulation, it will return to Marseille from where it first left, by means of the canal joining the two Oceans. Each nation has canals . . . [through which] gold and silver will perpetually pass.

Saint-Evremond's satire indicates that the arguments expressed by the directors of the East India Company were neither especially new nor particularly radical; they appear to have been part of a long-established undercurrent of opposition, temporarily brought to the surface by acute economic difficulties and contradictions within the mercantilist system.

A further indication of the widespread and intense character of merchant opposition during the 1680's may be seen in their demands for freedom from government interference in matters of trade. On 5 October 1685, Marillac, intendant at Rouen, wrote Controller General Le Pelletier that he had consulted with two powerful merchants, Thomas Le Gendre and Antoine Asselin. They had advised him:

The greatest secret is to leave trade entirely free; men are sufficiently attracted to it by their own interests. . . . Never have [manufactures] been so depressed, and trade also, since we have taken it into our heads to increase them by way of authority.[77]

This was no isolated statement. On 29 August 1686, Dugué de Bagnols, intendant in Flanders, wrote a bitter protest against an edict of 15 August 1685 imposing a 20 per cent duty on imports from the Levant. Goods carried on French ships which had not been in *entrepôt* in Italy or elsewhere, were exempt from the tax if they entered the ports of Marseille or Rouen. The law was directed against English and Dutch ships which undercut French merchants by transporting cargoes picked up in Italy and selling them at low prices in Dieppe, Dunkirk, Le Havre, and other Atlantic ports. This activity was also particularly damaging to fishermen from Saint-Malo and Dunkirk who sold their North Atlantic catch in Marseille and transported Levantine goods to ports in Spain and along the Atlantic and channel coast. Yet, despite these seemingly sound reasons for the law, Dugué insisted that textile industries in Lille and Dunkirk, dependent on imported cotton goods and thread, should not be made to pay for the failure of Marseille merchants to compete successfully with the English in the Levant: merchants in Lille and Dunkirk should be permitted to buy what they needed from English ships until such time as French businessmen could sell Levantine goods at competitive prices. Indeed, it could be taken as a general principle that

Trade can flourish and subsist only when merchants are free to procure the merchandise they

[77] Boislisle, *Corr. des con. gén.*, I, 54-55.

need in the places where they are [sold] at the lowest price, and every time we wish to compel them to buy in one place at the exclusion of all others, merchandise will become more expensive and trade will consequently fall into ruin.[78]

Even if the maxim *laissez faire et laissez passer* were not actually coined during the first part of Louis XIV's reign by Thomas Le Gendre, the rich Rouen merchant, as Turgot would have us believe,[79] Dugué certainly stated the argument. And this should occasion no surprise, for the idea had been gaining ground since at least 1654, the date when Paris merchants submitted a formal remonstrance to the King. Opposition to fundamental mercantilist principles, becoming increasingly apparent during the course of Colbert's ministry, continued to grow more intense and more widespread in the years immediately following his death. Convinced that prosperity could be restored only if the state accorded the greatest possible freedom to businessmen in the exercise of their trade, merchants, after 1683, transformed the term "liberty of commerce" (an expression frequently employed by Colbert) into a slogan directed against

[78] A.N., Archives de la Marine, B7 492, ff. 201-204.

[79] A. Oncken's history of the phrase *laissez-faire*, presented in two lectures delivered before the Historical Society of Berne in 1886, is discussed at length by Hazel Van Dyke Roberts, *Boisguilbert: Economist of the Reign of Louis XIV*, New York, 1935, pp. 339-360. According to Oncken, Turgot, when he said that "No one knows the words of M. Legendre to M. Colbert: Laissez-nous faire," was referring to Thomas Le Gendre, the rich merchant of Rouen. Evidence from the notarial minutes at Rouen tends to confirm Oncken's assertion: on 3 April 1692 the Turgot family sold sixteen houses to Thomas Le Gendre (Minutes Cavé). Other acts show that the two families knew each other very well. If Turgot simply said M. Le Gendre, a name as common as Brown in English, without further precision, he was in all probability referring to the man his grandparents knew so intimately.

the continuation of that minister's program to control all aspects of economic activity. In the next chapter we shall see how aristocrats, also opposed to the
crown's centralizing mercantilist policies, thought
favorably of the merchant position. Indeed, they expanded the meaning of "liberty of commerce" to
include not merely freedom from government intervention in merchant affairs, but the abolition of tariffs and all barriers interfering with the universal
natural laws governing economic and human relations.

CHAPTER V

THE ORIGINS AND DEVELOPMENT OF CHRISTIAN AGRARIANISM, 1684-1697

THE DECADE following Colbert's death saw divergent factors combine so as to produce an active and intensely devout political group which developed both an ideology and a program for reform. At this time of public protest a Christian agrarianism found its immediate inspiration in a new kind of criticism which had been first, but very briefly, expressed by Fénelon's friend, Claude Fleury, in 1670-1675, during the worst years of Colbert's administration. Attention was drawn to Fleury in 1687 because the reports of investigating commissions of that year appeared to confirm his arguments. It was this convergence of thought and circumstance, the apparent conformity of theory with fact, which inspired reformers in 1688 to submit a memoir to Louis XIV containing judicious paraphrases from both Fleury and the subsequent report of 1687. This memoir provided the basis for an ideology and a program for reform. From the point of view of developed theory the memoir was totally inadequate, but for the history of ideas, the document is of major importance. All of its principal arguments were incorporated in the more fully elaborated form of Christian agrarianism which Fénelon developed after the great famine of 1693-1694.

i. THE REPORT OF 1687

The problem of rural depression, most urgent in the years immediately following Colbert's death, often proved perplexing to government officials because they had no means to measure its precise extent. In this regard there is an important exchange of letters in 1682 between Colbert and Morant, intendant in Provence. During the first decades of the reign, Colbert, receiving frequent complaints from intendants that a region could not meet this or that fiscal obligation, often expressed skepticism and even frank disbelief. He knew that the well-known popular hatred of taxes was matched only by peasant ingenuity in seeking to avoid payment. Occasionally peasants even succeeded in persuading the intendant that they were destitute when they were not. Report of such tactics prompted Colbert to answer Morant in the following terms:

> His Majesty has not been persuaded of this province's great misery nor has much credence been given to the inflated terms of exaggeration . . . met with in all letters. . . .
>
> If you wish individually to judge well and reasonably if there is misery in the province, consider whether population has declined in the cities, if trade, if marriages have diminished, if the price of offices, lands and houses has decreased. . . .[1]

Taking the Controller General at his word, Morant wrote an unexpected reply on 7 November 1682; it merits particular attention, because Colbert's sugges-

[1] Pierre Clément, *Lettres, instructions et mémoires de Colbert*, 7 vols., Paris, 1861-1882, IV, 141-142.

tions, actually applied by Morant, became standard procedures for the great, publicized investigating commissions of the following decade. Explaining that he had personally applied "the methods you kindly showed me to be the most certain for revealing the true state of cities and the strength or feebleness of provinces," Morant concluded that his jurisdiction was impoverished to a dangerous degree. "Games, feasts and all other occasions for spending are almost entirely abolished." People did not even speak of "their terrible losses because they don't gamble any more." Funerals for distinguished persons of quality, ceremonies "conserving a certain elegance for the longest time," had become simple and austere. Only a few ordinary ceremonies had taken place. Moreover, "I see neither expensive furniture nor any recently erected handsome buildings in Aix or in any other of the principal cities."[2]

[2] *Ibid.*, pp. xxii-xxiii. Earlier, on 12 September 1670, Colbert instructed the intendant at Tours, Voysin de la Noiraye, to examine "how the peasants are dressed, their furniture, and see if they are more joyous on holidays and at weddings than they have been in the past" (*ibid.*, II, Part II, p. 551, n.1).

Charles de Sainte-Maure, Marquis de Salles, Duc de Montausier (1610-1690) was appointed governor to the Dauphin in September 1668. Sometime between 1668 and 1679, Montausier composed several thousand maxims of instruction for the Dauphin (B.N., Fds. fr., n.a., MSS 10629-10639). One of them reads as follows:

De se faire rendre compte exactement par les Intendans et par les gouverneurs, les magistrats, par les gentilhommes, par les bourgeois et par les paysans . . . de l'état des provinces, de la richesse ou de la pauvreté, de la joye ou de la tristesse, de la fasson dont vivent des nobles et des peuples de la campagne et des villes, si c'est opulemment ou commodément, ou petitement et avec incommodité; si on s'y réjouit, si on y fait des fetes, si on s'y divertit dans les familles et en public, si on y est bien ou mal meublé, si l'argent y est rare ou non, si le commerce y fleurit ou y languit, ce qui l'empeche ou le favorise, il faut qu'il s'informe de beaucoup d'autres choses de cette nature, par lesquelles il peut voir l'Etat ou sont ses sujets, pour se conduire et prendre ses mesures sur

Morant's letter stands at the beginning of a series of events which transformed the problem of rural relief into a burning public issue. The greater part of Colbert's ministry, as we have seen, was a period of abundant harvests and depressed cereal prices. Small farmers and agricultural workers, particularly hard hit, found it increasingly difficult to meet the *taille*, the *gabelle*, and other fiscal charges requiring a money payment, and many of them went into debt or fell behind in their taxes. At this point, with cash reserves depleted, they were especially vulnerable to crop failure. Fixed charges paid in kind (the tithe, seignorial dues, etc.) would consume most of a meager harvest, and the farmer would have neither enough cereal to feed his family until the next harvest nor sufficient funds to purchase grain at the high prices brought about by scarcity. One of these abrupt transitions from several years of abundance and depressed farm income to a year of scarcity and high prices occurred in 1684-1685.[3]

The consequences were disastrous. On 31 March and on 19 April 1684 La Reynie, Lieutenant General of Police in Paris, received two anonymous memoirs which, describing a desolate countryside, explained that poverty-stricken peasants, many of whom were fleeing the realm, were "no longer able to pay taxes."[4]

---

cela afin de les assister et pourvoir aux besoins de tout le monde à propos (B.N., Fds. fr., n.a., MS 10632, f. 276).

[3] See the tables in Pierre Goubert, *Beauvais et le Beauvaisis de 1600 à 1730: contribution à l'histoire sociale de la France du XVIIe siècle*, Paris, 1960, p. 403, and also the numerous elaborate graphs in the accompanying volume. See also the tables and graphs in M. Baulant and J. Meuvret, *Prix des céréales extraits de la Mercuriale de Paris (1520-1698)*, 2 vols., Paris, 1960-1962, II.

[4] A. de Boislisle, *Mémoire de la généralité de Paris*, Paris, 1881, pp. 764-767. The documents raise the issue of emigration of non-Protestant Frenchmen. Warren C. Scoville, *The Persecution of the Huguenots and French Economic Development 1680-1720*, Berkeley

Even foreign travelers such as Gilbert Burnet, Bishop of Salisbury, wrote in September 1685: "On the way from Paris to Lyon I was astonished by such great misery. . . . Everywhere one meets nothing but wretched hovels, torn clothes and emaciated faces. . . . *Even the towns* are terribly affected" by rural misery.[5] Around the same date a French gentleman wrote to Louvois, Minister of War, explaining how, "zealous for the glory of his sovereign and devoted to the salvation of his country," he traveled on his own initiative "through all the provinces of France." The good man saw "nothing but calamities": on every side he met "abandoned farms, ruined nobles, bankrupt merchants, desperate creditors, and destitute peasants." The latter had neither fire nor food nor "other means of subsistence; the children ordinarily perish from hunger."[6] Finally, in 1685, the Paris merchants presented a memoir to the crown. Describing measures they thought essential "for the reestablishment of trade," the merchants insisted that "the first and most urgent remedy . . . is for His Majesty . . . to relieve the countryside. If the inhabitants of the *plat*

---

and Los Angeles, 1960, pp. 170-171, discusses the problem only briefly. In fact quantities of references to this phenomenon may be found in source material of earlier years. In the text of a tariff promulgated in 1648, for example, speaks of an "infinite number of little people . . . obliged to transfer their domiciles to foreign countries" (Isambert, Jourdan *et al.*, *Recueil général des anciennes lois françaises . . . jusqu'à la révolution de 1789*, 29 vols., Paris, 1821-1833, XVII, 72-84); French concern with emigration was evident long before the revocation of the Edict of Nantes.

[5] Gilbert Burnet, *Voyage de Suisse, d'Italie et quelques endroits d'Allemagne et de France*, 2d edn., Rotterdam, 1688, pp. 2-3.

[6] The copy of this text in the War Archives (A¹ 795), pub. by G. Servois, *Annuaire Bulletin de la Société de l'Histoire de France*, 1870, VIII, 185-187, is dated January 1686. Another copy with one or two interesting variants, dated 1685 and entitled "Mémoire touchant l'Estat présent de la France," is at the B.N., Joly de Fleury, MS 2510, ff. 61-62.

pays [agricultural areas] are restored to their former condition . . . they will come into the cities and procure honestly the things most necessary to pass the winter."[7]

The poor harvest of 1684-1685 was followed immediately by several consecutive bumper crops, driving prices to an unprecedented and catastrophic low in the years 1687 to 1689.[8] It was at this time that La Bruyère wrote his dramatic description of the peasantry:

> Dispersed over the country certain wild animals, males and females, are seen bent over the ground which they turn with an invincible persistency. They have articulate voices, and when they stand upright they disclose human faces, and in truth they are men. At night they retire into dens where they live on black bread, water and roots. They spare other men the pain of sowing, of cultivating and of reaping in order to live, and thus deserve not to lack the bread which they have sown.[9]

However literary, La Bruyère's picture did not, on this occasion at least, materially distort the facts. It is fully confirmed by the report of a team of government officials investigating conditions in the Generality of Orléans and the four *élections* of Maine, which were part of the Generality of Tours.[10] The Commission said that poverty was widespread, the rural

[7] Boislisle, *Mémoire de la généralité*, p. 769.

[8] Goubert, *Beauvais et le Beauvaisis*, p. 403 and accompanying volume of graphs. M. Baulant and Jean Meuvret, *Prix des céréales*, II.

[9] This well-known passage first appeared in the 1689 edition of *Les Caractères*.

[10] "Mémoire des commissaires du roi sur la misère des peuples et les moyens d'y remédier," pub. in Boislisle, *Mémoire de la généralité*, pp. 781-786.

areas desolate. "We rarely see games or other diversions in villages or in the countryside; all languishes, everything is sad." Houses fell "into ruin," because the owners were unable to keep them in repair. They reported a general exodus from the countryside: people who abandoned their homes because of poverty were joined by others leaving the realm "because of religion." Among those who remained there was scarcely "a peasant who owns anything at all . . . and worse we no longer see any rich *laboureurs*," so necessary for the proper exploitation of farms. "Today no one [lives in the country] except poor share-croppers who have nothing. The landlords must supply them with beasts, provide food, pay their *tailles* and accept as payment in return the entire portion of the [share-cropper's] harvest, which is sometimes inadequate." Rural folk were vulnerable to the first misfortune: "A hail-storm, sickness and a thousand other accidents reduce these poor people to beggary. And the landlords on their side can do nothing because of expenses, advances and the loss of their animals, not to speak of the ones stolen by those *misérables*." Everywhere peasants were living "on bread made of black grain; others who do not even have this live on roots and boiled grass mixed with flour from barley and oats with some salt." Industries which "used to bring a lot of money to the regions where they were established, permitting so many people to live, have diminished considerably." In short, there was "a universal decline in the orders of every estate . . . and this requires prompt remedy." The Commission urged that more money be sent to the provinces: even though receipts from tax farms had not diminished, investigation had revealed that the fiscal machine had operated more ruthlessly, seeking every last taxable resource. "Individuals have almost no more money; this is why it is so difficult to sell [goods] in commerce and why the *seigneurs* have so much trouble in obtaining income from their lands. . . ."

Confirming the opinion expressed by the Paris merchants in 1685, the Commission clearly explained that prosperity would be restored to both town and country only if the purchasing power of France's provincial population were raised.[11] The contents of this report were quickly divulged and they pro-

[11] The clearly expressed consciousness of the relation between rural poverty and general economic decline raises a point which should be made in the controversy concerning the validity of C. E. Labrousse's theory of industrial crises in the old regime. Arguing from statistics gathered from the second half of the eighteenth and the first part of the nineteenth century, Labrousse, in his *Esquisse du mouvement des prix et des revenus en France au XVIIIe siècle*, Paris, 1932, said that industrial crises in the old regime were caused by poor harvests. High prices brought about by the scarcity were profitable only for large landowners; the majority of the rural population spent all their money in order to keep alive. Little purchasing power remained for other things. David S. Landes (see his article "The Statistical Study of French Crises," *Journal of Economic History*, X, [1950], 195-211, and his more recent debate in the same journal with André Danière, XVIII, [1958], 317-344) has objected that poor harvests did not affect all small rural interests with equal severity; he thinks some modest country folk may even have been in a position to profit from high cereal prices. Moreover, argues Landes, the shift of a greater proportion of revenue from the small landowners to the richer areas of the population would affect industry adversely only if the concentration of wealth became excessive. Perhaps these points are well taken for the last part of the eighteenth century when rapidly expanding foreign trade brought immense sums of money into the countryside. It is certain that greater income made rural folk less vulnerable to years of abundance and scarcity in the eighteenth century than they had been a hundred years before. Famines were a thing of the past during most of the second half of the eighteenth century; they were frighteningly common in the seventeenth. And if many people in the earlier period lacked money to stay alive, how many more who survived felt inclined to spend their slender reserves on anything but the barest necessities? This is precisely what the Paris merchants were complaining about. Whatever may be its weaknesses for the eighteenth century, Professor Labrousse's theory is admirably applicable to the reign of Louis XIV.

vided the reform movement with solid documentary evidence for a radically new approach to problems of political economy. It is important to emphasize here, however, that the documentary foundation merely supplied factual support for theories developed from an entirely different source. This is why the first reforming literature, written in 1688, contains substantial paraphrases from both the report of 1687 and from the earlier writings of thinkers whose political, economic, and social views were an integral part of wider philosophical thought.

ii. CLAUDE FLEURY: EARLY AGRARIAN CONCEPTS

Having reviewed the general conditions which helped prepare for the emergence of a comprehensive and coherent philosophy of opposition during the decade following Colbert's death, we can now examine in more detail the factors contributing directly to the development of cardinal ideas in the reform movement. Between 1688 and 1695 the aristocracy elaborated and transformed anti-mercantilist doctrines into a fully matured political ideology. The immediate sources for their theories may be divided into two distinct categories. First, a series of ideas expounded in writings dating from approximately 1670-1675 directly influenced, sometimes almost word for word, several critical sections of texts written by aristocratic reformers slightly more than a decade later. Second, the scattered letters and official documents concerning rural poverty, especially the report submitted by the investigating commission of 1687, provided the nobility with an impressive documentary and factual basis for its point of view. These sources explain in detail how the most abstract ideas became associated with specific grievances and daily experience in such a manner as to create the impression of perfect conformity of theory with fact.

Although Fénelon, Belesbat, and Boisguilbert were the more significant spokesmen writing between 1688 and 1695, there were others who remain anonymous. In general, despite important differences, these men were united by basic concepts which can be classified as "agrarian." One premise fundamental to their otherwise frequently divergent theories was the idea that the soil is the source of all wealth and that the rate of industrial production—indeed, the index of all economic activity—varies directly with agricultural prosperity. This was of course contrary to the principles laid down by Montchrétien, Laffemas, Richelieu, La Gomberdière, Jean Eon, Foucquet, and Colbert. Nothing was more fundamental to the mercantilist tradition than the conviction that industry, which was overwhelmingly rural, alone could stimulate trade, attract money from abroad, and cause it to circulate throughout the realm, carrying prosperity from the remotest districts of the countryside to the King and back, in a circuit kept in motion by the labor of a fully employed population. The mercantilist program was above all an attempt to bring relief to depressed areas by increasing industrial production; in contrast, Fénelon, Belesbat, Boisguilbert, and other aristocratic spokesmen insisted that the constant efforts to increase industrial production, far from relieving rural distress, actually intensified misery in the countryside, reduced the purchasing power of most Frenchmen and caused a general decline in all sectors of economic life, industry included. From our perspective it is clear that mercantilists were quite as concerned with ameliorating rural conditions as were their aristocratic opponents; but the mercantilist emphasis on industrial production as the means of bringing prosperity to the provinces persuaded reformers that men like Colbert systematically favored industry *at the expense* of agriculture—a misconception which has been transmitted down to the present day even by some of the most reputable historians.[12]

Some time between 1670 and 1675 Claude Fleury, theologian, moralist, historian, man of letters, and intimate friend of Fénelon, wrote a few pages entitled *Pensées politiques*.[13] The first line states that "the goal of politics is to render a people happy": many individuals composed a people, but the factors making one person happy were no different from those applicable to the whole of society. Who was the happiest among Frenchmen? "The man for whom we are looking to serve as a kind of example of a happy people is first of all a *laboureur* living from his flock and the fruits of his land." He enjoyed "an honest liberty." Necessities were possessed in abundance; but, because they were "born of his labor," he remained satisfied and sought neither luxury nor

[12] "L'agriculture ne compta . . . que dans la mesure où elle touchait au ravitaillement et à l'industrie" ed. E. Préclin and V. Tapié, *Le XVIIᵉ siècle*, "Clio" series, Paris, 1949, p. 229. That Colbert was not always misunderstood has been attested by the Vicomte Jean Paul Alban de Villeneuve-Bargement. This nineteenth century aristocrat recognized and praised Colbert, saying that through support of industry and commerce, the Controller General hoped to promote rural prosperity, thereby stimulating agriculture. The reference, which I owe to the courtesy of my colleague, Richard Soloway, may be found in *Economie Politique Chrétienne, ou Recherche sur la nature et les causes du paupérisme, en France et en Europe, et sur les moyens de le soulager et de le prévenir*, Bruxelles, 1837, pp. 18, 121.

[13] The full text of this small essay appears in the abridged editions of Fleury's *Oeuvres*; I am here using the one edited by M. Aimée-Martin, Paris, 1837, pp. 547-549. Guy Thuillier, "Economie et administration au Grand Siècle," *La Revue Administrative*, LVIII (1957), 350, n.14, believes it was written between 1670 and 1675. No indication on this point is given by François Gaquère, *La vie et les oeuvres de Claude Fleury 1640-1723*, Paris, 1925.

the "superfluous." The *laboureur's* independence made it possible "for the country to live without the cities but not for the cities to live without the country."

Cities, Fleury wrote, were "needed for security and for sociability"; they should, however, be "small and close to one another rather than large and distant." Urban population should be determined "by the number of citizens required to cultivate the surrounding countryside, returning to town at night, along with a small number of artisans and merchants necessary to support them." Large cities were most undesirable: "The multitude of inhabitants is such that most of them do not know each other, they have no ties, no friendship; often, even those living under the same roof become suspicious [of one another] and take continual precautions. This is no longer a society." Large cities were "a confused amalgam of the best and the worst"; they were the foci of disproportionate concentrations of wealth." One oversized urban center was sufficient "to exhaust entire provinces"; it attracted all the wealth, consumed the very life-blood of the state, and caused the "rest of the body [politic] to wither away."

If large cities were pernicious because they drained the countryside of wealth necessary to maintain the whole of society, foreign conquest was equally injurious because it increased the proportion of arable soil to the number of inhabitants, dispersing their energies over expanded wastes of uncultivated territory. Political strength rested on production from the soil which in turn varied directly with the number and density of the farming population: "It is the number of men and not the expanse of territory which determines the power of the state." Foreign conquests weakened the kingdom:

It is better to command a hundred men on a fertile island of two leagues than to be alone on an island of two thousand leagues. Thus he who governs a hundred thousand men in ten leagues of country will be more powerful than he who has two hundred thousand dispersed over a hundred leagues. More there are men, more will they cultivate the soil, if it is not totally unfertile. When this is the case they strive to subsist through manufacture and trade. Holland is an example, whereas the states of the Turk, being poorly populated, do not have a force proportional to their extension.

These few pages throw light in two principal directions. First, considered in the context of his other writings, the *Pensées politiques* reveal both the internal and external factors which caused Fleury, between 1670 and 1675, to oppose the pessimistic implications of mercantilist doctrine with arguments prescinded from anti-skeptical and anti-Machiavellian thought. Second, direct paraphrases from the *Pensées politiques* appear, along with further paraphrases from the Commission's report, in an anonymous text submitted to the King in February 1688. This manuscript and several other documents, no one of which constitutes by itself a fully developed theory, collectively presented both an ideology and a program for reform. The *Pensées politiques* are in some important ways an extension of Fleury's *Réflexions sur les oeuvres de Machiavel*.[14] A devoutly religious man, Fleury struggled with the problem which the author of the *Prince* had posed so clearly for posterity: given the nature of man, how can government be at once both effective and moral? It has been shown

[14] Also a very short essay which appears in full in Aimée-Martin's edition, pp. 562-568.

how this question, intensely debated, was intimately connected with a more general controversy concerning the place of human reason in the scheme of creation. Pyrrhonians—men who, like Gabriel Naudé were most contemptuous of reason—insisted that the unrestrained exercise of power alone is capable of retaining the centrifugal forces set loose in society by intellectual pride, the ultimate source of man's depravity.[15] Fleury, strongly influenced by Plato and Descartes, opposed the Pyrrhonian contempt for reason; he also rejected Machiavelli's demand that politics be divorced from ethics. But no matter how intimate people made the relation between the character of reason and the nature of government, the two issues were never identical, and Fleury could not, therefore, directly refute Machiavelli by arguing against skeptical disparagement of reason. Instead, Fleury felt compelled to devote his most skillful discussion to prove ethics inseparable from politics.

The anti-skeptical implications of his position, however, drove Fleury toward a political view which, while not novel, was nevertheless infrequently expressed. Declaring ethical government possible because man was not fundamentally depraved, Fleury, following the logic of his position, went on to declare that the exercise of justice led humanity down the path of virtue and ultimately to the good life. Machiavelli's Prince was a godless tyrant who did not understand that the first principle of government is to improve human nature, thereby contributing to universal happiness.

> But you [Machiavelli] say that if the Prince is good he will not survive because men are bad. First, they are for the most part neither very

[15] See Chapter I, above.

bad nor very good. . . . Moreover, you, who
wish to govern, have the duty of making them
better: this is the goal of true politics. . . . Raise
your mask and confess that you do not teach
politics, but tyranny; you do not seek to render
a people happy. . . .[16]

Taken together, the arguments expressed in the
Réflexions sur les oeuvres de Machiavel and the
Pensées politiques now make clear a fundamental
trait which would characterize reformers of every
description. Since the days when Richelieu sponsored
Louis Machon's *Apologie pour Machiavel,* the doctrines of the *Prince* had not only become identified
with those of mercantilism, but by 1670 they were
the official ideology of government. The shadow of
the Sun King loomed ominously at this time on
Europe's political horizon. Meanwhile, an overwhelming majority of Frenchmen suffered intensely
from a disastrous economic crisis. Under these pressures Fleury expanded his anti-skeptical arguments
against Machiavelli to include attacks on mercantilist doctrine and foreign conquest. Mercantilism,
identified with ideas expressed in the *Prince,* came
in this way to be intimately related with disputes
over the ultimate problems concerning man's nature. And reformers, including even the earliest
critics who are as widely separated as Lartigue and
Fleury, however diverse in their opinions, all represented one side in the growing struggle between
those who saw the state primarily as an instrument
of order and those who believed government was
obligated to help man achieve the good life. Reformers of both spiritual and secular persuasion,
without exception, championed positive views of

[16] *Oeuvres*, p. 565.

government and voiced optimistic convictions about human nature. Religiously minded mercantilist critics, the group around Fénelon on one hand expanded Fleury's agrarian statements into almost physiocratic principles, while, on the other, they directed anti-skeptical discussion against Bossuet, the official spokesman who provided theological justification for absolutism. Meanwhile, secularly inspired reformers, to be described in the following chapter, transformed agrarian arguments and a number of themes expressed by earlier figures, especially by Lartigue, into an anti-Christian philosophy which, more than any other body of writings, contained the ideas and attitudes made familiar by eighteenth century *philosophes*. This, in the most general terms, is how diffuse intellectual currents, going back directly to at least the middle of the sixteenth century, converged about 1670 to 1675, under intense external pressures, to form the ideological foundations for subsequent movements of political opposition to Louis XIV.

iii. THE MEMOIR OF 1688: FÉNELON, CHRISTIAN AGRARIANISM, AND POLITICAL CONSPIRACY

On 23 February 1688 an anonymous *Mémoire sur les Finances* was submitted to the King.[17] The first lines inform His Majesty that "a wise and Christian ruler, governing according to reason alone, considers nothing but the good of his people, whom he is obliged to render happy." France, however vast her resources, was not endowed with inexhaustible wealth; "we cannot therefore raise taxes without limit." Receipts "this year, 1688, total 115 millions . . .

---

[17] There are two copies of the manuscript at the B.N., Fds. Fr. MSS 1735 and 11,149. For all practical purposes the two documents are identical.

26 millions remain in the provinces while 89 millions enter the royal treasury." By examining the "present state of France" the wisdom of these fiscal demands could be judged. Nothing of course could be learned from "the splendor of Paris or Versailles"; the most reliable information could be obtained from "a true inspection of the countryside and from [consulting] the reports of the Commissioners who were despatched to the provinces by the King in 1687.[18]

> Everywhere we see houses in ruin, abandoned hovels in villages and closed shops in towns, virtually no new buildings anywhere. . . . There are no games or diversions. The number of cabarets have diminished. Manufactures decrease every day; in several towns they have ceased entirely, the workers reduced to mendicity. Fewer students are in schools because of the lack of means to support them. There is even a shortage of priests in most of the dioceses. And the difficulty of marrying has created several unworthy ecclesiastics . . . who dishonor the Church. Dowries in small towns are no longer given in money, but in land or sharecrops. . . .
>
> Almost no rich *laboureurs* may be found; indeed, few peasants remain who own land . . . they [the *laboureurs*] can no longer furnish horses and livestock . . . nor anything necessary for exploitation of large farms. . . . Landlords must furnish everything: feeding the peasant, paying his *taille*, accepting in exchange part of the harvest. The peasant leaves share-cropping as poor as when he started. Badly cultivated farms bring in less profit; the buildings fall in ruin. Most of the land in France appears on the auc-

[18] B.N., Fds. fr. MS 11149, pp. 1-13.

tion block. . . . Wool-bearing animals have fallen sharply in price, often the beasts are returned from market for want of a buyer. . . . The poor frequently have no bread, not even the blackest; lately they have been compelled to live off roots or gleanings. Most of them no longer possess even some furniture on which [the tax collector] may levy executions. They sleep on straw in the clothes on their back, frequently half-naked. Haggard, thin and languishing, having neither provisions to live nor anything in reserve, all are driven to beggary. . . . Is this the flourishing state of the realm about which we hear so often?[18a]

Depopulation, found by the commissioners "to be considerable," caused disastrous consequences. A marriage, for example, produced normally two or three children; "extreme misery . . . , however, causes fewer children to be born and brings about the death of many more." Were rural life "a little easier and marriage more practicable each [family] would follow natural inclination, the number of men would grow every day and they would cultivate the earth with all possible care." Returning pros-

[18a] *Ibid.*, pp. 13-17. An anonymous work published in 1687 (*Histoire de la décadence de la France*) contains the following lines:

Les paisans n'y mangent de la viande que . . . trois ou quatre fois l'an. Le reste du temps ils n'ont que du pain noir, et quelques légumes. . . . Cependant ce n'est pas faute de prendre de la peine, ils travaillent depuis le matin jusques au soir, mais les besoins de l'Etat sont si grands, qu'il faut que chacun donne une partie de sa substance pour y subvenir.

Voila l'image fidele du bonheur de la France; et je laisse à juger apres cela, si l'on doit etre plus attaché à son Prince, qu'à sa femme et à ses enfans (pp. 221, 236).

In the *Siècle de Louis XIV*, 2 vols., Paris, 1878, I, 295, speaking of foreign policy in 1688, Voltaire exclaimed: "Voilà . . . le roi . . . au comble de sa grandeur. . . ."

perity would even attract foreigners to reside in France, leading them "to seek the domination they now fear so much." Finally, in a direct paraphrase from Fleury, the writer explained how France's strength would increase in proportion to the growth of her population:

> The power of the state consists in the number of inhabitants and not in the expanse of territory. The greater the size of a state the more there are frontiers to guard, and further is the distance from the center to the extremities. One hundred thousand men in ten leagues of country are more powerful than two hundred thousand in fifty leagues. It would be a much more splendid conquest to repopulate a town in the middle of the Kingdom such as Meaux or Estampes . . . than to take a town on the frontier where the inhabitants will not cherish France in their hearts for a long time and who can be kept subject only at great cost. . . . One has but to see the difference between Spain and Holland and also the extreme feebleness of the Turks.[19]

The wealth of states was created when "little people profit sufficiently from their labor to accumulate a surplus. The poor who cultivated, who worked in manufactures, who engaged in retail trade" provided the source of treasure and power. Such activities were impossible unless men had "hope for profit," without which they would despair and "sink into idleness and mendicity." It would not "take much to ruin a peasant but also very little is required to enrich him." If ten écus remained at the end of a year he could buy a cow "then two and later a pair of oxen or horses according to the nature of the soil"; before

19 *Ibid.*, pp. 19-21.

long he would become a big farmer. "His children will grow, help with the work and increase his wealth. They in turn will marry and create other families who will grow in proportion." Moreover, the farmer would be aided by the industrial worker. If a weaver with modest savings were to build a small trade and hire one or two helpers, he would purchase the farmer's hemp, cloth, grain, and wine. Agricultural prosperity would "flow from the country into the towns."

If the *taille* or other imposts, however, deprived the farmer or artisan of a modest annual profit, he would "remain always poor." Vulnerable to the first misfortune, "a hailstorm, a frost, a flood or the death of livestock,"[20] his meager resources would diminish continually. Lands would be poorly cultivated. "Commerce will languish and the provinces will deteriorate to the point where we now see them." It could be countered that the King did not store up monies collected in revenue; he spent them as rapidly as they were received, causing treasure to flow through the realm in "a perpetual circulation." The anonymous author said this mercantilist axiom was a specious objection: "To know the truth let us examine how money enters and leaves the provinces." Taxes were not the only cause of rural impoverishment. What of the great seigneurs, the *abbés commendataires*, and other officeholders "who live for the most part in Paris": they along with judicial and financial officers residing in this enormous city drew revenue from estates situated in all parts of the realm.

[20] "Il n'aura plus de quoy résister aux accidents ordinaires d'une gresle, d'une gelée, d'une inondation, d'une mortalité de bestiaux, de l'insolvabilité d'un débiteur" (p. 25). The passage from the report of 1687 is as follows: "Une maladie, une gresle et mille autres accidents qui arrivent à ces pauvres gens les mettent à l'aumone." Paraphrases of this type are most frequent.

Private rural income pouring into Paris was one factor to consider, while another was the enormous sums spent for troops and fortifications guarding France's vast frontiers. Part of this money went into other countries, some of it returned very slowly to Paris by means of the passage of soldiers who "frequently carry off more than they leave." In short, both individuals and the state drained the provinces of money; the former squandered it amidst the luxurious splendor of Paris and the Court, while the latter dispersed the earnings of its subjects in recently conquered provinces or desolate frontier regions. The insatiable maw of Paris and the false glory of war consumed the life-blood of France; this was why "income from land diminishes day by day and grain has reached the lowest price in the memory of man."[21]

Urban concentration and the luxury trade were related evils, and their injurious effect on the whole of French society was incalculable. Incomes enjoyed by private individuals residing in Paris or at Versailles was of little benefit to public finance or to trade because they were spent largely on luxury items. The city literally sparkled with expensively ornamented carriages, inlaid furniture, clothes made with silver and gold lace, magnificent plate, and any number of useless gewgaws which should be melted down and put into circulation.[22] Luxury was ultimately responsible for "the misery of the people." It had "ruined an infinity of individuals who spend more than they earn." The prodigality of the great

[21] If the document were not dated, this phrase alone would make one think irresistibly of the disastrous abundance in the harvest year 1687-1688.

[22] In December 1689 Louis XIV, wishing to set an example, sent his gold and silver table service to the mint to be melted down and coined.

had been emulated by the robe and even by the petty bourgeois. Life had reached the point where "you no longer plan your expenses according to what you have but according to what others do." People consumed five years of income in two or three months. They then lived at the expense of their fellows: borrowed without repaying, gambled, and committed "a thousand other bad artifices." Such virtues as honesty and integrity had long been held in contempt.

Evil consequences flowing from luxury were not confined merely to gentlemen and bourgeoisie. Merchants and artisans who supplied them had to extend credit, "often losing everything." Frequently a creditor would borrow in anticipation of payment from a debtor; there developed "a veritable chain of debts, creating a situation where one bankruptcy causes several others." Indeed, the largest part of "wealth in Paris exists only in people's imaginations." True, considerable money did pass from hand to hand, but this circulation was not so useful as it would be in the country. The ease of earning money attracted "a prodigious multitude from all parts of the realm, and this is one cause for desolation in the provinces." Moreover, high prices in Paris also contributed toward disproportionate concentration of wealth in that city. An income sufficient to make a peasant rich would barely enable an artisan to subsist. Also, people working in luxury industries wished "to imitate those whom they serve." Thus an income necessary to satisfy one goldsmith would make wealthy the *laboureurs* of an entire province. Yet even in Paris the luxury trade was established on a fragile base because consumption of luxury goods was determined by fashion. A caprice could put the wigmakers out of work overnight, to say nothing of the ribbonmakers, furriers, hatters, etc. The farmer's work was "useful for himself and for others, and things which are useful multiply naturally." In contrast, artisans employed in luxury trade manufactured "sterile" products. If the great "number of valets, chair-porters, artisans of every sort with whom Paris is filled, lived in the country or were able to return," they would bring both wealth and labor to France's uncultivated fields. Unless some overriding duty kept them in Paris, measures should be taken to make both great and small reside in the country.

In addition, it was especially urgent that the King reduce both taxes and unnecessary expenditures. At the same time the crown should, as far as possible, undertake public works in the provinces such as roads and hospitals, particularly in winter so that "the little people may live." Commerce and industry "should be favored by letting them follow their natural course without restraint."[23] Ministers should be careful lest "excessive precautions" to prevent money from leaving the realm would "infuriate foreigners and ruin trade; we recently have had some unfortunate experiences in this regard." Also, the King should not resort to the immoral practices suggested to him by financiers. The creation and sale of offices, their suppression and resale, alienations of public domains, forced loans and "all other devices invented over the past one hundred and sixty years" should be abolished. Whatever immediate advantage these measures might have, they served only to destroy His Majesty's credit in the long run. Also, the author explained that apart from being economically injurious, dishonest financial practices violated the moral law binding on all rulers:

I leave aside reasons of conscience and the ter-

[23] B.N., Fds. fr., MS 11149, p. 43.

rible judgment to which Princes are brought before God when by negligence, love of pleasure
or to satisfy false glory they have put themselves
in the necessity of having to contract such debts;
because whatever color you may wish to put on
them, no other law of contracts is applicable to
sovereigns than that governing the dealings of
their subjects. . . .

We leave to the piety of the King to examine
seriously before God, to Whom he will one day
render account, the expenses absolutely necessary for the conservation of the State, and without which the Crown will be in peril. . . . Those
who judge only from the outside find it difficult
to believe, however, that the state of the Kingdom has so changed during the past fifty years
that we must spend in peacetime three times
more than was required at the height of the [last]
war. If there are expenses for which the utility
to the State is not commensurate with the sacrifices they impose on the people, how will they
be justified in the presence of Him Who judges
all sovereigns?

Finally, the author warned Louis XIV that a more
immediate danger faced the crown should he persist
in his perverse and misguided policies:

It is most important that the nobility be protected from ruin. Poverty strikes down courage
which is the soul of the aristocracy; or if it [cour-
age] remains, it turns in fury and desperation
ready to explode the moment authority is less
firm. A ruined nobility is capable of risking any
enterprise where it either will perish or flourish
once again. Such was the fate of Julius Caesar

and of those who helped him upset the Roman Republic.[24]

This memoir submitted to the King, which elaborated agrarian anti-mercantilist arguments earlier outlined by Fleury, on the documentary bases provided by the report of 1687, expressed the views of men who, penetrating into intimate and powerful circles at the Court and within the administration, were at the head of a conspiracy to reform government in France. The leaders were François de Salignac de la Mothe-Fénelon, appointed preceptor to the children of France in 1689, the Duke of Beauvillier, member of the all-powerful *Conseil d'en Haut* and Director of the Council of Finance, and the Duke of Chevreuse, later trusted adviser to Louis XIV. These men, profoundly hostile to the crown's policies and fundamentally opposed to mercantilist theory were at first allied with individuals who, while holding opposite views on principles of political economy, were united by family ties and by a common hostility to a government dominated by the Le Tellier family. On 18 March 1686 Colbert's son, Seignelay, Minister of the Navy, wrote his exiled cousin, Desmaretz: "We are all assembled, Monsieur, and we believe that you must come to Dampierre as soon as you receive this message."[25] Dampierre was the residence of the Duke of Chevreuse who, like the Duke of Beauvillier, married one of Colbert's daughters. After this date Desmaretz played an important part in an early and concerted attempt to influence directly the formulation of government policy. Beauvillier had been appointed head of the Council of

[24] *Ibid.*, pp. 27, 46-47, 50-51, 54-55.
[25] Saint-Simon, *Mémoires*, ed., A. de Boislisle, 41 vols., Paris, 1879-1928, VII, 562.

Finance in 1685; and at the end of March 1686, Desmaretz, now in Paris, wrote:

> Monsieur the Duke of Beauvillier who has had me work on all matters concerning finance, received my memoirs with satisfaction. Other people have told me that he has spoken [about them] to the King, and even in Council in presence of His Majesty.[26]

Desmaretz' memoir on finance was the first of a series of important documents, dating from 1686 to November 1693, sent to Colbert de Croissy, the deceased minister's brother and Secretary of State for Foreign Affairs.[27] Some of these papers were copied by a clerk and one or two remain unidentified; the most important manuscripts, however, were written either by Desmaretz himself or composed under his personal direction. One of these writings is an abbreviated version of the memoir submitted to the King on 23 February 1688. It reveals that in the very earliest stages, the reform movement was in part an expression of family-faction rivalries at Court. At least three-fourths of this manuscript, the title written in Desmaretz' hand and the text copied by a clerk, is a direct paraphrase of the memoir addressed to Louis XIV in February 1688, which, discussed above, contained paraphrases from Fleury and from the report of 1687; there is, nevertheless, an important difference between the two documents.[28] The passages

26 *Ibid.*, p. 524.

27 Archives Aff. Et., mém. et doc., France, 991 (papiers Colbert de Croissy). The documents are enumerated and briefly described by Boislisle, *ibid.*, pp. 564-565.

28 A. de Boislisle, who published Desmaretz' memoir (*ibid.*, VII, 566-571), wrote: "J'ai dit que ce morceau si intéressant pouvait etre de l'année 1687; j'ajouterai maintenant qu'une rédaction plus étendue en fut, selon toute vraisemblance, mise sous les yeux du Roi au com-

omitted by Desmaretz and the manner in which others are paraphrased make his arguments resemble less those of a disinterested reformer than of a potential Controller General seeking above all to oust a rival and discredit the regime. Desmaretz makes no mention of how Kings are accountable before God, nor does he speak of "unfortunate experiences" connected with protective tariffs and failure to allow trade to take its "natural course." And most important, Desmaretz says nothing about the possible uprising of a ruined and desperate nobility. Instead, Colbert's nephew concentrated exclusively on purely agrarian themes, holding the administration responsible for both rural poverty and general economic decline. The memoir of 23 February 1688 placed responsibility for economic distress squarely on Louis XIV's foreign and domestic policies; in contrast, Desmaretz argued that the Sun King was being served by incompetent ministers.

Far from opposing mercantilist doctrine, Desmaretz held steadfastly to traditional principles of political economy. (Two decades later, however, when the ideas expounded by reformers had gained immense headway, Desmaretz, then Controller General, reversed his position, announcing his approval of unrestricted international trade.)[29] In a brief paper

---

mencement de l'année suivante, que nous en possédons encore le manuscrit original, daté du 23 février 1688" (citing B.N., Fds. fr. MS 1735). Recognizing the similarities in the two documents, Boislisle overlooked the very significant passages which *do not* appear in Desmaretz' version of the memoir.

[29] In 1712 Desmaretz wrote Nicolas Mesnager, special envoy in England and formerly the first deputy from Rouen to the Council of Commerce in 1700, the following letter:

Je vous avoue que je ne crois pas qu'il y ait à craindre des suites préjudiciables au commerce de la France en donnant à toutes les nations une égalité réciproque. Mon opinion est que, plus on donnera de facilité aux étrangers de nous communiquer

about the causes for the scarcity of money, written in the autumn of 1693, Desmaretz exclaimed that those who export precious metals commit a crime meriting *le dernier supplice*;[30] foreigners had increased their cash reserves by amounts corresponding directly with the rate of decrease in France's stock of precious metals.[31] Elsewhere Desmaretz said that "trade is not a simple exchange of merchandise, the

leurs marchandises et les productions de leur pays, plus on facilitera le débit des notres. L'uniformité et la liberté en fait de commerce font toujours la richesse du pays ou elles sont établies (quoted from the papers of the Controller General, E. Lavisse, "La fin du règne, 1685-1715," *Histoire de France*, Paris, 1911, VIII, 218).

Another administrator who was intensely mercantilist, and about whom much is said in Chapter VII below, Jean Pottier de la Hestroye, also had a change of heart at about the same time as Desmaretz. Indeed, Pottier even admits the error of his previous position:

Le sieur de la Hestroy raporte les raisons qui l'ont porté à revoir les Mémoires qu'il avoit faits immédiatement après la Paix signé à Riswick pour le restablissement du commerce de france, d'y changer et d'y augmenter quelque chose.

Il avoue qu'il s'estoit trompé, qu'il avoit proposé mal apropos d'éloigner les holandois de france, ayant reconnu depuis qu'ils ne luy doivent pas etre tout a fait inutiles, par raport au débit de ses denrées, manufactures et marchandises superflues, qu'elle a intérest de débiter aux estrangers. (Bibliothèque de l'Arsenal, MS 4069, avertissement.)

Elsewhere, in the second part of his *Réflexions sur le traité de la Dixme de M. Le Maréchal de Vauban*, Paris, 1716, pp. 76-77, Pottier wrote passages about the "liberty of trade" which would not have been out of place in the several anti-mercantilist writings discussed in the remainder of this work. The fact that even high-ranking administrators admitted that the principles to which the government had held firm for over a half-century were mistaken would seem to indicate that the death of the Sun King in 1715 symbolized the ideological as well as the financial bankruptcy of the *ancien régime*. The causes for this collapse are made abundantly clear in the following pages.

[30] Aff. Et., mém. et doc., France, 991, ff. 207-208.
[31] *Ibid.*, f. 208.

difference must be paid in money."[32] Similarly, the person whom Croissy had summarize the several memoirs written by Desmaretz explained that domestic trade, "while necessary and good produces nevertheless no increase or decrease [in wealth] for the state as a whole":[33] foreign trade, export, would alone enrich France. But this view did not prevent the writer from supporting Desmaretz' agrarian arguments.

In this way agrarianism, family ties, and a common hostility to the Le Telliers caused Beauvillier and Chevreuse at first to join with men who did not fundamentally oppose established principles of political economy. But the alliance did not long endure. Fénelon rapidly made the two dukes aware of the full anti-Machiavellian and anti-mercantilist implications of agrarian theory. These three men led a powerful conspiracy, an intrigue at Court, aimed ultimately at transforming government from a repressive symbol of order to a positive force for the good life. The initiative at first appears to have been taken by Fénelon in January 1689. He was then a religious director to Madame de Maintenon. One passage in a long letter about her spiritual life reveals Fénelon's political preoccupations: he was intent on increasing the influence of his friends at Court in order to be able to reach the Monarch more directly:

The King behaves . . . according to impressions

32 "Mémoire de M. Desmaretz sur l'état présent des affaires," *Correspondance des Contrôleurs-Généraux des finances avec les intendants des provinces 1683-1715*, ed. A. de Boislisle, 3 vols., Paris, 1874-1897, I, 545.

33 "On entend par le commerce celuy qui consiste à envoyer des denrées ou des manufactures dans les pays estrangers, car celuy qui se fait d'une province à une autre au dedans du royaume, quoy que bon et nécessaire ne produit néanmoins aucune augmentation ni diminution par rapport au général de l'Estat" (Aff. Et., mém. et doc., France, 991, ff. 224-225).

he receives from people who surround him and from those in whom he confides his authority. It is of capital importance that you lose no opportunity to surround him with reliable people who will act in concert with you to have him [the King] perform his duties, the true extent of which he has no idea.

. . . When you can increase the credit of Messieurs de Chevreuse and de Beauvillier you will have struck a great blow. It is for you to determine when the moment is opportune.[34]

Madame de Maintenon lost no time. Beauvillier was appointed Governor to the children of France in August; he immediately named Fénelon as preceptor. Fénelon in turn called on his intimate friend Claude Fleury to assist him in the task of educating the royal children, especially the Duke of Burgundy who appeared likely to become the next King. The cabal's rising influence during these years (1688-1691) may be measured by the declining fortunes of the Le Tellier family. The Chancellor had died in 1685. In 1688 Madame de Maintenon exclaimed that her presence "seemed to irritate" Louvois,[35] Le Tellier's son, who was Minister of War and at the same time controlled industry and internal economic affairs. On 4 October 1689, Seignelay entered the *Conseil d'en Haut*. Two years later Louvois was on the verge of disgrace; his fortuitous death in 1691 saved him from humiliation. Meanwhile, Controller General Le Pelletier, who owed his position to the Le Tellier family, thought it wise to resign in 1689. Finally, in 1691, when Louvois had disappeared from the scene, Beauvillier entered the all-powerful *Conseil*

---

[34] Madame de Maintenon, *Lettres*, ed. M. Langlois, 5 vols., Paris, 1935-1939, III, 302.

[35] Quoted by Lavisse, *Histoire de France*, VIII, Part I, 150.

d'en Haut; and it was no accident that Louvois's old enemy, Arnauld de Pomponne, accompanied the Duke into the Council as a new member.

When Beauvillier named Fénelon preceptor in August 1689, France had recently entered into the War of the League of Augsburg. Already suffering from farm surpluses and depression, France now found her Atlantic trade, which had received a tremendous impetus under Colbert, reaching a peak in 1688,[36] seriously interrupted by hostilities.[37] For a while there was hope that naval supremacy would protect the new commerce;[38] but after the French defeat of La Hogue in June 1692, the government made an important change in naval strategy. Pontchartrain, the new Controller General and also Min-

---

[36] The growth of the Atlantic trade under Colbert is the subject of an excellent study by S. L. Mims, *Colbert's West India Policy*, New Haven, Conn., 1912. The subject is also discussed in Henri Sée, *Histoire économique de la France*, 2 vols., Paris, 1939-1942, I. More recently the archivist of Charente Maritime, M. Delafosse, "La Rochelle et les Isles au XVIIᵉ siècle," *Revue d'histoire des colonies*, XXXVI, 1949, 238-281, has shown that the port's Atlantic commerce increased from four annual departures for the West Indies in the period 1642-1648 to forty-five in the period 1678-1686.

[37] Statistical studies in individual ports support this view. Professor Jean Delumeau, "Le commerce Malouin à la fin du XVIIᵉ siècle," *Annales de Bretagne*, LVI (1959), 263-286, demonstrates that war had a disastrous effect on the port of Saint-Malo, especially for ocean commerce and far-flung fishing expeditions. Delafosse, "La Rochelle," obtained similar results in his study. Georges Scelle, *La traite négrière aux Indes de Castille*, 2 vols., Paris, 1906, II, 191, says that war severed the French West Indies from their normal sources of slave labor. Unfortunately, however, material on the Nine Years War is sketchy in comparison with the thorough studies done on the War of Spanish Succession by J. S. Bromley, "The French Privateering War, 1702-1713," *Historical Essays 1600-1750 Presented to David Ogg*, London, 1963, pp. 203-231; and "Le Commerce de la France de l'Ouest et la Guerre Maritime (1702-1712)," *Annales du Midi*, LXV (1953), 4-66. Until such work is published, knowledge about the precise extent to which privateering interfered with seaborne trade will remain speculative.

[38] This point is discussed in Chapter VII, section i, below.

ister of the Marine, argued that continued mainte-
nance of the magnificent fleet built up by Colbert
and his recently deceased son, Seignelay, was too
heavy a financial burden, especially in light of the
great losses just sustained at La Hogue. Instead of
fighting the maritime powers with ships of the line,
hordes of privateers should be sent to prey upon enemy commerce. Receipt by the crown of a commission on each prize, moreover, would transform naval
operations into a source of revenue rather than an intolerable expense.[39] Whatever the merits of Pontchartrain's argument, one consequence of this policy became immediately clear: unrestricted warfare against
English and Dutch merchantmen further reduced
France's international trade. Only nine months after
the disaster at La Hogue, Pontchartrain received the
following letter from the intendant at Bordeaux:

> Only two foreign vessels have sailed from this
> port, and even they were loaded only with
> wine . . . for Rochefort. Nothing has been
> charged for export, whereas during the same sea-
> son in 1692, twenty-two foreign ships had sailed
> and sixty-nine remained in port. The harvest,
> as mediocre as it was, cannot be sold; it will be
> lost unless a foreign fleet arrives.[40]

The unprecedentedly intense campaign against
Anglo-Dutch trade had put Colbert's ideal of national self-sufficiency to the test. This decision to

[39] "M. de Pontchartrain ne sentant pas la Marine de France assez
forte surtout depuis l'affaire de la hogue pour tenir tete à celle des
Ennemis, essaya de mettre la course en honneur. Il mit des officiers
du Roy de distinction . . . à la tete de quelques armemens particuliers, y fit prendre intéret au Roy qui entroit en part de la perte
et du profit des Armateurs" (B.N., Fds. fr., n.a., 21261, ff. cclxv-
cclxvi).

[40] Boislisle, Corr. des con. gén., I, 312.

launch privateers on a grand scale was identified with the mercantilist assertion that France, while providing the rest of Europe with sustenance, was independent from all other powers.[41] The action was badly timed, however, for in the very next year, 1693, the realm was gripped by a great famine. The kingdom grew desperately in need of imports from abroad, and ministers were obliged to issue large numbers of passports permitting trade with the enemy in exchange for wheat and other cereals.[42] On 16 June Beauvillier, now both Director of the Council of Finance and member of the *Conseil d'en Haut*, told Louis XIV that "rehabilitation so essential to the interior of the Kingdom" placed France before the "absolute necessity of making peace"; and he accompanied his admonitions with a detailed program for negotiating with the allied powers.[43] Two months later Madame de Maintenon, exclaiming, "I would give everything for peace," assured her correspondent that "the King . . . wants it as ardently as we."[44] She

[41] See Chapter VII, section i, below, especially pp. 385-391.

[42] The extent to which this is true can be gathered from the Archives of the Marine, deposited at the National Archives, series B². Volumes 88 through 97 are filled with letters concerning the extraordinary issue of passports permitting trade which would ordinarily be prohibited in exchange for the import of foreign grain. The *Mercure historique*, La Haye, February 1694, p. 155, contains the following observations: "On a tiré des pays étrangers tout autant de grains qu'il a été possible. Il en arriva encore à Dunkerque trente vaisseaux le mois passé, qui venoient de Danemarc et de Suede."

[43] "Mémoire . . . au roi pour recommander un moyen de conclure la paix," in Georges Lizerand, *Le duc de Beauvillier, 1648-1714*, Paris, 1933, App. III, 583, n.1.

[44] A. Geffroy, *Madame de Maintenon d'après sa correspondance authentique*, 2 vols., Paris, 1887, I, 242. The agitation for peace at this time was strong. In October 1692 Mme de Maintenon exhorted prayers for peace (*ibid.*, I, 229). The *Mercure historique* for April 1694 states: "Bien qu'on soit sévere à punir en France tous ceux qui ont la hardiesse de parler ou d'écrire contre le Gouvernement, il

was probably correct. Louis XIV rapidly entered into serious peace negotiations, and the character and extent of the concessions which France was willing to make speak much for Beauvillier's influence.[45] But conferences lagged and the war continued. Fénelon found the situation intolerable. In an anonymous, famous, and impassioned letter, addressed to the King but meant as a severe reproach to Beauvillier and to Madame de Maintenon for not bringing sufficient pressure to bear upon their sovereign, Fénelon explained why peace was not obtainable:

> Sire . . . for the past thirty years your . . . ministers have violated and overturned all the ancient maxims of state in order to raise your power, which was theirs because it was in their hands, to the highest possible point. We no longer heard of the State nor of its rules; they only spoke of the King and his pleasure. They have increased your revenues and your expenditures to the infinite. They have elevated you to the heavens . . . and impoverished all of France so as to introduce and maintain an incurable and monstrous luxury at Court. They wanted to raise you on the ruins of all classes in the State, as if you could become great by oppressing your

---

est néanmoins impossible de se taire dans l'état ou sont les choses. La misere générale arrache quelquefois des plaintes de la bouche ou de la plume des personnes les plus patientes et les plus soumises. On voit courir à Paris de tems en tems quelques écrits, tantot sur la cherté des bleds, tantot sur la rareté de l'argent, tantot sur les arrérages des payments, tantot sur les nécessitez de la paix, ou sur d'autres sujets de cette nature" (pp. 397-399). In June of the same year the *Mercure* declared: "La principale [chose] est la paix, que tout le peuple non seulement de Paris, mais de tout le Royaume souhaite avec le dernier empressement, parcequ'il ne s'en peut plus passer" (p. 293).

[45] This point is brought out in some detail by Lizerand, *Le Duc de Beauvillier*, pp. 170-176.

subjects on whom your Grandeur is founded. . . .
They have known no other rule, neither for
administering the interior of the realm nor for
negotiating abroad, than to threaten, to crush
and to destroy all who resist them. . . . They have
rendered your name odious, and have made the
entire French nation intolerable to our neighbors. We have conserved no ally because we
wanted only slaves. For the past twenty years
we have caused bloody wars. For example, Sire,
we undertook a war against the Dutch in 1672.
*I cite this war in particular because it is the
source of all the others.* . . . It is true, Sire, that
subsequent peace treaties seemed to have re-
paired this injustice . . . , but treaties signed by
the vanquished are not signed freely . . . they sign
with the knife at their throat. . . .

Meanwhile your people, whom you ought to
love as your children . . . are dying of hunger.
Cultivation of the land is virtually abandoned,
the towns and the countryside are becoming
depopulated; the crafts are languishing and no
longer nourish their workers. All trade is
crushed. You have destroyed half the true
strength . . . of your state in order to defend
vain conquests abroad. Instead of exacting
money from this poor people you should be
charitable and feed them. France is nothing but
a vast hospital, desolate and without provisions. . . .

The people . . . who so loved you . . . have lost
their . . . confidence in you, even their respect. . . . Sedition is spreading slowly everywhere. . . . Paris . . . is not even exempt. Magistrates are obliged to tolerate the insolence of
agitators and cause money to flow secretly in

order to appease them; thus we pay those whom we ought to punish. You are reduced to the shameful and deplorable extremity of either allowing sedition to grow and spread unpunished or to massacre inhumanely the people whom you have driven to desperation by exacting from them, for your wars, the bread which they have endeavored to earn with the sweat from their brows.[46]

Thoroughly aroused, Fénelon did not remain content with a single letter; but Louis XIV, now old and difficult, was no longer the principal object of his attention. Instead, the Archbishop and his friends, Beauvillier and Fleury, all responsible for the Duke of Burgundy's education, concentrated their efforts on the boy who might one day become King of France. Fénelon's instructions on the fundamental principles of government and trade at first took the pleasant form of a novel wherein were recounted the mythical adventures of young Prince Télémaque,[47] who, before becoming King, traveled through the

[46] The letter is published in full by Charles Urbain, *Ecrits et lettres politiques de Fénelon*, Paris, 1920, pp. 143-157. The fact that Fénelon did not see the inside of the Bastille suggests that Louis XIV never actually received it. The lines criticizing Beauvillier and Mme de Maintenon are as follows: "On avait espéré, Sire, que votre conseil vous tirerait de ce chemin si égaré; mais votre conseil n'a ni force ni vigueur pour le bien. Du moins Mme de M. . . . et M. de B. . . . devaient-ils se servir de votre confiance en eux pour vous détromper; mais leur faiblesse et leur timidité les déshonorent et scandalisent tout le monde." Since the King was most probably not the true addressee, it appears reasonable to conclude that the missive was in fact meant for Beauvillier and Mme de Maintenon. Moreover, as we shall see below, the letter was in Mme de Maintenon's possession in 1695.

[47] Composed sometime between the last months of 1694 and the last months of 1696, *Télémaque* was not published until April 1699 (see introduction by A. Cahen, *Télémaque*, 2 vols., Paris, 1927).

lands of antiquity. He was curious and asked many questions; for example, how did the Phoenicians become masters of the world's commerce? Mentor, a wise man, answered:

> Become loved by all foreigners. Above all never do anything to interfere with trade in order to turn it to your views. The Prince must not concern himself [with commerce] for fear of hindering it. He must leave all profits to his subjects who earned them, otherwise they will become discouraged: the King will draw sufficient wealth from treasures entering the realm. Trade is like certain springs: if you turn them from their course they will dry up. Profit and convenience can alone attract foreigners to your shores; if you make trade difficult and less useful for them they will gradually withdraw and not return, because other people, profiting from your imprudence, have attracted them to their lands and have accustomed them to getting along without you.[48]

In the distant capital of Salente, home of King Idomenius, "the liberty of commerce was entire." Every-

[48] *Télémaque,* vol. I, Bk. III, 121-122. Significantly enough this passage is almost immediately preceded (77 previous lines) by a eulogy of Amsterdam, thinly disguised as a description of the ancient town of Tyre: "Cette grande ville [Tyre] semble nager au-dessus des eaux et être reine de toute la mer. Les marchands y abordent de toutes les parties du monde, et ses habitants sont eux-mêmes les plus fameux marchands qu'il y ait dans l'univers. Quand on entre dans cette ville, on croit d'abord que ce n'est point une ville qui appartienne à un peuple particulier, mais qu'elle est la ville commune de tous les peuples et le centre de leur commerce. . . . Dans ce port on voit comme une forêt de mâts de navires, et ces navires sont si nombreux qu'à peine peut-on découvrir la mer qui les porte. Tous les citoyens s'appliquent au commerce, et leurs grandes richesses ne les dégoutent jamais du travail nécessaire pour les augmenter."

thing entered and left with complete freedom; trade "was similar to the ebb and flow of the tide."[49]

[49] *Ibid.*, vol. II, Bk. X, pp. 88-89. Luxury items are the one restriction on the ideal of total free trade. Fénelon uses the term "liberty of commerce" to mean both the absence of state interference in international trade and freedom for the merchant to manage his affairs free from government control. Both concepts are made clear by Narbal, admiral of the Tyrian fleet, who complains how his state has fallen under the rule of the tyrant, Pygmalion:

> Au lieu d'ouvrir, suivant notre ancienne coutume, ses ports à toutes les nations les plus éloignées dans une entière liberté, il veut savoir le nombre des vaisseaux qui arrivent, leur pays, les noms des hommes qui y sont, leur genre de commerce, le prix de leurs marchandises, et le temps qu'ils doivent demeurer ici. Il fait encore pis; car il use de supercherie pour surprendre les marchands et pour confisquer leurs marchandises. Il inquiète les marchands qu'il croit les plus opulents; il établit, sous divers prétextes, de nouveaux impots. *Il veut entrer lui-même dans le commerce, et tout le monde craint d'avoir quelque affaire avec lui.* Ainsi, le commerce languit; les estrangers oublient peu à peu le chemin de Tyre, qui leur était autrefois si doux: et, si Pygmalion ne change de conduite, notre gloire et notre puissance seront bientot transportées à quelque autre peuple mieux gouverné que nous (Vol. I, Bk. III, pp. 123-124, italics added).

The similarity of this passage with a few lines Fénelon wrote a decade previously in 1686, when he was on a mission in La Rochelle, is positively striking:

> J'entans dire de tous les costez que les commis des fermiers du Roi genent trop le commerce. Chaque intéressé qui passe ici fait pour sa compagnie de nouvelles regles. Les marchands ne savent tous les jours a quoi s'en tenir, souvent on leur tend des pieges, et puis une confiscation les met au désespoir (B.N., Fds. fr., n.a., MS 507, f. 47).

Fénelon returned frequently to this theme. In his "Examen de conscience sur les devoir de la Royauté, composé pour l'instruction de Louis de France, duc de Bourgogne," in *Ecrits et lettres politiques*, ed. Urbain, pp. 29-79, Fénelon writes:

> N'avez-vous point accordé aux traitants, pour hausser leurs fermes, des édits ou déclarations, ou arrêts, avec des termes ambigus, pour étendre vos droits aux dépens du commerce, et même pour tendre des pièges aux marchands et pour confisquer leur marchandises, ou du moins les fatiguer et les gêner dans

Fénelon's anti-mercantilist opinions were an integral part of a general philosophy, much more elaborate than Fleury's loosely associated ideas. Relating religious optimism with political opposition, in a manner recalling the entire *dévot* tradition, Fénelon brought about a thorough integration of anti-skeptical argument with agrarian attacks on mercantilist doctrine. Internally, the Archbishop joined mystical emotion to logic; externally he sought to transform society and government in the image of philosophical principles. Like Malebranche, Fénelon believed ideas were nothing less than the presence of God in the minds of men. All knowledge, in his view, was therefore knowledge of God, and salvation synonymous with omniscience. Omniscience, however, was intelligible only in mystical (as distinguished from rational) terms. Ideas could be either the object of reason or of contemplation; and the contemplator directed his attention exclusively to the divine character of thought. Disciplined and sustained mental effort permitted the mystic to think of the divine, conceived to be actually within him, in such a manner as to experience a sense of participation. Losing its discursive and conceptual character, thought would become pure abstraction: God is both the object and the cause of all mental activity. Union with the divine is achieved; and the mystic comprehends the finite through and by virtue of his absorption into the infinite. He knows all, yet he reasons not. The universe itself participates in the spirituality of man. The phenomenological world, existing for the use of man, is animated with the spirit of the Creator. Original sin, however, has affected us in such a way

---

leur commerce, afin qu'ils se rachètent par quelque somme. C'est faire tort et aux marchands et au public, dont on anéanti peu à peu par là tout le négoce (art. XXII, p. 52).

that passion clouds our understanding to the point
where we are unable to see the Lord's immediate
presence at almost every step.

> Oh my God! If so many men do not discover
> Thee in this great spectacle Thou givest them
> of all nature, it is not because Thou art far from
> any of us. Every one of us feels Thee, as it were,
> with his hand; but the senses, and the passions
> they raise, take up all the attention of our minds.
> Thus, Oh Lord, Thy light shines in darkness. . . .
> All nature speaks of Thee and resounds with
> Thy holy name. But she speaks to deaf men
> whose deafness proceeds from the noise and clut-
> ter they make to stun themselves. Thou art
> near and within them; but they are fugitive and
> wandering, as it were, out of themselves. . . .
> Thou art to them an unknown God. . . . Oh
> misery! Oh dismal night that surrounds the chil-
> dren of Adam! Oh monstrous stupidity! Oh con-
> fusion of the whole man! Man has eyes only to
> see shadows and truth appears phantom to him.
> What's nothing is all, and what's all is nothing to
> Him. What do I behold in all nature? God! God
> is everywhere, and still God alone. When I think,
> Oh Lord, that all being is in Thee, Thou ex-
> hausteth and swallowest up, Oh abyss of truth,
> all my thoughts.[50]

Being at once in mind and in nature, God is the
source both of spiritual and natural law; therefore
the mystic, participating in the divine, that infinite
nature within himself, communes and is also one
with all creation in the glory of Him, the Almighty.
The union of the microcosm and macrocosm is com-

[50] *Traité de l'existence et des attributs de Dieu*, ed. A. Aulard,
Paris, 1874, pp. 109-111.

plete. This glorious achievement, now enjoyed by the fortunate few, is the ultimate goal toward which all mankind must strive. It is here, in his *Treatise on the Existence of God*, that Fénelon early joins an anti-mercantilist drive for the unity of all peoples to arguments attacking skepticism. On one hand, the Archbishop emphasizes how "the human race is but a single family dispersed over the face of the earth"; and, on the other, he explains that reason, which is "independent and above man, is the same in all countries." Literally present in the mind of both the savage and the Christian, God unites the whole of humanity in a common basis of understanding.[51] Moreover, as men are brought together in God through universal reason, so the Almighty joins them to each other by providing natural highways for trade and communications. Water, the oceans, for example,

which seem to be placed in the midst of lands

[51] "Ainsi, ce qui paraît le plus à nous, et être le fond de nous-mêmes, je veux dire notre raison, est ce qui nous est le moins propre, et qu'on doit croire le plus emprunté. Nous recevons sans cesse et à tout moment une raison supérieure à nous, comme nous respirons sans cesse l'air, qui est un corps étranger, ou comme nous voyons sans cesse tous les objets voisins de nous à la lumière du soleil, dont les rayons sont des corps étrangers à nos yeux.

"Cette raison supérieure domine jusqu'à un certain point, avec un empire absolu, tous les hommes les moins raisonnables, et fait qu'ils sont toujours tous d'accord, malgré eux, sur ces points. C'est elle qui fait qu'un sauvage du Canada pense beaucoup de choses comme les philosophes grecs et romains les ont pensées. C'est elle qui fait que les géomètres chinois ont trouvé à peu près les mêmes vérités que les Européens, pendant que ces peuples si éloignés étaient inconnus les uns aux autres. C'est elle qui fait qu'on juge au Japon comme en France que deux et deux font quatre. . . . C'est elle par qui les hommes de tous les siècles et de tous les pays sont comme enchaînés autour d'un certain centre immobile, et qui les tient unis par certaines règles invariables, qu'on nomme les premiers principes, malgré les variations infinies d'opinions qui naissent en eux de leurs passions, de leurs distractions et de leurs caprices pour tous leurs autres jugements moins clairs" (*ibid.*, pp. 66-67).

to make an eternal separation between them is, on the contrary, the common rendezvous of all people on earth. . . . It is by that trackless road, cross the bottomless deep, that the old world shakes hands with the new; and that the new supplies the old with so many conveniences and riches. The waters, distributed with so much art, circulate in the earth, just as the blood does in a man's body.[52]

And as the sea was "a link joining the society of all peoples," so the earth produced its wealth in such a manner that men depend upon exchanging the fruit of their labor.

It is the effect of a wise overruling Providence that no land yields all that is useful to human life. For want invites men to commerce, in order to supply one another's necessities. Want therefore is the natural tie of society between nations; otherwise all peoples would be reduced to one sort of food and clothing, and nothing would invite them to know and visit one another.[53]

The dependence of one area on the products of another was a natural cause for unity among nations; foolish man, however, had increasingly resorted to the manufacture of unnecessary luxury goods. This policy, born of pride and cupidity, caused material and moral impoverishment. Worst of all, the luxury trade, instead of creating bonds between men, destroyed all that which unites them. It sowed discord and, exciting the passions, drove men to draw their sword against their brothers. Speaking to the ancient and simple Boetians, Télémaque, for example, reported:

[52] *Ibid.*, pp. 13-14.   [53] *Ibid.*, p. 10.

When we talk to them of peoples possessing the art of erecting superb buildings, making furniture of gold and silver, textiles embroidered with precious stones, exquisite perfumes, tasty delicacies, instruments capable of delightful harmony, they answer in these terms: it is most unfortunate that these people have wasted so much labor and industry to corrupt themselves! Superfluous goods soften, intoxicate and torment those who possess them, and they tempt those who are deprived to acquire them through injustice and violence. Can we call good a luxury which serves only to make men bad?. . . . Such men are jealous of one another, eaten by secret and cowardly desires, agitated continually by ambition, by fear, by greed, incapable of pure and simple desires because they are slaves to so many false necessities on which they cause all their happiness to depend.[54]

Elsewhere, taking advice from Mentor, King Idomenius "banished" all luxury crafts from Salente. "Artisans who were employed in these pernicious occupations served in agriculture, in commerce or in the small number of trades which are necessary." Such laws guaranteed the happiness of a people:

Ambition and avarice are the only source of unhappiness: men wish to possess everything, rendering themselves miserable by their desire for the unnecessary; if they would live simply and be content with satisfaction of genuine needs, we would see *everywhere abundance, joy, peace and union.*[55]

[54] *Télémaque*, Vol. I, Bk. VII, pp. 328-329.
[55] *Ibid.*, Vol. I, Bk. V, pp. 187-188, italics added.

Some princes, through pride or through ignorance, followed policies directly contrary to those which nature and reason demonstrated to be the ones which would make their subjects both prosperous and happy. Above all, kings must understand that "power is measured by the number of people, not by the expanse of territory." There could not be too many people because the land would return harvests in proportion to the number of hands which work the soil: the earth was a "good mother who multiplies her gifts according to the number of children who merit her fruit by virtue of their labor."[56] Fénelon returns again and again to this theme stated earlier by Fleury. The ancient King Inachus, for example, said:

> Apply yourself to multiplying the natural riches in your realm. . . . Cultivate the land in order to have great abundance. . . . In this way you will put yourself in a position never to fear poverty. The more you have children the richer will you become, so long as you render them industrious: the earth is inexhaustible, she increases her fecundity in proportion to the number of inhabitants who take the trouble to cultivate: she repays everyone liberally for all his pains.[57]

But strange as it might seem, there were kings who encouraged the production of luxury goods at the expense of agriculture. Indeed, in order to amass great treasures so that they might be absolute at home and embark on conquest abroad, these insen-

[56] *Ibid.*, Vol. I, Bk. V, p. 187.
[57] *Ibid.*, Vol. II, Bk. XIV, p. 367. On the next page the wise Erichtonius fears that money "vous fera mépriser l'agriculture, *qui est le fondement de la vie humaine et la source de tous les vrais biens,*" italics added.

sate rulers imposed ruinous levies on the countryside, impoverishing the nobility,[58] driving rural populations to despair, and exhausting the entire realm. Such a tyrant, instead of loving his people and leading them down the path of virtue, would draw out their life substance and ultimately bring about the very seditions and uprisings which he most feared:

> What a detestable maxim it is to seek order in nothing but the oppression of one's own people! Not to instruct nor lead them to virtue, never to be loved by them, to terrorize them to the point of desperation, to place before them the horrible alternative of either never being able to breathe freely or to throw off the yoke of your tyrannical domination: is this the right way to reign without disorder? Is this the true path leading to glory?[59]

[58] "La noblesse, dont tout le bien est en décret, [on the auction block] ne vit que des lettres d'Etat" (Letter to Louis XIV, in *Ecrits et lettres politiques*, ed. Urbain, p. 150). Fénelon emphasizes the importance of the nobility in *Télémaque*:

> Mettez au premier rang ceux qui ont une noblesse plus ancienne et plus éclatante. Ceux qui auront le mérite et l'autorité des emplois seront assez contents de venir après ces anciennes et illustres familles, qui sont dans une si longue possession des premiers honneurs. Les hommes qui n'ont pas la même noblesse leur céderont sans peine, pourvu que vous ne les accoutumiez point à se méconnaître dans une trop prompte et trop haute fortune, et que vous donniez des louanges à la modération de ceux qui seront modestes dans la prospérité. La distinction la moins exposée à l'envie est celle qui vient d'une longue suite d'ancêtres.
>
> Pour la vertu, elle sera assez excitée, et on aura assez d'empressement à servir l'Etat, pourvu que vous donniez des couronnes et des statues aux belles actions, et que ce soit un commencement de noblesse pour les enfants de ceux qui les auront faites (Vol. II, Bk. X, pp. 92-94).

Citizens in the ideal state of Salente were divided into seven hereditary classes.

[59] A similar rhetorical question is asked in the *Mémoire* of 23

Remember that those countries where sovereigns are most absolute are those where they have the least power. They take all and ruin everything. They are sole possessors of the entire state, but the whole realm languishes. The countryside is uncultivated and almost deserted, towns diminish every day, trade stagnates. . . . The King's absolute power creates as many slaves as he has subjects. . . . This monstrous power swollen to its most violent excess cannot endure; it has no support in the heart of the people. It has wearied and irritated the whole body of the state: it has compelled all the members to aspire ardently for a change. At the first blow the idol will fall, crack and be crushed underfoot. Contempt, hate, vengeance, defiance, in a word all passions will unite against so odious a rule. And the King who, in the midst of vain prosperity found no one sufficiently courageous to tell him the truth, now, in his misfortune, will find no one to excuse him nor defend him against his enemies.[60]

Finally, it is worthwhile to repeat, Fénelon believed foreign wars were the direct result of France's outrageous economic policy: "Sire, we undertook a war with the Dutch in 1672. I cite this war in particular because it is the source of all the others. . . ." Instead of working to unite mankind, France had made

---

February 1688: "N'ayant ny provisions pour vivre ny rien de réserve tout est plein de mendians. . . . Est-ce la donc ce royaume si florissant?" (p. 17.) In both instances the irony is directed against the idea that the mercantilist program can bring either prosperity or glory.

[60] *Ibid.*, Vol. II, Bk. X, pp. 126-130. Earlier in the reign, François Bernier explained that the "causes principales de la décadence" of the states of Asia came directly from "the aveugle passion [of kings] d'estre plus absolus que ne permettent les loix de Dieu et de la nature . . ." (François Bernier, *Voyages* . . . , 2 vols., Amsterdam, 1679, II, 321).

herself the enemy of all Europe. "War is the greatest of evils." Cursed were those rulers who "augment the power of their peoples" at the expense of their neighbors and sought a "monstrous glory" in the blood of their brothers. Such individuals, "far from being demigods, are not even men; they must be an execration to all the centuries by which they thought themselves so admired. Oh! how kings must beware of the wars they undertake!"[61]

Generalities alone, however, did not suffice. Fénelon, along with the Duke of Beauvillier, charged "one of the cleverest men of this century" to write a remarkable book, meant exclusively for the eyes of the Prince and his instructors. It was designed to teach the Duke of Burgundy "all that which is necessary to know thoroughly about . . . the state which he will one day govern." Some attention would also be devoted to other kingdoms, but "what will make this work a curiosity and of an infinite utility is . . . that it will be filled with all the treaties made between . . . the nations of Europe, the infractions committed, their causes and the sequels of all the wars and all the woes which have arrived, and that which might have been done to avoid them." The principal objective would be to get at the "naked truth": "We will, for example, bring several letters of princes and their principal ministers, uncovering the secret causes of their actions, the particular views they held, often greatly different from the interests of state . . . and those of their master."[62] Unfortunately, the prospec-

[61] Quoted from *Télémaque*, by P. Lorson, "Guerre et paix chez Fénelon," *Le XVIIᵉ siècle*, Nos. 12-14, Numéro Spécial: Fénelon et le tricentenaire de sa naissance 1651-1951, 1951-1952, p. 210.

[62] "Mémoire sur l'éducation des ducs de Bourgogne, d'Anjou et de Berri, rédigé en 1696 par le marquis de Louville, gentilhomme de la marche du duc d'Anjou," in Fénelon's *Oeuvres*, ed. Saint-Sulpice, 4 vols., Paris, 1843, IV, 80-84.

tive author of this unusual work, François Le Blanc,[63] died before completing his task.

Le Blanc's identity not only explains much about the intentions of the men who employed him, but also throws light beyond himself, making clear the relations of Fénelon's group with another more important intellectual figure. Le Blanc, author of a monumental treatise on money,[64] was appointed historian to the children of France in 1696. He is the person whom the Marquis of Louville called "one of the cleverest men of this century." In all likelihood, Le Blanc was personally acquainted with Pierre Daniel Huet, Bishop of Avranches and sometime preceptor to the Dauphin.[65] In 1694, the year the great

[63] See Fénelon's letter to Fleury, 19 March 1696, *ibid.*, IV, 79.

[64] *Traité historique des monnoies de France depuis le commencement de la monarchie jusqu'à présent*, Paris, 1690. Another edition was published at Amsterdam in 1692.

[65] Huet was, in a sense, Le Blanc's predecessor; before becoming Bishop, Huet was appointed preceptor and historian to the Dauphin by the Duke of Montausier, who was then governor of the royal child. At this time Le Blanc was also in the service of the house of Montausier.

Moreover, Claude Fleury was Huet's colleague in the service of Montausier. In fact, Montausier was also personally sympathetic to many of the ideas expressed by the group around Fénelon. G. Thuillier, "Manuscrits inédits du XVIIe siècle: les 'maximes politiques' du Duc de Montausier," *La Revue administrative*, May 1962, pp. 262-272, has recently called attention to several thousand political maxims which the Duke composed sometime between 1668 and 1679. Many of them could have been written by Fénelon. Indeed the following maxim, chosen very much at random, is even reminiscent of the Archbishop's style:

S'il [the King] n'estime pas qu'il y a plus de véritable gloire à bien affermir son Etat, à le rendre tranquille, paisible, riche, opulent, bien réglé et bien uni, à y faire régner la justice, l'équité, et l'ordre, à en bannir la violence, l'insolence, les vols, la fraude, les intrigues, les cabales et les séditions, à y faire fleurir le commerce, les lettres, la vertu et la bonne foi, à en assurer le dehors et le dedans par de bonnes places bien fortifiées, bien entretenues, . . . à se faire respecter et honnorer par ses voisins, et aimer par ses sujets, qu'à mettre tout sans

famine ended, Huet severely criticized mercantilist policies, which he mistakenly thought to have originated with Colbert. Huet argued that excessive protection prevented foreign, especially Dutch, shipping from carrying off French agricultural products. Moreover, this policy was not only economically injurious, but it struck at the heart of Dutch commerce, thereby provoking tariff wars between the two countries which in turn led to armed conflict.

This treaty [tariff agreement of 1662] made French and Dutch merchants hope for a substantial increase in a commerce which was useful and advantageous to both nations. But their hopes were mistaken . . . , toward 1664 . . . we raised entry duties on divers foreign merchandise without respect to the treaty of 1662. Already for the past few years we had proposed to enter upon a commercial policy hitherto unknown. We decided to sell much to our neighbors and buy nothing from them. One must confess that we could not have invented a more handsome design to fill France with gold and silver. Unhappily, however, experience has demonstrated that it was not practicable. . . .

I think we can say that these trade quarrels were in part the cause of . . . this last war be-

dessus dessous pour faire des conquetes, qu'à agrandir ses frontieres et à se rendre redoutable à tous les autres Princes qui se liguent contre luy, qui cherchent à luy nuire de tous cotez, et qui le mettent luy et son royaume en état d'etre ruinez au premier accident, qu'à faire des guerres perpétuelles qui mettent tout à feu et à sang; qu'à vivre en une éternelle inquiétude, et faire vivre les autres en une perpétuelle misere; qu'à voir toutes les familles de son Royaume en deuil, et qu'à estre exposé d'un cruel et perpétuel remords de conscience, d'etre cause de tant de maux et à l'obligation indispensable d'en rendre compte à Dieu (B.N., Fds. fr., n.a., MS 10629, f. 212).

tween France and the United Provinces. Its declaration was followed by the most rigorous and the longest interdiction of trade, on one side and the other, that has ever been known because it has lasted for nearly seven years. And it is to be feared that it has taught the Dutch that they can get along without our products. The future will show if after peace they will again take the road to France with as great a number of merchant vessels as before, and if they discharge us of as many of our products and manufactures as in the past.[66]

Le Blanc's views may well have been influenced by those of Huet. First, Beauvillier directed him to write a substantial abridgment of the learned Bishop's memoirs.[67] At the same time, Le Blanc's personal thoughts

[66] Bibliothèque municipale de Rouen, MS 225, Collection Montbret, ff. 58-61. There are numerous copies of this manuscript. In Paris: B.N., Fds. fr., MSS 646, 18597 and 23022; Bib. de l'Arsenal, MS 4496; Aff. Et., mém. et doc., Hollande, 49; Bib. Thiers, MS 30. Copies also exist in at least two other municipal libraries outside of Paris: Rennes, MS 155. Reims, MS 955. In 1712 Huet published a slightly modified version of this manuscript, at Rouen, under the title: *Le grand trésor historique et politique du florissant commerce des Hollandois dans tous les états et empires du monde.* There is no doubt about the factual character of this document; indeed, it provided the principal source for Henri Sée's description of Dutch commerce at the end of the seventeenth century, "L'activité commerciale de la Hollande à la fin du XVIIᵉ siècle," *Revue d'histoire économique et sociale,* XIV (November 1926). The value of Huet's manuscript for economic history, however, should not obscure its author's purpose; to demonstrate how the Dutch became masters of the world's commerce! And his explanation does not differ in principle from the one used to make Télémaque understand the reasons for "Phoenician" prosperity.

[67] The copy of Huet's manuscript at Rouen has the following note on the last page: "Ces mémoires m'estant tombez entre les mains j'en ay fait une copie pour me servir dans l'occasion. Mr le B . . . qui en est autheur et qui avoit fait cet abrégé par ordonnance du Roy dont il estoit pensionnaire, pour en donner une première idée à Mgr. Le Duc de Beauvilliers, estant mort avant

seem clearly expressed when peace negotiations opened at Ryswick in 1697. He then wrote Beauvillier that "nothing less than a perfect reconciliation with the Dutch" was necessary for France's economic rehabilitation. Colbert's notorious tariff of 1667 must be reduced. Indeed, it was common knowledge that this pernicious trade barrier had precipitated France's economic decline: "All the merchants in the realm recognize that the decadence of our trade and of our manufactures began with the tariff of 1667."[68] These thoughts would probably have been developed at greater length had Le Blanc lived to write his curious history for the Duke of Burgundy.

While Fénelon no doubt agreed with Le Blanc's opinions, he thought that data about present conditions would provide a more apposite critique of state policy. As important as history might be, "it is not sufficient to know the past"; "you must," said Fénelon, "also know the present. Do you know the number of men who compose your nation; how many women, how many workers, how many merchants . . . ? What

---

que d'y pouvoir donner la dernière main, y a laissé plusieurs choses en blanc que je n'ay pu remplir. Il paroît que ces mémoires ont esté fait en 1694." The fact that François le Blanc died suddenly in 1698 while in the service of Beauvillier appears to establish the identity of "Mr le B. . . ." It is true that a literal reading suggests that "Mr le B. . . ." wrote both the original work and the abridgment; Huet's authorship of the original manuscript, however, is certain. We can only suppose that the confusion is due to awkward wording. So far as the abridgement itself is concerned, variations from the original text are slight and over three-fourths of Huet's work was copied verbatim.

[68] "Lettre de Mr Le Blanc sur le commerce," Archives du Château de St. Aignan, Fds. Beauvillier, MS 255. I am here again indebted to the kindness of Monsieur le duc de la Roche-Aymont for permission to consult his private archives. Le Blanc's opinions appear to have had some notoriety. At the B.N., Clairambault, MS. 286, f. 103, there is an "extrait d'un troisième mémoire de Mr de Foucherolles contre Mr Le Blanc pour faire voir que Mr Le Blanc établit mal à propos la prospérité du commerce de France. . . ."

would you say of a shepherd who did not know the size of his herd?" A king must also know the character of his subjects, "their principal customs, their liberties, their commerce and the laws of their divers traffic in the interior and outside of the kingdom. . . . A king ignorant of all these things is but half a king: his ignorance renders him incapable of correcting that which is not right; his ignorance causes more harm than the corruption of men who govern beneath him."[69]

Largely because Fénelon held these views, Beauvillier, on 12 February 1697, wrote a circular letter to all the intendants in France.[70] It began as follows: "Knowledge of the interior of the kingdom, being an

[69] "Examen de conscience . . . , in *Ecrits et lettres politiques*, ed. Urbain, pp. 35-37.

[70] Edmond Esmonin, "Les mémoires des intendants pour l'instruction du duc de Bourgogne," *Bulletin de la société d'histoire moderne*, 8 January 1956, admits that the above partially quoted passage provides "tout le schéma du questionnaire de février 1697" (p. 15). We do not know, however, precisely when the *Examen* was written; it is generally agreed that it probably dates from before Fénelon's disgrace on 1 August of the same year. For this reason Professor Esmonin casts doubt on Fénelon's authorship of the circular letter, and concludes that there is no reason to question the face of the document which states that Beauvillier himself was the author. It is indeed possible that the Archbishop did not personally draft the letter, but this is not important; the inquiries sent to the intendants arose out of preoccupations which the two men shared completely. Indeed, one question, if more elegantly phrased, could have been found in *Télémaque*: "Ports: Entrées en détail, abord d'étrangers, commodité ou incommodité de leurs commerces, quesce qui [sic] les gene, quesce qui pourroit faciliter ou augmenter le négoce" (quoted by Esmonin, *ibid.*, p. 16). There is one further consideration. No positive evidence suggests that either Beauvillier or Fénelon personally drafted the list of questions contained in this letter. Does it not appear that such a task was precisely the kind of service for which Le Blanc was employed? The questions were expressly designed for the instruction of the Duke of Burgundy, and the object of their inquiry fell within the scope of the remarkable history which Le Blanc was to write for the instruction of the young prince.

extremely important part of the education of M. the
Duke of Burgundy, I humbly pray you, sir, to send
me toward the end of the year an ample and detailed memoir answering the articles in the enclosed . . . questionnaire." The nineteen articles accompanying this letter were designed to obtain the
kind of information which Fénelon thought essential
for competent direction of state affairs. The inquiry
was, however, unofficial. Beauvillier did not invoke
royal authority: the intendants were to write memoirs
for the instruction of the Duke of Burgundy, and it
was in his capacity as governor of the young prince
that the minister launched the investigation.[71] Interestingly enough, the response from the intendants
was almost unanimous.[72] When Colbert had undertaken a similar inquiry a generation previously, officially and in Louis XIV's name, he had received a
comparatively small number of answering reports.[73]
The three decades which separate the two inquests
were among the most difficult in French history. Perhaps the conscientious efforts to satisfy Beauvillier's
demands indicate that the overworked intendants also
hoped the Duke of Burgundy would one day bring
better government to France.

iv. THE QUIETIST CONTROVERSY:
ANOTHER DIMENSION TO REFORM

The reaction to Fénelon's activities, leading ultimately to his disgrace and exile on 1 August 1697,

[71] This point is stressed by Professor Esmonin: "L'enquête est
faite en dehors de l'administration régulière, les mémoires n'ont pas
de caractère officiel, ils sont simplement officieux, au même titre
que les renseignements qu'un intendant peut être appelé à donner
à un particulier" (*ibid.*, p. 17).

[72] The one exception was due to the premature death of the intendant from Perpignan.

[73] See E. Esmonin's introduction to his edition of Voysin de la
Noiraye's *Mémoire sur la généralité de Rouen*, Paris, 1913.

centers principally on the Quietist controversy. The intense character of this dispute, involving the two leading religious figures in France, Bossuet and Fénelon, and the widespread passion it aroused is enough to suggest that more than a few doctrinal points were at stake. In fact, the quarrel raised basic issues with ramifications affecting many areas of thought; it was nothing less than the first large-scale encounter between the forces of tradition and those of reform. Negative versus positive conceptions of government— based on pessimistic and optimistic notions of human nature—were now, for the first time, an expression of open political struggle. So fundamental a conflict is, of course, complex. Indeed, historians are still writing contrary interpretations of the confused body of sources which relate to the great battle between Fénelon and Bossuet. Some emphasize political aspects of the question;[74] others, the religious.[75] Distinctions of this kind, however, are to some extent misleading because they did not exist so clearly at a time when men saw immediate political implications in what today appears as the most remote type of theological argument.

The facts of the Quietist affair have been frequently recounted; therefore only the briefest attention will be given here to the details of an unusually complex story. But even the most summary account must begin with a few words about the career of Jeanne-

[74] M. R. Schmittlein, *L'aspect politique du différend Bossuet-Fénelon*, Baden, 1954. A hastily written, often inaccurate and impassioned polemic against Bossuet which adds nothing new to our understanding of the problem.

[75] Louis Cognet, *Crépuscule des Mystiques: le conflit Fénelon-Bossuet*, Tournai, 1958. This fine book, the first of a projected two-volume work, provides an excellent introduction to the religious background of the controversy. Moreover, no other historian has presented so complete and straightforward an account of the events leading up to the struggle between Bossuet and Fénelon.

Marie Bouvier de la Motte, better known as Madame Guyon.[76] Jeanne-Marie entered into an unhappy marriage when she was fifteen with a man twice her age, Jacques Guyon, Seigneur du Chesnoy, son of the engineer responsible for constructing the canal de Briare. Her intense mystical experiences, first occurring in the early years of marriage, embarrassed and annoyed Monsieur Guyon; it was not until his death in 1674 that Jeanne-Marie, now a wealthy young widow, could give free reign to her religious vocation. Her activities during the next decade antagonized powerful ecclesiastical figures, particularly Jean d'Arenthon of Alex, Bishop of Geneva, and Bishop Camus of Grenoble, later appointed Cardinal. Moreover, these enmities were intensified by the publication of Madame Guyon's mystical treatises, *Les Torrents* and the *Moyen court et très facile pour l'oraison, que tous peuvent pratiquer et arriver par là à une haute perfection*, sometime between 1683 and 1685.

The second work, *Moyen court*, explains that "nothing is more easy than to have God and to taste Him. He is more within us than we are inside ourselves. He wishes to give Himself to us more strongly than we desire to possess Him. There remains only the method to seek Him, which is as easy and natural as breathing."[77] From this premise Madame Guyon went on to describe step by step how the individual may abandon himself entirely to the divine presence Who is within and Whose infinite spirit extends outward, penetrating and exalting every part of creation. True prayer is interior communion with God. Neither confession nor any other religious observ-

[76] Except where otherwise indicated, I have depended entirely on Father Cognet's work (*ibid.*) in describing the events leading up to the Council of Issy in 1694.

[77] Quoted by Cognet, *ibid.*, p. 96.

ance is a substitute for that totally passive state in which the soul receives the "divine effusion" present inside us all.

The book was immensely popular, fifteen hundred copies being distributed in the Grenoble region alone. But hostility to the young widow grew apace with her popularity. Compelled to leave Grenoble, Madame Guyon arrived in Paris in July 1686. One year later, François La Combe, a Barnabite priest enjoying an intense spiritual intimacy with Madame Guyon, was arrested and imprisoned in the Bastille, destined never to regain his liberty. The man who obtained the *lettre de cachet* for the Barnabite's arrest, François de Harlay de Champvallon, Archbishop of Paris, a person held in wide contempt for his worldly life and dissimulating ways,[78] never made clear the charges against La Combe; Harlay was also equally mysterious about the reasons which led him to order Madame Guyon's arrest shortly after La Combe's imprisonment. Meanwhile, friends were active on Madame Guyon's behalf. The intervention of her twenty-five-year-old first cousin, Marie-Françoise-Silvine Le Maistre de la Maisonfort, proved decisive. Mademoiselle de la Maisonfort was a member of Saint-Cyr, the religious establishment for daughters of impoverished aristocratic families established in 1686 and directed by Madame de Maintenon. Having long disliked Harlay, she caused Madame Guyon to be released from prison on 13 September 1688. A few days later the mystic was received at Saint-Cyr by Madame de Maintenon, the Princess of Harcourt, and the Duchesses of Chevreuse, of Beauvillier, and

[78] Fénelon's letter to Louis XIV carried the following reference to Harlay: "Vous avez un archevêque corrompu, scandaleux, incorrigible, faux, malin, artificieux, ennemi de toute vertu et qui fait gémir tous les gens de bien" (*Ecrits et lettres politiques*, ed. Urbain, p. 154).

of Béthune-Charost—Foucquet's daughter and Madame Guyon's old friend. This group of aristocratic ladies, who looked toward Fénelon as their spiritual director, understandably enough, arranged a meeting between the mystic and the future Archbishop.

Fénelon shortly became persuaded that Madame Guyon was divinely inspired. His own spirituality developed in the light of her mystical teachings; and to the end of his life, Fénelon never denied his veneration for this woman. Indeed, the fundamental mistake made subsequently by Fénelon's enemies was to underestimate the Archbishop's intense loyalty. Admired by Fénelon as "a prodigy of sainthood and doctrine" and surrounded by a powerful but sincerely devout group of aristocratic ladies, Madame Guyon rapidly became a kind of spiritual authority. Her book, *Moyen court*, circulated freely at Saint-Cyr. At the same time Madame de Maintenon had copies made of long passages from Fénelon's letters addressed to her; these "secret notebooks" contained spiritual advice inspired directly by Guyonian mysticism. Fénelon's well-known theology of "pure love," subsequently called Quietist, is the direct product of his personal and peculiar interpretation of Madame Guyon's teachings.

The astonishingly rapid rise of Madame Guyon's influence at Saint-Cyr, at first accepted by Madame de Maintenon, shortly caused her considerable alarm. In September 1687 both the person and doctrines of the Spanish priest Molinos had been condemned in Rome by the Papal Inquisition. Molinos' writings, *Defense of Contemplation, The Accord of Fatigue and Repose in Prayer* and *The Spiritual Guide* contained views capable of being interpreted as dangerously similar to those held by Madame Guyon. And a man like Harlay, the Archbishop of Paris, for example, would be only too anxious to point out how Saint-Cyr was infected by the heretical teachings of a person whom he, the ever-vigilant Harlay, had sought to silence at an early date.[79]

The gravity of the issue becomes clear when it is remembered that Molinos' condemnation had been a major issue in the protracted and intense struggle between Louis XIV and Innocent XI. The Sun King had been particularly irritated by Innocent when the latter, in 1678, refused to recognize Louis XIV's claim to the *régale*, the right to temporal revenues of vacant bishoprics. The *régale*, however, was only one dramatic incident in a number of Franco-Papal quarrels which all had their source in the crown's claim to exercise absolute dominion over the clergy's temporal wealth.[80] Innocent XI's prolonged and stubborn resistance provoked Louis XIV to convene the French clergy in a national council; and in 1682 this body issued the well-known four articles reaffirming the crown's temporal powers and appealing to the old theory of conciliar supremacy. The conflict continued and grew increasingly bitter: on one side Innocent refused to recognize episcopal and other religious appointments; on the other, anti-papal feeling ran high.

Relations became most strained, however, during the years 1687-1693. Long sympathetic to the teach-

[79] Antoine Adam, *Histoire de la littérature française au XVIIe siècle*, 5 vols., Paris, 1949-1956, V, 141-142, explains that Harlay's intentions were made clear when "il voulut soumettre à la Sorbonne le cas de conscience suivant: si un prince chrétien pouvait souffrir auprès de ses enfants un précepteur soupçonné de quiétisme." No one, least of all Madame de Maintenon, could think this question a mere academic point.

[80] "Toutes les difficultés avaient une cause commune: la croyance du souverain à son domaine absolu sur tout le temporel de l'Eglise de France" (Jean Orcibal, *Louis XIV contre Innocent XI*, Paris, 1949, p. 6). The author provides full documentation for this point.

ings of Molinos, Innocent XI had been among the Spanish mystic's most staunch supporters. In order to embarrass the Pope, Louis XIV, working principally through his Ambassador, Cardinal d'Estrées, brought great pressure on Innocent to condemn Molinos. This was finally accomplished on 2 September 1687. In January, however, Omer Talon, General Counsel [*Procureur Général*] for the Paris *Parlement*, reminded Innocent that the Bull condemning Molinos's teachings had not yet been published. Moreover, Talon reprimanded the Pope for taking no public measures against Cardinal Petrucci and other well-known friends of Molinos. Furious at the Pontiff for foiling Louis XIV's plans concerning the appointment of an Archbishop at Cologne who would be loyal to France rather than to the Emperor, Omer Talon also accused Innocent of indirectly favoring Protestant heretics and of directly supporting the Jansenists. Meanwhile, a French officer, the brutal Marquis de Lavardin, under orders to refuse recognition of the Pope's withdrawal of extra-territorial rights in Rome, extended unduly French territorial jurisdiction in Rome, cruelly repulsing the Swiss Guards. The Papal Nuncio left Paris without troubling even to take formal leave. Finally, at the beginning of 1688 Louis XIV was informed secretly that he and his ministers were also included in the excommunication decreed against the Marquis of Lavardin. Colbert de Croissy returned the Sun King's answer in October of the same year by sending troops to occupy Avignon.[81]

Innocent XI died on 12 April 1689; Franco-Papal quarrels were not resolved, however, until after four years of negotiations. Madame Guyon's influence at Saint-Cyr reached its height during the period 1689-

[81] *Ibid.*, pp. 11-47.

1693, clearly the most inopportune time for Madame de Maintenon to be suspected of supporting precisely those doctrines which Louis XIV had gone to such trouble to have condemned. Madame de Maintenon moved cautiously. In the fall of 1692, working through her confessor, Bishop Godet des Marais, religious head of Saint-Cyr, Madame de Maintenon tried to isolate and reduce the influence of those women who openly espoused Fénelonian or Guyonian mysticism. But Mademoiselle de la Maisonfort, stubbornly resisting all efforts to work against the new spirituality, angered Madame de Maintenon who, holding Madame Guyon responsible for the young lady's insubordination, requested that the mystic never again visit Saint-Cyr. Fénelon approved of this measure; he, too, thought it prudent for Madame Guyon to appear as if she had no relation with the institution. Moreover, the same prudence which caused Madame de Maintenon to exclude Madame Guyon drove the mystic's friends to seek approval of her doctrines from distinguished religious authorities: Madame Guyon clearly needed protection against the enmity of the Archbishop of Paris and against the hostility of doctrinaire anti-mystics like the Cartesian, Pierre Nicole, who early expressed his fundamental opposition to the new spirituality. Powerful support had to be found somewhere, and fairly rapidly, in order to avoid further public controversy over Madame Guyon's teachings. Therefore, in July 1693, Fénelon turned to his friend and teacher, Jacques-Benigne Bossuet, Bishop of Meaux, generally conceded to be the very incarnation of orthodoxy.[82]

---

[82] It is strange that Father Cognet, overlooking these external pressures (described so well in Orcibal, *Louis XIV*) remained puzzled about Fénelon's choice of Bossuet in his search for independent approval of Madame Guyon's doctrines. It is true that Bossuet was clearly no mystic; but many a mystic had been canonized and there

At first, Bossuet seemed favorably impressed with Madame Guyon, but outside factors soon helped to persuade the Bishop to pursue the mystic as if she were the Devil's agent on earth. The stage was being prepared for a mighty struggle in which the figure of Madame Guyon would become overshadowed by the clash of two immensely powerful personalities. During the summer of 1693 Mademoiselle de la Maisonfort's continued obstinacy had caused tension to rise at Saint-Cyr; finally in September, Madame de Maintenon summoned Bossuet. On the 25th of the same month the Bishop departed for his country estate with a large package containing Madame Guyon's writings. Returning to Versailles in January 1694, he interviewed Madame Guyon to whom he now showed unmistakable hostility. A short time later in early February, Bossuet visited Fénelon in the latter's apartments at Versailles; and in the presence of the Dukes of Beauvillier and Chevreuse, the Bishop of Meaux spoke disparagingly of Madame Guyon, doing his best to persuade the future Archbishop to withdraw his support from her. Bossuet appears to have been shocked to find his arguments so coldly received: "I retired astonished to see so fine a mind in admiration before a woman of such feeble lights, whose merit is so small, whose illusions are so palpable and who acts the role of a prophetess."[83] Meanwhile, Madame de Maintenon was busy at Court: gossip about Madame Guyon spread rapidly. People accused her of everything from witchcraft to the basest of immoral acts. Deeply hurt, Fénelon wrote Madame de Maintenon, "You are full of self, like Lucifer." A

was no reason for Fénelon to foresee the intense hostility of so intimate a friend. Indeed, given the urgency of the situation, it behooved Fénelon to seek out the most narrowly orthodox among the colleagues whom he respected.

[83] Quoted by Cognet, *Crépuscule des mystiques*, p. 190.

short time later Madame de Maintenon explained to Godet des Marais: "I am greatly chagrined to see that God wishes to separate me totally from the abbé Fénelon."

Understandably, Madame Guyon demanded an opportunity to defend herself against outrageous and slanderous attacks on her character: she requested that her moral life be publicly examined before an impartial tribunal. Unwilling to risk an encounter on these grounds, Madame de Maintenon and Bossuet refused the request and demanded instead that Madame Guyon's doctrines, not her life, be scrutinized by the authorities. The tribunal was quickly organized with royal approval; sessions were held at Issy from July 1694 through 10 March 1695. They were secret because the case should have properly come before the Archbishop of Paris, known to be jealous about infringements of his authority. Bossuet presided at the Issy proceedings where he attacked Madame Guyon's writings with surprising fury and a relentless singleness of purpose. Fénelon did not hesitate to defend the person to whom he owed so much of his spiritual development. Devoting all his energy and his immense talents to this task, the Archbishop of Cambrai proved a formidable opponent for Bossuet.

Neither differences in personalities, however great, nor the pressure of political events are by themselves sufficient to explain the intensity of the conflict. Both men realized that far-reaching issues of the most fundamental importance were at stake.[83a] Bossuet was

83a Earlier in the century, Richelieu imprisoned Jean-Pierre Camus, Bishop of Belley, for defending a theological position similar to the one adopted subsequently by Fénelon. Indeed, the Archbishop early explained to Bossuet:

"M. Le Camus, évêque de Belley, ami intime de saint François de Sales, et qui déclare avoir été son disciple pendant quatorze

no mere puppet in Madame de Maintenon's hands. Her enmity against Madame Guyon and Fénelon served only to reinforce the Bishop's determination to fight against what, according to his convictions, were profoundly disturbing implications, both theological and political, of the new spirituality. Fénelon spoke of universal reason, of the divine presence both in nature and in the human mind, of ultimate union with the eternal and of the way to guide men toward virtue and finally to pure love. Nowhere could one find, as in Bossuet's *Politique tirée de l'Ecriture Sainte*, how man, depraved by original sin, is plagued with an intractable nature; impervious to all external influence, according to Bossuet, human beings can be governed only by a divinely appointed authority enjoying a monopoly of force which it exercises for the general good. In contrast, Fénelon wished to limit sovereignty by rules more definite and precise than the general welfare: the state is bound by the same moral laws as those governing the humblest subject in the realm. Where the Archbishop cursed the ruler who "augmented the power of his peoples" at the expense of his neighbors, Bossuet pointed both to the great David, who enriched his realm with booty from subjected kingdoms,[84] and to the wise Solomon,

---

ans, fut accusé depuis l'an 1639 jusqu'en 1642, d'enseigner l'illusion sous le nom du pur amour. On lui disait, Monseigneur, presque tout ce que vous me dites. On assurait qu'il voulait faire oublier le paradis et l'enfer, étouffer l'espérance et la crainte, enfin saper les fondements de la religion" (Première lettre de Mgr. l'Archevêque de Cambrai pour servir de réponse à celle de Mgr. de Meaux, *Oeuvres Complètes*, edit. Gosselin, II, 635). See Henri Brémond, *La Querelle du Pur Amour au temps de Louis XIII*, Paris, 1932, and Gabriel Joppin, *Une querelle autour de l'Amour pur, Jean-Pierre Camus, évêque de Belley*, Paris, 1938.

[84] "David nous en est encore un beau modèle. Ses victoires étoient marquées par les dons magnifiques qu'il faisoit au sanctuaire, qu'il enrichissoit des dépouilles des royaumes subjugués.

"La belle chose de voir ce grand homme après avoir achevé glori-

who established his rule on mercantilist principles.[85] Where Fénelon declared the entire human race a single family, Bossuet, insisting on the permanent division of society into self-contained political units, declared love of country and devotion to the state the first duty of a Christian subject.[86] The difference was not merely political: it proceeded directly from diametrically opposed views about the nature of man and his relations with God. Fénelon was both the last of the great seventeenth century French mystics and a leader of the first large-scale encounter between those who were convinced that moral progress was possible and those who denied that human efforts

---

eusement tant de guerres . . ." ("Politique tirée des propres paroles de l'Ecriture Sainte," *Oeuvres complètes de Bossuet*, ed. F. Lachat, 31 vols., Paris, 1864, XXIII, Bk. V, art. IV, prop. II, 649).

[85] Solomon, recognizing "la nécessité du commerce pour enrichir son royaume," at first kept the peace and entered into an alliance with Tyre, the most experienced maritime nation. Later, however, "quand les Israêlites furent instruits par eux-mêmes dans les secrets du commerce, *ils se passèrent de ces alliés* . . ." (*ibid.*, XXIV, Bk. X, art. I, prop. III, 193, italics added).

[86] "La parole est le lien de la société entre les hommes, par la communication qu'ils donnent de leurs pensées. Dès qu'on ne s'entend plus l'un l'autre, on est étranger l'un à l'autre. . . . Voilà donc le genre humain divisé par langues, et par contrées: et de là il est arrivé qu'habiter un même pays et avoir une même langue, a été un motif aux hommes de s'unir plus étroitement ensemble. . . .

"La société humaine peut être considérée en deux manières. Ou en tant qu'elle embrasse tout le genre humain, comme une grande famille. Ou en tant qu'elle se réunit en nations. . . . La société considérée de ce dernier sens, s'appelle *société civile*. . . . Quiconque . . . n'aime pas la société civile dont il fait partie, c'est-à-dire l'état où il est né, est ennemi de lui-même et de tout le genre humain" (*ibid.*, XXIII, Bk. I, pp. 487-488, 514-515).

Elsewhere Bossuet says:

"Si l'on est obligé d'aimer tous les hommes, et qu'à vrai dire il n'y ait point d'étrangers pour le chrétien, à plus forte raison doit-il aimer les concitoyens. Tout l'amour qu'on a pour soi-même, pour sa famille et pour ses amis, *se réunit dans l'amour qu'on a pour sa patrie*, où notre bonheur et celui de nos familles et de nos amis est renfermé" (*ibid.*, Bk. I, art. VI, p. 505, italics added).

could significantly alter man's fundamentally corrupt nature. At bottom, this was the issue between the movement for reform and the forces of tradition.[87] The following pages show how the doctrines of Fleury and Fénelon, agrarianism and anti-skepticism, with all its optimistic and political implications, were adopted by secularly inspired reformers who transformed them into themes which will stand at the very heart of Enlightenment thought in France.

[87] Henri de Boulainvillier expressed perhaps most clearly the issue separating Bossuet from the men who, religiously inspired or not, wished to change government in France.

Il n'est personne . . . qui ne reconnoisse les conséquences malheureuses du pouvoir despotique soit par son propre sentiment, soit par les exemples des Monarchies d'Orient, ou meme par celui des Romains. Ainsi je pense que tout homme non intéressé, et d'ailleurs suffisament éclairé, regardera le sisteme politique d'illustre Bossuet Eveque de Meaux, comme un des plus honteux témoignages de l'indignité de notre siecle, et de la corruption des coeurs, contre lesquels l'érudition et les lumieres de l'esprit ne donnent point de secours, que l'artifice ne puisse détourner et employer contre la vérité meme. Il n'y a rien en effet de si mauvaise foi que l'abus perpétuel qu'il a fait des Textes de la SAINTE ECRITURE, *pour forger de nouvelles chaines a la liberté naturelle des hommes*, et pour augmenter le faste et la dureté des Rois. Il est vrai que pour mettre son sisteme à couvert d'une détestation universelle, il a fait une tres belle et tres magnifique peinture des obligations de la Royauté, mais c'est à mon avis, ce qui découvre mieux le faux de cet ouvrage, *parce que ce sera toujours la partie dont les Princes prendront le moins de connoissance, pendant qu'ils feront valoir à force celle qui regarde la soumission* (*Lettres sur les anciens parlements de France que l'on nomme Etats-Généraux*, 3 vols., London, 1753, I, 67-69, italics added).

Thus Boulainvillier also clearly thought that something more than divine law and the general welfare was needed to limit the exercise of power. Unlike Fénelon, however, Boulainvillier did not believe moral law sufficiently precise to serve this function. In his mind historical truth, revealing all past abuses on the "original" and "natural" limitations of power is a more certain protection against the growth of despotism.

CHAPTER VI

SECULAR REFORM:
UTILITARIAN PHILOSOPHY AND
AGRARIAN THEORY

PREVIOUS discussion of passages from Pierre Nicole and Jean Silhon has shown how men, sometimes devoutly inspired, separated ethics from theology in such a way as to judge human behavior according to a criterion of social usefulness. The good or bad character of an act was determined by the degree it benefited society as a whole. And from the point of view of political thought, utilitarian theory was also associated with Machiavellian and mercantilist doctrine. Just as social usefulness, defined as enlightened self-interest, replaced virtue in the realm of ethics, so did the "general interest" supplant traditional ideals of justice in politics. In other words, "self-interest" in the one field became "reason of state" in the other. Finally, it may be remembered that these ideas gained acceptance during the first half of the seventeenth century when royal authority seemed to offer a fragile protection against the forces of anarchy. The urgent need to keep the peace, to exert more control over human activity, gave rise to theories which subordinated the ideals of virtue and justice to the more practicable criteria of utility and the general interest. And out of this drive for more effective government came attempts

to formulate theories which would make human behavior more predictable. Again Pierre Nicole was
the outstanding example. He said the social order,
existing without justice (its only purpose being utility), was a purely natural phenomenon. Indeed, for
him society functioned in the same manner as Cartesian vortices: ethics and politics were problems in
physical theory; men acted according to laws governing the course of the planets and the rhythm of the
tides.

But this current of ideas so compatible with centralization and with mercantilist doctrine must be
contrasted with a second stream of seventeenth century utilitarian thought which provided the foundations for elaborate anti-mercantilist theories. This
current of utilitarian thought formed an important
intellectual movement which, despite the strange silence of scholars, played a central role both in the
particular development of the reform movement and
in the more general history of the Enlightenment.
Becoming highly developed and surprisingly systematic near the middle of the century, the new ethical
and political philosophy merged with the agrarian
theories made popular by Fleury and the group
around Fénelon. In this expanded form, it expressed
more fundamentally than any other body of contemporary doctrine the ideas and attitudes traditionally
associated with French society in the mid-eighteenth
century.

i. EARLY UTILITARIAN PHILOSOPHY

In 1598 Antoine Hotman, brother of the famous
François Hotman, published an essay which was shock-
ingly contrary to established teachings. The text,

"Deux paradoxes de l'amitié et d'avarice,"[1] can be rapidly summarized. According to Hotman, a passionate attachment for another person is both immoral and contrary to reason.[2] Moreover, the exclusive character of friendship is a "great cause of division and discontent," interfering with "the duty we owe to the public."[3] Consisting as it does in an "affection directed especially toward some rather than toward others,"[4] friendship is a kind of civic treason, contrary to the natural law governing human relations: the Golden Rule.[5] To assert, as many do, that love for another person is a consequence of our love for God is grossly mistaken, for "as praiseworthy as is our love for God, I think it is vituperable when directed toward

[1] *Opuscules françoises des Hotmans*, Paris, 1616, pp. 113-183.

[2] "Car elle [l'amitié] est contraire à la vertu, d'autant que la vertu consiste au résistement et reiglement de nos affections, et non pas au relaschement et augmentation d'icelles" (*ibid.*, p. 153). Concerning reason, Hotman says friendship "nous faict perdre tout discours de raison" (*ibid.*, p. 114).

[3] *Ibid.*, p. 114.

[4] *Ibid.*, p. 115. In the same paragraph, Hotman specially emphasizes this point: "La pluspart disent, qu'une vraye et entiere amitié ne peut estre qu'entre deux ou trois, comme si de la société, qui est infinie au genre humain, on avoit extrait toutes les forces, pour les assembler en un petit endroit, affin qu'estans pressées, elles ayent plus d'effect entre deux ou trois personnes."

[5] "Et puis que la loy naturelle nous commande de faire à autruy comme à nous mesmes, qu'est-il besoin d'amitié qui nous incite de nous contenir en ce devoir par instinct sensuel (on p. 132, *ibid.*, "l'amour" is defined as "une impression et affection de quelque chose en nostre fantaisie" occasioned by emotional responses analogous to those engendered by sensual impressions) particulierement envers un ou deux, puisque la raison nous y doit contenir envers tous? Car au contraire il semble que la recommandation en un particulier soit une exception du général, de sorte que si vous incitez quelqu'un de faire à son amy du mieux qu'il luy sera possible, il semble que vous l'excusiez, si envers un autre il ne se comporte en pareil devoir, qui est un inconvénient contre raison, et contre la loy de justice, qui veut qu'on rende à un chacun ce qui luy appartient, et que l'on se comporte envers autruy comme on voudroit estre fait en son endroit" (*ibid.*, pp. 139-140).

men, none of whom are imbued with anything we desire from the Deity."[6]

The belief that friendship among men is unrelated, indeed contrary to man's love for God is essential to Hotman's further and, in 1598, most extraordinary argument that the "passion" to grow rich is an admirable quality, in fact an emotion necessary for the development of both moral virtue and civic responsibility. This aspect of the text can be examined more profitably, however, when we recall briefly in what respect Hotman's notion of love conflicted with accepted teachings. Traditionally, friendship among men was derived directly from a love of God. Thus, for example, when earlier in the century Juan Luis Vivès (1492-1540), exclaimed, "who loves not man certainly does not love God,"[7] he expressed a view identical with St. Thomas Aquinas' explanation of divine and human friendship: "Since every law aims at establishing friendship, either between man and man, or between man and God . . . love of one's neighbor includes love of God."[8] Moreover, intellectuals frequently emphasized that it was precisely the concept of charity, a love extended to another for the sake of God and *without expectation of a quid pro quo*, which particularly distinguished Christian society from pagan antiquity. Thus Henricus Cornelius Agrippa (1486-1535) wrote in the spirit of many Christian humanists when he said

Jesus Christ teaches that we should . . . love our

[6] *Ibid.*, p. 115.

[7] *L'Aumonerie*, Lyon, 1583, p. 84. Elsewhere, Vivès said: "Il a esté crucifié pour tous les hommes et pour chacun d'eux en particulier. Ne présumez pas de pouvoir jamais luy estre agréable si vous haïssez quelqu'un de ceux qu'il a tant aimer" (*L'Introduction à la Sagesse*, Paris, 1670, p. 231. In this edition the Latin pages are faced by a French translation).

[8] *Summa Theologica* I, II, q. 99, a. 1. ad. 2.

enemies . . . and give to those who ask. In contrast, the philosophers [of antiquity] would give only to those who can return in kind.[9]

No one can by his own will become more loved by God than another; all human souls are equal before Him.[10] And for this reason Luis Vivès and Thomas More, for example, thought wealth should not be distributed in a manner contrary to the love God seeks to infuse into man for his neighbor. Worldly goods are a divine trust; men are entitled to the use, not the ownership, of material possessions.[11] The unconditioned property right is contrary to the first

[9] *Déclamation sur l'incertitude, vanité et abus des sciences*, Paris, 1582, p. 219. After exclaiming that "la Charité" is "l'unique précepte" in the "cité Chrestienne," Vivès said that Europe's failure to exercise charity causes Christendom to differ only in name from pagan society: "Et véritablement nous n'avons rien changé des citez payennes, excepté le nom. A la mienne volonté que nous n'eussions augmenté les vices, nous oyons ce: Faites bien à ceux qui vous haïssent, et priez pour ceux qui vous calomnient et persécutent" (*L'Aumonerie*, pp. 85-86).

[10] "Qui pourra exprimer combien est folle et aveugle la présomption de ceux qui se vantent d'estre de parfaits Chrestiens, et qui osent se préférer à tous les autres, en ce qui regarde l'exécution et l'accomplissement des loix divines.

"Puisque d'une part nul n'est asseuré d'avoir une vertu solide et véritable, ni s'il est digne de la haine, ou de l'amour de Dieu, et que de l'autre il ne scait pas si celuy auquel il a l'insolence de se préférer n'est pas plus riche que luy en grace et en dons célestes. . . . C'est pourquoy Dieu n'a point voulu que l'homme fust juge d'un autre homme ni que celuy qui n'a pas assez de lumiere pour découvrir parfaitement le fond de son coeur se donnast la liberté de vouloir pénétrer et étendre sa censure jusques dans les consciences des autres, il s'est reservé à luy seul ce jugement. . ." (Luis Vivès, *L'Introduction à la Sagesse*, p. 225).

[11] "Parquoy, sçaches que quiconque possede des dons et présens de nature, si avec son pauvre frere il communique, . . . il les possede de droit et de la volonté et institution de nature. Mais si au contraire il n'en communique rien, . . . *il est larron et ravisseur et nature convaincu et condamné de la loy. Veu qu'il occupe et détient ce que nature n'a procrée à son profit particulier*" (Luis Vivès, *L'Aumonerie*, p. 73, italics added).

principles of charity because it presupposes the personal enjoyment rather than the Christian *use* of riches. The point is crucial: no matter how eloquently More and Vivès spoke of injustice in a society where a few are wealthy and vast numbers are destitute, the two men emphasized repeatedly that excessive wealth is as dangerous to the souls of the rich as it is unjust to the poor. Everyone should live a simple life. The *Utopia* did not describe a society of universal abundance; on the contrary, More would abolish all luxury.[12] In short, both More and Vivès were spokesmen for a traditional concept which is part of the Christian idea of charity: dependence upon purely temporal objects impoverishes the spirit because it directs man's emotional being away from the love for God and for man.[13] Friendship becomes indistinguishable from charity. Indeed this is precisely how Lucien Febvre described Erasmus' definition of Christianity: "Bread among the ancients was the symbol for friendship. It was broken in company in order to unite men in a sacred bond. Thus did Christ act among his disciples. Erasmus goes even further. He says that this is the origin of the act where Christ distributes bread to His disciples, consecrating among them a perpetual friendship. . . . We know the fine definition which Erasmus, elsewhere, gives of Chris-

---

12 See J. H. Hexter, *More's Utopia: the Biography of an Idea*, Princeton, 1952, especially pp. 66-71, 90-91. Similar views are expressed by Vivès, *ibid.*, see the section entitled: "Réformateurs et de la police et réformation," pp. 137-180.

13 "Les choses de la terre estant de leur nature incertaines, fragiles, passageres, nullement durables et sujettes à mille changements ne méritent point nostre estime et nostre affection. . ." (Vivès, *L'Introduction à la Sagesse*, p. 121).

Elsewhere Vivès says: "Amasser avec tant d'ardeur ces choses extérieures qu'on appelle biens de fortune, n'est ce pas faire le mesme que si un piéton se chargeoit et s'accabloit de meubles et de paquets inutiles" (*ibid.*, p. 131).

tianity: *nihil aliud quam vera perfectaque amicitia.*"[14] Wealth was created for the use of all, and the exercise of charity will unite men in a common love for God and for each other.[15]

Antoine Hotman's views stand in stark, indeed almost grotesque contrast to these time-honored principles. Declaring that "it is best to be as rich as one can," Hotman further asserted: "I maintain that anyone who rejects the wealth which brings convenience into our lives is unnatural and does not know what it is to live."[16] The arguments supporting this astounding position are of immense interest because other texts will reveal them to be an essential part of one of the earliest direct links with the French Enlightenment. Nothing, wrote Hotman, has been more universally condemned through the ages than the zealous pursuit of wealth, yet, paradoxically, nowhere in the entire body of jurisprudence can there be found a law condemning "someone for having avidly enriched himself by legitimate means."[17] In fact the contrary is true: "The laws themselves invite men to do good, by offering wealth as a spur and recompense, deterring men from evil by threatening them with the loss of their goods."[18]

[14] *Le problème de l'incroyance au XVIe siècle: La religion de Rabelais*, Paris, 1962, p. 347.

[15] "Que nulle considération du monde ne puisse jamais affoiblir, ni encore moins vous faire perdre ces justes et nobles sentiments de la charité Chrestienne. N'ayez egard ny à la diversité de la nation, ny au lieu de la naissance, ny à la famille, ny à la profession, ny a l'estat de la personne, ni aux défauts de l'esprit" (Luis Vivès, *L'Introduction à la Sagesse*, p. 237).

[16] "Je soutiens que quiconque rejette les richesses qui nous apportent les commoditez de nostre vie est desnaturé, et ne scait que c'est de vivre" (*Opuscules françoises*, p. 169).

[17] *Ibid.*, p. 156.

[18] "Et de fait les loix mesmes invitent les hommes de bien faire, en leur proposant pour guerdon et recompence les richesses, et les déterrant du mal par menaces de la perte de leur bien" (*ibid.*, p. 158).

Some people, it is true, say avarice causes us "to forget God" or to become *peu charitable*. To these objections, however, "it is easy to reply that . . . such inconveniences are accidents which may or may not happen."[19] For example, an intemperate use of wine is necessarily harmful, but the avid pursuit of wealth, having no physical effects, is not necessarily injurious.[20] On the contrary, said Hotman, a full purse is essential to a virtuous life. Dividing *les biens de ce monde* into health, virtue and wealth, Hotman explained that the first two qualities are innate. Their opposite terms, sickness and vice, refer to no malevolent presence; they indicate merely the absence of attributes naturally inherent in all men:

> Vice is an evil and evil is a privation . . . not an essence. Thus viciousness is not a quality . . . in man, but it is an absence of that . . . which ought to be in him. . . . Nature . . . has created us with virtue. . . . We have . . . from our childhood . . . an inclination to do good, such that if we do evil it is against nature. Especially since we can by ourselves become virtuous by following the course and the precepts of nature. . . . Thus we can say that virtue cannot be acquired, but it is preserved . . . and vice does not exist as something acquired, but as the privation of what one should naturally have.[21]

Health and virtue, being innate, are qualities men take for granted. In contrast, wealth, "the one and unique acquisition we can make in this world,"[22] is

[19] *Ibid.*, p. 159.

[20] "Mais de richesses on n'en peut trop avoir et n'y a point d'excez, parce que des richesses il ne sort rien qui puisse offenser nos corps ny nostre esprit" (*ibid.*, p. 160).

[21] *Ibid.*, pp. 163-164.

[22] *Ibid.*, p. 163. On the same page, Hotman wrote: "Reste donc

desired most ardently. Indeed, men will sacrifice their inborn qualities in order to acquire wealth. Such action is misguided, but preoccupation with money among men of modest means is such that for them *"c'est chose presque impossible d'estre sain et vertueux."*[23]

Amassing a private fortune not only helps to build moral character, but it also performs a positive public service. The rich provide employment for the poor; they endow educational institutions. Also, by purchasing positions in government, wealthy men will ultimately infuse prosperity, culture, and virtue throughout society:

> He who is rich can do good by becoming always more wealthy. . . . He employs servants and mercenaries who earn a livelihood by augmenting his wealth. He becomes master of a *seigneurie*, of a Province, even of a Kingdom. And being *un homme de bien*, he formulates fine constitutions and ordinances so as to keep everyone in their place. He establishes Magistracies and Offices to punish malefactors. . . . A rich man can build Colleges and support learned men.[24]

In sum, Hotman contended that the unbridled pursuit of private gain is virtuous because men, having no love for one another, can define virtue only in terms of actions useful to society. Traditionally, excessive dependence upon temporal objects was said to produce spiritual impoverishment. To assert, in contradiction, that the good life cannot be attained without acquiring substantial wealth, is to deny the

---

que des trois sortes de biens cy-devant specifiez, les deux premiers qui sont la vertu et la santé ne s'acquierent pas, ains seulement la troisieme espece de bien est en acquisition."

[23] *Ibid.*, p. 169.   [24] *Ibid.*, pp. 173-174.

transcendental character of good and evil, to declare human behavior devoid of intrinsic moral worth. An act is by itself neither good nor bad. In this context, Hotman's statement that, through "offers of recompense" and "threats of loss," the laws "themselves" spur men "to do good" and "deter them from evil," must be considered as a piece with his argument that nature, not God, implants the seeds of virtue in men at birth. For good and evil would not be socially determined if they extended beyond the realm of nature. Hotman is unquestionably one of the earliest European figures to argue explicitly that social usefulness is the ultimate ethical criterion.

Hotman's essay bears a striking resemblance to several aspects of a curious and very different kind of text. A few months before his death in 1596, Jean Bodin wrote a short treatise entitled, *Le paradoxe moral . . . Qu'il n'y a pas une seule vertu en médiocrité, ny au milieu de deux vices.*[25] In this work, Bodin separates the spiritual from the worldly order without at the same time denying the presence of a divine influence on earth. Every being, says Bodin, is created for some good (*bien*) and for some purpose (*fin*). He defined a good as something enjoyed, as that "which is profitable" to a creature; in contrast, a purpose (*fin*) is a principle external to the agent, its *raison d'être*. Upon this distinction Bodin built two parallel orders of values, internal and external, ultimately converging in God since no value is superior to the Divinity in the hierarchy of either order. Moreover, every point on the internal hierarchy of the good corresponded to a point on the external scale of purpose. Bodin explained this correlation when he discussed how the subject of moral science, defined as

[25] Here using 1604 edn.

"the happiness of man," is related to the purpose for which man was created: the glory of God.

Since every earthly good is enjoyed for something beyond itself (only God is absolute and can be enjoyed for His own sake) it follows that "everything which is good must also be useful, and if it is not useful it is also not good."[26] Indeed, everything which exists is good, therefore useful. Evil is merely the privation of being, and what doesn't exist can have no use. Similarly, vice has no existence for the word designates only the absence of virtue.[27] Moreover, virtue is a purely natural quality which, if allowed to develop freely, will lead men to the happy life:

> Nature has imbued really no vice in our souls.
> . . . All the elements of virtue are implanted in
> our souls, and if they are not prevented from
> growing . . . we can guide ourselves toward true
> honor and come very near to the happy life.[28]

Bodin said explicitly that man can execute God's commands by free will alone, without the aid of divine grace; indeed, this is how man attains happiness.[29] Here the faculties of will and of reason play

[26] "Tout ce qui est bon doit estre utile aussi; que s'il n'estoit utile, aussi ne seroit-il pas bon" (*Le paradoxe moral*, p. 12).

[27] "Or nous avons enseigné que le mal se définit par privation, pourtant est-il nécessaire que les vices soient définis par privation des vertus. . ." (*ibid.*, p. 54).

[28] *Ibid.*, pp. 81-82.

[29] *Le paradoxe* is written in the form of a dialogue between father and son (*Père et Fils*). Speaking through the former, Bodin writes:

F. Declarez moy s'il vous plaist quel est le devoir de l'homme par lequel on atteint à la vie heureuse?
P. Faire les commandemens de Dieu.
F. Mais qui fait les commandemens de Dieu?
P. Quiconque voudra or tous le doivent vouloir.
F. Cela est-il en la puissance de l'homme?
P. Pourquoy non? Autrement si on commandoit une chose im-

a special role which Bodin discusses in the context of what he calls the theological and philosophical "virtues." The philosophical virtues, consisting of prophecy (through inspiration of the Holy Spirit), wisdom, science, prudence, and art, are purely intellectual and were therefore familiar to pagan antiquity. Reason is thus concerned only with distinguishing truth from error whereas the will, "greater not only than reason but greater than understanding," can tell good from evil,[30] a function placing it close to the theological virtues (faith, hope and charity) which were unknown to the ancients.

Although the will cannot effect a union with God because the Deity is external to man,[31] it can nevertheless make clear the correspondence between the internal order of good and the external order of purpose: the conformity of truth with good and of evil with falsity. The *jouissance* of the sovereign good is the greatest happiness possible. It comes from an "excellent" love, the love in turn is derived from a

---

possible, ce ne seroit pas commander. . . . Pensez-vous qu'il y ait jamais eu Législateur si stupide ou inique qui voulut commander ce qu'on ne scauroit faire?

. . . .

F. Je ne voy pas qu'aucun puisse accomplir les commandemens de Dieu sans l'aide divine?

P. Pourquoy l'entendement humain par les graces divines qu'il a receues dès le commencement de son origine, ne pourra sans aide extraordinaire de Dieu user de la droite raison, fuyr les choses vilaines et embrasser les honnestes (*ibid.*, pp. 39-43)?

[30] *Ibid.*, pp. 63-64. The clearest wording on this point is in the 1598 edition: "il n'y a point de péché s'il n'est fait une franche volonté, qui est non seulement plus grande que la raison, ains aussi que l'entendement" (p. 51).

[31] "De combien a mieux escrit le sage, que Dieu est tres-prochain à ceux-là qui l'ayment ardemment. Il n'a pas dit qu'il fut uny à eux. La nature divine ne le sçauroit souffrir, si nous ne voulons advouer que les hommes deviennent dieux, et les Dieux hommes" (*ibid.*, p. 30).

knowledge of God, the knowledge of God from an understanding of His laws, works, and actions, and, finally, this understanding from *"cette divine lumiere, qui rayonne plus abondamment sur ceux qui ont le plus assemblé de vertus en un."*[32] In other words, he who of his own free will executes God's commands shall bring the internal order, contained within himself, into correspondence with the external, transcendental order of purpose, permitting *la droite connoissance de Dieu,* the ultimate human experience.

Bodin said the will stands toward the human being as does a legislator toward his country.[33] And, like Antoine Hotman, this view must be taken as an integral part of Bodin's conviction that the seeds of virtue are implanted in every child by nature—not God. For virtue must be natural if it is to become

[32] *Ibid.,* p. 53.

[33] Speaking of the individual soul, Bodin defined justice as rendering "à chaque partie de l'ame ce qui luy appartient" (*ibid.,* pp. 96-97). The dialogue then turns to justice in society:

> F. Mais veu que la justice, par laquelle on rend à chacune partie de l'ame ce qui luy appartient, est une justice générale, qui . . . fomente toutes les vertus souz son embrassement. . . . Sous quel genre sera celle là qui se produit en dehors qui rendast à chacun le sien entretient la concorde és Citez, qui commande recercher les choses communes pour le commun, et rendre les propres aux particuliers?
>
> P. Il appartient à la discipline du Droit qui pour ceste occasion s'appelle Jurisprudence. . . . Elle ne gist pas seulement à juger, mais aussi en la defence de ceux qui sont oppressez par les plus puissans, en l'obeissance des particuliers envers les Magistrats, és devoirs mutuels des particuliers entre-eux mesmes, qui s'appelle d'un nom péculier moral ou éthique. . . . Car pourquoy ce sont les richesses octroyées de Dieu immortel, sinon pour les distribuer aux souffreteux? Pourquoy la puissance, si ce n'est pour défendre les foibles? L'art de commander est la principale partie de prudence appellée politique, qui regarde le gouvernement public (*ibid.,* pp. 97-98). In other words, justice stands toward the body politic as does the will toward the soul.

synonymous with utility. Although Bodin did not go so far as Hotman in denying that transcendental values are applicable to everyday life, his unorthodox views are clearly a step in that direction.[34] Perhaps Bodin's concept of friendship, standing midway between Aquinas and Hotman, is indicative of his generally anomalous position: "Friendship is a mutual love tending toward the enjoyment of things honest or dishonest, from which it appears that friendship is no virtue in itself."[35] Only a step is required to transform "mutual love" into the "mutual interest" which Hotman described.

If positive law can lead men to the good life, then good government can bring about halcyon days of peace and plenty. In any event this is what we read in a treatise by Louis Turquet de Mayerne: *La monarchie aristodémocratique ou le gouvernement composé et meslé des trois formes de légitime république*, Paris, 1611. Professor Roland Mousnier, calling attention to this unusual work, first written in 1591, has said that "all the traits" of Turquet's elaborate blueprint to establish a new kind of Estates General designed to function somewhat like a Constitutional Assembly, *"font penser irrésistiblement à la philosophie des lumières, bien des traits évoquent l'oeuvre des assemblées bourgeoises de la Révolution française."*[36] If Mousnier may have rather overstated the case, it remains clear, nevertheless, that Turquet wrote in a manner at least compatible with eighteenth century social engineers. Thinking true aristocracy was more

[34] Thomas N. Tentler, "The Meaning of Prudence in Bodin," *Traditio*, 1959, xv, 365-384, discusses the extent of Bodin's unorthodoxy.

[35] *Ibid.*, pp. 111-112.

[36] "L'Opposition politique bourgeoise à la fin du XVIe siècle et au début du XVIIe siècle: L'oeuvre de Louis Turquet de Mayerne," *Revue historique*, 1955, CCXIII, p. 15.

a product of virtue than of birth, Turquet described a democratic system to recruit nobility from among all members of the population. His emphasis upon a career open to talents was, as Mousnier points out, expressed in a bourgeois spirit. If a person, for example, in whom nature has implanted "a vehement inclination" to amass "great riches by art and diligence," should "employ" his wealth "splendidly . . . he will . . . be worthy of advancement to the highest honors of government, those which *donnent degré et pied ferme à la noblesse.*"[37] Turquet said his plan for the democratic selection of aristocracy, would provide a "common purpose for citizens, noble or non-noble, who, having attained indifferently . . . public honors and dignities, unite the parts of their Estate in friendship by the equality of right."[38] Such an arrangement is dictated by nature. Indeed, according to Turquet, the *insigne ignorance* about nature's laws is an obstacle to social improvement among "all nations of the earth." Education is the key to moral and political progress. If only "individuals could receive enlightenment and the people *une bonne réformation* we would no doubt see in a generation or two *un siecle d'or remply de tout bien désirable,* all of which depends upon the dexterity, magnanimity and charity of princes."[39] In short, individually or collectively, men in society are as good or as bad as their governments.

The writings of Hotman, Bodin and Turquet fall into one of two general categories in the backgrounds to early utilitarian philosophy. The second influence lies in controversies which raged around the problem of the relation of the passions to evil. The Augustinians thought the passions, originating with the Fall,

[37] *La monarchie aristodémocratique,* p. 86.
[38] *Ibid.,* p. 405.   [39] *Ibid.,* p. 87.

were sinful and could not be controlled by reason. The Jesuits, taking a contrary view, denied all connection between evil and the passions which, they insisted, were ruled by intellect and will. The Jesuit Father Pierre Le Moyne, for example, writing in 1645, explained that "passion is universal . . . , as old as the world." [Do you think] "love has a different color in Ethiopia than in France? . . . Are hatred and anger less cruel under our skies than under those of the savages?" Moreover, Le Moyne said, similar emotions could be observed among animals, and in all instances they came from the "pursuit of pleasure and the avoidance of pain." These passions were "natural," neither good nor bad because "they have limits." In contrast, Le Moyne emphasized that passions "arising from opinion," where the object of satisfaction went beyond mere sensual pleasure and pain, might become evil because such passions arose in the intellect which has no intrinsic bounds. Reason alone could hold them in check.[40]

The conflicting positions of the Augustinians and the Jesuits were directly connected to contrary views about society and government. Those who argued that the passions were evil and beyond the control of reason also believed society was superior to a "state of nature" because only civil government was capable of keeping the peace. Convinced that savages lived in the worst of all possible worlds—a kind of Hobbesian nightmare—the Augustinians defined society above all in terms of its repressive functions. In contrast, if good and evil were largely a product of intellectual activity, then society, the only place where culture was possible, might be seen in educative and

[40] *Les peintures morales*, 2d edn., 2 vols., Paris, 1654, I, Bk. III, chap. 4, 307-325.

positive terms. Here the state of nature would be undesirable not only for its anarchy but also because the inhabitants were uncivilized. Thus Le Moyne described the savage in the following terms:

> He is without eyes for the beauties of nature, and for those of the arts . . . ; the rarest statue . . . would not be treated more civilly by him than a tree trunk. His other senses are neither less crude nor less savage. . . . Honor and glory are ideas unknown to him. He is generally ignorant of all that which can give pleasure and contentment.[41]

Pursuing this line of thought somewhat further, Le Moyne insisted that reason stood in the same relation to will as the King to his ministers: in both cases the subordinate agency acted only in accordance with the powers received from the ruler. By equating government with reason (much the same way, incidentally, as did Bodin and Descartes' friend, Jean Silhon) and arguing at the same time that good and evil were a product of intellectual activity, the Jesuit more than suggested that both reason and virtue, fully developed, could exist only in civilized society. Good and evil, vice and virtue, were purely social phenomena. These startling implications of Jesuit doctrine and of writings such as those of Hotman, Bodin and Turquet did not escape the notice of contemporaries. Indeed, they helped prepare the ground for the construction of far-reaching utilitarian theories in the middle of the seventeenth century. A most unusual document in this regard is an anonymous manuscript, containing no hint even of the author's profession or social status, in the Bibliothèque Sainte-Geneviève in Paris entitled, *Abrégé de politique où il est traité de*

41 *Ibid.*, Bk. VII, chap. 2, 620-624.

l'origine des sociétés civiles, de la puissance des Princes et du devoir des sujets.[42]

Internal evidence reveals that the manuscript, which, as suggested by the title, is an abridgment of a larger work, was written sometime between 1668 and 1679.[43] The original treatise is lost; and, apparently, only three copies of the shorter version exist.[44] Yet a curious circumstance demonstrates that the missing text had influence which went far beyond the neglected manuscripts which remain in the Bibliothèque Sainte-Geneviève. An anonymous book, bearing the seal of royal privilege, was published in Lyon in 1687. The second sentence of its lengthy title is very close to that of the abridgment: *Essais de morale et de politique où il est traité des devoirs de l'homme considéré comme particulier, et comme vivant en société. De l'origine des sociétés civiles, de l'Autorité des Princes, et du devoir des sujets. Divisés en deux parties.* The second part of the book, corresponding in content with the second sentence in the title, although differing substantially from the manuscript, contains an entire chapter which is identical, word

[42] MS 2215.

[43] The author writes (p. 85): "et lorsque le Roy dans sa derniere guerre de Flandre fit publier un petit livre en forme de manifeste, où il justifioit ses droits sur ces pays bas. . . ." The only official publication corresponding to this description is: *Renonciation non valable que la reine de France a faite de la succession à la couronne d'Espagne et des pays qui en dépendent*, Paris, 1667. The first page states explicitly that the king had published this manifest "pour informer toute l'Europe de la justice de ses droits." And since the manuscript specifies: "le Roy dans sa *derniere* guerre de Flandre . . . ," the document must have been written sometime between 1668, the year in which the War of Devolution ended, and the ending of the Dutch War in 1679. The royal publication is described in E. Bourgeois and L. André, *Les Sources de l'histoire de France au XVIIᵉ siècle 1610–1715*, 8 vols., Paris, 1913-1935, IV, art. 2940, pp. 306-307.

[44] They are at the Bibliothèque Sainte-Geneviève: MSS 2215, 3082, 2997. The citations which follow are taken from MS 2215.

for word, with a chapter in the abridgment written two decades previous.[45] Neither the *first sentence* in the title of the 1687 book nor the corresponding subject matter in the first part appear in the earlier abridgment, but the opening lines of the abridgment show that the author had discussed the topic in his original full-length version. All of which strongly suggests that the book published in Lyon was based upon the missing work, not upon the abridgments. At the end of the last century, George Lacour-Gayet,[46] who was unaware of the earlier abridged copies and their markedly different content, demonstrated that the book published in Lyon had considerable influence in France. However tenuous the connection, the evidence would indicate a continuous and fairly broad current of thought.

The opening lines of the manuscript describe ethics, "the art of living well," as a discipline concerned with man either as an individual *per se* or as "a member of Civil Society." The former study he called "monastic," the latter "political." Indicating that he had previously discussed "monastic" ethics,[47] the author turned his attention to politics. He began by saying that since all men living in a state of nature were born with equal rights, no person was superior to another and, in the absence of positive law, every individual was "guided by the light of his natural reason." To understand what is permitted by natural reason, it was "necessary to distinguish natural law from natural right." The former was a positive duty to perform or not to perform a particular act; the

[45] Compare chap. 35 in the second part of the book with chap. 30 in the second part of the manuscript.

[46] *L'Education politique de Louis XIV*, Paris, 1898, pp. 382-384.

[47] "La morale qui considere l'homme comme particulier J'appelle monastique et c'est celle que j'ay traitter jusqu'à présent," p. 1.

latter was a voluntary power to do or not to do something.[48]

Natural law, according to the author, imposed two positive obligations on man: "to love God above all and to love ourselves after God." Anything not contrary to the love of God and to self-love was, by definition, a natural right. And since natural reason alone inspired men with knowledge of law and of right, it follows that they can act legitimately only according to this reason. Therefore, in all matters not related to the love of God, men were bound by love for themselves to act in ways useful to themselves: "That is to say it is our proper utility which must be the Rule and the basis for all our reasoning. Therefore the rule and the measure of natural right is utility."[49]

What obligations does the love of God impose upon man? Writing in a manner reminiscent of Antoine Hotman, the author denied that relations among men should be governed by man's love for God. "To love someone," says St. Thomas, "is to wish him some good." Yet God is the source of all good; men were therefore powerless to wish Him something which could be to His benefit. But love also produced esteem for the object loved; love for the Almighty must consist in esteem for His infinite perfection and readiness to obey His will. "But in the natural state we suppose . . . God makes no law or positive command; it follows therefore that the obedience due Him while in that state does not consist in obedience to any particular point. It is only necessary to be ready always to obey Him when it shall please Him to command."

Having defined natural obligations to God by saying in effect that it is sufficient to love and think well

[48] *Ibid.*, pp. 3-4.   [49] *Ibid.*, pp. 5-6.

of Him, the author turned toward the second rule of natural law: every man must love himself after loving God. Where love of God took the form of esteem and obedience because He is infinite and perfect, self-love caused the imperfect individual to seek benefit for himself; he wished "to procure all the goods, advantages and conveniences which are not only necessary, but are useful for his preservation." Moreover, if God issued no positive commands in a state of nature and if nothing which man can procure could possibly be contrary to his love for God because the Almighty lacks nothing, it was clearly unreasonable to neglect or "prejudice one's own utility and conservation" in the name of love for God. Fasting or vows taken by monks, for example, were clear abuses of the love men owed themselves. Men may act to their disadvantage only in order "to acquire a greater benefit or avoid a greater pain." To kill another in self-defense is to choose the least inconvenient of alternatives, but suicide would be as flagrant a violation of natural law as is mortification of the flesh.[50]

Since every man in a state of nature was born with equal rights and with no authority to command another, it also followed that no one had more right to property than another. Were this not so, what tribunal could rule in a particular dispute and by what authority could it judge in favor of one or to the prejudice of another? The author was obliged to agree explicitly with Hobbes that force would then be the only arbiter. Self-love invested each with an equal right to seek by violence to possess all and to subjugate his neighbor. In short, nature was a "state of fear, of alarm and of war of all against all."[51] Since the state of nature was a condition of anarchy it

[50] *Ibid.*, pp. 6, 10-12.   [51] *Ibid.*, p. 32.

would be contrary to the principle of reasonable self-love and utility. Therefore, if men could, by means other than armed conflict, place themselves in a position where they would not fear one another, "natural reason dictates that they embrace" such procedures. And if all men renounced their natural rights with respect to possessing everything and subjugating everyone, no person would have cause to fear his neighbor: "Everyone would then live in peace." But a peace accomplished by means of mutual promises to forbear from exercising individual natural rights, and to remain content with the *status quo* would signify that man had left the state of nature and, by submitting himself to the law of contracts, had entered civil society.[52]

Although agreeing with Hobbes about the way man left nature and entered society, the author's views of man and society diverged sharply and frequently anticipated those of Locke. First, laws arising out of "pacts and conventions" were as natural as those governing men outside of society: in both states natural reason guided human behavior. Therefore, a study of society was largely the application of the second rule of natural law (the duty to love oneself) to the principles of contract. All contracts involved promises but all promises were not contracts. In order to be irrevocable a promise must be made under certain conditions. The promiser, for example, must have a preexisting right to dispose of the thing which he promises. Also, "that which is promised must be reasonable because unreasonable promises are not binding, on the contrary the parties are bound to re-

[52] "Nous allons donc parler doraisnavant du droit des gens, et comme son fondement est la cession mutuelle, que les hommes se font les uns aux autres du droit qu'ils ont tous a tout, il nous faut parler d'abord de cette cession, et de les différentes especes" (*ibid.*, p. 34).

pudiate them because honoring an unreasonable promise . . . is to persist against reason which is vicious [conduct]." The object of the promise must be "useful and advantageous" to both parties because no one could reasonably bind himself to another without receiving some advantage in exchange.[53]

At this point the author's concept of "advantage" merits particular attention. Whether he knew it or not, his arguments were undermining the established mercantilist belief that one man's profit is necessarily another man's loss.[54] And, more generally, his insist-

[53] "L'objet de la promesse doit etre quelque bien, car si c'est un mal, la promesse est déraisonnable, et par conséquent elle est nulle, or le bien doit etre un bien indifférent, c'est-à-dire, qu'on puisse faire et ne pas faire; car si c'est un bien nécessaire et auquelle on soit obligé de sa nature et qu'on ne puisse omettre sans manquer à son devoir, il est inutile de sy obliger par promesse, puisqu'on le doit d'ailleurs" (p. 39).

[54] Most frequently, it is true, scholars have understood the axiom to mean one *country's* loss is necessarily another country's gain, a concept supported at first glance by the idea that circulating wealth creates general prosperity within one state. But the documents show clearly that throughout the seventeenth century mercantilists applied this principle to individuals as well as to countries. Montchrétien in 1615 wrote: "One man's loss is another man's profit. This is true and is better known in matters of commerce than anywhere else" (see Chapter I, above). At the end of the century, in 1698. Pottier de la Hestroye, speaking of "the perpetual circulation of wealth," wrote: "The state profits from the loss of one and the gain of others" (see Chapter II, above). In other words, an increase in the volume and rate of monetary circulation would be to the advantage of all subjects (and to the state through indirect taxation) even though each individual transaction, that is every time money passed from one hand to the other, necessarily involved profit and loss. Later in this chapter, Belesbat attacks precisely this position.

In this connection it is interesting to note that in the sixteenth century Antoine Hotman, recognizing an incompatibility between the unbridled pursuit of wealth and the belief that one man's loss is necessarily another's gain, tried clumsily to deny the validity of the traditional view:

Quand à ce que l'on pourroit dire que l'avaricieux bien qu'il ne se face point de tort, faict toutesfois dommage au public,

ence upon the reasonable and above all the utilitarian character of contracts as the source of all social relations, carried him far along the path toward views of society popular a century later. Discussing the problem of "advantage" the author said: "Here under the name useful we mean not only natural and gross advantages but also those which might in any way prove beneficial. A reputation of being liberal and charitable, for example, is very advantageous . . . , thus a man may perform good deeds from the sole motive of appearing to be charitable." Similarly, to pass for *un homme de parole* must also be considered advantageous and, other things being equal, the desire to be known as an *honnête homme* "is by itself sufficiently powerful to oblige one to keep a promise." In short, all contracts rested upon the fundamental principle of utility; no agreement was binding unless

the advantage is such, with respect to him who promises and to him to whom the promise is

---

d'autant qu'il ne se peut enrichir qu'un autre n'appauvrisse, et comme l'on dict jamais personne ne gaigne que un autre ny perde; d'autant que nous ne pouvons pas tous estre riches. Mais telles objections n'ont aucune apparance, d'autant que moyennant qu'un homme riche soit homme de bien, les autres n'en sentiront aucun dommage. . . . Et à dire vray un homme riche n'a rien plus que les autres hors le commandement et le choix, qui sont à la vérité de grandes commoditez: mais elles ne nuysent de rien au public, d'autant que cela n'empesche pas que les autres ne puissent estre accomodez et chacun selon son rang peut honnestement vivre et qui voudra gouster de ces commoditez, qu'il s'efforce d'estre riche. Car moyennant que ce soit sans faire tort à autruy et sans injustice, plus y aura de riches en ce monde, plus y aura de gens de bien, quoy que soit de gens qui pourront estre vertueux et à leur aise philosopher. De sorte que pour satisfaire à nostre premiere promesse il n'y peut avoir d'inconvénient en l'acquisition des grandes richesses: ainsi au contraire pour venir au second poinct, plus un homme est riche, plus il est heureux, et plus il a de moyen de bien faire (*op.cit.*, p. 179).

made, that it can reasonably be preferred to the pain and inconvenience the promiser engages to undergo. . . .

Therefore when the inconveniences are greater than the advantages promised to one and to the other, the promise is no longer binding. Because, according to our principles, it is reasonable to suffer an inconvenience only in order to acquire a greater advantage or to avoid a greater inconvenience.[55]

Since utility was a principle which, by definition, prohibited men from alienating their rights to the necessities of life, no one in a state of nature could therefore reasonably give up his natural right to everything in order to enter civil society if, in his new state, he would be deprived of the necessities of existence. Consequently those men living in society who were deprived of necessities were not bound by contract and must be considered as living in a state of nature where they had as much right to any piece of property as anyone else. It could therefore be stated as a general principle that

natural reason requires that men do not refuse to one another things which are necessary; it [natural reason] commands instead that men give to others that which is necessary if, by doing so, they do not put themselves in the same necessity. And one must give *à pur et à plein*. . . .[56]

[55] *Ibid.*, pp. 40-41.

[56] *Ibid.*, p. 55. Insofar as the author suggests here that all rights, even those relating to property, are defined and originate in the community, he may seem at first glance to anticipate Rousseau more than Locke; but the crucial concept of an organic unity is missing. Moreover, the author points unmistakably toward Locke for whom the property right was indefeasible because man brought it with him into society. The author's view is that if a person in civil society is deprived of property rights he exercised in a state of na-

It was not without cause that the Church Fathers said: "The poor have a right to the wealth of the rich. Charity is a command of natural reason."[57]

Although very brief, the author's thoughts about commerce are of particular interest. Contractual problems arising out of things which were necessary and things which were useful were closely connected to economic theory. All commerce involved some form of exchange. "And at bottom whether an exchange is made for money or for another thing in nature it is always a sale and a purchase, because money takes the place of the thing in nature. Money after all has no utility by itself but only in so far as it can procure the things of nature; therefore it is merely a question of language."[58] Necessity and utility determined the price or value of an article. With respect to necessity, we have just seen that the principle of utility was inapplicable; therefore the price of commodities essential for life should be controlled. In contrast, the rule of the open market applied to all unnecessary things: they could be sold at whatever price they would fetch.

What factors determined the price a product would fetch on the open market? It was against the principle of utility that any product be sold for more than its worth. And in determining how much an article was worth, men must distinguish between "physical" and "moral" value. St. Augustine had observed that a man would "pay more for a horse than for a slave." Frequently a worthless souvenir was valued more dearly than the finest stallion from the royal stables. Clearly,

---

ture, that is those he took with him into society, then the social pact is ended so far as that individual is concerned. To be sure, the author speaks only of "les choses nécessaires," but the parallel seems sufficiently close to be worth noting.

[57] *Ibid.*, p. 75.   [58] *Ibid.*, p. 53.

"men do not esteem things for themselves." Price was determined by "moral value" which in turn was ascertained:

> by the utility which we receive, by the pleasure obtained, by the need or desire which we have. . . . Also he who sells must estimate the thing in proportion to what it is worth for him. . . . He must figure the labor put into the thing which he sells, the need he has for the article and the profit or loss which he will receive.
>
> It is therefore what the article is worth with respect to both the buyer and the seller which determines the value and the price.[59]

In other words, assuming an ideally free market, goods would not sell for more than "they are worth" because self-love, guided by natural reason, would protect men from paying more than "true value" received for any purchase. According to the criteria of utility, the buyer could not reasonably act against his own interests.

The author carried this line of thought no further, and it is not clear whether he understood how readily such reasoning could lend itself to the most extreme anti-mercantilist theories. Be that as it may, aristocrats soon began to insist that France's economic difficulties were created by ministers who did not understand that commerce would thrive only when government did not interfere with its operations. And these arguments were integrated into a larger philosophical framework wherein the principles of utility played a central role.

In addition to these anti-mercantilist implications the manuscript abridgment is significant in other ways for subsequent theories of political opposition.

[59] *Ibid.*, pp. 59-60.

The author derived fifteen rules of moral conduct from the principle of utility. The burden of his argument was that since everyone originally had equal rights and would not have given them up without acquiring in exchange some corresponding advantage, men in civil society were bound to safeguard the interests of others in the same manner as they would have others safeguard their own. The golden rule has here a special meaning: it is a precise description of the terms of the original contract establishing the state of civil society. Like Antoine Hotman and Pierre Le Moyne, the author appears to suggest that good and evil, vice and virtue may be best understood as purely social phenomena. And, although the anonymous author here again did not pursue further the economic implications of his argument, subsequent reformers insisted that the golden rule is the natural law of trade in civil society. Moreover they identified the golden rule with the principle of utility, transforming this maxim into a natural law of reciprocity whose universal application destroyed not only the mercantilist distinction between domestic and foreign trade, but also provided a powerful impetus to the familiar, now wholly secular, drive for world and cosmic unity.

Another theme linking early utilitarian thought with later theories of political opposition may be found in the section of the manuscript which discusses the power of the Prince and the duties of his subjects. For the most part, the author here adopted Hobbes's point of view: the unrestricted exercise of authority was the only means by which government could prevent men from reverting to their original state of nature. The duty of a prince was to keep the peace and guard against all that which might be injurious to the general interest. And the general interest, conceived as merely another name for reason of state, was "the first and only principle for all actions of Princes."[60]

If government functioned only according to its interests (here the author starts down a path Hobbes did not venture), punishments for actions detrimental to the community should be imposed in each case so as to satisfy the public welfare, the particular interests of the wrongdoer, and the injured parties. In other words legal sanctions, both criminal and civil, should be derived exclusively from the principle of utility:

> This utility must be understood with respect to the person who committed the fault or with respect to the others.
>
> The utility of punishment with regard to the guilty one consists in preventing him from falling again [into the same error].
>
> The utility with respect to the others consists as much in sheltering them from insult as in preventing them from falling into the same error.
>
> In considering the utility of the punishment with respect to the guilty one, he must suffer a penalty sufficient to deter him from committing the same fault, and a penalty is considered capable of impeding an action when it is greater and incurs more damage or pain than the action can bring profit or pleasure.
>
> If we measure the penalty by the utility which others receive by being sheltered from insults, we must take notice of the ease . . . or profit which may be enjoyed by the fault committed, or the greatness of the damage suffered and proportion the penalty accordingly.[61]

[60] *Ibid.*, 2d part, p. 81. Several pages are paraphrased from Hobbes.
[61] *Ibid.*, 2d part, pp. 59-60.

This is not yet a theory of government and society based upon the principle of "the greatest happiness," but it is a step in that direction. The following pages show how this line of thought, clearly developed, became central to an ideology of opposition which struck not only at mercantilist doctrine, but also directly at all the values traditionally associated with the *ancien régime*.

ii. BELESBAT: ANTI-MERCANTILIST THEORY AND THE PRINCIPLES OF UTILITY

Charles Paul Hurault de l'Hôpital, known as the Seigneur of Belesbat, a great grandson of Catherine de Médicis' venerable Chancellor, submitted six memoirs to Louis XIV in September 1692.[62] Despite the diversity of topics, his writings taken together form a kind of loose unity which may be treated as one work. His apparent obscurity and his almost certain eccentricity[63] did not keep Belesbat's writings

[62] These documents are bound in a single volume (B.N., Fds. fr., MS 1205) along with other papers composed at various dates between 1694 and 1702. Serious scholarly attention had been devoted to Belesbat on only one occasion: Albert Schatz and Robert Caillemer, "Le mercantilisme libéral à la fin du XVIIe siècle en France. Les idées économiques et politiques de M. de Belesbat," *Revue économique et politique*, XX (1906), 29-70, 387-396, 559-574, 630-642, 791-816. As the title of their article indicates, the authors did not go beyond the purely political and economic aspects of Belesbat's writings: and their failure to do so has led them to mistake seriously both the intent and significance of the writer's treatise. The subsequent pages show how Belesbat's political and economic thought takes on a special meaning when seen as an integral part of a much wider current of ideas.

[63] The following description by Saint-Simon, although more vivid, agrees substantially with other contemporary observations about Belesbat: "C'était une manière d'éléphant pour la figure, une espèce de boeuf pour l'esprit, qui s'était accoutumé à se croire courtisan, à suivre le roi dans tous ses voyages de guerre et de frontière, et à n'en être pas plus avancé pour cela" (*Mémoires*, ed. A. de Boislisle, 41 vols., Paris, 1879-1928, XIII, 306). Belesbat died unmarried on 15 February 1706.

from being known. Copies and lengthy extracts of his work may be found in Paris,[64] Grenoble,[65] Rouen,[66] and Nantes.[67] One memoir aroused sufficient notice to provoke an anonymous person to address a refutation to the president of the Paris *Parlement*.[68] Moreover, a letter by Belesbat to Controller General Pontchartrain reveals that the King's ministers were also acquainted with some of Belesbat's writings.[69] Finally, evidence exists which suggests that Belesbat's ideas may have had a wide audience in the fashionable salon.[70]

[64] B.N., Fds. fr., MS 7009.

[65] Bibliothèque Municipale, MS 807. It is a beautifully bound full-length copy.

[66] Bibliothèque Municipale, Collection Montbret, MS 3450. Authorship here is attributed to Belesbat's father Henri de l'Hôpital. This is not possible because the earliest memoirs are explicitly dated September 1692 (f. 75) and Henri de l'Hôpital died on 13 March 1684 (A.N., Minutier Central, Etude XC, 267, 27 March 1684).

[67] Bibliothèque Municipale, MS 1154. These substantial extracts are ascribed in Nantes to the Marquis de Breauté, an impoverished noble who, after a vain search for the philosopher's stone, died in 1708 from the poisonous effects of one of his personal alchemical remedies. Since Breauté is known to have written on related subjects (see Saint-Simon, *Mémoires*, XVI, 424, n.4), it is possible that he copied from Belesbat extracts which were later attributed to the unfortunate marquis.

[68] B.N., Fds. fr. MS 16736, ff. 265-272.

[69] A.N., G⁷ 695. The letter, written shortly after the Capitation in 1695, is in part as follows:

Monseigneur,

Il y a un an, ou environ, que je remis au Roy un mémoire concernant plusieurs affaires nouvelles dont il pouvoit revenir à Sa Majesté des sommes tres considérables. Sa Majesté vous le remit entre les mains Monseigneur pour le voir; depuis ce temps, je n'ay fait aucune démarche pour cette affaire. Mais ayant appris que vous aviez résolu, Monseigneur, de faire une affaire sur les toiles qui font une partie de mon mémoire, je vous supplie tres humblement de vouloir bien que je vous remette les Etats et mémoires concernant cette affaire à Monsieur de Caumartin à qui j'en ay parlay pour en faire son raport. . . .

[70] François Thimoléon, Abbé de Choisy, Belesbat's first cousin,

Belesbat declared that France's long economic decline was caused largely "by the divers quarrels we
have had with Holland for the past twenty-five years
or so."[71] He was convinced that "if we change and
adopt an entirely contrary [policy] . . . France will
become more opulent than ever." It was not by cap-

---

had organized at his home in the Luxembourg gardens one of the
first political *salons* in France; and the topic discussed by the
learned assemblage in April 1692, four months before Belesbat submitted his memoirs to the King, was entitled, "the present state of
the kingdom of France." If so many other people subsequently knew
of Belesbat's writings, it would seem possible that this knowledge
was also shared by the intellectuals who met every Tuesday after-
noon at his cousin's home. The documentation for this statement
is as follows. The Bibliothèque de l'Arsenal, MS 3186, contains fragments of a "Journal de l'assemblée de Luxembourg" written by
the abbé de Choisy. The term Luxembourg refers to the palace
which was Choisy's residence (A.N., Minutier Central, Etude CXII,
420A, 6 January 1701). The significance of the club, having among
its members, for example, Fontenelle and Charles Perrault, is discussed by Gustave Lanson, "Le rôle de l'expérience dans la formation de la philosophie du XVIIIᵉ siècle en France," *Revue du mois*,
IV, 410. Also in E. Carcassone, *Montesquieu et le problème de la
constitution Française au XVIIIᵉ siècle*, Paris, 1927, chap. 1.

Even if Choisy did not provide a forum for his cousin's views,
the Abbé's own thoughts were on occasion quite similar. Speaking
of Colbert, for example, Choisy wrote:

> Il crut que le royaume de France se pourroit suffire à lui-meme,
> oubliant sans doute que le Créateur de toutes choses n'a placé
> les différens biens dans les différentes parties de l'univers qu'afin
> de lier une société commune, et d'obliger les hommes par leurs
> interets à se communiquer réciproquement les trésors qui se
> trouveroient dans chaque pays. Il parla à des marchands et leur
> demanda en ministre les secrets de leur métier, qu'ils lui dis-
> simulerent en vieux negocians. Toujours magnifique en idées et
> presque toujours malheureux dans l'exécution . . . il établit
> toutes sortes de manufactures qui coutoient plus qu'elles ne
> valoient (ed. M. de Lescure, Paris, 1888, *Mémoires*, 2 vols., I,
> pp. 92-93).

[71] B.N., Fds. fr., MS 1205, f. 4: "Les divers démesles que depuis
environ vingt-cinq ans nous avons eu avec la holande, estant une
des diminution des Richesses de la France, j'ay cru que pour establir
solidement la parfaite Intelligence si utile aux deux nations, il
estoit nécessaire d'esclaircir à fond leurs véritables interests. . . ."

turing or destroying the commerce of other nations that states would become rich; governments would acquire wealth and power only by encouraging trade which conformed to their "true interests" as defined by nature. The Dutch, for example, established on a territory so exiguous that it was "not even worth the price of its own upkeep," and with scarcely "any clergy, nobility or office-holders and with little revenue from land have no alternative but to invest almost all their wealth in trade." And since Dutch government rested entirely upon this activity, trade constituted their one "true interest." In contrast, the vast realm of France was so fertile that the people could "never consume even two-thirds of its production"; the remainder must be exported. Indeed, the extent to which agriculture, as distinguished from commerce, conformed to France's "true interests" could be seen from both the social structure and the proportion of national wealth invested in trade. There were six orders of society: the clergy, the nobility, the office-holders, the merchants, the artisans, and the peasants.[72] Of these only the merchants were concerned with trade, and even among them it was "rare that a family enriched by business continues [in its profession] for several generations." These facts, concluded Belesbat, demonstrated that France was provi-

[72] This was not an empirical observation; two separate traditions have long conceived of society as divided into six parts. Aristotle seems to be the most ancient (*Politics*, VII, 8, 1328 b, 3ff.), but there is also a neo-Platonic tradition: "Now it is not without cause, that we divide our present commonweale into sixe manner of labours, and sixe kind of men. For the number of sixe by the doctrine of *Pythagoras*, is the first and cheefest of perfect numbers, and the first number of equality. . . . Moreover, it is not without great reason, if our present commonweale and city be made perfect by sixe manner of Citizens, seeing the excelent and most mighty god in times past brought to perfection the universal building of this worldly house in sixe daies." Guillaume de la Perrière, *Mirrour of Policie* . . . , (f. 124).

dentially destined to supply the agricultural products needed by the Dutch in exchange for merchandise they brought to French ports. When misguided ministers understood that nature compelled the state to "take measures to have the Dutch reestablish the center of their commerce" in France, the United Provinces would be "persuaded that, far from wanting to oppress them, France wishes only to preserve their liberty and to accord full protection to their trade." Hostilities would end because France would no longer threaten their "true interest," trade.[73]

The complementary character of the Dutch and French economies, declared Belesbat, revealed only part of a divine network of reciprocal interests binding all powers into a universal pattern of economic interrelations: "There is nothing that one [country] lacks which the others do not produce. . . . God in His infinite wisdom, having created men for society, has so well divided them that they cannot do without one another."[74] Restrictions on trade only upset the natural interdependence of states. Therefore merchants should be free to engage "in the commerce of their choice." It could be taken as a general rule that the natural resources and the character and distribution of capital investment in a country determined the economic activities naturally suited to its population and defined, at the same time, the "true interests" of state. Colbert and his successors, foolishly attempting to compete in the area nature reserved for the Dutch, upset the natural division of international labor, creating enemies abroad and attacking vital interests at home. A glance at the tax rolls would demonstrate that the loss of trade caused by this absurd policy was largely responsible for the poverty of the people who, standing with respect to the King

[73] B.N., Fds. fr., MS 1205, ff. 4-6.   [74] *Ibid.*, f. 1.

as tenant farmers to the proprietors of their land, could no longer supply great revenues to the nobility and to the state as they had in the past: the *taille* "was one third higher at the peace of the Pyrenees and the people were infinitely richer; their misery therefore has another cause which I attribute to the loss of trade."[75]

If commerce would thrive only after merchants everywhere were permitted to trade where and when they found it profitable, it would become clear, according to Belesbat, that the King's ministers were mistaken in their belief that one country's profit was necessarily obtained at the expense of another. Moreover, Belesbat demanded the same freedom for merchants in internal affairs. When the state ceased to intervene in the everyday activities of merchants, an age of prosperity would necessarily ensue. "It must be taken as a principle that liberty is the soul of commerce, without which . . . good harbors, great rivers and . . . fertile [lands] are of no use. When liberty is absent nothing is of any avail."[76] The gist of Belesbat's argument is that nature had provided for the distribution of wealth by countless numbers of transactions which caused the products of one place to be exchanged for those of another both within and without the realm. Every transaction, either domestic or foreign, required complete freedom because it was carried out in special circumstances by merchants whose fortunes depended partially upon the secret and unique procedures by which each conducted his business. No one should be permitted to interfere with the affairs of merchants.[77] One man's profit would not be necessarily another's loss. Detailed regulation, far from protecting the market from unfair competition,

[75] *Ibid.*, f. 43.   [76] *Ibid.*, f. 6.   [77] *Ibid.*, ff. 103-105.

would only destroy the liberty and good faith essential to any flourishing trade:

> If people are to become rich, the lands which they inhabit must be made to produce more than they can consume, and they must be permitted to market the surplus. Great fertility is of no use without this outlet . . . and since the wealth of the state depends upon this outlet, it is necessary to speak of commerce before describing the means whereby the country can be made fertile.
>
> We call commerce an exchange between men of the things they mutually need. It is divided into two kinds: that which is practiced between the inhabitants of a single country and that which is carried on with foreigners. In both the principles for success are the same. And despite the fact that there is an infinite number of ways in which to practice trade, all different, they are founded on a great liberty, large capital investment, a lot of good faith, much application and a great secrecy. Each merchant, having his particular views, in such a way that he who profits from a sale of his products, does not prevent the one who buys them from profiting considerably by disposing of them, after a time, in the manner which he had [originally] planned. Thus the entire success of commerce, consisting as it does in liberty, large capital investment, application and secrecy, prevents princes from ever intervening without destroying the principles. And it is for this reason that they must always give to commerce in general a vigorous protection without ever entering into a single detail for any reason whatsoever.[78]

[78] *Ibid.*, f. 103.

Belesbat thought freedom and prosperity could come about only as a result of far-reaching reforms in government and society. He also explained that such vast changes should be discussed in the light of wider philosophical considerations:

> To reason solidly on a matter it is necessary to examine it from its origins in order to establish principles from which we can draw exact conclusions. This is what leads me to begin this work by examining what is a state, the different kinds which exist, what is the nature of men who belong to them, the interests of princes, those of their states in general, and the interests of those who have a place in government.[79]

Here Belesbat revealed the powerful influence of early utilitarian thought. Thinking the Prince God's representative on earth and an hereditary monarchy incomparably superior to other forms of government, Belesbat explained that because kings, however great their power, were unable to do everything themselves, they were "obliged to employ individuals who are frequently governed by interests very opposed" to those of their sovereign. To control these people effectively

> Princes must establish as a principle . . . that men have neither good nor bad qualities in the last degree . . . and since they act only in accordance with their interests, [princes must] oblige them by the certitude of rewards always to do good and by the certitude of punishment never to do evil.[80]

If rewards and punishments were calculated according to the degree of conformity or deviation from

[79] *Ibid.*, f. 96.   [80] *Ibid.*, f. 97.

the just and equitable "rules and maxims" of good government, the ruler would not only be well served but the entire society would eventually become penetrated with virtue. "Like other men [ministers are] people of habit and [are] led by their interests." They were certain to avoid all bad actions if the slightest deviation were punished according to the spirit in which it was committed. In a case of mere inadvertence or negligence, for example, the Prince could "never be too indulgent . . . , the greatest geniuses often commit serious faults"; but a premeditated violation could "never be punished too severely." Even the most pedestrian of ministers, capable of but the slightest reflection, would in the course of time become inured through force of habit and by the guidance of his own interests to perform only virtuous acts. The people, having before them the perpetual example of virtuous rule and prospering mightily under the free operation of economic laws, would become "united and attached to [their Prince] from their own inclination." The love of their sovereign, whose interests were "inseparably united" with their own, would in turn cause them to admire the rules and maxims of equity and justice upon which their own happiness and well-being depended. In this way "the larger part of the inhabitants of a state will become *Gens de Bien*."[81]

Carrying early utilitarian thought to unexpected

---

[81] *Ibid.*, ff. 97-98. Some lines from Pierre Charron's *De la Sagesse*, edn. Paris, 1886, Bk. II, chap. 3, pp. 320-321, written almost a century earlier, are suggestive of Belesbat's views: "[La] Nature a disposé toutes choses au meilleur estat qu'elles puissent estre . . . de sorte que qui la suyvra ne fauldra [ne manquera] point d'obtenir et posséder son bien et sa fin. . . . Les hommes sont naturellement bons, et ne suyvent le mal que pour le proffit ou le plaisir: donc les législateurs, pour les induire à suyvre leur inclination naturelle et bonne, et non pour forcer leurs volontés, ont proposé deux choses contraires, la peine et la récompense."

lengths,[82] Belesbat did more than say that what is useful is just or that utility is the operation or execution of the golden rule embodied in the social contract establishing civil society. He converted utility into a metaphysical principle meaning justice in action. Since all men were motivated purely by their interests and all interests were created by nature, "justice" or "utility" could be defined as the satisfaction of human interests in the manner prescribed by nature. Universal justice therefore could be defined as that state when men become conscious that all people's interests were everywhere properly protected. In sum, where early utilitarian theory explained that "justice renders to each his own,"[83] Belesbat said that justice is the manner by which nature does render to each his own. Moreover, justice, the satisfaction of people's interests, was possible only if government were made to conform to natural law and the King's sovereignty "restored" to its natural form of undivided splendor:

> As in nature all the power and all the qualities in their last degree of perfection terminate in God, Who is in a manner of speaking the metaphysical zenith, similarly in states, power and authority must terminate in the Prince, who is the representative image of the divinity.[84]

The plenitude of royal authority would alone bring into play that universal harmony of interests uniting ruler and ruled in common love and enjoyment of

[82] The organic character of Belesbat's concept of the unity of interest between ruler and ruled does give the impression of an early version of the *volonté générale*.

[83] Bibliothèque Sainte-Geneviève, MS 2215, p. 90. The formula is of course traditional; in the utilitarian context, however, justice has no transcendental dimensions. It is a purely social phenomenon.

[84] B.N., Fds. fr., MS 1205, f. 48.

just and prosperous government. When a mighty prince organized society so as to bring all of its parts into their natural relations with the productive forces of the earth, the interests of people everywhere would be satisfied. His glorious reign would inaugurate a period of universal justice where civil and international strife were unknown. The [present] European, indeed world-wide, conflict, for example, was totally unnecessary. In the conduct of his affairs, the King must understand that war, like poverty, was the product of confusion created by policies contrary to the natural order of things:

> His [Louis XIV's] interests both with respect to his subjects and to foreigners, appear to me after very great reflection, to be all equally founded on equity and on the exact observation of the laws. And I am ready to prove by past and present examples that all that which has been committed contrary to justice, has never been useful to kings or to the state: and if for a time it could have appeared advantageous, the inconveniences which followed have proved invincibly the contrary. . . .
>
> We can conclude from all that which I have observed that the King's one and unique interest is to guide all his actions according to justice and equity; that, since our policy in the past has united all Europe against France, the only way to disunite them is to adopt one [policy] entirely different, founded on this maxim: ONLY THAT WHICH IS JUST CAN BE USEFUL.[85]

Belesbat's conversion of utility into a metaphysical principle, which formed an integral part of his anti-mercantilist theories, was also intimately connected

[85] *Ibid.*, f. 55. Upper case letters used by Belesbat.

with his views about philosophy and religion. Taking up much the same position as Montaigne, Belesbat declared that all heresies and most libertine thought were caused by men who

> never having reflected on the narrow limits of their minds and their small knowledge, have with intolerable presumption and pride wished to explain the mysteries notwithstanding the Bible where it appears that Jesus Christ never wished to do this.[86]

Mysteries should be believed "without reasoning" because they were "beyond human understanding." Instead of vainly speculating about such matters, men should turn to more useful thoughts. "There are an infinity of effects," having purely natural causes, that remained unexplained. Men ate and drank, for example, yet no one had really "penetrated the manner by which the nutriment is distributed to the various parts of our body. Why don't we think more about matters useful for our Conservation?"[87]

The world men live in is here for their use; nature presented man with a multitude of problems which, by definition, were explicable in terms of simple cause and effect. So far as faith was concerned,

> God's purpose . . . was, by hope of rewards and by fear of punishment in the next life, to make men more perfect. And to this end Jesus Christ became man in order to teach that which is necessary to earn eternal happiness. The Bible teaches us the road to follow.[88]

The "true theology of Christ," according to Belesbat, consisted in the moral principles found in the sacred

[86] *Ibid.*, f. 133.   [87] *Ibid.*, f. 136.   [88] *Ibid.*, f. 133.

book.[89] Indeed, apart from our duty to love God above all else, "the entire science of Religion" consisted in treating others as we would have them treat us.[90] In other words, propounding a most extreme point of view, Belesbat expressly denied the fundamental mystery of the Redemption; he said that philosophy is useful for making man happy in this life, while religion prepares him for paradise in the next through a calculus of reward and punishment.

Having explained that the principle of utility is literally justice in action both in heaven and on earth, Belesbat turned to a closer examination of how the natural interests of princes and their subjects may be satisfied. The King had six true interests, his subjects four; and by following his own interests, the King necessarily satisfied those of his people because "there is an inseparable union" between the two. Indeed, "it is on this inseparable union that the remedies and principles which I proposed have been established."[91] The half-dozen interests of the crown could be compressed to four: the King must be able to obtain "all the money he needs," his subjects must increase in number, they must love him to the point where they would be willing to die in his service, and neighboring peoples must seek rather than fear his domination. The subject's interests consisted in being comfortable, being sheltered from all sorts of injustices and vexations and aided in his necessity.

In this section, more than anywhere else, Belesbat incorporated into his views the agrarian arguments expounded by the group around Fleury, Beauvillier, and Fénelon. The influence is certain. Apart from similarity of argument, Belesbat even suggested to

[89] *Ibid.*, f. 137.   [90] *Ibid.*, f. 144.   [91] *Ibid.*, f. 43.

Louis XIV that, if his Majesty wished the advice of a third party, he should consult with M. de Beauvillier.[92] On occasion, for example, Belesbat explains what appears to be short paraphrases from earlier Christian agrarian writings: "The power of Princes lies in the number of men they command and not at all in riches or in the expanse of their states. The Turkish empire is seven or eight times larger than France" but its thinly spread population provided the state with little power.[93] Elsewhere Belesbat explains at greater length how proper agricultural exploitation would increase national wealth, cause population to grow both more numerous and more prosperous, and unite ruler and ruled in an indissoluble and felicitous union. The inauguration of a glorious reign of justice and plenty would cause peoples from neighboring states to seek to live under the laws of so beneficent a government:

> Taxes in almost all states are levied on persons, on land and on agricultural products. Therefore, the more a state is populous the more there are taxpayers, the more the [fruits of the earth] are consumed the better cultivated are the lands, which can produce nothing that is not useful, even the poor lands continue to produce. All this shows that the wealth of princes comes from the fertility of their states, and fertility from proper cultivation, and proper cultivation depends [in turn] on the great number [of people] employed. Consequently, princes who know their true interests will do everything in order to conserve and increase the number of their subjects, to enrich and render them happy. And peoples from neighboring states, knowing of the happiness of

[92] *Ibid.*, f. 85.   [93] *Ibid.*, f. 45.

his subjects, will wish to be governed by so good a prince.[94] All this proves invincibly that the interests of princes and the general interests of their subjects are inseparable.[95]

In matters pertaining to revenue, according to Belesbat, the King stood in the same relation to his subjects as a proprietor stood with respect to his tenant farmers: in both cases the people would pay their charges more easily when they were rich.[96] It followed also from this proposition that the aristocracy, the most ancient and honored proprietors of France, men motivated by interests identical with those of the crown, were uniquely qualified to participate in affairs of state. Unlike officials who came "from the bed of the people," men of quality had independent means and were therefore less tempted to amass private fortunes at public expense. Indeed, says Belesbat, the history of France revealed that "the grandeur, power and long duration of this monarchy come from the nobility, which, until recently, has always had a principal part in government,

[94] The manuscript of 23 February 1688 contains the following lines:

> Si la vie estoit un peu commode à la campagne et les mariages faciles chacun suiveroit l'inclination naturelle, et le nombre des hommes croissant toujours, ils cultiveroient les terres avec tout le soin possible, et enfin on auroit besoin de décharger le royaume par des colonies dans des pays de l'obéissance du Roy, que si la curiosité de la jeunesse, ou l'inquiétude de la nation en attiroit quelques uns dans les pays étrangers, ils reviendroient bientot en france y trouvant la vie plus commode. *Cette commodité y attireroit mesme les Etrangers et leur feroit désiré notre domination qu'ils craignent si fort maintenant* (f. 19, italics added).

[95] B.N., Fds. fr., MS 1205, f. 98.

[96] "Les peuples sont à l'égard du roi ce que les fermiers sont aux propriétaires; quand ils gagnent dans leurs fermes, ils payent exactement. De meme les peuples étant riches payent aisément les impositions" (*ibid.*, f. 43).

the command of armies and the administration of justice."[97]

If the nobility no longer held its traditional place in society, it would be a misfortune caused above all, says Belesbat, by the subversive aggrandizement of ministers and their subalterns who sought continually

> to be absolute masters in their departments, to direct them at their pleasure, to employ only those who are totally dependent upon them and to this end destroy the order, forms and maxims of government so that, being restricted by nothing, they can go more surely about their business in the [resultant] disorder and confusion.[98]

This evil, complained Belesbat, had "gone to such excess in France that it is one of the principal causes

[97] *Ibid.*, ff. 113-114. One of Montausier's political maxims, written for the Dauphin's instruction, reads as follows:

S'il [the King] ne tient pas la main exactement et avec un tres grand soin à empecher la Noblesse de se ruiner comme elle fait, et s'il ne cherche pas tous les moyens imaginables pour cela, parmi lesquels ce n'en seroit pas un peu considérable de faire que jamais les roturiers, marchands, gens de finances, de négoce et de robe, s'ils ne sont nobles au moins de quatre races, ne puyssent ni tenir ni acheter de biens nobles, de terres, ni de seigneuries. . . . Au lieu qu'on void aujourd'hui, non seulement le bien de la commune Noblesse, mais encore celui des plus grands seigneurs du Royaume passer entre les mains des gens de robe, de finances, et meme de personnes de la lie du peuple, et l'on soupire en voyant porter à des fils de misérables bourgeois les plus beaux noms des meilleures maisons du Royaume, et sous lesquels tant de personnes sont illustres dans l'histoire, s'appelant le Marquis, le Comte, et le seigneur d'un tel ou d'un tel lieu; ce qui confond toutes choses, relevant des faquins, et abbaissant des gens illustres: [le Roi devrait] avec affection et constance chercher tous les moyens qu'il pourra inventer et qu'on pourra lui proposer pour remédier à un désordre si général et si préjudiciable à l'Etat (B.N., Fds. fr., n.a., MS 10632, f. 111).

[98] *Ibid.*, f. 102.

for the impoverishment of the state, the misery of the people and, I dare say, for the great number of enemies whom we have on our hands."[99] Among the many abuses Belesbat sought to remedy, he clearly believed none were so dangerous as rapid administrative growth. His large-scale reforms were concerned directly with this problem.

Above all, Belesbat sought to answer the following questions. How could higher officials be chosen more selectively? What institutional changes were required to make the structure of government conform more nearly to the interests of crown and people? According to the author, the proper distribution of appointments was impossible without a thorough knowledge of the character and capacities of every candidate. Such information would be available if the education and upbringing of future functionaries were entrusted to the state from early childhood. Such a program, although clearly impracticable for the entire population, was "nevertheless the one and unique method of knowing men thoroughly." Selection should be restricted to children of noble birth and from families having "sufficient wealth to purchase offices in the judicature: because it is from these two orders that those who participate in government are drawn." So far as other children were concerned the best possible education would be provided by apprenticeship in the professions of their fathers.[100]

The creation of state-run training academies for the children of nobility, a proposal which, incidentally, had been made by the aristocracy in the early years of Richelieu's administration,[101] was to be ac-

---

[99] *Ibid.*, f. 103.   [100] *Ibid.*, ff. 98-99.

[101] "En 1627, au moment où se sont terminés les troubles qui depuis 1610 avaient souvent les nobles pour auteurs, au moment où s'est réunie une assemblée de Notables, beaucoup de nobles se sont

companied, said Belesbat, by large-scale institutional reforms. The most important proposal was a plan to replace all ministerial posts with a series of councils charged to direct closely individual administrative departments. And significantly, Belesbat states explicitly that the purpose of this reform was to destroy the crown's mercantilist program.[102] His other

---

groupés pour présenter au Roi par l'intermédiaire du Maréchal de la Force, une requête demandant une série de mesures. Les nobles désiraient être associés au gouvernement royal, c'est-à-dire que l'on fasse appel à eux pour le recrutement des Conseils; . . . ils voulaient qu'on leur réserve une part importante dans les postes de commande de l'armée et aussi dans la distribution des bénéfices ecclésiastiques; ils voulaient pour se rendre digne de remplir ces fonctions la constitution de collèges spéciaux pour la jeune noblesse et même ils préconisaient l'institution dans chaque province de 'censeurs de nobles,' c'est-à-dire de certains nobles qui auraient la surveillance de la conduite des autres. Ce programme fort intéressant fut présenté au Roi en 1627." Paul Vaucher, *Etude sur la France de 1598 à 1660*, Centre de documentation universitaire, Paris, 1960, p. 63. See also V. L. Tapié, *La France de Louis XIII et de Richelieu*, Paris, 1952, p. 210. Five years later, in 1632, Philippe de Béthune, *Le conseiller d'Estat ou recueil des plus générales considérations . . .* , Paris, p. 275, pleads for the same reform. The idea seems to derive from at least the middle of the sixteenth century. See Henri Hauser, *François de la Noue (1531-1591)*, Paris, 1892, p. 171.

102 [Ministers in the past] regarderent ny regles ny mesures, manquerent de parolle à tout le monde, firent touttes les injustices imaginables, et traitterent avec une hauteur insupportable tous les princes et estats de l'Europe, ce qui a causé cette haisne universelle contre la France bien plus sans examiner si le Royaume pouvoit seul sans le secours des autres pays faire le Comerce. Ils ruinerent autans qu'ils purent celuy des estrangers, et croyant y pouvoir proffiter, pour en estre les seuls maistres. Ils firent faire des Compagnies et ne donnerent des Congez et des permissions de trafiquer de certaines marchandises dans de certains pais qu'à ceux qui leur plaisoient, ce qui mist au désespoir tous les négotians et obligea les estrangers à retirer la plus grande partie de leurs effects et à tascher de se passer de notre Comerce, mais au bout de quelque temps, voyant que malgré l'establissement de nos manufactures, leurs nouveaux traffics, ils ne laissoient pas de s'abismer, et que malgré les traittés qu'ils avoyent faits avec nous ils estoient plus ruinés par la

plans for reform resemble the better known projects of earlier *Frondeurs*.[103] Establishment of councils in the central government would be paralleled by simultaneous reforms in the provinces, for the most part, the suppression of intendants. The intendants' financial duties—deemed by Belesbat to be their only important function—would be assumed, as they had earlier been, by the *trésoriers de France* under the immediate direction of the governor or lieutenant general. Abolition of the intendancy would destroy "ministerial tyranny," and the money spent for its upkeep could be used to restore office-holders in provincial government to the time-honored functions of which they had been unlawfully deprived.[104] Finally, once freed from bureaucratic tyranny, France could adopt policies which, according to Belesbat, conformed to those universal principles governing the fortunes of all states.

In order to establish more firmly the absolute authority of the King and his new councils, Belesbat

---

paix que par la guerre, ils ouvrirent les oreilles aux propositions du prince d'Orange, espérant par le boulversement de la France remédier aux maux qui les accablent, et comme j'attribue leur réunion, et la diminution de nos richesses à la conduite que l'on a tenue, il est certain, que si l'on en change et que l'on en prenne une toutte contraire fondée sur la justice et la bonne foy, nos ennemis se désuniront, feront la paix, restabliront le Comerce et par ce moyen le Royaume deviendra en peu de tems plus opulent qu'il n'a jamais esté. Pour parvenir à l'exécution de ce desein, Je crois qu'il seroit à propos que le Roy entre [dans] son Conseil d'estat en creast quatre autres, pour le destail des affaires, un pour les affaires ecclésiastiques (B.N., Fds. fr., MS 1205, f. 57).

Belesbat here enters immediately into a detailed consideration of his project for conciliar government.

103 One of these early pamphlets, however, A. Ctesiphon, *Le labyrinthe de l'estat, ou les véritables causes des malheures de la France*, Paris, 1652, p. 18, states that "la véritable cause de nos malheurs est le défaut d'un conseil pareil à celuy d'Espagne . . . ."

104 MS 1205, f. 62.

devoted considerable space to attacking the claims
of the magistrature, showing at the same time profound resentment against a judicature staffed largely
by nobles who were not of the Sword. Opposing par-
lementarian views about registration of royal decrees,
Belesbat declared them to be totally without foundation in either history or jurisprudence. Here he distinguished the "ancient" *parlements* which, representing the entire nation

> were composed of the greatest *seigneurs* and the
> principal prelates of the realm, convoked by our
> kings who assisted in person, and where all the
> important affairs of state were treated. Those at
> present, however, are but simple courts of jus-
> tice, established in divers provinces . . . , com-
> posed for the most part of *roturiers* and very
> few nobles and ecclesiastics, to whom our kings
> have given the power to judge cases arising in
> their jurisdictions . . . without having any part
> in government. Thus it is pure illusion when
> they confound themselves with the ancient *parle-
> ments*, arrogating . . . all their rights, proclaim-
> ing themselves tutors of kings, and pretending
> that ordinances, edicts and declarations cannot
> be executed without first being registered in
> their courts.[105]

The alleged right to register royal edicts was not,
according to Belesbat, the only outrageous pretension
of the judicature. The equally false principles that
"their authority must never be questioned and . . .
that they are not accountable for their [judicial] opinions" permitted magistrates to administer justice in
a manner conforming entirely to their own interests.
Magistrates' revenues were swollen by deliberate mul-

105 *Ibid.*, f. 177.

tiplication of lawsuits: "Money and credit . . . prevail over right and reason." The abuses, "which oppress, ruin and destroy an infinity of families," ran directly counter to the King's interests, united to those of his people. The remedy, Belesbat believed, was clear: magistrates should be made to obey the law.

Concerning recruitment, Belesbat suggested that when a father was ready to purchase a judicial office for his son, the crown conduct an inquiry into the aptitude of the candidate. So far as the magistrates themselves were concerned, they should be compelled to respect all royal decrees (issued by the aristocratic councils which replaced ministerial departments) irrespective of parlementary registration. And in the daily administration of justice, every magistrate should be obliged to indicate the precise authority and texts upon which each of his decisions was based. Moreover, when a given piece of legislation could be understood in more than one sense its interpretation should be a matter for the appropriate royal council and not for the individual judge. The magistrate's function should consist of nothing more than the application of the law to particular cases; it should be a mechanical procedure and subject to rigid control.[106]

The one remaining area of major reform concerns Belesbat's four projects to direct the larger portion of church revenues to public assistance. The author wrote scores of pages, displaying an overwhelming erudition in an effort to prove that ecclesiastical property belonged to the body of the church; the clerics were entitled only to the use of temporal possessions. During the course of time churchmen "usurped" this wealth and assumed property rights over it. In these circumstances the King should com-

[106] *Ibid.*, f. 80.

mand that these riches be used to relieve the poor
in accordance with the teachings of the primitive
church. Belesbat's several projects discussed different
methods whereby the crown could assume direction
of ecclesiastical revenues and employ part of the
clergy to administer a public assistance program.[107]

Belesbat's writings are particularly valuable in helping us understand the development of secularly inspired aristocratic opposition to Louis XIV's government. Most striking is the increasing power and
elaboration of anti-mercantilist theory. No previous
writer had so emphasized the idea of a natural harmony of interests governing both domestic and international relations. At every opportunity Belesbat
enlarged nature's jurisdiction at the expense of state
authority. Superficially his plea for liberty from government intervention seems inconsistent with the
idealization of an all-powerful prince. Yet in his discussion of the natural identity of interests between
ruler and ruled, Belesbat clearly interprets power to
mean the ability to organize society so that each part
functions with respect to the others in a manner
prescribed by its natural relations with the productive
forces of the earth. In other words, royal power varies
directly with the crown's ability to give free play to
the operation of natural laws. And, consistent with
himself, Belesbat interpreted the course of administrative growth from Francis I to Louis XIV as a study
in the progressive disintegration of royal authority.[108]

107 See particularly the following memoirs: "De l'origine des biens
d'Eglise et de leur usage," "Projet pour soutenir la guerre avec les
revenus ordinaires du Roy," "Mémoire sur l'état présent de la
France."

108 "Les guerres civiles, qui ont déchiré la France depuis cent quarante ans, ont répandu partout un esprit de désordre et de confusion, en telle sorte que personne n'est demeuré dans les bornes
de son état, de son devoir et des fonctions de sa charge" (*ibid.*, f.
81). Continuing, Belesbat wrote that the monarchy had, in the same

The picture of an absolute prince ruling in accordance with the felicitous commands of natural law seems, of course, to herald the enlightened despotism theories of eighteenth century physiocrats.[109] Aside from that, it is more important to understand why Belesbat's opinions reflect a particularly significant turning-point both in the development of the reform movement and in the more general history of French thought. Most revealing is the absence of any argument concerning the luxury trade. Until now, whether from religious motives or from a general class antagonism to increasing urban wealth and government centralization, aristocratic opposition to mercantilist theory placed a strong emphasis on anti-luxury arguments. In contrast, Belesbat accepted the world of trade very much as he found it. He believed that exchange for luxury items came under the same natural laws as those governing commerce in any other domain. The distinction between good and bad trade, he felt, had disappeared and that in its stead, the doctrine of utility had become the expressed fundamental criterion governing economic and, indeed, all human relations.[110]

It is difficult to exaggerate the importance of this profound change of attitude. Belesbat's expansion of familiar utilitarian principles into a comprehensive

---

period, given up its authority piecemeal to ministers, functionaries of every description, and the *parlements*.

[109] This point is made by Schatz and Caillemar, "Le mercantilisme libéral," in a section entitled, "Absolutisme de Belesbat et absolutisme physiocratique."

[110] It is revealing that Belesbat's unexpectedly indulgent attitude toward the venality of offices is compatible with his view of luxury. Despite an immense pride in being a direct descendant of Michel de l'Hôpital, a man who condemned venality as a veritable curse—the "ruin" of the state—Belesbat, like Montesquieu later, accepted venality with only a few expressions of mild "regret."

theory of nature and society represented something more than mere speculation. It was a program for political action based upon a philosophy consciously antagonistic to all the fundamental principles which had hitherto characterized the *ancien régime*. Unlike Fénelon, Belesbat was as free from traditional ethics as he was devoid of Christian faith: his utilitarianism was a violent rejection of the contemplative ideal, his view of the Redemption a mockery of the central religious mystery. Here for the first time we are confronted with a general assault against the political regime and against all the ancient values with which it was associated.

iii. THE MERGER OF FISCAL REFORM WITH AGRARIAN THEORY AND THE ECONOMICS OF UTILITARIAN PHILOSOPHY, 1688-1695

Pierre le Pesant de Boisguilbert, a Rouen magistrate, was another major agrarian theorist writing at about the same time as Belesbat. The parallels between the two men are suggested by the curious origin of some of their major ideas. Belesbat's theories, although mostly written in 1692, expressed, as we have seen, many of the agrarian themes first developed at length in a memoir presented to the King on 23 February 1688. Similarly, Boisguilbert's views (his first work was published in 1695) are to some extent foreshadowed in a companion piece bound with the memoir of 1688. The document, which despite its audacity seems also to have been submitted to Louis XIV, contains several passages dealing with fiscal reform. They are also the most traditional and restrained in an otherwise fiercely vehement writing. The manuscript shows that in 1688 it was impossible to say, as did Boisguilbert in 1695, that fiscal reform was no longer concerned merely with better methods of levying, assessing, and collecting taxes and had become instead an integral part of a wider body of anti-mercantilist economic doctrine. The point is fundamental: a comparison of Boisguilbert's works with the earlier writing of 1688 reveals how the magistrate's important contribution both to the reform movement and to the history of economic thought was in great part a product of utilitarian philosophy.

The companion piece to the memoir of 1688, a year when cereal prices plunged to an all-time low,[111] was written by an unidentified but much disgruntled noble. His first lines repeat a theme common to agrarian critics of the Sun King:

> The force of a state, even the power of the Prince who governs it, does not consist in possessing great expanses of territory, but in having well cultivated lands capable of nourishing a very large number of people. Thus the multiplication of people and the cultivation of land in order to nourish them properly is infinitely preferable . . . to all conquests which could extend the state. . . . Other things being equal . . . , it is certain that a small state would be more powerful than one which is larger, because the forces of the first would be more concentrated and more able to aid each other without effort. There would be fewer frontiers to guard and each frontier could be more promptly defended by all the forces drawn from the center. . . .[112]

[111] See the tables in Pierre Goubert, *Beauvais et le Beauvaisis de 1600 à 1730: contribution à l'histoire sociale de la France du XVIIe siècle*, Paris, 1960.

[112] This second memoir is bound with the one presented to the King on 23 February 1688, discussed in the previous chapter. The quotation is from B.N., Fds. fr., MS 11149, p. 65; an identical copy is also bound with the duplicate of the memoir submitted to the King (B.N., Fds. fr., MS 1735).

The writer expressed the familiar argument that the Paris luxury trade, draining the countryside of labor and wealth, created depressed rural conditions and caused population to decline; this, in turn, adversely affected all economic life. In sum, "avarice for money is the root of the evil . . . , causing a notable damage to the State which does not grow wealthier when money leaves one purse and enters another but becomes genuinely impoverished by the diminution of natural riches."[113] Perhaps, writes the author,

> the King is not unhappy to see people of quality reduced, because of luxury, to a pitiful state and in a continual need for him. But he must also consider how this necessity causes souls to become base, mercenary and capable of all sorts of indignities. This baseness of soul which gives hope for obedience must also create fear of treason and revolt. . . . What is more dangerous than to have gone beyond the limits of honor for the sake of interest and to be restrained only by fear . . . it is a mine ever ready to explode. There are other methods whereby the nobility can be made dependent. For example, paying for their children's education . . . , making royal service easy to enter, advantageous, and to give great prestige to those who distinguish themselves. . . .
>
> One must not imagine that it is possible to crush entirely the nobility. This corps is the force of the state . . . during an absolute reign it may seem crushed but as soon as authority shows the slightest enfeeblement, [the nobility] will rise up with violence and its long period of subjection . . . will only serve to have made it more intractable.[114]

[113] *Ibid.*, p. 78.   [114] *Ibid.*, pp. 80-83.

In short, both the power of the state and the tranquility of the realm required that the King abolish the luxury trade, encourage marriage among the nobility by assuring the education of its children, and, finally, make it possible for a gentleman with little money "to be able to live a simple life without dishonor."

In commerce according to the 1688 memoirist, "those most experienced say that the great secret is to interfere in nothing": when the crown directs trade "by authority all economic activity declines." High tariffs caused international commerce "to deviate and it never returns to its original course." It was therefore "necessary that the King favor commerce without wishing to obtain any profit: he will always draw sufficiently from the opulence of his state." The writer went on to discuss with considerable force the agrarian anti-mercantilist arguments popular with both the group around Fénelon and, a few years later with Belesbat.[115] He introduced a concept, however, which, although sometimes encountered with merchants, appeared neither among Christian agrarians nor in Belesbat: commerce, being

[115] There are some passages which would not have been out of place in *Télémaque*:

> Pour les étrangers il ne faut leur donner aucun ombrage c'est par la fidélité, la sureté, l'aisance du commerce qu'ils viendront à nous. . . . Il n'y a que l'égalité, la liberté, la regle qui puisse faire la liaison et la confiance sans laquelle tout languit. Il faut qu'ils puissent entrer, sortir, venir, ne venir pas, acheter des uns et des autres, payer en marchandises, ou en argent. Surtout qu'ils soient seurs que nous ne courrons jamais sur leurs marchés que nous ne voulons point nous rendre nécessaires et nous passer d'eux. Tout cela est odieux et les excite à se passer de nous. . . .
>
> Les pays ont été faits si différents par la main du Créateur afin qu'ils eussent besoin les uns des autres et que ce besoin entretienne l'union. Qui veut par ambition détruire cette commodité réciproque trouble et révolte tout *(ibid.,* pp. 97-99).

able to thrive only where it was free, flourished more in a republic than in a monarchy where it "languishes" under the oppression of authority.[116]

The author certainly did not intend to suggest by this remark that a republic is superior in form of government to a monarchy. From the context, he clearly meant to say that an aristocracy, being more numerous and more powerful in a monarchy and receiving its traditional source of income from land, creates a type of society where foreigners are encouraged to exchange their goods or money for agricultural surpluses. Therefore, in a republic where the aristocracy, and consequently agriculture, play a minor role, the relative volume of merchandise trade would be greater than in a monarchy. There was no remedy, he thought: the cause lay in the very structure of society; nothing, therefore, could be more foolish than the futile efforts of Colbert and his successor to capture Dutch trade.

Perhaps the most interesting aspect of the document is the way it foreshadows how agrarian theory was later to merge, in Boisguilbert and to a much lesser extent in Vauban,[117] with projects for fiscal reform.

[116] *Ibid.*, p. 91. For merchant statements to the same effect see, for example, Archives de la Guerre, vol. 2649 (*papiers* de Chamlay). See also A.N., MS F[12] 641, quoted by R. B. Grassby. "Social Status and Commercial Enterprise under Louis XIV," *The Economic History Review*, 2d series, XIII (1960), 38.

[117] A military engineer of great talent, Marshal of France, Sébastian le Prestre de Vauban is also well-known for his *Projet d'une dixme royale*, written in 1698 and published in 1707. The striking characteristic of this treatise is its extraordinary attention to statistical detail and procedure. Vauban is the most distinguished figure in a tradition which began with military engineers like Fabert and Terwel (See above, Chapter IV). But this is the extent of his contribution to the reform movement prior to his death in 1707; after that date the condemnation of his book made Vauban a posthumous hero for the opposition movement to Louis XIV. In fact, however, Vauban's ideas did not differ in principle from those of Colbert. We shall

At first glance, it seems quite unexceptional, at a date when cereal prices were at an all-time low and the countryside was without financial resources, that people complained about taxes and suggested remedies for existing inadequacies in fiscal policy. Indeed, a decade prior to Vauban's *Project for a Royal Tithe* the author revealed that people already had long been debating about a scheme "whereby the King could, in exchange for all his levies, take a certain portion such as a tithe on all the natural riches growing in his kingdom."[118] The question which should be posed here—and we shall see its importance—is: when, and under what precise circumstances, did projects for fiscal reform cease to be primarily concerned with better methods of levying, assessing, and collecting taxes and become instead an integral part of a wider body of anti-mercantilist economic doctrine?

During the first half of the seventeenth century mercantilist writers strongly emphasized the idea of monetary circulation. It may be remembered, for example, how Richelieu thought it necessary to adjust indirect taxes to the rate of circulation in such a way

---

see in the next chapter that he was one of the most ardent supporters of mercantilist theory and practice. Although sufficiently influenced by agrarian principles to insist that agriculture is the source of all wealth, Vauban was also convinced that an equitable and efficient fiscal system would permit France to approach the mercantilist ideal of complete economic autarky. In sum, Vauban's influence as a reformer, in the sense of being opposed to the Sun King's government, did not exist until after his death when the reform movement hailed him as a martyr to its cause. Prior to this time he was, if anything, a defender of government policy.

118 "Je ne parle point icy d'une chose qui a esté tant de fois agitée qui est que le Roy pourroit pour tous ses droits prendre une certaine portion comme la dixme de toutes les richesses naturelles qui croitroient dans son royaume, il en feroit les fermes; comme il fait aller [il s'agit] de ses droits, il seroit par là intéressé à favoriser l'agriculture pour augmenter ses revenus et le commerce pour en rendre le débit plus facile" (pp. 109-110).

as to maintain price levels at a point assuring the greatest possible volume of general public consumption and consequently maximum revenues for the crown. Moreover, it long remained axiomatic that the velocity of monetary circulation varied directly with the rate of industrial consumption. The volume of commercial transactions involving agricultural products was, in mercantilist opinion, the result of money made available through the sale of industrial products.[119] The first serious attack on this view, appeared in Lartigue; they were then developed in Fleury and elaborated in the memoirs of 1688. These critiques asserted that the luxury trade, taking up the bulk of industrial production, hindered and impeded the flow of money. These people also insisted on contrasting the "true" value of "natural wealth" with the illusory value of artificial riches.

The conclusion toward which such arguments were vaguely pointing, however, was not arrived at until 1695, when Pierre le Pesant de Boisguilbert advanced the theory in the *Détail de la France,* that the velocity of monetary circulation varied directly with the volume of agricultural rather than industrial consumption.[120] No idea could have placed govern-

---

[119] Richelieu's concern to keep sales taxes from impeding business, and the underlying mercantilist assumption that revenue for agriculture was provided by the sale of manufactures were both treated more extensively in Chapter I, above.

[120] This is the basic theoretical principle of the *Détail de la France,* published in 1695:

> Tout le fondement et la cause de toutes les richesses de l'Europe sont le blé, le vin, le sel et la toile, qui abondent en France; et on ne se procure les autres choses qu'à proportion que l'on a plus qu'il ne faut de celles-la. . . .
>
> Et quand il [l'argent] produit de l'utilité, ce n'est point dans le coffre, mais en le gardant le moins qu'il est possible; et comme c'est la consommation, dont il n'est que l'esclave, qui mene sa marche, du moment qu'elle cesse, il s'arrete aussitot, et demeure comme immobile. . . . De façon que

ment tax policy in a more unfavorable light while, at the same time, putting previous theories of fiscal reform in a totally new dimension. When men thought that industry was the pump which caused money to circulate, they also reasoned that indirect taxes on farm products in commerce were harmless so long as they were kept proportional to the rate of industrial production.[121] But according to Boisguilbert, impositions on farm products were nothing less than criminal: indirect taxes dried up the very source from which flowed the nation's wealth. Now, for the first time, criticism of fiscal policy became an integral part of a wider body of economic doctrine.

How did Boisguilbert come to formulate this principle lying at the very heart of his thought? The magistrate's writings clearly reveal that the most original aspects of his thought were consciously derived from utilitarian philosophy. Explanation of this interpretation must begin by comparing Boisguilbert's concept of wealth with that of most previous agrarians. So long as "natural wealth" was opposed to arti-

---

tous les revenus d'industrie cessent tout à fait, et l'argent, qui forme pour autant de revenus qu'il fait de pas, ne sortant point des fortes mains, arrete entierement son cours ordinaire; ce qui met le pays dans une paralysie de tous ses membres, et fait qu'un Etat est misérable au milieu de l'abondance de toutes sortes de biens. Ce sont la des effets que les pauvres ressentent les premiers, mais qui se communiquent ensuite imperceptiblement à tous les autres membres de l'Etat, meme aux plus relevés, ainsi que l'on a fait voir par ces Mémoires (pp. 173, 211).

Unless otherwise indicated, all references are to E. Daire's edition of Boisguilbert's works in *Economistes financiers du XVIIIe siècle*, Paris, 1843.

121 Furthermore, it may be remembered that the tendency to resort to indirect taxes was reinforced by the long established conviction that products circulating in trade were the surplus remaining after necessities had been consumed. See Chapter III, above.

ficial or illusory riches it was impossible logically to conceive of a principle determining the value of *all* goods, luxury or otherwise, as a function of the volume of agricultural consumption. And it is for this reason that Boisguilbert took special care formally to define a different concept of wealth: "True wealth consists of a full enjoyment, not only of the necessaries of life, but even of all the superfluities and all that which can give pleasure to the senses."[122]

Having disposed of the distinction between good and bad wealth[123] Boisguilbert, like Belesbat before him, declared that agriculture created an identity of interests between ruler and ruled:

> No one can doubt that the bases and origin of revenue for all princes in the world is the same as that for their subjects who, properly speaking,

[122] *Dissertation sur la nature des richesses*, p. 403. The *Détail* contains a similar definition: "la richesse . . . n'est autre chose que le pouvoir de se procurer l'entretien commode de la vie, tant pour le nécessaire que pour le superflus" (p. 210). All of Boisguilbert's writings are treated as a unit, although they were written at different dates. There is an excellent bibliography in a thorough but very pedestrian study by Hazel Van Dyke Roberts, *Boisguilbert: Economist of the Reign of Louis XIV*, New York, 1935. Despite a considerable amount of scholarly attention no one has placed Boisguilbert in a wider context, and because historians have persisted in treating him largely as an isolated figure, they have failed to see those characteristics of his work which are most unique and most significant.

[123] Polemics about the nature of wealth may well have been carried on during the entire course of the century. Eustache de Reffuge († 1617), ambassador to the United Provinces during Henry IV's reign, wrote a manuscript of considerable interest, "*Recueil des plus générales considérations servans au maniment des affaires publiques*" (B.N., Fds. fr., MS 19050), wherein the following lines are contained:

> Toutesfois chacun n'est pas d'accord en quoy consiste la richesse d'un Estat.
> Les uns l'ont mesurée par les grands Tresors, les autres par le revenu, d'autres par la fertilité du pais (p. 180).

are merely their tenant farmers, sovereigns being able to receive more or less [revenue] according to the extent that those who cultivate the earth are capable of earning money from the products [of the soil].[124]

Just as agriculture joined state and people so did it bind the fortunes of one subject with another. The income of the lawyer or artisan varied directly with that of the farmer:

All wealth in France is divided into two kinds, wealth from the products of the land and wealth from industry, and the latter rises or descends in proportion to the first. In this manner the . . . fruits of the earth give work to lawyers, doctors, actors and the smallest artisan, of whatever trade he may be. . . .[125]

Sufficient proof for this statement could be supplied, thought Boisguilbert, by simply pointing to the deplorable course of events since the day when Colbert took office. After that fateful date the personal incomes of lawyers, doctors, and artisans had decreased continually, and to this day (1695) "the cause remains the same, . . . the diminution of revenue from the products of the land, which is not . . . half of what it was in that time [when Colbert took office]."[126]

Why had land values and rural income declined so persistently? Because [said Boisguilbert] misguided ministers, unable to understand that "consumption and revenue are one and the same thing," had pursued a monstrous fiscal policy which, exhausting the countryside of all resources, had brought about a corresponding depression in every area of economic

[124] *Factum de la France*, p. 272.
[125] *Détail*, p. 173. [126] *loc.cit.*

life. To assert that "for forty years we have not declared an open war on consumption and on commerce
is to maintain that the Seine does not pass through
Paris."[127] This point is crucial: Boisguilbert's analysis
of "consumption" is nothing less than a conscious
attempt to describe how the natural law of utility
governs all economic relations, both national and
international.

From the purely technical point of view, Boisguilbert said that consumption, occurring only when
money changes hands, was a function of circulation.
In his words, "wealth . . . consists in a continuous
commerce, so that neither land nor works are ever in
a moment of repose."[128] But further analysis, he explained, revealed that the passage of money from one
person to another, when circulation was totally free,
was the direct expression of natural justice, that universal law requiring each to do unto others as he
would have them do unto him. In other words, given
an ideally free economy, the golden rule governed
domestic and international trade; it was nature's
means of imposing an order or "police" in human
affairs, restraining each member of society from pursuing his natural inclination, originating from the
Fall, to take unfair advantage of his neighbor:

> Since wealth is a continual exchange from man
> to man, from trade to trade, from region to re-
> gion and even from kingdom to kingdom, it is a
> frightful blindness to seek the cause of misery
> elsewhere than in the cessation of this trade. . . .
> Everyone preserves this [universal] wealth by
> [looking after] his private interests, contributing
> at the same time, although it is the last thought

[127] Letter to the Controller General, 1 July 1704, pub. in A. de
Boislisle, *Corr. des con. gén.*, II, 536.
[128] *Traité des grains*, p. 391.

361

to enter his mind, to the general good from which . . . he must always obtain his individual utility.

A police is required to enforce concord and the laws of justice among so great a number of men who seek only to destroy them, and to deceive and surprise each other from morning to night, seeking continually to establish their opulence upon the ruin of their neighbors. But it is nature alone which can keep this order and maintain peace; all other authority spoils everything when it mixes in affairs, however well-intentioned it may be. Jealous of her operations, nature seeks immediate vengeance by causing a general disorganization the moment she sees that, through interference, we defy the lights and wisdom of her operations. Her first intention is for all men to live comfortably by their labor, or by the labor of their ancestors. . . .

Thus, in order to accomplish this plan, everyone, both buyer and seller, must profit equally. . . . Nevertheless we cheat so much, as may be seen at any market, before concluding [transactions] . . . that each merchant, wholesale or retail, would prefer that the profit . . . , instead of being shared as it should, remain entirely for himself, although it cost the wealth and even the life of his compatriot. . . . No one . . . realizes that by failing to act in accordance with the Evangelical maxim: *by the rule with which ye measure others, so shall ye be measured*, it will happen that by wanting to obtain goods at the expense of our neighbor so shall we be obliged to part with our own in the same manner. . . .

Nature, therefore, or Providence, can alone make [men] observe this justice, provided once

362

again that no one whoever he may be interferes. And here is how she accomplishes the task. First she establishes an equal necessity to buy and to sell . . . , thereby making a desire for profit the very soul of the transaction; and by virtue of this equilibrium [the mutual and equally strong desire to profit and necessity to sell and to buy] each will come to a compromise. . . .

It has been said, and it is repeated again, that for this happy situation to exist, all things and all products must be continually in equilibrium, maintaining proportional prices in relation to one another. . . . But . . . the moment anything which is in equilibrium like a balance, receives on one side the least increase, the other is immediately carried as high as if there were no [weight] there at all.[129]

In short, the moment authority extended favor to one party or product "all is lost, both for him who profits from the other's misfortune and for him who suffered [loss]."[130] Boisguilbert returns to this theme again and again: "Trade is nothing but reciprocal utility; and all parties, buyers and sellers, must have an equal interest or necessity to buy or to sell."[131]

It would be difficult to imagine a clearer example of how utilitarian philosophy influenced the develop-

[129] *Dissertation sur la nature des richesses*, pp. 408-409.
[130] *loc.cit.*
[131] *Traité des grains*, p. 392. Elsewhere the author wrote:

Pour entretenir l'harmonie sur laquelle roule toute la consistance des peuples et des Etats, et par conséquent les revenus du prince, il ne faut point qu'une partie passe l'autre; c'est-a-dire qu'il est nécessaire que la balance soit si égale dans tous ces commerces, que tout le monde y trouve pareillement son compte (*ibid.*, p. 355).

See also *Dissertation sur la nature des richesses*, p. 422; *Traité des grains*, pp. 378, 387-388, 390; the *Détail*, p. 234.

ment of economic theory among secularly inspired reformers. Prior to Belesbat and Boisguilbert, criticism of the traditional concept that any profit is necessarily obtained at another's expense was formulated largely in moral terms. So long as this was true, so long did the concept of luxury dominate economic thinking in anti-mercantilist literature. Just as moral condemnation appeared weak when confronted with arguments based on *raison d'état,* so did warnings about the economic consequences of the luxury trade seem inadequate when compared with the entire body of mercantilist theory. But now, for the first time, reformers no longer thundered against the curse of Mammon nor did they lecture on the pernicious influence of Machiavelli. Instead, they attacked mercantilist doctrine on its own terms with a comprehensive, wholly secular, and systematic philosophy of opposition.

If the new ideological assault on traditional doctrines of political economy was secular in character, this does not mean that religion was a matter of indifference. On the contrary, utilitarian philosophy had, as we have seen, clear anti-Christian implications.[132] While theories of utility remained purely speculative in character, as in the case of the manuscript abridgments at the Bibliothèque Sainte-Geneviève, they were simply another theme in the complex intellectual currents of the day. The matter was entirely different, however, when utilitarian thought merged with agrarian theory: anti-Christian ideas now, for the first time, formed an essential part of a political movement. Perhaps no other development had a stronger influence and more portentous implications for the future of French society during the Age of the Enlightenment.

[132] See discussion earlier in this Chapter.

The role of utilitarianism in the general development of aristocratic reform may now be made clear. Among the critics of mercantilism there were two groups: some men were above all antagonistic to a new ethic which they identified with Machiavellian principles; others opposed universalist arguments against the view of a world order made up of hostile self-contained political units. The first group, led by Fénelon, were devout men who insisted on placing personal salvation before public welfare, and they were profoundly hostile to any theory legitimatizing immoral acts on grounds that they benefited the common weal. Moreover, they declared that kings are bound by the same moral laws as those governing their most humble subjects. Finally, although Fénelon displayed some universalist tendencies, it was clearly impossible for him to reconcile his theological emphasis on the unique character of Christian mysteries with the concept of a fundamental oneness behind all apparent religious diversity, which so characterized the familiar drive for world and cosmic unity since the days of Postel.

Those men who were most influenced by universalist arguments, and least interested in defending the uniqueness of Christianity, did not place personal salvation above the public welfare. Instead, they identified social and political behavior with the operations of nature, making it possible to define good and evil in purely social or "natural" terms. Moreover, they held, since virtue and vice were products of environment, which in turn could be defined ultimately as nature, different environments would produce varying proportions of moral characteristics; there was a kind of natural selection among nations. It was Jean de Lartigue who first combined these views into a plan for an aristocratic, anti-mercantilist,

and nationalist mission for the union of mankind under the beneficent rule of the French crown. He
clearly sought to dissociate belief in the predestined
superiority of Frenchmen from the general context
of state centralization. This position led him in 1664
to formulate a positive view of the role of government: superior to any other people, the French would
rule the world when their King made the reforms
required to bring his subjects to that degree of virtue
and happiness necessary for their armies to communicate the good life to all humanity. No other monarchy, he maintained, was capable of this task because France occupied a unique geographical position which molded the personality of her subjects so
that they were specially fitted for world leadership.

And here it is important to remember how Lartigue insisted that "virtues and vices come from ways
of life . . . , ways of life from temperament, temperament from climate and elemental qualities, and all is
reduced . . . to Nature, where one must search as if in
the source, the origin of all our movements and our
. . . knowledge as well as our good and bad qualities."
By insisting that human nature is essentially the
product of environment, Lartigue not only approached the utilitarian view that good and evil could
be understood as purely social phenomena, but he
also consciously formulated a position directly opposed to the mercantilist view that government had
primarily repressive functions in society. Thus, while
making vice and virtue a political matter, Lartigue
at the same time identified national expansion with
the civilizing mission of the entire French nation.

Lartigue's writings were the first protest against
mercantilist theory to be based squarely on the principle that the quality of government is measured by
the happiness of its subjects. And, in contrast to the

mercantilist concept of expansion at the expense of the foreigner, Lartigue, substituting nature for government, made conquest part of natural law: the happiness of Frenchmen was now intimately connected with the felicity of mankind in general. Writing in the very early 1660's, Lartigue's preoccupation with traditional concepts of luxury, vice, and virtue prevented him from giving meaningful social and economic content to natural law. Yet, by dissociating nationalism from the general context of political centralization, he gave a universal applicability to the ideals identified with national expansion, and in this manner helped prepare the way for the formulation of theories, such as utilitarianism, which attacked French institutions in the name of all humanity.[133] Two decades later, when utilitarianism merged with agrarian theory, Belesbat—like the author of the anonymous memoir of 23 February 1688—wrote very much in the tradition of Lartigue: both were convinced that domestic reform, giving the aristocracy a leading role in a society governed according to natural law, would usher in a period when peoples from other countries would of their own accord seek to live under the rule of so happy a government. It was in this way that utilitarian thought,

---

[133] An undercurrent of opposition to nationalistic sentiment may be seen as early as 1648 when Cyrano de Bergerac observed: "Un honnest homme n'est ny François, ny Aleman, ny Espagnol, il est Citoyen du Monde, et sa patrie est par tout" (quoted from a letter to the son of F. de la Mothe le Vayer by F. Lachèvre, *Les oeuvres libertines de Cyrano de Bergerac*, 2 vols., Paris, 1921, II, 280). Later when the wars of Louis XIV had contributed toward creating xenophobic sentiment, La Bruyère, like Fénelon, insisted that universal reason caused men to think the same everywhere: "La prévention du pays, jointe à l'orgueil de la nation, nous fait oublier que la raison est de tous les climats et que l'on pense juste partout où il y a des hommes" (quoted from the *Caracters*, by C. G. Picavet, *La diplomatie française au temps de Louis XIV, 1661-1715*, Paris, 1930, p. 143).

and the secularly inspired branch of the reform movement, grew to be an integral part of a peculiar kind
of nationalism which, denying the supremacy of state
in society, exalted the role of the nation, casting
the French people as leaders in mankind's progress
toward universal brotherhood and the good life.

The terms "good" and "truth" were synonymous
with the word "nature." We have seen how, according to Lartigue, cosmic regularities, all "movements
of this admirable machine," made the science of politics a study independent of "private opinion and imagination," guided only by "nature's works and operations." Later, in the absence of traditional but troublesome concepts like vice, virtue, and luxury, Belesbat
was able to describe human behavior as a universal in-
terplay of interests, the dynamics of which were determined by the same principles as those governing the
course of planets and the rhythm of the tides. The
golden rule, he believed, had a comprehensive validity for men in this world and in the next, just as, to
use an analogy, Newton's inverse square law described
matter and motion both on earth and in the infinite
reaches of interstellar space. Nature and truth were
not only one, they were also simple and devoid of
mystery; easily understood by any reasonable person,
a Frenchman or a Hottentot. Local traditions, political and religious, he considered pernicious and unnatural because they emphasized the differences
among men, created conflicting loyalties, and obscured those universal laws governing the harmony
of peoples and of the cosmos. Thus, by applying utilitarian doctrine to many of the same premises as
Lartigue, Belesbat substituted the golden rule or the
principle of utility for the mystery of the Redemption; he drew the full anti-Christian and anti-traditional implications contained in this complex stream

of ideas and emotions which led men to seek virtue in the service of a political cause and to identify national expansion with the spread of truth.[134]

[134] This attitude, more or less distorted, was increasingly reflected towards the turn of the century. Consider, for example, a passage from the superficial writings of Charles-Auguste de la Fare (1644-1711):

> Quel est donc mon dessein? C'est de faire comme un Tableau de la vie humaine. Il ne s'agit pas ici de ce que les hommes doivent penser et faire, il s'agit de ce qu'ils pensent de ce qu'ils font et de ce qu'ils sont capables de faire, et d'en juger par ce qu'ils ont fait. . . . Il est question de présenter des objets réels, où chacun puisse se reconnoître, et reconnoître les autres: et peut être arrivera-t-il, que mettans devant les yeux cette multitude de routes différentes que les Hommes prennent pour arriver à leur bonheur, les plus simples et les plus droites seront suivies, sinon par la plus grande, au moins par la plus saine partie. C'est ce qui a fait dire que le livre du Monde [nature] étoit le plus utile de tous les Livres, parce que c'est le seul qui peut par expérience montrer le véritable chemin de la Félicité, qui n'est et ne peut être autre, que la Vérité et la Vertue (*Mémoires et réflexions sur les principaux événemens du règne de Louis XIV*, Rotterdam, 1726, pp. 6-7).

Around the same date, sometime during the first decade of the eighteenth century, Henri de Boulainvillier was asked, perhaps by Fénelon (see Renée Simon, *Henri de Boulainvillier 1658-1722*, Paris, 1951, p. 195, n.4), to write an abridged version of the memoirs submitted by the intendants for the education of the Duke of Burgundy. The preface to this work, *Etat de la France*, contains the following passage:

> Mes idées sur le bien public, sur l'engagement dans lequel naissent tous les particuliers d'y contribuer de toutes leurs forces, sur l'amour presque surnaturel qu'ils doivent à leur patrie me firent imaginer [this treatise], . . . Je pensois encore que de ce meme détail on pourroit receuillir les moyens de perfectionner l'Art et la Nature pour porter le bonheur des Peuples bien plus loin qu'il a été possible de le faire aller dans les Siecles passez. . . .
>
> En effet, quels avantages ne doivent pas couler naturellement de cette Connoissance? Le Prince qui en aura fait une étude judicieuse, non seulement . . . aura la satisfaction de Commander, d'etre obéi, mais il aura celle de rendre ses peuples heureux, et . . . d'augmenter leur félicité proportionellement à leur mérite . . . il sera l'Arbitre universel de la Guerre et de la Paix.

There is another aspect to the relation between the utilitarian concept of good and evil and a view of the cosmos. It may be remembered that utilitarian doctrine received powerful confirmation from the Epicurean revival which began with Gassendi in the 1640's. Epicurean philosophy posited not only a purely social ethic, but it also played a major role in helping to create the now corpuscularian and infinite universe during this age of scientific revolution. Ancient atomism was "the only developed cosmology available to replace an increasingly discredited scholastic world view; atomism was firmly merged with Copernicanism as a fundamental tenet of the 'new philosophy' which directed the scientific imagination."[135] Where Descartes was the first to apply atomism to a Copernican universe systematically, Gassendi, his almost exact contemporary, provided a psychological and social dimension to the corpuscularian cosmos by rehabilitating Epicurus and focusing human intellect on the task of structuring sense impressions created by the impact of tiny atoms whirling in space. However traditional and devout Gassendi may have been, it is understandable that a more worldly disciple, Saint-Evremond, believing man neither wholly good nor irremediably bad, established a social ethic and an idea of progress on Epicurean and Gassendist sensational and atomistic theory of knowledge. Thus the corpuscularism which "transformed seventeenth century science"[136] also provided a kind of scientific or cosmological confirmation of the revolutionary social and political ethic which was utilitarianism. One could not attack mercantilist doctrine with arguments against the luxury trade without at the same time

[135] T. S. Kuhn, *The Copernican Revolution, Planetary Astronomy in the Development of Western Thought*, Cambridge, Mass., 1957, p. 237.
[136] *loc.cit.*

denying Epicurus and thereby appearing to deny the new Copernican infinite and corpuscular universe. And if a person took this position during the period 1688 to 1692, for example, when the well-known quarrel between the "ancients" and the "moderns" had reached its most violent and intense phase,[137] he ran the risk of being called something similar to what Voltaire later called Pangloss: a metaphysico-theologo-cosmolonigologist.

In contrast to the secularly inspired reformers, the Christian agrarians remained unshaken in their contempt for a social ethic without religious bases and they retained their profound hostility to the luxury trade. Fleury and Fénelon could not be more emphatic on these issues. Even in their positive view of government, Fleury and Fénelon differed fundamentally from the utilitarians: no Christian agrarian attempted to support the idea of moral progress on earth by denying original sin and the mystery of the Redemption. This would be attacking directly the very foundations of faith. The areas of agreement that did exist arose out of common aristocratic opposition to the crown. Thus, allowing for the large exception of the luxury issue, we can say that aristocratic reformers were united in their purely agrarian attack against the mercantilist system.

[137] The fact that the more literary quarrel was most strong during the years when the reform movement, also in great part a struggle against tradition, was at its height, does suggest that the two phenomena were not unconnected.

CHAPTER VII

NEW DIMENSIONS TO REFORM

THE WAR of the League of Augsburg, Europe's first
World War, marks the beginning of a perceptible
and ultimately fatal period of decline for the *ancien
régime*. From the opening of hostilities to about 1695,
years when war and famine seemed to exact their
heaviest toll, the government followed the most rigorous mercantilist policies. This was also the time when
the reform movement entered its mature phase under
the leadership of Fénelon, Belesbat, and Boisguilbert.
Meanwhile, spokesmen wishing to defend the crown
against its critics developed more militant and aggressive forms of mercantilist doctrine. At first traditionalists directed small tracts and pamphlets
against aristocratic reformers. But after 1695 the merchant, who had become immensely rich and powerful
at the expense of political authority, entered the ranks
of opposition and demanded an end to mercantilist
restrictions. As might be expected, the shifting social
structure of opposition provoked changes in the arguments of those defending established points of view.
Merchant power and antagonism posed a direct and
immediate threat to the fundamental mercantilist
principle that effective central control over all aspects
of the economy is a condition essential to national
prosperity. Convinced that France would enter a
period of political decline unless merchant activities
were brought under prompt control, administrators,

profoundly alarmed, wrote lengthy treatises expounding mercantilist thought with more system, and in a manner more extreme, than had ever been done before.

Placed on the defensive for the first time, the crown was thrown into confusion. First, the administration turned violently against what appeared to be the most powerful group of aristocratic reformers, the coterie led by Fénelon. Secondly, ministers, no longer possessing Colbert's supreme self-assurance, exhibited fatal indecision, consulting merchants about even the most fundamental principles of trade. Meanwhile, there was a fragmentation of authority and several different agencies undertook the task of economic regulation. Unable either to appease or to control the business community, the government established a Council of Commerce in 1700, from which merchants publicly unleashed a torrent of pent-up criticism. Never before had public discussion about matters of state been so widespread and intense: the highest questions of policy became the proper subject of market place debate. Moreover, there is evidence to suggest that the wider philosophical views associated with aristocratic reform, especially utilitarianism, began to penetrate the merchant world when they joined the ranks of political opposition. Thus the aristocracy, which more than any other class depended upon the sanctity of tradition, inspired a powerful anti-traditional and anti-Christian movement, leading ultimately to the destruction of the social system which gave them so privileged a place among their fellow countrymen.

i. CROWN-MERCHANT RELATIONS AND GOVERNMENT REACTION TO REFORM, 1689-1695

Between 1689 and 1695 the administration was torn by conflicting views which were to some extent connected with personal rivalries. At the heart of the controversy was the question whether taxes should be lowered in depressed rural areas or, instead, whether government should make a more determined effort to increase monetary circulation in the poorer regions through the stimulation of greater industrial production and higher volume of export. A second and related area of debate, the navy, was also the principal subject of contention between the Colbert and Le Tellier families. Wishing to make France a major maritime power, the Colbertists sought to raise industrial production at home through exploitation of colonial markets. In contrast, army men opposing this position argued, as did Vauban, for example, that France could get along with minimal imports from the colonies or elsewhere if rural distress were alleviated by adequate fiscal reform. Expensive ships of the line, they argued, were useless, and should be converted into privateers, sea-going marauders which, if launched in sufficiently large numbers, would destroy Anglo-Dutch trade. The French defeat at La Hogue in May 1692 tipped the scales in favor of the anti-naval forces. Although the great famine of 1693-1694 showed the value of a navy capable of keeping sea lanes safe for ships carrying vital foodstuff to France, the crown nevertheless decided finally in favor of the anti-naval forces, undertaking at the same time a major program for fiscal reform in which the nobility would be taxed directly. In view, however, of the tremendous impetus which famine and impending tax legislation had given to aristocratic opposition, the government felt obliged to justify these far-reaching decisions. Thus the Colbertists, spokesmen for the most extreme mercantilist position, were supplanted after La Hogue by men who expressed army-inspired anti-naval views. But the substitution

was brief. Again predominant after 1696, the Colbertists pointed with alarm to the rise of the merchants
and to their open challenge to continued government
control of trade. Understanding that the approaching
Peace of Ryswick would cause traditional policies to
be seriously reexamined, the Colbertists expounded
mercantilist doctrine with unprecedented militancy
and with more system than ever before.

In 1689, the year when Le Pelletier (Controller
General and a creature of the Le Tellier family) decided to resign, Seignelay, Minister of Marine, tried
to obtain absolute control over every area of trade.
He supported his demands by arguing that a wholly
consistent mercantilist policy in all sectors of the
economy was possible only under total unity of direction. The document presenting these views is worth
some attention. The title alone indicates disagreement
between the offices of Controller General and the
Minister of Marine: *"Mémoire de Monsieur Seignelay
au sujet des contestations entre lui et le Controleur
Général sur l'administration des affaires du Commerce."*[1] The text is a peculiar composite of militant statements of mercantilist doctrine and personal
attacks against Le Pelletier.

> Matters of commerce must be directed by the
> Secretary of State who has the department in the
> charge of his office, to the exclusion of His
> Majesty's other ministers. Since all parts of trade
> have an indivisible connection one with the
> other, they must necessarily pass by the same
> hand in order to conduct them all on different
> occasions for the . . . general good . . . of every-
> thing concerning the internal and external
> [trade] of our subjects and against foreign enter-

[1] A.N., Archives de la Marine, MS B⁷ 495, ff. 550-552.

prises. . . . Despite the fact that rules leading to the great increase in navigation in recent years ought to be inviolably observed . . . those responsible for the administration of finance have not ceased to interfere with the functions of commerce and have opposed every proposal we have had occasion to submit before Your Majesty for remedying abuses or ameliorating the condition of His subjects, all of this on pretext of the interests of the General Farms. . . .

Since this state of affairs cannot continue . . . without infinite injury . . . it is only just that we propose His Majesty rule that everything concerning commerce either directly or indirectly be controlled by the Minister in charge.

Commissions investigating poverty in the countryside sent out, as we have seen, by Le Pelletier demanded important reductions in fiscal duties, *especially indirect taxes*. In contrast, Seignelay insisted that money be pumped into the provinces through increased industrial production and a greater volume of foreign trade:

M. le marquis de Seignelay from the first proposed to His Majesty the means to reestablish the manufactures of the realm, the value of agricultural products increasing with the [greater] consumption at home and abroad of cloth, woolens, silk stockings . . . , tanneries, . . . coal mining, glass works and other things which foreigners used to sell in France to the exclusion of the merchandise and produce of [our] kingdom.

Thus, the struggle between Seignelay and the Controller General was more than a matter of mere personal rivalry: it concerned policy decisions based on conflicting assumptions about economic theory.

The controversy was also reflected in another area. Merchants had long objected to undue government meddling in business affairs. Le Pelletier thought their grievances could be satisfied in some measure if they were heard in a traditional Council of Commerce. Seignelay squarely opposed the suggestion: he declared that "this Council could only multiply the diversity of advice and cause difficulty."[2] Colbert's son thought prosperity possible only if the state could control every aspect of economic activity, regulating all its parts like a smooth-running machine. Contradictory advice from conflicting merchant interests, he contended, would be injurious to the general welfare and could be therefore of no possible benefit to the crown.

Seignelay told the merchants that instead of complaining they would do better to cooperate more actively in the government program to capture the Atlantic trade from the maritime powers. The Ministry of Marine's optimism about achieving this goal, possible only if France became supreme on the seas, was simply boundless prior to the defeat of La Hogue. Seignelay had raised the navy to an even greater splendor than had his father. Superior to the combined Anglo-Dutch forces, the French fleet won several naval engagements during the early years of the war, 1689-1691. One of these victories on 22 July 1690, for example, caused De Lagny to exclaim: "The King's naval forces have prevailed over those of the

[2] In 1698 or 1699, someone, acting under instructions, submitted a history of Councils of Commerce to De Lagny, still Director General of Commerce (*ibid.*, B⁷ 499, ff. 390-392). After saying that the Council established during Colbert's ministry did not last long, the author explained that later, "M. Le Pelletier Controleur Général des Finances l'ayant proposé, feu M. de Seignelay fit connoitre que ce conseil ne pouvoit que multiplier la diversité des avis et causer de l'embarras. . . ."

English and the Dutch, gaining the mightiest advantage ever won in any battle during the past century. . . . His Majesty finds himself master of the seas."[3] Time and again the naval despatches for these years contain glowing accounts of the supremacy of French seapower.

Seignelay's confidence in the navy lay at the heart of his program for national recovery; internal economic activity had to be organized so that France would be able to take the fullest possible advantage of the Atlantic trade. As early as 9 January 1688, for example, Seignelay gave Denis Pierre Faulconnier, merchant from Dunkirk, along with Pierre François Surmont, François Surmont, and Christian Libert, merchants from Lille, the exclusive privilege of carrying merchandise from French Flanders to Cadiz in order to take business away from foreign shippers. The document, however, also provided that in order

> to give [the undersigned merchants] occasion to extend their commerce and to aid them in meeting initial expenses in establishing enterprises, His Majesty accords them permission to send two vessels a year to Guinea and the African coast to trade for negroes and to carry them to New Spain, and, in case they cannot all be sold, His Majesty permits their sale in the French West Indies.[4]

In short, the merchants did not need to worry about how unprofitable it might prove to carry merchandise from Flanders to Cadiz, as demanded by the government, because the state would permit them to recoup their losses in the allegedly lucrative slave trade, an activity possible only with the protection of French seapower.

[3] *Ibid.*, B7 64, ff. 141-142.   [4] *Ibid.*, B2 64, ff. 11-13.

This is merely one case; there are many examples of Seignelay's efforts to stimulate recovery by organizing France's economy around the needs of the Atlantic trade. On 23 July 1690, for instance, De Lagny wrote a woolen manufacturer that "the empire on the seas won by the King's victorious arms, will render future English and Dutch trade very difficult. From all these reasons, you can clearly see that we will have first choice of [Spanish] wool and at a cheaper price." Moreover, in view of the "advantages won over enemies on land and sea," De Lagny directed the manufacturer, the Sieur Barthe, to expand his facilities in order to house and to provide labor for new workmen.[5] De Lagny also explained that the victory won off Dieppe "cannot help but bring favorable consequences, above all for the islands [Antilles] which the King will be in a position to help more effectively." Again in December 1690, the Director General repeated carefully to his agent in India, Pilavoyne, the role of the colonies in the larger scheme of French policy:

> I must never cease repeating to you . . . that you must pay special attention to creating the greatest possible market for the manufactures, fruits and agricultural products from France, and to furnish us with divers merchandise which are most necessary such as drugs, spices and finally all those things which you know we are obliged to purchase from the English and Dutch. . . . Our industry will be judged badly . . . if we depend always on our neighbors.[6]

Never had the traditional goal of mercantilist policy—relief for depressed rural areas through increased industrial production and export from the

[5] *Ibid.*, B7 62, ff. 136-137.   [6] *Ibid.*, f. 193.

countryside—appeared to depend so urgently and totally on a naval establishment of immense size.[7] Indeed, the only justification for the huge expenditures necessary to maintain costly fleets was the argument that, however expensive, the country would be economically worse off without adequate sea power. Those who questioned this position with the greatest vigor were, understandably enough, enemies of Seignelay. And no man was more skeptical about the value of the navy than Le Tellier's son, Louvois, Minister of War and Director of Industry. His argu-

[7] Nowhere is this stated more explicitly, perhaps, than in the following paragraphs from a letter De Lagny wrote on 1 August 1690:

Je ne fais pas de difficulté de vous dire touttes mes pensées le plus que je puis, suivant ce que j'ay de connoissance des reglements, des convenances génaralles du commerce du royaume par rapport aux Isles et des intérests généraux et particuliers des habitans desdites Isles balancez sur les convenances du royaume, et enfin sur que je puis scavoir des sentimens de Monseigneur le Marquis de Seignelay qui embrasse touttes les considérations imaginables.

Ce qui rend les Isles aussy considérables qu'elles sont à l'Estat, c'est qu'outre l'employ qu'elles donnent à une infinité d'hommes et particulièrement de matelots qu'on trouve dans les besoins comme à present, elles déchargent pour la subsistance des hommes qui y sont ou qui trouvent de l'employ dans les différentes fonctions de son commerce d'une prodigieuse quantité de denrées superflues de France dont le débit donne moyen aux sujets du Roy de subsister de leur part et de payer les charges publiques, et par échange des marchandises desdites Isles qu'il faudroit que nous tirassions des estrangers qui profiteroient du prix de leur valeur par l'argent qu'ils emporteroient au préjudice de l'Estat dans lequel on ne scauroit trop s'appliquer à le conserver.

Le commerce et l'establissement desdites Isles portent d'autant plus de considération qu'il porte en soy un besoin réciproque qui se peut remplir sans le secours des estrangers, sur quoy j'estime qu'il faut toujours avoir en veue d'entretenir ces besoins, affin qu'une partie ne se pouvant passer de l'autre, touttes ensemble concourent plus facilement à l'entretenir et l'augmenter (*ibid.*, B[7] 62, ff. 144-146).

ments gained increasing weight after Seignelay's death in 1690. Under his leadership, opposition to the navy grew so strong that one of Seignelay's most distinguished officials, François d'Usson de Bonrepaus, former intendant general of the marine, minister plenipotentiary, ambassador extraordinary and lieutenant general of France's combined naval forces, believed it necessary to write a defense of the navy on 20 June 1691, one year before the disaster at La Hogue when the French were still most hopeful of being supreme at sea!

Bonrepaus' memoir, addressed to Louis XIV personally,[8] opened by attacking those who opposed the establishment of a strong navy.

> They have wished to persuade Your Majesty that it is in his interest to abolish great naval expenditures because we can defend our coasts without cost.
>
> Those who think this way, I dare say, know nothing about navigation and trade neither within nor without your realm. . . .
>
> What will happen to [our] commerce . . . when the English and Dutch become masters of the sea? . . . No more industry, . . . your revenues will diminish everywhere and Your Majesty's subjects . . . reduced to the last extremity.
>
> . . . Your Majesty will be compelled to conclude a peace with [the maritime powers] on terms they wish to impose. . . .
>
> I come now to the motives which could have driven Messieurs the *Maréchal* de la Feuillade, the [Marquis] of Louvois and the Count of Pontchartrain. I will not dissimulate before Your

---

[8] The document is one of several memoirs by Bonrepaus conserved at the A.N., series K, carton 1360.

Majesty what I think and what is most probable. M. de Louvois' ambition has long inspired in him an extreme desire to destroy the Marine, not only to increase his [power], as much as possible, but principally to have no rival to combat who is near Your Majesty.

Bonrepaus accused La Feuillade of seeking Louvois' favor, and he said that Pontchartrain, the new Controller General and Minister of Marine, thought Louis XIV would allow his son to inherit the direction of maritime affairs if the navy was small and the responsibilities not too great.[9]

Anxious to impress the Sun King with France's need for a great fleet, Bonrepaus discussed briefly the history of French naval power. Since the Peace of the Pyrenees, "Your Majesty has worked . . . and employed 350 millions" to build a great navy. From that time, "increasing the trade of her subjects and consequently diminishing that of the others," France had become "absolute master of trade and navigation." Indeed, the decisive victory in the Channel on 10 July 1690[10] against combined Anglo-Dutch naval forces left "no doubt in all Europe about the superiority of Your Majesty on the seas." Considering the "grandeur of the navy," the immense sums spent, it seemed "surprising to find some Frenchmen advising the King to diminish or even renounce the only establishment by which [national] abundance may be maintained." Entirely ruined during Mazarin's administration, a recently constructed navy had enabled "your Kingdom to get along without foreigners while [at the same time] reducing them to the necessity of

9 Pontchartrain disliked doctrinaires; this may have been a factor in his "opposition" to the Colbertist tradition.

10 The reference is probably to the battle of Beachy Head, won on 30 June 1690.

coming to purchase [our] surplus agricultural products and textiles." Finally, this advantageous position had been due above all to colonial trade:

> No one ignores that trade with the colonies, is
> carried on with flour, wines, spirits, meat, salt
> and textiles from the realm without employing
> money, and returning in exchange for all this
> merchandise are those things which at one time
> we were compelled to purchase with money from
> the foreigner. . . .
>
> Finally we see today that Your Majesty has de-
> veloped his maritime forces to the point of ren-
> dering him absolute master of the sea, defeating
> in the Channel the combined Anglo-Dutch mari-
> time forces. . . . When France had no seapower
> we saw her humiliated and at the mercy of her
> enemies . . . desolate and always extending an
> imploring hand to her neighbors, begging for
> help. . . . When a navy is created you see the same
> Kingdom take on a new face: power, grandeur,
> glory and abundance return. Her kings impose
> law everywhere, they become the arbiters of
> Europe and the most distant nations seek their
> alliance. . . .

Pleading the cause of a mighty navy, Bonrepaus
reaffirmed Seignelay's program for national recovery
through seapower and colonial trade. One year later,
in May 1692, France suffered the defeat of La Hogue.
Moreover, the great famine of 1693-1694 which
quickly followed caused the government to anticipate
drastically reduced revenues in the immediate future.
In these circumstances many people thought the cost
of a huge navy prohibitive. Others were of the opposite opinion. The former favored an all-out privateering campaign against the maritime powers; the

latter desired to continue the Atlantic trade with adequate naval protection. Thus on 1 June 1692, a few weeks after La Hogue, a merchant in Nantes, the Sieur Bourville, wrote Pontchartrain a letter explaining in effect that France's manufactures were worthless without accompanying seapower.[11]

Although financial pressures were great, political factors may well have played an important role in the decision to sacrifice the navy and engage in large-scale privateering.[12] Whatever the reasons for the decision,

[11] "Mémoire touchant les deux moyens proposés à Monseigneur de Pontchartrain pour faire rentrer l'argent qui est sorti de France" (A.N., G7 695).

[12] At the height of the controversy Madame de Maintenon threw her influence on the side of the anti-naval forces. In July 1694, the month when the conferences at Issy first convened, famine conditions had ended and France, no longer dependent upon imported cereals, could prepare for large-scale privateering; this was the crucial time for decision. Meanwhile, Madame de Maintenon was busy grooming the next Controller General, Michel Chamillart. Formerly Master of Requests, intendant at Rouen, appointed in 1690 to one of the four newly created posts of intendants for finance, Chamillart was unexpectedly chosen by Madame de Maintenon to become intendant at Saint-Cyr. In July 1694, while in this capacity, he was ordered by Madame de Maintenon to prepare the budget for 1695, not for Saint-Cyr, *but for all of France* (see Mme de Maintenon, *Lettres*, ed. M. Langlois, 5 vols., Paris, 1935-1939, IV, 286-287). Whether the budget prepared by Chamillart became official is not known, but it is certain that the draft he prepared for Madame de Maintenon contained drastic reductions in naval appropriations. Indeed, Madame de Maintenon so insisted on this point that Chamillart went to unusual lengths to justify measures which would deal a fatal blow to the navy:

> You told me to speak with entire liberty. You have even ordered me to talk to you of things about which I have only a mediocre knowledge. . . . During the past few days I have had occasion to speak at great length with people in the profession. And conversations with them have proved so instructive that I have drafted a new memoir which I have the honor to send you. It will certainly not be to M. de Pontchartrain's taste who, up to now, has not been able to resign himself to abandon the King's vessels to adventurers and who apparently looks upon this abandonment as the ruin

however, it was clear that unrestricted warfare against enemy shipping would reduce foreign trade, and fewer exports meant a further cut in rural income. Tax reform was imperative: unable to procrastinate any longer, Louis XIV's ministers reluctantly set about to find some way to oblige privileged classes to contribute something to the war effort. The result

---

of the marine. I would surely be of the same sentiment . . . if the King were able always to maintain a fleet; but it seems more worthwhile to make use of the vessels we have than to leave them idle on the pretext of a glory which is purely imaginary (see the document published *in extenso* by G. Esnault, *Michel Chamillart contrôleur général des finances et secrétaire d'état de la guerre 1699-1709: correspondance et papiers inédits*, 2 vols., Le Mans, 1884, I, 5-9).

Bonrepaus had accused Pontchartrain of opposing expenditures necessary to maintain a great fleet; whatever Pontchartrain's position, it was clearly not so extreme as to demand, as did Madame de Maintenon and Chamillart, that the royal navy be turned into privateers.

Madame de Maintenon's activities with Chamillart are intimately connected with the break in her relations with Fénelon. It is no accident that Louis XIV's wife turned her attention to Chamillart in 1694 when it first became clear that Fénelon could never be made to disavow Madame Guyon. The Quietist controversy, destroying Madame de Maintenon's intimate relations with the powerful dukes of Beauvillier and Chevreuse, caused her most reliable contacts at Court (apart from the King, who disliked women meddling in state affairs) to disappear almost overnight. Madame de Maintenon turned to Chamillart because she was seeking above all to reestablish her influence in government by insinuating a creature of her own into a high position of state. She favored the anti-naval position probably because it appeared as the most likely policy Louis XIV would follow when government was in desperate financial straits. Helping to destroy the navy was above all a means to get her protégé into power. But she may also have been motivated in this direction by the fact that in the struggle between the recently deceased ministers, Seignelay and Louvois, she had been Seignelay's most powerful protector. The last Minister of Marine was, after all, a brother of the duchesses of Beauvillier and Chevreuse: the family tie might have proved to be an awkward reminder of Madame de Maintenon's previously intimate relations with the group led by Fénelon.

was the Edict of 18 January 1695, known as the first Capitation. The aristocracy felt immensely threatened. We have discussed the amplitude of its opposition, especially during the critical years 1692-1695; what remains to be examined is the administrative reaction to this storm of criticism.

More militant and aggressive forms of mercantilist doctrine were formulated as direct replies to the new attack against the established principles of political economy. The earliest statements of traditionalists were written by men whose pens were for hire, like the impoverished Courtilz de Sandras who more than once accepted payment for writing against a position he had previously defended; moreover, he often showed great skill in arguing both sides of an issue.[13] He was hired in 1693 to defend the policies of the late Colbert. At first, perhaps because his sponsors had not fully thought out a reply to their critics, Courtilz did not go beyond a restatement of all that was well known in Colbert's thought. The prestige of the first Controller General was invoked and he was made to say: "I know very well that against my opinion it is objected that should we try to dispense with the foreigner he will do without us . . . one must be ignorant to talk like this."[14] But it was not until two years later, in 1695, that critics received an answer from Courtilz designed to come to grips with their objections; by this time traditional ideas had been reworked to con-

[13] See B. N. Woodbridge, *Gatien de Courtilz sieur de Verger: étude sur un précurseur du roman réaliste en France, The Johns Hopkins University Studies in Romance Literature and Languages,* Paris and Baltimore, 1925, VI, p. 21.

[14] *Testament politique de messire Jean Baptiste Colbert, ministre et secrétaire d'état, où l'on voit tout ce qui s'est passé sous le regne de Louis le Grand jusqu'en l'année 1684, avec des remarques sur le gouvernement du royaume,* La Haye, 1693, pp. 494-495. Two other editions were published in 1695 and 1697.

form with army-inspired anti-naval views. Although many of the phrases had a familiar ring, the theory which emerged would not have received Colbert's approval. Indeed, Courtilz, whose subsequent imprudences landed him in the Bastille, may have been deliberately provocative when he entitled his book, *The Political Testament of the Marquis of Louvois*,[15] because it is certain that the position here developed corresponds well to the practices and politics of Colbert's well-known antagonist.[16]

Courtilz made Louvois say: "Your Majesty must never lose sight of the alliance between war and trade. They are the two pillars which together uphold the edifice of state; one cannot fall without shattering the other by its collapse." In the measure that "war drains blood from the body of the state, trade will furnish the nourishment necessary to form new blood."[17] Indeed, without war, France's commerce would be in even more desperate straits. During peace, in England

---

15 (Cologne, 1695). Another edition was published in the same year in Brussels.

16 E. Spanheim, *Relation de la Cour de France en 1690*, ed. E. Bourgeois, Lyon, 1900, p. 345, speaking of Louvois, explained:

> Plein d'ailleurs d'une présomption qu'il a tirée des succès passés, il s'en est formé une idée sur laquelle il fonde ceux pour l'avenir, savoir: une grande confiance sur les forces de la France et sur la foiblesse de ses ennemis. . . . Ministre merveilleusement vigilant, actif, ferme, appliqué, entrant dans tout le détail . . . n'épargnant ou ne négligeant rien pour y réussir, que, d'autre part, il a peu de droiture dans ses intentions, peu de maturité ou de toute la réflexion due dans ses conseils, peu d'équité dans ses projets, peu de modération dans sa conduite, et, en un mot, qu'il y apporte plus de violence et de prévention que de justice et de bonne foi.

The severity and rigor with which Louvois applied and interpreted mercantilist policies after his death is described by Germain Martin, *La grande industrie sous le règne de Louis XIV*, Paris, 1898, pp. 218-222; also in Charles Woolsey Cole, *French Mercantilism 1683-1700*, New York, 1943.

17 *Testament politique* . . . , pp. 506-507.

and especially in Holland, "all men capable of bearing arms are employed in maritime trade." This was
not true in France, where the nobility did not understand that trade "always has an air of war and conforms with the noble ardour of a bellicose heart"; it
did not "deserve the penalty of derogation." By continuing hostilities against the maritime powers, "Your
Majesty . . . diverts an infinite multitude of people
who would otherwise be employed in trade. . . . In
contrast there is not one officer in Your Majesty's
troops, nor one soldier who [during peace] was destined for the navy."[18] Should peace come, enemy armies, presently employed "to resist Your Majesty"
would disband and the men would "dedicate themselves to navigation." This could be easily proved:
at sea the English and Dutch, "the most experienced
nations in the universe," were strongest; yet, allied
together, what had they accomplished? "In what part
of the world have they ruined the trade of your
subjects?" By compelling enemy forces to do battle on
land, France would protect her maritime interests.[19]

Those who believed that high tariff barriers would
keep foreigners from French shores and prevent landowners from selling agricultural surpluses abroad had
fallen victim to enemy propaganda. "Foreigners are
jealous because Your Majesty has established manufactures in his kingdom which hitherto had existed
only in their territories, permitting them to draw
immense sums from Your subjects. . . . Now, having
lost their profits, they threaten to stop coming to
France and cease to purchase our products to which
they have grown accustomed." If they tried, "you will
see what will happen." France needed nothing from
them which she could not procure elsewhere. Yet they
had "an extreme need for [France's] wines, for her

18 *Ibid.*, pp. 514-516.　　　19 *Ibid.*, pp. 516-517.

spirits, and her cereals. . . . Can they easily do without her wools, her hemp, her textiles which she has in so great abundance and which are so necessary for them?" There was nothing to fear. "We can, with complete assurance, establish in Your Kingdom all foreign manufactures, or get along without those we do not establish, without having our neighbors cease to come and carry away our products" as they had in the past.[20]

France, Courtilz continued, was self-sufficient and had the strength to weaken her enemies not only by defeating their armies but especially by destroying their sea-borne trade. Here Courtilz echoed the naval controversy so recently carried on between the Colbert and Le Tellier families. The author had Louvois say: "Of all states bordering France there are two whose power . . . resides exclusively in their fleets."[21] To attack their naval strength directly would be senseless. Sea engagements would "serve only to enfeeble Your State, uselessly consume Your finances, and remove sailors needed for more favorable occasions."[22] And those occasions would be exploited by corsairs who would wage "certain combats which may be called private. . . . We must surprise enemy merchant fleets and destroy them if they cannot be captured."[23] Thus, while the state directed its principal strength toward land combat where "Your Majesty has already succeeded so well," enemy commerce would be weakened on two fronts. On land, armies would divert men who otherwise would contribute toward enemy prosperity by being employed in navigation; on the ocean, privateers stalking the sea lanes would multiply in the measure that their rich prizes would finance construction of more vessels.

[20] *Ibid.*, pp. 534-537. [21] *Ibid.*, p. 565.
[22] *Ibid.*, p. 571. [23] *Ibid.*, p. 572.

Courtilz did not discuss privateering any further. But as one might expect in view of the Louvois-Seignelay rivalry, a more eloquent spokesman on this subject was an army officer: Sébastien Le Prestre de Vauban, author of the famous *Dixme Royale*.[24] In November 1695, he declared that the English and Dutch, France's "true enemies," not content "to wage war by land and sea, incite all the countries they can [against France] by means of money. This money does not come from their realms; . . . commerce alone attracts it." By means of "a prodigious quantity of vessels" the maritime powers had become "master and dispenser of the most valuable money in Europe, of which the largest part certainly remains in their hands." This created "their abundance" and permitted them to continue the war against France. "In a word, here is the source of all our difficulties, and against this evil we must employ every possible force and industry." Superior enemy forces demonstrated that open naval combat was futile; privateering, however, "a subtle and hidden kind of ocean conflict, . . . can strike directly and sever the sinews of war." This strategy

---

[24] Interestingly enough, the penchant for projects for privateering and for fiscal reform among army officers was carried on after Vauban by Jules Louis Bolé, Marquis de Chamlay. In 1702 he wrote a memoir urging an all-out privateering campaign, observing at the same time how successful such action had been during the War of the League of Augsburg (see Michel Chamillart, *Correspondance et papiers inédits*, ed. G. Esnault, 2 vols., Le Mans, 1884). For Chamlay's role in fiscal reform see Stanislas Mitard, *La crise financière en France à la fin du XVIIᵉ siècle: la première capitation, 1695-1698*, Rennes, 1934. Chamlay's advice on commercial matters also seems to have been taken seriously. On 28 August 1702 Denis P. Faulconnier, a merchant from Dunkirk who fairly flooded the Controller General with the most extreme mercantilist projects, presented a paper entitled: "Pour entreprendre l'exécution du projet présenté par le sousigné à Mgr. de Chamillart pour ruiner le commerce et la navigation des Hollandois." On page two there is written "et examiné par Mons. de Chamlay" (A.N., G⁷ 696).

would prove "infinitely advantageous": the enemy would not succeed in preventing the destruction of his trade, and he would be unable to "retaliate because we, [self-sufficient], have but little foreign commerce." France must be resourceful and prove herself capable of "fighting this battle to the end."[25]

Privateering, after it had taken on the character of unrestricted warfare against enemy shipping, had a peculiar effect on the debate between reformers and traditionalists. The issue became less a matter of tariffs and more a question of war and peace. Belesbat, Huet, Fleury, Fénelon, and the many other agrarian reformers, secularly or religiously inspired, viewed the unhampered pursuit of international trade as necessary to maintain peace and prosperity both at home and abroad. In contrast, Vauban and men like Bonrepaus who remained attached to the navy of Colbert and Seignelay, as well as those who employed Courtilz de Sandras to write the *Political Testament* of Louvois were alike convinced that prosperity abroad meant bankruptcy at home. To them trade and war were simply different methods of enriching the realm at the expense of its neighbors. Commerce was primarily a contest for power. But the signing of a treaty at Ryswick on 20 September 1697 brought the merchants, who grew rich and powerful during the war, into the ranks of opposition. The emphasis of argument shifted again, this time from war back to trade. And traditionalists, especially the Colbertists, now directed their attacks against the merchants. Here

[25] Mémoire concernant la caprerie: la course et les privilèges dont elle a besoin pour se pouvoir établir, les moyens de la faire avec succes sans hasarder d'affaires générales et sans qu'il en puisse couter que tres peu de chose à sa Majesté," dated 30 November 1695, ed. Rochas D'Aiglun, *Vauban, sa famille et ses écrits. Ses oisivetés et sa correspondance*, 2 vols., Paris, 1910. The quotations which follow in the text are taken from Vol. I, 454-461.

mercantilist doctrine received its most elaborate and extreme expression. The spokesmen for these views can be understood, however, only after the magnitude of merchant ascendancy and the relation of merchant opposition to the growth of public opinion has been made clear.

ii. MERCHANT ASCENDANCY AND THE GROWTH OF PUBLIC OPINION, 1695-1700

From the earliest years of Louis XIV's personal reign, merchants had protested bitterly against government intervention in business affairs; but so long as they remained weak, their discontent had only limited political significance. After 1688, however, the situation changed rapidly: merchants grew immensely powerful during the War of the League of Augsburg. By 1698, business influence in government had reached unprecedented heights, and merchants were demanding official recognition of their new place in society. They insisted that their prestige and social status be improved by new laws, and they clamored for institutional reforms designed to give them an official voice in directing the economic affairs of the realm. By the Peace of Ryswick the phrase "liberty of trade" was no longer a mere protest against ministerial oppression. It was a war cry, a militant slogan in a powerful campaign to sweep away all obstacles from the path of profit-making. Anti-mercantilist theory, instead of reflecting grievances and impotent opposition, now symbolized a profound transformation in society. Merchants had previously criticized traditional thought about political economy because they, like the aristocracy, feared and resisted the seemingly ineluctable progress of royal centralization. But now businessmen spoke from strength, and their memoirs must be interpreted in the light of their rapidly growing importance.

The merchant's relations with government, indeed his role in society, took on a special character during the War of the League of Augsburg. Some suggestion of his new power may be seen in a changed attitude toward chartered trading companies. During Colbert's ministry, it may be remembered, the Controller General encountered strong resistance and was frequently obliged to compel merchants to invest in these newly established enterprises. The situation remained substantially the same after his death. During the last five years or so of the century, however, when every great colonial company without exception was either founded or reorganized, merchants, instead of avoiding membership, did their best to join as many trading companies as possible. The reasons are clear: earlier, when the state dominated the business community, a directorship only made the merchant more vulnerable to government pressure. Later, when merchant influence reached high into administrative circles, a directorship was no longer regarded as a kind of forced service, placing the businessman at the mercy of the King's ministers. On the contrary, the director would then use his position to bring more immediate pressure to bear on the administration.

Among the merchants purchasing directorships between 1696 and 1701, years which mark a new era in chartered companies, several bought such an office in two or more enterprises. On 19 January 1697, for example, Samuel Bernard and Antoine Crozat became directors in the East India Company,[26] as well as being the new directors of the Companies of Guinea

26 A.N., Minutier Central, Etude CXV, 294.

and of Santo Domingo.[27] Similarly, the financiers Pierre Thomé, Etienne Landais, Vincent Maynon, and Jacques de Vanolles were directors in both the Guinea and Santo Domingo Companies;[28] moreover, Landais and Vanolles held the same positions in the South Sea Company.[29] Finally, a letter—dated 13 November 1697—from Jérome Pontchartrain, Secretary of State for the Marine, to Jean Saupin demonstrates that it was the merchants who took the initiative, at least on one occasion in entering and, perhaps, even in organizing a company:

> I received the letter you wrote to me on the fourth of this month. I consent with pleasure that you enter into the Guinea Trading Company; but nothing has yet been done. And since it will be established without my entering into any details, it is necessary that you address yourself to M. du Ruau-Palu[30] and to the others in the event that you desire to purchase an interest.[31]

This merchant initiative was symptomatic of a profound change in the relations between state and trade, minister and merchant. The transformation, revealing both the extent of the new power and much about the manner in which it was acquired, can be shown only by examining the careers of several individual merchants who grew from relatively moderate fortunes and political impotence to vast wealth and

[27] A.N. Min., Etude LXV, 156, 15 June 1703. For the Guinea Company see George Scelle, *La traite négrière aux Indes de Castille*, 2 vols., Paris, 1906, I, App., doc. 4, 691.

[28] *Ibid.*, for the Santo Domingo Company, A.N., Min., Etude LXV, 156, 15 June 1703.

[29] A.N., Min., Etude XCVI, 20 June 1702.

[30] Vitry la Ville du Ruaupalu, a director of the Guinea Company prior to its subrogation in 1701.

[31] A.N., Archives de la Marine, B[2] 121, ff. 207-210.

influence in the highest government circles. Moreover, these biographical sketches show that unprecedented government dependence upon the business
community was a substantial factor in the merchants
rise as a group. And these radical changes were all
the more striking because they occurred within the
brief period 1693 to 1697. The lives of Thomas Le
Gendre in Rouen and Samuel Bernard in Paris, for
example, provide an illustration of how immense
wealth and influence was built up during the middle
and later years of the war. Moreover, a short account
of some lesser figures shows that other people similarly
engaged shared, although on a smaller scale, the prosperity enjoyed by Le Gendre and Bernard. Thomas Le
Gendre (1638-1706) was the most distinguished representative of a long line of merchant-bankers whose
history has been traced back to the early sixteenth
century.[32] From his father he inherited vast interests
stretching from Canada to Morocco and to the Guinea
coasts, but it was under his own direction that the
fortunes of the house of Le Gendre reached their
peak. As a banker he handled huge sums, on one
occasion making advances which amounted to 110,000
livres or, when calculated in modern money values,
more than $200,000.[33] Should a purchaser require a
ship, Thomas Le Gendre was always known to have
some for sale.[34] His reputation was extensive. Mer-

[32] Georges Vanier, "Une famille de grands marchands Rouennais
aux XVIe et XVIIe siècles: les Le Gendre," *Société libre d'émulation
du commerce et de l'industrie de la Seine-Inférieure*, Dieppe, 1950,
has written a genealogical study of this family.

[33] Archives de la Seine-Maritime, Min. Cavé, 10 July 1692, loan of
110,000 livres to Bruno Emanuel de Motteville . . . conseiller du
Roy en ses conseils, Président à Mortier en sa cour du parlement de
Normandie. According to Professor Meuvret, one livre in the late
seventeenth century is equivalent approximately to $1.80 to $2.00
today.

[34] Sale of ship to Senegal Company, 11 June 1677, A.N., Min.,
Etude XCIX.

chants at Amiens complained that he had an absolute monopoly on the import and sale of alum from the Levant.[35] When the King of Sweden sent an agent to France to purchase material for the manufacture of textiles, the French government referred him to Le Gendre.[36] He was frequently called upon to arbitrate disputes between merchants, both French and foreign.[37] The extent of his international connections caused La Bourdonnaye, intendant in Rouen, to observe: "The Sieur Le Gendre has correspondents in every possible place and his wealth runs from four to five millions."[38]

More significant perhaps is the letter of ennoblement received by Le Gendre immediately after his conversion to Catholicism in 1685.[39] It indicates how famous this merchant was. "Being well informed that Thomas Le Gendre, bourgeois of our town of Rouen, is among those of our kingdom who carry on the greatest ocean commerce . . . we are pleased to grant him a mark of honor which he can pass on to his posterity and which will render him equal to the nobles with whom he may associate, without, at the same time,

[35] Archives du château de Saint-Aignan, Fonds Beauvillier, 283, f. 48.

[36] A.N., Archives de la Marine, B² 107, f. 670.

[37] Archives de la Seine-Maritime, Tabellionage (2d quarter), 23 April 1680. On 20 August 1680, *loc.cit.*, Le Gendre was chosen to arbitrate differences between merchants from Rouen, from The Hague and from Venice.

[38] "Mémoire de la Bourdonnaye intendant de Rouen," pub. by Boulainvillier, *Etat de la France*, 6 vols., London, 1737, IV, 129. In November 1692 the same intendant wrote that Le Gendre had "une correspondance universelle" (A.N., G⁷ 494). Boisguilbert also commented upon Le Gendre's wealth, *Correspondance des Contrôleurs-Généraux des finances avec les intendants des provinces 1683-1715*, ed. A. de Boislisle, 3 vols., Paris, 1874-1897, II, App. 91, 537.

[39] See Vanier, "Une famille," pp. 101-102, 115.

impeding him from continuing his trade."[40] During the next year, 1686, he was made official correspondent for the crown and on 1 March summoned to Versailles for consultation with ministers of state.[41] On 28 March 1688, Le Gendre received a letter from Seignelay informing him that His Majesty had resolved to increase the commerce of the East India Company, "and above all to strengthen it by new stockholders of known and consummate experience in great trading enterprises. His Majesty, whom I had the honor of informing about the reputation which you have among the principal merchants, directed me to write to you that he wishes you to enter into this Company and that you take stock like all the other directors."[42] Le Gendre obeyed; he bought 60,000 livres of stock and took his place among the other directors.[43]

At this date, despite his unquestionable stature, there is no indication that Le Gendre wielded unusual influence in government; if anything, the evidence suggests the contrary. His requests for special consideration about shipment of merchandise on foreign vessels were refused on a number of occasions.[44]

[40] The letter of nobility is reproduced *in extenso* by Vanier, *ibid.*, pp. 101-102.

[41] A.N., Archives de la Marine, B2 57, f. 142. La Lande Magon from St. Malo was also summoned at the same time, see Chap. IV, p. 219, n.62.

[42] *Ibid.*, B2 65, f. 228.

[43] See Paul Kaeppelin, *La Compagnie des Indes Orientales et François Martin*, Paris, 1908, pp. 211-212, n.6.

[44] For example, on 5 January 1686 Le Gendre's request for authorization to send a vessel from Saint-Malo to Cadiz was refused (A.N., Archives de la Marine, B2 57, f. 13). On 3 March of the same year he was denied permission to load textiles on an English ship (*ibid.*, f. 151). For another refusal on 21 July 1694, this time concerning loading of merchandise on a Danish vessel, see *ibid.*, B2 99, f. 158.

By 5 January 1698, however, the picture had changed dramatically. The Secretary of State for the Marine, Jérome Pontchartrain, wrote to Le Gendre from Versailles:

> The commissioners whom the Estates General [of the United Provinces] have named to work out the tariff which must be drawn in execution of the Treaty of Ryswick have arrived here. Before entering into conference with them I would be very happy to take your advice on matters concerning the commerce in which you are engaged. It will be necessary for you to come here for a visit; please make it as soon as possible because in the event that we pass something contrary [to your interests] it would be difficult to come back on a question that has already been decided.[45]

How did Thomas Le Gendre grow so powerful in the decade between 1688 and 1698? The answer seems to lie partially in the fact that he was among those Protestant merchants who remained in France after the revocation of the Edict of Nantes by converting to Catholicism. Many of these businessmen had intimate relations with Huguenot refugees, often members of their own family who established themselves abroad. In a period when confidence played an important role in international transactions, the former Protestant merchant was particularly favored by a large number of reliable foreign correspondents. During the War of the League of Augsburg the govern-

[45] *Ibid.*, B2 131, f. 25. On Thursday, 23 January 1698, the *Gazette de Hollande* carried the following entry: "Le sieur Le Gendre fameux banquier de Rouen est venu ici [Paris] pour s'aboucher avec les deux commissaires des Etats Généraux des Provinces Unies qui sont ici pour les affaires du commerce."

ment had increasing need for services which only a merchant with such connections could provide. The early 1690's, for example, were years of poor harvests and famine, and the crown did its utmost to procure foreign grain. Normal commercial intercourse with the United Provinces and the countries to the north were severed by war. Moreover, although it was common throughout the early modern period to trade with the enemy, an intensified privateering campaign interfered with even the traditional wartime relations between merchants of belligerent powers.[46] In these circumstances, the administration turned to men like Le Gendre. During the winter of 1692, Pontchartrain ordered the president of the Rouen *Parlement*, Montholon, to contract with Le Gendre for the import of grain. Montholon replied that Le Gendre, the only merchant in Normandy upon whom the government could depend for sizable imports, expected answers from his foreign correspondents within three weeks.[47] The results were impressive. From 1693 to 1694, dozens of vessels loaded with grain from the Protestant countries of Scandinavia and Holland sailed into French ports for the "account of Thomas Le Gendre."[48]

[46] An intelligent and detailed attempt to explain the joint effort of England and the United Provinces to suppress the trade of France was written by Sir George N. Clark, *The Dutch Alliance and the War Against French Trade, 1688-1697*, Manchester, 1923.

[47] "Quand j'ay eu l'honneur de vous rendre compte de l'entretien que j'avois eu avec le sieur Le Gendre suivant vos ordres, je n'ay parlé de la Bretagne que pour ne rien oublier. Il n'a aucune pensée pour tirer des bleds que des pays estrangers, dont il espere des responses dans trois semaines. . . . Je n'en ay parlé à aucune autre personne, estant le négociant le plus sur qui soit icy" (A.N., G7 494). See also A. de Boislisle, *Corr. con. gén.*, I, arts. 1126, 1238.

[48] See, for example, A.N., Archives de la Marine, B2 88, f. 211; *ibid.*, B2 97, f. 193; B2 98, f. 351. In this last reference there is also the following letter from Pontchartrain to Chamillart, then intendant of finances: "Je vous envoye monsieur une lettre que m'escrit

Other merchants, like Samuel Bernard, who co-operated with Le Gendre in rendering similar services,[49] were also newly converted to Catholicism after the Revocation.[50] Bernard profited immensely from the fact that other members of his family had chosen to retain their religion and change their nationality. His brother-in-law, Estienne Soullard, who was a Paris banker in 1681,[51] later exercised the same profession in London.[52] Jacques Herquelin, another brother-in-law,[53] went to Frankfort[54] and subsequently established his banking business in Leipzig;[55] Herquelin's

---

le Sieur Thomas Le Gendre sur une affaire dont il marque que vous avez connoissance. Je vous prie de vouloir bien prendre la peine de m'en parler quand nous travaillerons ensemble parce que je serois bien aisé de luy faire plaisir et justice à cause du soin qu'il se donne de faire venir des bleds."

Some idea of the amount of cereals imported at this time may be gained from a passage in Pottier de la Hestroye, lt. general of the Admiralty in Flanders at Dunkirk:

En 1693 et 1694 La France manquoit du bled, la disette étoit générale dans nos Provinces, c'étoit le fort de la guerre, c'étoit en apparance le moment fatal à la France. . . . Cela les a-t-il [the Dutch] empeché d'en envoyer en France, en se servant des vaisseaux Suédois, et Danois, ou de leurs vaisseaux masqués du pavillon des nations neutres, et meme de leurs propres vaisseaux portant pavillon hollandois? Combien le Roy n'a-t-il pas fait expédier de passeports pour les recevoir en France, les registres du secrétaire d'Estat pour la Marine, qui les a expédié, en sont pleins, aussy bien que ceux des sièges d'Admirauté des ports où ils arrivoient (Bib. Mun. de Poitiers, MS 548, pp. 50-52).

[49] A.N., G7 494-497 contains many references in this regard.

[50] See the document reproduced in Herbert Lüthy, *La Banque protestante en France de la Révocation de l'Edit de Nantes à la Révolution*, Paris, 1959, I, 68-73.

[51] A.N., Min., Etude IX, 470, 21 November 1681.

[52] *Ibid.*, 564, 29 November 1705. The act contains the phrase "tous absents du royaume pour fait de religion." See also *ibid.*, 538, 12 August 1698.

[53] *Loc.cit.*

[54] *Ibid.*, 490, 3 October 1686.

[55] *Ibid.*, 535, 8 February 1698.

brother Pierre, a merchant, moved to Breslau.[56] Samuel Bernard's own brother, Pierre, also a banker, moved to Frankfort;[57] and another brother, Gabriel Bernard, fleeing first to Leipzig,[58] later managed to establish his banking firm in Strasbourg.[59] These people soon coordinated their activities to their mutual advantage. On 3 October 1686, Samuel and all his refugee relations, with the exception of Soullard, concluded transactions with third parties amounting to 269,000 livres, a sum roughly equivalent to a half million dollars today.[60] The crown early became interested in this ability to amass capital when money was scarce; and, probably with a view to increasing the domestic stock of precious metals, the Controller General and De Lagny, Director General of Trade, secretly gave their approval on 29 November 1688 to Bernard's illegal purchase of interests in Spanish galleons for himself and on behalf of others whose names remain unknown.[61]

The government found Bernard's services increasingly useful. His connections with Northern and Central Europe proved invaluable for importing

56 *Ibid.*, 490, 3 October 1686.   57 *Ibid.*, 538, 12 August 1698.
58 *Ibid.*, 490, 3 October 1686.   59 *Ibid.*, 538, 12 August 1698.

60 *Ibid.*, 490, 3 October 1686. Lüthy, *La Banque protestante*, I, writes: "La carriere du banquier de la Cour reposait sur le fait qu'il savait trouver du crédit sur toutes les places d'Europe, où le roi avait besoin de fonds pour sa diplomatie, ses subsides où ses armées, et qu'il était le seul à la trouver. D'où tirait-il [Bernard] ce crédit? Nous n'en savons rien, mais ce n'est certainement pas de sa boutique de marchand-drapier de la rue Bourg-l'Abbé qu'il délaissait en 1687 pour s'établir banquier. La seule hypothèse plausible, quoique indémonstrable, reste celle dont le journal de Barbier, au moment de la mort du financier [January 1739], s'est fait l'écho: "On dit que sa fortune a commencé dans les troubles des huguenots qui furent obligés de se retirer et dont il avait la correspondance pour les affaires" (pp. 74-75).

61 A.N., Min., Etude IX, 511, 23 October 1691.

naval supplies. Bernard furnished hemp from Riga,[62] and provisioned ports like Brest, Rochefort, and Toulon with masts and naval stores of all kinds.[63] But his most spectacular activities during this period were connected with intensified privateering campaigns. An individual merchant-privateer's ability to continue his operations depended largely upon the facility with which he could dispose of his prizes profitably. Men like Bernard, Le Gendre, and many others here played a crucial role: they often assured the privateer an immediate cash payment of a sum 25 per cent higher than the officially estimated value of the captured merchandise.[64] Cargoes of exceptional value, however, posed difficult problems of finance. On 23 October 1695, for example, Pontchartrain requested Bernard "to encourage his friends" to buy shares in the fabulous prizes captured by the Marquis de Nesmond and by the Sieur Beaubriand L'Evesque. The minister also expressed great pleasure that Bernard had already taken steps to encourage his associates by personally undertaking to purchase a substantial interest.[65] Nesmond's prizes alone were sold to Bernard for a price presently equivalent to over $4 million (2,100,000 livres);[66] he subsequently resold them for 5 million livres.[67] No record has been discovered of the sale value of Beaubriand's prizes, but the notarial minutes reveal that Bernard, along with the East India Company, had bought a one-sixth share which was valued at 1,243,720 livres.[68] Bernard had other

[62] A.N., Archives de la Marine, B2 109, ff. 224, 263.

[63] *Ibid.*, B2 116, ff. 141-142.

[64] A.N., Min., Etude XCIX, 344, 7 February 1697. See also A.N., Archives de la Marine, B2 117, ff. 710-711.

[65] A.N., Archives de la Marine, B2 104, f. 555.

[66] A.N., Min., Etude XCIX, 344, 7 February 1697.

[67] A.N., Archives de la Marine, B2 112, f. 441 bis.

[68] A.N., Min., Etude XCIX, 346, 21 October 1697.

similar investments but the figures are not yet available.[69] Most significant, however, is the fact that Bernard's participation in financing the purchase and marketing of captured enemy prizes, along with his vast network of international correspondents, proved so valuable to the crown that Pontchartrain, in 1696, secretly gave him sole authority to provision all of France's maritime forces.[70]

[69] A.N., Archives de la Marine, B2 117, f. 661. He seems also to have sold captured vessels to the navy (A.N., Min., Etude LII, 22 February 1696).

[70] The letter in which this offer is made, revealing the extent of Bernard's influence, is worth quoting at length.

Je suis fort étonné de n'avoir point encore receu de lettre de vous depuis vostre départ de Paris. Je vous prie de me faire scavoir exactement tout ce qui se sera passé dans la vente de vos marchandises à Nantes dans un grand détail, tant par raport au prix de la vente que par raport aux Cabales que vous aurez pu découvrir, et à la conduite des directeurs de la Compagnie [des Indes]. En un mot ne me laissez rien ignorer sur cela.

Mandez moy ce que vous pensez pour les vivres de la marine, il commance à estre temps de prendre des mesures pour cela, et vous scavez que je serois bien aise que vous en fussiez chargés. Songez aussy à trouver un homme capable de vous aider, et de son crédit et de son travail, et mandez moy sur cela vos veues affin que je dispose toutes choses pour terminer cette affaire à mon arrivée à la cour. Evitez *surtout de rien parler à personne. Je vous dis à personne sans exception pour des raisons que je vous expliqueray.*

En travaillant avec Monsieur de Bonrepaux qui retourne ambassadeur en Danemark sur ce qui concerne le commerce de France en ce pays, nous sommes convenus qu'il seroit d'une tres grande Utilité pour le Royaume d'y introduire nos draps et les marchandises que nous retirons des Isles françoises de l'amérique, telles que sont le gingembre, le sucre, l'indigo. Et il me dit meme qu'il croyait que cela se pourroit exécuter facillement, et avec proffit mais nous sommes convenus qu'avant de passer outre il estoit nécessaire d'essayer par une petite quantité pour voir si ces marchandises auroient le débit. J'ay cru qu'il vous convenoit mieux qu'un autre de suivre cette veue, et de la mettre à exécution. Vous comprenez assez combien les suites en seroient advantageuses au Royaume, et aux négotians, et je connois trop vostre zele pour doubter que vous n'y entriez

The affairs of Bernard and of Thomas Le Gendre, who also engaged in privateering transactions involving huge sums, were similar to the smaller scale activi-

avec plaisir; le détail de cela est trop long pour vous le mandez et j'ay chargé monsieur de Salabery de vous en instruire à vostre retour à Paris. . . . Et comme Monsieur de Bonrepaux s'est chargé d'en procurer le débit il sera nécessaire que vous luy mandiez le nom du marchand à qui vous ferez adresser en ce pays la affin qu'il puisse suivre cette affaire. J'oubliois de vous dire qu'il faut bien se garder de vendre dans le commencement ces draps comme estant de France mais bien comme estant de Hollande affin de ne pas faire d'abord un grand mouvement dans le commerce. Il faut aussy que les sucres que l'on envoyer en ce pays la soient rafinez. Je suis persuadé que je ne vous dis rien la qui vous soit de nouveaux, mais j'ay mieux aymé vous dire des choses que vous scavez desja que de vous laisser rien ignorer de ce que je scay sur cela.

Mandez moy je vous prie en détail tout ce que vous ferez par raport à cette affaire. En cas que vous preniez le party de la suivre vous me ferez plaisir de prendre vos draps de la manufacture du sieur Costagnier de carcasonne qui a sans contredit la meilleure manufacture qu'il y ait en France.

Si vous avez des nouvelles ou s'il vous vient quelque nouvelle idée soit par raport à la marine, soit par raport au commerce, vous me ferez plaisir de m'en faire part (A.N., Archives de la Marine, B² 112, ff. 353-355, italics added).

The above letter was written on 13 May 1696. By 30 November of the same year Bernard began secretly to supply French maritime forces behind the name of one Jean Robert Tronchin, a merchant-banker who later joined the rest of his family in Geneva (A.N., Min., Etude XCIX, 377, 29 September 1707). For Bernard's early connections with Genevan merchants, see *ibid.*, Etude IX, 472, 10 April 1682, and 506, 9 August 1690. After concluding a series of contracts with Pontchartrain, minister of the marine, Tronchin made the following declaration before the notary: "Jean Robert Tronchin bourgeois de Paris . . . déclare que le marché qu'il vient de faire avec Sa Majesté sous l'acceptation de Mgr. de Pontchartrain ministre et secrétaire d'Estat de la marine pour la fourniture aux troupes de mer pour le service de Sa Majesté . . . est pour et au proffit de Sieur Samuel Bernard, intéressé dans les affaires de Sa Majesté, auquel en la passation du dit marché il n'a fait que prester son nom à sa réquisition et pour luy faire plaisir." This declaration is dated 29 March 1697 (Etude XCVI), but there is no doubt that it applies to the contracts of 8 February 1697 and of November 1696 (*ibid.*).

ties of other businessmen.[71] Here an account of several
lesser careers shows that merchants were interrelated
on a truly national scale, forming an intensely powerful pressure group. There was, for example, a mer-
chant-banking family headed by one Nicolas Baudran
who lived in Paris, rue Michel le Comte. His principal customers included most of the leading merchant-
privateers in the active port of Saint-Malo.[72] Information about Baudran's previous religious convictions
is lacking; but his intimacy with Dutch merchants
was such that he was able to have them come to
France during the height of the war to buy cargoes of
captured English prizes.[73] He and his son-in-law,
François Arson, also owned substantial interests in
many of the vessels which hunted the sea lanes for
enemy shipping.[74] His name appears frequently in
the complicated transactions surrounding the sale of
Nesmond's and Beaubriand's prizes, where Baudran
acted for himself and on behalf of other investors
from Saint-Malo and from Nantes.[75] All the evidence

[71] Le Gendre's purchase of one prize on 14 May 1691 amounted to
230,000 livres (A.N., Min., Etude XCV, 45). See also B² 125, ff.
316-317.

[72] Such names as those of Noël Danican Sieur de l'Espine, Nicolas
Magon Sieur de la Chipaudière, Nicolas Magon Sieur de la Lande,
and Julien Eon Sieur de la Villebague appear frequently in the
numerous acts of the Baudran family which are to be found in
Etude XCIX.

[73] Pontchartrain, on 19 November 1695, wrote the following letter
to Baudran: "J'ay receu la lettre que vous m'avez escrit le 7 de ce
mois. Le Roy veut bien permettre aux particuliers qui vous ont
escrit d'hollande de venir en france pour se trouver à la vente des
cinq prises angloises venant des Indes qui sont à Brest et au Port
Louis pourveu que vous respondiez de leur conduitte pendant qu'ils
y seront. C'est à dire que parmy eux il n'y aura aucun Espion. Sur
ce pied vous n'avez qu'à m'en faire scavoir les noms et je vous
envoyeray des passeports pour eux" (A.N., Archives de la Marine,
B² 109, f. 435).

[74] A.N., Min., Etude XCIX, 337, 5 November 1694.

[75] *Ibid.*, 344, 7 February 1697.

suggests that Baudran's business prospered.[76] More important, however, is the fact that his growing wealth was no isolated phenomenon; indeed, it was precisely because his customers from Saint-Malo and Nantes grew rich in the pursuit and capture of English and Dutch merchantmen that Nicolas Baudran's affairs flourished in the manner that they did.

Another example of merchants who became prosperous during this period is the career of Joachim Descazeaux du Hallay in Nantes. He assumed direction of the house of Descazeaux on 1 January 1689. Business was bad and the family faced ruin on several occasions. When Joachim's father who was Assistant-Mayor, died in 1693, the son inherited nothing but debts.[77] By 1700 he had become rich and was elected

[76] The size of Baudran's transactions increased as the war advanced; by Ryswick he had grown to be a veritable man of "affairs." Noël Danican, for example, passed the equivalent of a half million dollars worth of transactions through Baudran on 7 March 1698 (Etude XCIX, 347).

[77] Archives de la Loire-Atlantique, E. Supplément, dossier Descazeaux et famille. An act of succession dated 1693 contains the following statement:

Il est ainsy que noble homme Pierre Descazeaux ancien sous maire de la Ville demeurant de Nantes seroit décédé le 30 novembre 1693 lequel a laissé trois enfans de son mariage avec demoiselle Marie Françoise à présent veuve, Scavoir Nobles Gens Pierre Julien Descazeaux, sr. de la Foliette; Joachim Descazeaux sr. du Hallay et demoiselle Françoise Descazeaux, Epouse de n.h. Jean Choumis sr. de Kervesan con^{er} du Roy trésorier antien des fouages et autres deniers Royaux et l'évesché de Vannes. . . .

Or est-il que ledit deffunt Sr. Descazeaux avoit depuis son mariage fait un grand Négoce qui n'ayant pas toujours bien réussi par les pertes considérables qu'il auroit faites, tant par Banqueroutes, prises de ses Navires en mer, par les ennemies de l'estat, qu'autrement, en sorte que des dettes surpassoient la Valleur de ses biens, ne pouvant agir avec autant de liberté qu'il faisoit auparavant, à cause de ses ages fort avancés, et de ses fréquentes malladies desquelles il est enfin décédé, il aban donna le Négoce qui fut repris par ledit sr. du Hallay qui

deputy to the newly established Council of Commerce in Paris, where he became distinguished for a memoir which we will examine later. Joachim was associated early with Thomas Le Gendre and with Samuel Bernard.[78] Moreover, he frequently acted in cooperation with Noël Danican, Sieur de l'Espine, *armateur* from Saint-Malo. Their ship, the *Comte-de-Toulouse*, returned from a smuggling trip to Mexico on 9 June 1694 loaded with gold and silver and pulling in tow an English prize, the *William-Henry*.[79] Descazeaux also had interests in the ships *Le Furieux* and *Le Vaillant* which returned in 1693-1694 with a prize, the *Princess of Denmark*.[80] Also on 14 August 1694 Joachim seems to have had a share in four prizes taken "from the enemies of the state."[81] Elsewhere his warehouses were used as depots for storing booty prior to their sale and distribution.[82] Finally, the records also show that Descazeaux was able to outfit about a dozen

---

commença de prendre la conduite des affaires le premier Janvier 1689 et les géra sous son nom jusqu'au 31 décembre 1691, qui sont trois ans. Dans le commencement il se vue plusieurs fois en danger de succomber sous le faix des dettes, cependant s'étant acquis des amis, sous le crédit desquels il travailla si utilement qu'il acquitta des dettes de la Communauté de ses pere et mere jusqu'à la somme de 77.965£ 15ˢ. . . ."

[78] Jacques Saint-Germain, *Samuel Bernard le banquier des rois*, Paris, 1960, p. 137 shows that Descazeaux was a business associate of Bernard in 1706. And Monsieur J. Meyer at Nantes has very kindly told me that the Admiralty records show that Descazeaux armed a ship named the *Bernard* in 1703. M. Nieuhof shows (B 4672) that on 9 July 1691 Descazeaux acted as agent in Nantes on behalf of Thomas Le Gendre.

[79] Archives de la Loire Atlantique, B 4741. I am indebted to the generosity of Doctor Kerneis for this and much other information concerning Descazeaux.

[80] *Ibid.*

[81] *Ibid.*, B 4897. I am here again indebted to Monsieur J. Nieuhof for graciously sharing with me the results of his research concerning privateering in Nantes.

[82] *Ibid.*, B 4886, 28 June 1690.

vessels for the Atlantic trade; his fortune was made largely from the Newfoundland fishing banks and privateering between 1694 and 1698. When he arrived in Paris in 1700 for the first meeting of the Council of Commerce, Descazeaux was a wealthy man.

Closely related to privateering and prosperity in Saint-Malo and in Nantes was the most unusual career of Nicolas François Mesnager in Rouen. As early as 1682 he was associated with Eon de la Villebague and Guillaume Eon, well-known *armateurs* from Saint-Malo.[83] Indeed, Mesnager's connection with this port appears to have long been particularly intimate; on 26 January 1681, he gave François Moreau, uncle of Nicolas Baudran, fairly wide powers of attorney.[84] An inventory of Moreau's possessions at his death, on 13 April 1693, reveals a number of Mesnager's transactions with the Moreau-Baudran family whose business centered in Saint-Malo.[85] And on 18 June 1693, Mesnager gave Nicolas Baudran power of attorney just as he had done previously to his deceased uncle.[86] On 13 June 1692, Mesnager purchased the expensive office of *secrétaire du roi*[87] which, if retained for twenty years, conferred on the owner the legal status of hereditary nobility. Whatever the source of his wealth, it is certain that Mesnager continued his close relations with Saint-Malo interests: on 7 May 1698, he gave François Arson, Baudran's brother-in-law, the right to collect on his behalf monies from government

[83] Léon Vignols, "Le commerce maritime et les aspects du capitalisme commercial à Saint-Malo de 1680 à 1792," *Revue d'histoire économique et sociale*, 1931, XXX, 12-13.

[84] A.N., Min., Etude XCIX, 283.

[85] *Ibid.*, 333.

[86] *Ibid.*, Etude XCIV.

[87] According to the Père Léonard the charge of secrétaire du roy cost 55,000 livres in 1694 (A.N. MS 768, "Portefeuilles du P. Léonard," Mélanges historiques).

bonds and other investments.[88] Mesnager was elected
deputy to the Council of Commerce in 1700, and subsequently his expert knowledge of the slave trade
caused him to be appointed special envoy to Spain, to
the United Provinces, and to England.[89] Finally,
Nicolas François Mesnager was one of the three minister plenipotentiaries who fixed their signatures to
the Treaty of Utrecht. It is difficult to believe that the
fortunes of Saint-Malo and the Moreau-Baudran family are entirely unconnected with the early period of
Mesnager's spectacular career.

The affairs of Antoine Héron, deputy to the Council of Commerce from La Rochelle, seem also to have
been linked to some extent with the Baudran family
and Saint-Malo. On 22 July 1698, he paid Baudran
28,759 livres "in settlement of a composition arrived
at verbally concerning all bills and letters of exchange
which they have respectively furnished in the past and
to this day."[90] Héron was also on very close terms with
the well-known privateer and Governor of St. Do-
mingue, Jean Ducasse.[91] And, like Mesnager, Héron
became particularly interested in the slave trade.[92]

The connection between privateering and the slave
trade is here of special significance because it shows
why business communities from Dunkirk to La Rochelle and Bordeaux became rapidly and profoundly
hostile to the central government. Until the War of
the League of Augsburg, slave-trading had proved to
be anything but lucrative. Shortage of capital, both

[88] A.N., Min., Etude XCIX, 348.

[89] See the many references in Scelle, *La traite négrière*, II, especially p. 477.

[90] *Ibid.*, 348.

[91] A.N., Archives de la Marine, B7 62, see ff. 14-15, 18. Concerning
Heron's interest in privateering see also *ibid.*, B7 60, f. 171.

[92] Emile Jourdan, *Ephémérides de La Rochelle*, 2 vols., La Rochelle, 1871, II, 5.

private and public, seems to have been one major difficulty.[93] After Ryswick, however, merchants along the entire length of the Channel and Atlantic coasts called for an end to chartered companies and demanded with astonishing vehemence and persistence the unrestricted right to trade for slaves on the West African coast in order to sell them in the New World. It is only reasonable to suppose that these men had acquired considerable capital during the war.[94] In this connection, it is particularly instructive to follow the activities of a merchant-privateer from Brest, Jean Saupin. His most trusted officer was René d'Arquistade, adopted son of Descazeaux du Hallay.[95]

[93] Colbert organized companies for the slave trade, as well as for other kinds of commerce, largely because private capital was inadequate for the task (see *Lettres, instructions et mémoires de Colbert*, ed. Pierre Clément, 7 vols., Paris, 1861-1882, III, Part II, 477). So far as the under-capitalization of the slave trading companies themselves are concerned, see Abdoulaye Ly, *La compagnie du Sénégal*, Paris, 1958, pp. 225-226. Also in this regard, Pottier de la Hestroye made the following observation:

> Nous ne faisons pas assez valoir ce Commerce [the slave trade] pour lequel nous avons quinze cens lieues de costes. Les Compagnies que nous avons établis, qui en donnent l'exclusion à tous les autres sujets, n'y ont pas assez d'établissement, *ils ne font pas pour cela un assez gros fond*, ils n'y envoient pas assez de vaisseaux. . . . (Poitiers, Bib. mun., MS 548, p. 426, italics added).

[94] In this regard there exists a most interesting document in the archives of the marine (B⁷ 219). It bears the fanciful title: "Projet sur le Chateau de la mine et Buenos Aires le seul Establissement que les Hollandois ayent à la Coste de Guinée 1696." The anonymous author begins by explaining that the interests of the privateer and those of the state are one: "Le principal objet que l'on doit avoir dans les armemens en course est de pouvoir joindre l'intérest de l'Estat avec celuy des particuliers." The remainder of the project concerns a plan to capture the "entire African trade" from the Dutch. The memoir, very primitively written, was almost certainly composed by a prospering *armateur* who was looking forward to supplying slaves to the Spanish colonies.

[95] S. de la Nicollière-Teijeiro, *La course et les corsaires du port de Nantes*, Paris, 1896, p. 65, shows that Jean Saupin had "comme

Throughout the war, Saupin was deeply involved in privateering; and, like so many other *armateurs*, he entered into relations with Thomas Le Gendre[96] and with Samuel Bernard,[97] through the latter's correspondents in Paris, the De Meuves brothers. Finally, Jean Saupin, as we have seen, took the initiative almost as soon as peace was concluded, and on 13 November 1697, requested permission to purchase a directorship in the reorganized Guinea Company.[99] Other merchants were not so fortunate; and, unable to enter the great trading companies, they resented their exclusion from what promised to be a lucrative area of commerce. It was they, men like Descazeaux du Hallay, who presented the most radical anti-mercantilist arguments in the Council of Commerce in 1700.[100]

---

second René d'Arquistade, futur maire de Nantes en 1735 et 1740." Doctor Kerneis, working from the parish records, has generously told me that d'Arquistade, who went to sea at sixteen years of age, was adopted by Descazeaux and was subsequently married in the chapel of Du Hallay to "his cousin," Germaine Françoise Descazeaux, on 29 May 1714.

96 A.N., Min., Etude XLIV, 162, 30 June 1702.

97 A.N., Min., Etude XLIV, 162, 30 June 1702.

98 See the numerous indications in Lüthy, *La Banque protestante*, I, *passim*.

99 A signatory to the Asiento in 1701 was one François Saupin, perhaps a relative of Jean Saupin.

100 Descazeaux's anti-mercantilist views are dealt with below. Their relation to the slave trade, both for himself and for other merchants, consists entirely in their battle against monopoly. In 1701, for example, the vision of a virtually insatiable demand for slaves in the Spanish Empire, now ruled by Louis XIV's grandson, made Descazeaux wax eloquent in his protest against monopolies:

Les compagnies privatives étoient bonnes il y a quarante ans, parce qu'alors les idées du commerce maritime étoient entierement perdus en France. . . .

[Now, however,] il est de la derniere conséquence, et pour l'intéret du Roi, et pour celui de l'Etat, de lever les exclusions et de laisser la liberté. . . .

La maxime fondamentale des compagnies privatives est tout

The heat which merchants injected into the long-standing controversy about questions of political economy is partially explained by the quasi-public character of a debate over issues in which they had a vital interest. Retired noblemen, bishops, generals, political pamphleteers, Protestant refugees, and spokesmen of all kinds had previously taken sides on matters which affected businessmen perhaps more directly than anyone else; yet until now the mer-

---

opposée au bien public, en ce qu'il est de leurs intérets de borner leur commerce à une certaine quantité. . . .

Quant à la compagnie de Guinée, l'indolence où elle a été pour son commerce de negres depuis qu'elle a joui de ces privileges, nous a privés de faire de grands progres dans le commerce et dans la navigation par rapport aux peuples de l'Amérique. Elle a tellement borné la fourniture des negres à ces peuples, qu'il n'y en a pas la dixieme partie de ce qui seroit nécessaire pour défricher les terres. . . .

Les Espagnols ayant tant d'empressement d'avoir des negres, quoiqu'il leur soit étroitement défendu de négocier aux Indes avec les étrangers, cependant cet appat leur fait tout surmonter, au point qu'il suffit de porter aux Espagnols, par exemple, cinquante negres, pour les engager à faciliter en secret une navigation de cinquante mille écus de marchandises de l'Europe, qu'ils payent en argent comptant.

Lorsque nous aurons la liberté de ce négoce, nous pourrons aussi former de telles habitudes, et meme au préjudice des autres nations, à present que Dieu nous a favorisés par ce grand événement qui a transféré la couronne d'Espagne à l'illustre sang du Roi (A. de Boislisle, *Corr. con. gén.*, II, 494-495).

Elsewhere a number of merchants exclaimed: "It is a most certain Maxim that nothing but Competition and liberty in Trade can render Commerce beneficial to the State; and that all Monopolies or Traffic appropriated to Companies exclusive of others are infinitely burdensome and pernicious. What advantage can *France* receive from the Guinea Company? . . . Will they sacrifice their interests to those of the State? . . . Will they not rather choose to sell a Negro for 500 livres rather than 120 or 150?" This passage is taken from the minutes of the early debates in the Council of Commerce (p. 503). They may be found in the notes which follow the manuscript version of Spanheim's (the Prussian Ambassador to Versailles) memoir entitled "Relation de la Cour de France," B.N., Fds. fr., n.a. 6828, pp. 499-579. These minutes were somehow

chants' voice had been weak. An understandable conviction that they also had a right to be heard was
thus strengthened by recently acquired wealth and
by the services they had rendered during the war.
Merchants had financed the privateering campaigns,
and they had procured cereals from abroad in times
of famine and imported naval stores during the height
of the war. The combination of unprecedented government dependence upon the business community
and the increasingly public character of controversies
concerning matters of trade made it difficult for the
crown to refuse to listen to the merchants.

Moreover, the approach of a general peace, and
especially the negotiation of commercial treaties with
the maritime powers, raised problems that went to
the heart of the controversy which had been assuming mounting proportions since Colbert's death. The
bases for France's future international trade were to
be laid down in these negotiations, and ministers
hesitated to make decisions on such complex matters
without consulting the merchant community. On 8
May 1697, for example, Jérome Pontchartrain wrote
to the intendant at La Rochelle, Michel Bégon: "I
beg you to confer immediately with the merchants."
And the extent to which Pontchartrain was per-

---

published for foreign consumption and curiously enough, one volume may be found without a title in the Seligman collection at the
Columbia University Library. The pages are printed in French and
faced by English translations. Professor Cole mistakenly used this
source in his *French Mercantilism*. He does not appear to have
been aware of Spanheim's notes and unfortunately he mistook this
published edition of minutes for the memoirs presented to the
Council of Commerce in 1700 (see Chap. V, p. 327, n.2). But of
interest here is the fact that Professor Cole makes mention of a
"similar but not identical" volume listed in the catalogue of the
Kress collection at Harvard, No. 4346. The book, actually entitled
*Memorials Presented by the Deputies of the Council of Trade in
France . . . 1701*, is not available at the Bibliothèque Nationale.

plexed and troubled by their anti-mercantilist demands may be seen from the question which he instructed Bégon to inquire into "as deeply as possible."

> If we permit the entry of foreign merchan-
> dise . . . in order to obtain foreign markets for
> French products, will the Advantage thus earned
> be reciprocal and equal on one side and on the
> other? Will not the Kingdom's trade suffer too
> considerably . . . I beg you give me the same
> advice regarding your proposals for the sale of
> merchandise from the American colonies [French
> West Indies] to foreign countries, and the most
> certain and simple methods of considerably in-
> creasing trade.
>
> I beg you to give me this as promptly as pos-
> sible and in the greatest detail of which you are
> capable. . . . You are aware of the extreme ur-
> gency of the matter and that there is not a mo-
> ment to lose.[101]

The indecision which caused the crown to solicit
advice from merchants about the most fundamental
principles of trade also increased the pressure for
some institutional arrangement whereby the business
community could be heard. The path leading to a
newly founded Council of Commerce was now open.
But the situation which caused the government to
call this body into existence was above all created by
the fragmentation of bureaucratic control. A major
expansion in the Atlantic trade since the last year
or so of the war,[102] and the need to reexamine the

[101] A.N., Archives de la Marine, B² 121, ff. 207-210.

[102] Perhaps the most dramatic evidence for the rapid expansion
of the Atlantic trade around the Peace of Ryswick is that furnished
by Pierre Goubert, *Familles marchandes sous l'ancien régime: les
Mottes et les Danses de Beauvais*, Paris, 1961. Here Goubert shows
conclusively that Beauvais, which from the nature of its commercial

principles which were to govern France's future foreign trade, helped to complicate the direction of economic matters to the point where they could no longer be effectively centralized under one man. The task of economic regulation was parceled out among several agencies. In 1696 Controller General Pontchartrain unburdened some of his responsibilities on his cousin Henri d'Aguesseau, former intendant at Languedoc, under whom he established a sort of superintendence of commerce. Moreover, when Pontchartrain became Chancellor in 1699, the control of commerce was again divided; this time between the Ministry of Marine, headed by his son Jérome, and the office of Controller General, then assumed by Chamillart. In short, it is out of this background of administrative indecision, further aggravated by a division of authority, that the Council of 1700 emerged. Its significance should not be obscured by its merely advisory functions: government policies were for the first time regularly scrutinized by a body of well-informed and experienced men, representing the major commercial centers of France.

An edict promulgated on 29 June 1700 declared, in part, that the "KING, BEING IN HIS COUNCIL, has commanded and commands that in the future a Council of Commerce will meet once every week."[103]

---

activity could not have been an isolated case, underwent in 1700 a transformation in its method of conducting foreign trade. Up to that date merchants in Beauvais had traded with Spain, Portugal, and the colonies only indirectly through Rouen, Saint-Malo, and Dieppe; around 1700, however, this activity picked up, and the Beauvais merchants traded directly with people in the ports of destination.

Testimony of contemporaries suggests the same pattern for Rouen around 1697. See, for example, the papers of Father Léonard (A.N., M 757, No. 3).

[103] The document was published in full by A. de Boislisle, *Corr. con. gén.*, II, 476-477.

Composed of "twelve [later thirteen] of the principal merchant-bankers in the realm" and headed by Henri d'Aguesseau, Michel Chamillart, and Jérome Pontchartrain, the Council of Commerce was originally a kind of economic parliament wherein were debated matters which concerned the official direction of affairs. When the first deputies, elected locally in ten principal towns[104] by their fellow merchants, arrived in Paris, many of them, particularly those from the Atlantic and Channel ports, brought the administration's policies violently into question, contributing powerful support to the forces of opposition. Intoxicated with recently acquired wealth and exasperated at mercantilist restrictions, deputies such as Joachim Descazeaux du Hallay from Nantes, argued vehemently and eloquently against the established doctrines of political econony:

> This chamber of commerce has caused universal attention, not only in the kingdom, but even more among foreign nations. The lords who compose it are among the first and best heads in the realm; the matter could be of no greater importance . . . it concerns the interest of the prince, the honor of the nation, the welfare of his subjects and the particular glory of the ministers in this Council. We have reason to be attentive to their decisions. . . . The first thing which we can wish in favor of commerce is liberty. . . .
>
> Liberty is the soul and element of commerce; she excites the genius and application of merchants who never cease to meditate on new methods to make discoveries and to found enterprises. [Liberty] kindles a perpetual movement which

104 The two Paris delegates were appointed by the King.

produces abundance everywhere. The moment we limit the genius of merchants by restrictions, we destroy trade. The Dutch, whom we can cite for an example, . . . have made it a law which they observe regularly, to assure that liberty reigns without restriction. It is by this artifice that they have made themselves masters of all the world's trade: we see them go even to the length of permitting free exit of gold and silver specie, a practice severely prohibited in other nations. Clever merchants understand that, by a necessary process, that which leaves will return by another route, and if the movement is properly observed it will produce a profit which will remain in the country and enrich the one that created it.

They [the Dutch] have in addition that prudent politic of scarcely charging commerce with duties: in case of need they draw subsidies from the general [economy]; they regard commerce as the heart of the state, as a precious body with which we interfere the least. They protect it with all their force, so as to impress their subjects that it is the most cherished of occupations, thus exciting them all to throw themselves into it as the unique method of both enriching themselves and of being able to support the charges of the state. If this maxim were well weighed, we could find it very proper, and, by the method of liberty, we would create marvels in commerce in France, as is done in Holland.[105]

Descazeaux not only stressed the identity of merchant interests with those of the state, but he further insisted that this was the reason why the crown ought to leave the businessman alone and not bother him

[105] A. de Boislisle, *Corr. con. gén.*, II, 482-483.

with a host of regulations. Here, as if he had not made himself clear, Descazeaux emphasized that "if he [a merchant] works for himself, he works for the King and for the state: we must not trouble him."[106]

Deputies from the other ports in western France presented memoirs which, while not so eloquent or so lengthy, were written very much in the same vein.[107] They all attacked traditional mercantilist principles at a time when ministers, struggling with the problems bequeathed to them by Colbert, no longer possessed his supreme self-assurance. Moreover, this ministerial indecision encouraged further public controversy, and the heat of debate helped to create the illusion that official rulings depended upon force of argument. Advice poured in from all quarters.[108] Those demanding change remained hopeful,

---

[106] *Ibid.*, p. 485.

[107] The one exception is the memoir submitted by Mesnager from Rouen. His position, apart from the issue of the slave trade, was entirely traditional. Most revealing, however, is the argument between Pottier de la Hestroye and Anisson, deputy from Marseille, in 1704. On the one hand Pottier insisted:

On ne regarde le Commerce que par raport a ce que le Royaume produit. Ce principe est Incontestable pour le bien de l'Etat. . . .

Les Marchands particuliers n'y trouveront pas peut-etre aussy bien leur compte que si l'entrée étoit Indistinctement ouverte a toutes sortes de Marchandises. . . .

Et je ne doute pas que dans le grand nombre de marchands qu'on a entendu, la plus grand partie n'ait beaucoup insisté sur cette liberté. . . . Mais persuadé que dans la veue de retablir Le Commerce en France, on pense moins a enrichir quelques particuliers que l'Estat en général, J'estably mes veues sur ce principe là.

In contrast, Annison exclaimed:

Enfin il est constant que le commerce d'un Estat ne peut estre fait au proffit s'il n'est entre les mains de négociants riches et capables de grandes Entreprises telles que sont les voiages de long course. . . . (B.N., Fds. fr., 14294, ff. 185-186, 17-18).

[108] A doctor in the small town of Boulogne-sur-Mer, for example, sent the following letter to the Controller General, Pontchartrain:

418

and their repeated efforts to impress the authorities with the correctness of their views only provoked, as the following section will show, more lengthy and often denunciatory replies from opponents. Matters of state had become a proper subject of concern for everyone. Thus political discussion in 1700, if not sufficiently widespread to form what is presently called a public opinion, was nevertheless a force important enough to prevent government in France from being the exclusive affair of the King and his ministers.[108a]

Monseigneur,

En allant voir un soldat à Ambleteuse et en venant le long de la mer, j'ay pensé à deux ou trois moyens pour ramener la prospérité du commerce, que je prends la liberté de vous adresser, s'il y'en a quelqu'un de votre gout, je ne demande point d'autre récompense qu'un employ pour mon fils. . . .

Blondet

Quoted from the papers of the Controller General by Germain Martin, *La grande industrie*, p. 251, n.2.

Elsewhere an apothecary named Gaschet presented two lengthy and abominably written memoirs to Pontchartrain, one of which he claimed was written by another apothecary twenty-three years previously (A.N., G7 695).

The documents are full of proposals of every conceivable or outlandish kind.

[108a] One of the Duke of Montausier's political axioms (written for the Dauphin sometime between 1668-1679) suggests that if one cannot speak of public opinion in earlier seventeenth century France, there was at least a widespread sensitivity to the manner in which the crown addressed the subjects of the realm:

S'il [the King] ne scait pas que rien ne choque si fort les esprits, et n'éloigne tellement les coeurs de tout le monde, que les paroles de rudesse qui témoignent du mépris. La noblesse, les magistrats, les bourgeois, les villes et les peuples de la campagne sont sensibles au dernier point aux termes méprisans dont les Rois, ou leurs ministres, ou leurs gouverneurs se servent en leur endroit. Et on a veu de tres grands désordres arriver, et avoir de tres méchantes suites, seulement pour avoir dans des édits, des ordonnances, et d'autres écrits publics dit des choses désobligeantes, touchant la fidélité, l'affection, le courage, la capacité, l'utilité, ou les services des divers ordres des sujets qui composent l'état. Et si par conséquent il n'a pas

iii. REFORM AT ITS HEIGHT: THE CLASH OF IDEOLOGIES AND THE DECLINE OF AUTHORITY, 1695-1700

Confronted by the onslaught of aristocratic and merchant opposition and faced with the fact that matters of the highest policy had been transformed into issues for public debate, the government was plunged into confusion. Its reactions, hasty and inconsistent, often bore the earmarks of panic and bewilderment. Thus of all people it was Controller General Pontchartrain who, fearing that Fénelon's group at Court would subvert the negotiations at Ryswick, entered unexpectedly into the arena of religious controversy: he took what was in fact a conspiratorial initiative to cause the Archbishop's disgrace and exile. This action, following closely upon Fénelon's and Beauvillier's great inquest of February 1697, marked the beginning of both open political struggle and the public clash of ideologies. Meanwhile, the crown made fundamental compromises, indeed, capitulations to the nobility in fiscal matters and to the merchants in commercial policy. At the same time there was a fragmentation of administrative authority as control over economic policy was divided among several different agencies. It is against this background of popular polemic and rapidly declining royal authority that traditionalist spokesmen, writing immediately after Ryswick, viewed with genuine alarm the subversion of the established order. And their

---

les yeux ouverts, et ne tient pas la main extremement à ce que les secrétaires d'état, et tous les autres qui composent les patentes, et toutes ces sortes d'écritures publiques, parlent de la part du Roi avec douceur, humanité, considération, estime, et affection pour tous ces sujets. Car par l'indiscrétion de ceux qui tiennent la plume, . . . on peut donner des chagrins et des fantaisies aux peuples et à la Noblesse (B.N., n.a , MS 10633, f. 35).

elaborate memoirs reveal not only a sense of urgency and crisis, but profound ideological commitment to a most extreme interpretation of mercantilist doctrine.

Allegiance to ideological principles was a phenomenon which seems to have also appeared among merchants who entered the ranks of opposition. Some were imbued with an intense desire to display a knowledge of sophisticated reform doctrines. To be critical of government policies and to champion new ideas may well have become for them a means of social advancement. The rich *roturier* could seek acceptance in aristocratic society, his most cherished goal, by demonstrating a persuasion to the wider doctrinal implications of anti-mercantilist arguments. In this way the ideas traditionally associated with mid-eighteenth century French thought may have become of vital importance in 1700 to people who hardly understood their meaning.

It is difficult to exaggerate how intense and widespread the spirit of reform had become in the years 1695 to 1700. The Capitation of 1695 had created a serious crisis for the nobility,[109] to whom fiscal privileges were a genuine bulwark against royal oppression. Aristocrats took small comfort from official assurances, including a clause in the Edict, that the Capitation was a purely emergency measure enacted

---

[109] Typical of aristocratic attitudes toward the Capitation is the following outburst:

> Que la noblesse refuse de servir à l'Armée; que le Clergé ne soit plus si libéral du patrimoine des pauvres, quand le Roi le demande; que les gens riches et accomodez lui pretent point leur argent; que les Parlemens et les bonnes Villes opposent de tout leur pouvoir aux impots dont nous sommes accablez, à cette Capitation générale qui achève de changer le face de l'Etat: tout le monde en sera mieux. . . .

Quoted from the anonymous memoir, *Lettres d'un gentilhomme François sur l'établissement d'une Capitation générale en France,* Liège, 1695, pp. 9-10.

only for the duration of the war. Had not Bodin observed more than a century earlier that virtually all taxes, originally levied as mere provisional contributions, became "ordinary" because kings continued to demand their collection long after the reasons for their imposition had vanished? Yet, on 17 December, six weeks after the Peace of Ryswick, the government announced the repeal of the Capitation.[110] The promptness of this unusual act of state suggests the intensity of aristocratic pressure. Moreover, Louis XIV may even have taken pains to spread word of the impending repeal prior to the official pronouncement. Speaking of the marriage of the Duke of Burgundy to the Princess of Savoy, which took place on 7 December 1697, a nobleman, the Chevalier de Quincy, exclaimed:

> The entire Court came forth in extraordinary splendor, despite the fact that France has had to wage war for the past ten years against all the European powers. The King has kept the promises he made to suppress the Capitation as soon as peace would be concluded: [an act] which has earned him the affection and veneration of all his subjects.[111]

The Duke of Burgundy's marriage was associated with more than the repeal of the Capitation; in fact, it commemorated the conclusion of peace.[112] Many aristocrats were convinced that the Duke would some day bring better government to France. His marriage signified he was no longer a child, and the celebration of the wedding as a symbol of peace, coinciding as it

110 The Edict announced the repeal effective as of 18 April 1698.

111 *Mémoires*, ed. Léon Lecestre, 3 vols., Paris, 1898, I, 70.

112 See the comte d'Haussonville, *La duchesse de Bourgogne et l'alliance Savoyarde sous Louis XIV*, 4 vols., Paris, 1909, I, 151-156.

did with repeal of the Capitation, seemed to herald the dawn of a new era. Even administrators felt compelled to take heed of the widespread spirit for reform. In answer to a request for advancement, Pontchartrain wrote on 27 November 1697: "You can well imagine that immediately after the peace, when everyone talks about nothing but reform, the King cannot think of making a promotion."[113]

Peace treaties had long served as an occasion for internal reform. During the Dutch War, for example, the crown promised improvements after hostilities had ceased, and in fact Colbert did undertake major administrative changes following the Treaty of Nymwegen. The pattern was repeated in the years immediately after Ryswick; the difference lies in the fact that between 1679 and 1697 demands for reform arising from outside the administration had developed into ideological movements of political opposition. And the peace treaty, still seen by people both within and without the government as an opportunity to undertake reform, brought the crown into direct conflict with the forces of resistance. Nothing reveals this so much as the circumstances leading up to Fénelon's exile on 1 August 1697. It may be remembered that Fénelon and Beauvillier had launched one of France's greatest inquests *"for the instruction of the Duke of Burgundy"* on 12 February 1697.[114] This kingdom-wide inquiry was organized both with a view to reform and in anticipation of peace. Such activities were intolerable for Pontchartrain who, thinking the Dutch were difficult enough to handle in treaty negotiations without the added support of Fénelon and his pacifist free-trade followers at Court, worked actively toward the Archbishop's disgrace.

[113] A.N., Archives de la Marine, B^2 122, f. 399.
[114] See Chapter V, above.

To do this the Controller General joined forces with Madame de Maintenon in a determined attack against Fénelon. The details of the story begin in the year of the Capitation. When Harlay de Champ-vallon, Archbishop of Paris, died on 6 August 1695, Louis XIV was quarreling over a burning fiscal issue with some leaders of the clergy, particularly with two of Madame de Maintenon's protégés: Louis de Noailles, Bishop of Challons and the future Cardinal-Archbishop of Paris, and Godet des Marais, Bishop of Chartres, religious head of Saint-Cyr and Madame de Maintenon's confessor. Although the clergy had suc-ceeded in purchasing exemption from the Capitation rolls, royal fiscal policy since 1689 caused deep con-cern among several of its members. The crown's actions from the summer of 1689 to the beginning of 1695 were indeed of an alarmingly questionable character.[115] First there was the *droit d'amortissement*, a tax on land newly acquired by the clergy in pay-ment for all duties the crown would have collected had the land been purchased by people outside the clergy. In practice, the crown enforced this law only sporadically, when it desired large cash payments from the clergy. In 1641, for example, the Gallican church paid the *amortissements* due since 1620; now, on 5 July 1689, the moment had come for the clergy to pay the accumulated duties due since 1641. In December 1689, Louis XIV sent his table plate to be melted down and coined at the mint. Other owners of objects made of precious metals were supposed to emulate the royal gesture. Therefore, on 8 February 1690, the Sun King "being informed that there is much more silver in the churches than is necessary for the decency of

---

[115] All information concerning fiscal policy and the clergy has been taken from Albert Cans, *La contribution du clergé de France à l'impôt pendant la deuxième moitié du règne de Louis XIV, 1689-1715*, Paris, 1911.

divine service," had called upon the Archbishop of Paris to have an inventory made of objects in every church which could properly be sent to the mint. This action, which transformed a substantial portion of ecclesiastical wealth into liquid reserves, was immediately followed up in 1690 by a demand for a "free gift" of twelve million livres, four times the sum previously paid. For the first time since the Wars of Religion the clergy had to finance part of the payment through alienation of its lands.

Next came the "wood-cutting affair." As early as January 1691 a special syndicate of tax farmers were offering the crown four million livres in exchange for the right to collect fines for all violations of the forest code since its promulgation by Colbert in 1669. Until this time the forest code had scarcely been enforced at all, at least with regard to the Church;[116] and since the clergy had been exploiting over 500,000 acres of forest land for twenty-five years with little regard to Colbert's code, a tidy sum could be collected from sudden enforcement of this legislation. The prospect appeared especially tempting to the government in September 1693, when famine threatened all of France and the treasury looked ahead to lean years: the crown therefore accepted the offer of four million livres from the tax farmers. Finally, in 1695, again a year for voting the quinquennial "free gift," the government demanded ten million livres on one hand, and on the other, a supplemental annual payment of four million livres for the duration of the war in purchase of the right to be exempt from Capitation rolls. Once again the clergy resorted to financing fiscal payments through what amounted to alienation of its lands.

[116] See Paul W. Bamford, *Forests and French Sea Power, 1600-1789*, Toronto, 1956.

Pointed remarks began to appear in ecclesiastical literature. In May 1694, for example, the *Nouvelles ecclésiastiques* carried the following observation: "You are most correct in saying that we glimpse everywhere principles of Revolution in ecclesiastical as well as secular affairs."[117] More direct and more violent criticism, however, was addressed to Louis XIV personally by Bishops Godet des Marais and Antoine de Noailles toward the end of July 1695.[118] They complained less about the amount of taxes than the alienations to which the assemblies of the clergy resorted in order to finance payments to the crown.

> The alienations which the assembly has just made of the clergy's temporal [possessions] can cause not only her entire ruin . . . but are . . . strongly prohibited by the general councils under rigorous penalties. . . . The ancient rules observed by the Kings your predecessors and supported by your *parlements* declare that the estates of the Church cannot be alienated without . . . consent of the Holy See, especially when the alienations are substantial.

In the absence of consent from Rome, the bishops continued, alienations contracted by the clergy were "irregular" and therefore not legally binding. They hastened to add, however, that the crown's demands could be met more properly by other means: a tax of one-fifth, one-fourth, even one-third of annual income might be imposed on every ecclesiastical benefice—a device which would have the advantage of compelling the clergy "to lead a more

117 B.N., Fds. fr., MS 23504, f. 85.

118 The only known copy remaining of this letter is a first draft with extensive corrections which, in places, is quite difficult to read (B.N., Fds. fr., MS 23484, ff. 26-30).

ecclesiastical life, in this way fulfilling more than one duty." Should His Majesty persist in forcing the clergy to alienate church lands, however, consent of the Pope must be obtained.

Louis XIV had long and adamantly insisted that "kings are absolute lords and have naturally the full and free disposition of all the wealth possessed either by men of the Church or by secular subjects."[119] His anger upon receiving this document is reported to have been intense.[120] Up to now Louis had not personally met Noailles who, nevertheless, was appointed Archbishop of Paris on 6 August 1695, about a week after dispatching the letter, a fact which speaks much for Madame de Maintenon's influence, for she was the power behind Noailles's appointment.[121]

Having raised Noailles to a position where he could be of assistance, Madame de Maintenon lost no time in making use of the Archbishop. On 18 August, shortly after assuming his functions, Noailles received the following letter from her:

> Here is a letter from one of our friends, who knows a part of what is happening. You will keep this secret from all. Sometimes it is necessary to deceive the King in order to serve him; and I hope God will permit us to deceive him again, in a similar situation, *and in concert with you.*[122]

A deeply religious man, known for his ascetic life and devout spirit, Noailles was not altogether easy to handle. His sincere antagonism to Madame Guyon's teachings was of course the reason for Madame de

---

[119] Quoted from Louis XIV's memoirs by Esmonin, *La taille en Normandie*, p. 10.
[120] Documentation in Cans, *La contribution du clergé*, p. 28.
[121] *Loc.cit.*
[122] Langlois, *Lettres*, IV, 418, italics added.

Maintenon's favor. But Noailles' equally sincere hostility toward Louis XIV's government seems to have given his patroness some anxious moments. To inspire the prelate to be more prudent and circumspect, Madame de Maintenon sent him the letter wherein Fénelon accused Louis XIV of having turned France into a vast "hospital, desolate and without provisions."

> I am perhaps telling you, Monseigneur, many useless things, but I wish only to instruct you thoroughly about what the King thinks on all matters.
>
> Here is a letter which we wrote him two or three years ago . . . be sure to return it. It is well done; but such truths can not return him to the right path; they only irritate or discourage him. Neither one nor the other is good, but we must direct him gently where we wish him to go. I think if they had not estranged him from me, that we could have continued as we had begun five or six years ago. I do not deserve such happiness, but I would be happy to see it reserved for you.[123]

The last two sentences of this missive merit particular attention. Madame de Maintenon complained that people, presumably the group faithful to Fénelon, had estranged her from Louis XIV; she also hoped that Noailles would one day rise to the powerful position Fénelon used to enjoy. It is possible that Madame de Maintenon's cryptic phrases reveal that the King had heard something about her participation in the

[123] The letter was sent to Noailles on 21 December 1695. A few days later, on 27 December, Madame de Maintenon wrote him: "Je suis bien aise que vous trouviez la lettre que je vous ay confiée trop dure; elle m'a tousjours parue ainsy: *ne cognoisses vous point le stile?*" (*ibid.*, pp. 475-476, 478-479, italics added).

political activities of Fénelon, Beauvillier, Chevreuse, Fleury, Le Blanc, and Pierre Daniel Huet. Perhaps Madame de Maintenon's extraordinary efforts to destroy Fénelon's influence after the conferences at Issy can be partially interpreted as an attempt to calm Louis XIV's suspicions. If this is the case—and external supporting evidence does exist—we gain some idea of the power and importance of Fénelon's group. Indeed, given the fact that Louis XIV was an aging man who, in the normal course of events, would soon die, the small coterie surrounding the Duke of Burgundy could be considered a shadow government. This was at least the opinion of one contemporary, Charlotte-Elisabeth de Bavière, Princess Palatine and Duchess of Orléans. Writing after Bossuet had answered Fénelon's *Maximes des saints*, published in January 1697, Louis XIV's sister-in-law declared:

I thought that Monsieur de Meaux's [Bossuet's] book would prove diverting. From what he told me in conversation about the *affaire* Guyon, Monsieur de Cambrai [Fénelon] has taken her side only to hide his unmeasured ambition. All of this [the Quietist controversy] was but a front to govern the King and the entire court; nothing is more certain. They had decided to win over Madame de Maintenon, which was done in order to govern the king totally. At their homes we found entire lists of appointments placing their creatures in the most elevated posts. Religion was therefore the least of their worries. But as soon as Madame de Maintenon realized that Monsieur de Meaux had caught on to the plot, and the whole thing could turn badly, she grew afraid that the King would become aware of how he was governed by her; she turned about immediately and abandoned Madame Guyon and all her party. Then all came out in the light of day.[124]

Although the Princess was mistaken about religion being a mere screen for political conspiracy, her error was most understandable. Knowing nothing and caring even less about mystical doctrine, the worldly Princess thought Madame Guyon's spirituality the product of a demented soul: "That woman must be mad; I wonder why they didn't confine her to a lunatic asylum rather than in the Bastille."[125] The Princess was aware, however, that the Quietist controversy was associated with a political conspiracy. Seeing no other possible relationship, Louis XIV's sister-in-law drew what appeared to be the obvious conclusion: all the incomprehensible fuss about Madame Guyon's writings was a screen for a determined bid for power. However mistaken in her judgment of Madame Guyon, the Princess' testimony about the importance of the political conspiracy should be given some weight.[126]

One final bit of evidence suggests that contemporaries more strategically placed than Princess Pala-

124 Correspondance de Madame la Duchesse d'Orléans, trans. and ed. Ernest Jaeglé, 3 vols., Paris, 1890, I, 175-176.

125 Ibid., p. 173.

126 The Letters of Philip Dormer Stanhope, Earl of Chesterfield with the Characters, ed. John Bradshaw, 3 vols., London, 1893, II, 563-564, have the following passage:

Since my last to you I have read Madame de Maintenon's Letters; I am sure they are genuine. . . . They have brought me acquainted with the character of that able and artful lady, whom I am convinced that I now know much better than her directeur the Abbé de Fénelon . . . and I know him better too. . . . The Abbé though brimful of divine love, had a great mind to be the first Minister and Cardinal, in order, no doubt, to have an opportunity of doing more good. His being directeur at that time to Madame de Maintenon, seemed to be a good step towards those views.

tine not only assessed the situation in much the same manner, but even felt obliged to resort to political action. The struggle between Bossuet and Fénelon entered into its most acute stage by the time Fénelon published *Maximes des saints*. This was the Archbishop's first public defense of the teachings to which he and Madame Guyon had long held firm. Everyone awaited Bossuet's reply. The Bishop withdrew in silence. Unable to wait for Bossuet's answer, Controller General Pontchartrain in the company of Louvois' oldest brother, Maurice Le Tellier, Archbishop of Reims, took it upon himself to inform Louis XIV that his grandchildren were being educated by people holding questionable religious views.[127] Pontchartrain was known more for his buc-

[127] The Abbé Jean Phelipeaux, *Relation de l'origine, du progrès et de la condamnation du Quiétisme répandu en France*, 2 vols., n.p., 1732, I, 220, writes:

> M. Phelipeaux de Pontchartrain Ministre Secrétaire d'Etat, pour lors Controlleur général des Finances, et depuis Chancellier, fut le premier qui en avertit Sa Majesté. Il avoit une si mauvaise idée du livre, que quelque tems après, il dit au Père de S. Palais de l'Oratoire, qu'il n'y avoit que les flateurs outrés, ou les dupes de M. de Cambrai, qui pussent l'approuver. M. Maurice Le Tellier, Archevêque de Reims instruisit très particulièrement et plusieurs fois le Roi de tout le venin qui étoit contenu dans ce livre. Il auroit souhaité d'être chargé d'en poursuivre la censure, cherchant l'occasion de faire éclater son zele pour la bonne doctrine.

His testimony is confirmed by other contemporaries. Bossuet's secretary, the Abbé François Le Dieu, "Mémoire sur le Quiétisme," pub. E. Levesque, *Revue Bossuet*, VIII, supplément 7, 1909, pp. 19-56, for example, wrote:

> Son [Fénelon's] livre parut au milieu de ces dispositions favorables. Il fut d'abord donné à M. de Meaux, à Versailles par un homme de M. le duc de Beauvillier, le même jour que le roi l'avait reçu de la main de ce seigneur, qui en faisait les honneurs.
>
> M. de Meaux sans en avoir parlé à personne, revint à Paris deux jours après. Il persista quinze jours entiers dans le même silence à l'égard du roi et de tous ses meilleurs amis et affecta de demeurer à Paris lisant cependant le livre avec une grande

caneering, privateering, and slave-trading friends, some of whom married into his own family, than for his concern with mystical writings.[128] Also, until this occasion, Maurice Le Tellier had failed to demonstrate any unusual interest in theological dispute. Yet both these men felt called upon, even more urgently than Bossuet, to warn the King about Fénelon's allegedly unorthodox views. Their motives were unquestionably political. Pontchartrain's initiative appears to have been caused by fear that the peace negotiations at Ryswick would be subverted by the Archbishop and his coterie. The consequence of Pontchartrain's action was Fénelon's exile. The minister had successfully thwarted the group around the Duke of Burgundy at the moment when they could have been most influential. Thus, all the evidence suggests that Fénelon and his followers were, in the opinion of their enemies, more than a negligible political force. Indeed, they may well have constituted a shadow government.

---

attention. Mais le Roi avait été averti du bruit qui excitait déjà contre une doctrine si inouie, par M. de Pontchartrain, ministre et secrétaire d'Etat, contrôleur général des finances, aujourd'hui Chancelier de France et encore par M. de Reims qui en fit un grand éclat (p. 28).

Finally, the confirmation of d'Aguesseau's son emphasizes the tremendous stir which Fénelon's book caused. This was one of the supreme moments of the controversy:

Le livre des maximes des saints qui échappa à l'Archevêque de Cambray par l'imprudence et le zèle peu éclairé de ses amis, excita d'abord un soulèvement presque universel. . . .

Personne cependant n'osoit en parler au Roi, on craignoit le crédit de l'archevêque, . . . du duc de Beauvillier et de tout ce qui les environnoit. On craignoit même celui de Madame de Maintenon que l'on croyoit gouvernée par eux. M. de Pontchartrain fut le seul qui osa rompre ce silence trop politique . . .

(*Discours sur la vie et la mort*, pp. 145-146).

[128] Several references in M. E. W. Dahlgren, *Les relations commerciales maritimes entre la France et les côtes de l'Océan Pacifique*, Paris, 1909, describe Pontchartrain's friends and relations.

Most important in this regard is the public character both of Fénelon's great inquest of February
1697 and of his subsequent exile in August of the
same year: the Peace of Ryswick—concluded in a
widespread, heated debate—marked the beginning of
a period of open political struggle. Moreover, if the
Archbishop's exile announced the first public skir-
mish between the crown and the Christian agrarians,
the establishment of the Council of Commerce shortly
thereafter signified, among many other things, that
secularly inspired reformers had now also entered the
fray. The conflict assumed vastly greater proportions.
"Liberty of trade" became the battle cry for Christian
and secular aristocratic agrarians, as it was for the
merchants who demanded that government renounce
the ideal of directing France's economic life. Never
before had so many people insisted that the crown
should abolish all mercantilist restrictions. Only the
old-fashioned form of aristocratic and agrarian opposition, including Christian objections to the luxury
trade, stood in the way of complete agreement between both branches of the reform movement and the
merchants. But an objection of this kind was a small
matter, at least for the moment, in view of the tactical
advantage to be gained by common opposition during
a period of open struggle with the central government. The clearest indication of a closing of ranks
among reformers is the secret entry of Dugué de
Bagnols, the former intendant in Flanders who had
pleaded for free trade in August 1686, into the group
of conspirators around the exiled Fénelon on 22 June
1702.[129] Dugé had none of Fénelon's qualms about

---

[129] From his exile in Cambrai, Fénelon wrote a letter to Chevreuse,
which includes the following passage:

Je crois, mon bon duc, vous devoir dire ce que M. de Bagnols m'a prié de vous faire savoir. Il souhaiteroit de vous pou-

good and bad trade. Like Descazeaux, he wished to see the merchants free to buy and sell when and where they pleased.

Against the growing unity of opposition, administrators, especially those who had worked for Colbert or for his son Seignelay, pleaded the cause of mercantilist doctrine at length and in an entirely novel manner. Fearing the merchant above all other critics, they regarded as a product of merchant influence the clause in the newly concluded commercial treaty exempting Dutch ships from the long-established tax of 50 sous per ton. The spectacle of ministerial uncertainty, the presence of Thomas Le Gendre at the conference table where the Franco-Dutch tariff agreement was negotiated—a state of affairs which would have been unthinkable under Colbert or Seignelay, as would have been the exemption of Dutch trade from the tax—were understandably matters which caused grave concern among men who were convinced that effective state control over every area of the economy was a condition essential to national prosperity.

---

voir écrire en secret, et par des voies sures, pour diverses choses tres importantes au service du roi qu'il croit nécessaire que vous sachiez par rapport au pays ou il est. Il attend de savoir si vous le trouverez bon. Ce commerce de lettres ne vous exposera en aucune façon. 1o Il ne passera jamais par les hasards de la poste. 2o Vous ne serez jamais obligé de répondre rien qui ne put etre vu de tout le monde, si les lettres étoient ouvertes. 3o Il ne veut que vous informer du véritable intéret du roi sur les principaux points, afin que vous soyez plus en état de donner votre avis dans le conseil pour le bon succes des affaires. . . .

On 9 July 1702, Fénelon wrote to Chevreuse:

J'ai envoyé votre petite lettre ostensible à M. de Bagnols. Je compte, comme vous, qu'il est tres dévoué à un parti que nous n'aimons ni vous ni moi [Jansenist]: mais qu'importe! Il est tres éclairé dans les affaires; vous profiterez de ses vues. . . . Je vous supplie seulement de lui témoigner l'ouverture et l'estime qui peut etre sincere en vous pour lui en un certain degré . . . (Oeuvres, III, 763-764).

The most articulate among those holding this point of view was Jean Pottier de la Hestroye, lieutenant general civil and criminal of the Admiralty in Flanders at Dunkirk. Copies and abridgments of his voluminous writings may be found in several places.[130] Long extracts from Pottier's memoirs were included as part of personal correspondence between public-minded friends.[131] Indeed, substantial sections of the work which most concerns us here, a manuscript written in June 1700, entitled *"Mémoires touchant le commerce de la France et les moiens de le Restablir,"* turned up later in a memoir of 1715 allegedly written by John Law.[132]

[130] The earliest writing, which I have been unable to locate, seems to be the "Memoire du sr. de la Hestroy concernant les moyens d'assurer et d'augmenter le succez de la course" (B.N., Clairambault, MS 709, section entitled "Estat des Liasses qui sont entre les mains de M. d'Argenson concernant le Commerce et la Marine 1697," p. 681).

In 1698 Pottier wrote an extended treatise, "Mémoires touchant le commerce de la France et les moiens de le Restablir," Poitiers, Bib. mun., MS 548. Copies may be found at: Le Havre, Bib. mun., MS 259; Bib. de L'Arsenal, MS 4561 (with additions); *ibid.*, MS 4069 (a large extract with observations and replies); Aff. Et., mém. et doc., France, Supplément, MS 1999. These are all revised or modified and written between 1711 and 1715. A 92-page extract of the 1698 version may be found at Lyon, Bib. mun., MS 964.

In 1704 Pottier wrote a memoir in answer to others written by members of the Council of Commerce. It may be found at the B.N., Fds. fr., MS 14294, ff. 158-285. The title indicates the existence of a more extended version: "Extrait sur le second mémoire de M. de la Hestroye."

Finally in 1716, Pottier published a book entitled: *Réflexions sur le traité de la Dixme de M. le Maréchal de Vauban.*

[131] Lyon, Bib. mun., MS 964, pp. 93-94.

[132] Poitiers, Bib. mun., MS 548. Although this document is dated 1698 internal evidence reveals that it was in fact written in June 1700, very shortly before the establishment of the Council of Commerce on 29 June of that year.

The use of almost *verbatim* extracts from Pottier by John Law was kindly called to my attention by Professor J. M. Price. Cf. John Law, *Oeuvres complètes*, ed. Paul Harsin, 3 vols., Paris, 1934, II, 67-

Calling attention to his long and impressive experience high in the Naval Judiciary and on special trade commissions, this former appointee of Seignelay asserted that two diametrically opposed interests existed in all matters of trade. Pottier declared that a merchant's interest was often "false and contrary to the public welfare" whereas "the general interest of trade" was "real and has as its object only the [good] of the State." After all, "so long as he makes a profit, what does [the merchant] care if the State wins or loses?"[133] But this conflict of private with public interest did not exist universally; in the United Provinces, for example, business interests were identical with those of the government. Producing little on their own, the Dutch profited only by working for foreigners; in France the opposite was true: men in foreign employ, "as are almost all those whom we today call merchants,"[134] would ruin the kingdom because the profits earned from their transactions went abroad. Working for aliens abroad was the sole or principal source of revenue for both state and merchant in the Dutch Republic; there the two "walk in step, trade is absolutely free, nothing is forbidden. [Merchants] have no other rule but to follow their interests."[135] Even during the height of a war, Dutch businessmen traded with powers against whom they were fighting. But "if we suffered our subjects in France to sell arms and munitions to the enemy, what would become of the state?"[136]

---

259. Of the 192 pages in the published volume of Law's memoir, over 40 per cent are taken word for word from Pottier's manuscript of 1700. If one disregards the last 59 pages concerning the bank, then about 60 per cent of the remainder is a direct copy of Pottier's memoir.

133 Poitiers, Bib. mun., MS 548, pp. 4-5.

134 *Ibid.*, p. 47.   135 *Ibid.*, pp. 49-50.   136 *Ibid.*, p. 59.

The contrasting relations between government and trade within the two countries were a direct reflection of their conflicting international interests. Two considerations governed French economic policy: "enrichment of the State and of the individual." If at the end of a year, after exact calculation, more money was found to have been spent abroad than foreigners had left in the realm, the state could be considered as becoming poor.[137] Such a situation need never arise because France could "easily do without [the trade] of all other countries."[138] Whereas the "seven small provinces" of the Dutch Republic did not produce even "one-thirtieth" of the things necessary for national subsistence. If the Dutch had become powerful and rich, it was because "European nations, especially the French, have neglected their own interests. If they would open their eyes, waken from their torpor, they would regain the trade and navigation usurped by those clever [Dutch] merchants."[139] Indeed, no one knew this better than the Dutch, whose enmity toward France was first aroused by Colbert's clear-sighted policies. For, according to Pottier, European wars during Louis XIV's reign were caused by the Dutch, who tried desperately to prevent Colbert and his successors from demonstrating to other nations how more profitable it was to carry on international trade directly than to depend on the intermediary services of the United Provinces.

Most interesting in this connection is Pottier's brief account of Franco-Dutch relations between 1661 and 1697; more clearly than any other single source, he reveals how ideological considerations influenced more and more both domestic and foreign policy as mercantilist programs met with increasingly serious difficulties after Colbert's death.

[137] *Ibid.*, pp. 28-29.   [138] *Ibid.*, p. 32.   [139] *Ibid.*, pp. 33-31

The late Monsieur Colbert who had grand views for the good of France and for trade . . . first attracted many foreign artisans to establish manufacturing in the realm, so as to be able to do without foreign goods. He organized several companies for trade with foreign lands, in order to obtain raw materials which industry would need. Seeing few merchants . . . but many factors and agents employed by foreign merchants, he viewed the trading company as a most certain means of obliging the French to trade for themselves. . . . But his plans were interrupted by the war which began in 1672 and did not finish until 1678. What M. Colbert had commenced alarmed the Dutch, always alert to everything relating to trade. . . .

He [Colbert] died in 1683, leaving the execution of his plans to his ministerial successors. It was on these views and on these memoirs that we began to think seriously of doing without the foreigner and profiting from our own manufactures and from our fertile Provinces. . . .

The Dutch saw that they were going to lose France's trade, and they were fully aware of all the consequences about which I think I have sufficiently explained. . . . Unable to declare war against France alone, . . . they were obliged once again to reunite all of Europe. . . . In this way, and for other reasons known to everybody . . . , the last war came about. And now they have arrived at their goal because they have again obliged France to . . . destroy all that she has done to reestablish her trade.

The Dutch would like to put us back to the state we were in 1664, as if they had a right to limit the authority of the King by preventing him from establishing the duties he pleases in his own realm. . . .

There are many things to say about this last trade treaty signed at Ryswick. And if France so desired there is no lack of just and equitable reasons for not executing the clauses artfully introduced by the Dutch. They know that treaties, limiting the authority of a sovereign within his state, who has only God above him, deprive his subjects of the advantages they hold from nature. . . . Such treaties are contrary to natural law which is an immutable right . . . , that cannot be limited by civil law, that is to say by individual contracts. . . . Kings cannot make treaties which are to the prejudice of their subjects, like that, for example, [concluded] at Ryswick.[140]

Pottier thought the Treaty of Ryswick, particularly the clause exempting the Dutch from the tariff of 50 sous per ton, was a betrayal of traditional ideals.[141] In the course of his polemic, carried on for hundreds of pages, he elaborated a view of the mercantilist state and ethic which was more thorough-going and extreme than in any previous document. It was here that society appeared as the reflection of an inanimate power system of corpuscles and mechanical forces. Cosmic and human government were seen as primarily concerned with adjusting anonymous atoms and nameless interests indifferently here or there for the better functioning of the whole. It was also here that Pottier, while writing about luxury, made ex-

140 *Ibid.*, pp. 85-87, 94-97, 103-105, 121-123.

141 Vauban reveals a similar attitude, see "Etat des services de Vauban et abrégé de cet état," B.N., Clairambault, MS 1174, f. 31. For other arguments against, see A.N., Archives de la Marine, B7 498, ff. 399-402; A.N., G7 1686, "Mémoire sur la suppression du Droit de fret de 50 sols par tonneau."

plicit what he conceived to be the full social and political implications of mechanistic utilitarianism so compatible with mercantilist theory. When the rich spend money—even go into debt and eventually into ruin—by purchasing luxury goods, some people profit and the state always finds its advantage:

> Also the state benefits from the loss of one and the gain of others. The grandeur of a state is not to have individuals distinguished by their wealth, all subjects must be rich. . . . The gold and silver which a state must possess should be in the hands of every subject without distinction. It is not even wise politics to have subjects who think only of accumulating great savings; it distinguishes individuals too greatly and renders them idle and idleness is almost always accompanied by vices pernicious to the state and to the authority of the sovereign. . . . All subjects must work; in the state everyone must be occupied. The state is, properly speaking, a machine, the movements of which although different must be regulated without interruption; we cannot interfere with the movements without running the risk of destroying the state. Similarly subjects must act and work in a state to support it and to render it flourishing.
>
> The poor by hand and the rich by their purse, [spending] so as to make others work. The Rule, Charity and even Religion demand that the rich share . . . with the poor. Of what matter that the rich share their money gratuitously or by . . . spending uselessly for superfluities . . . it is a vice of their spirit which does no harm to the state. Far from losing, the state profits, everyone is able to find work and no one is useless, not even

those who impoverished themselves with unnecessary spending.[142]

Pottier held that the only luxury trade which should
be forbidden was that which impeded the circulation
of money, such as the use of precious metals for orna-
ments or embroidery. It should be taken as a general
principle, as a "maxim of State," that "the greatest
good is preferable even if it occasions some abuse, especially when the abuse is less considerable than the
benefit."[143]

Again and again Pottier attacked the familiar anti-
mercantilist arguments, and it is most significant that
he invariably made merchants, whose advice and pressure he thought responsible for the allegedly disastrous Treaty at Ryswick, spokesmen for the opposition.
A typical outburst was his proposal for a device to
establish firmer control over the import of foreign
goods. According to Pottier, King John in 1350 and
Henry III in 1588 issued *ordonnances* requiring foreign merchandise coming into the kingdom to be
stored in special warehouses located in the principal
towns of the realm. From here its distribution could
be controlled and an exact trade balance calculated
from information in the registers of these distribution
centers. But, Pottier exclaimed:

> I know well that such an establishment would
> cause those whom we regard in France as mer-
> chants, and who are not merchants because they
> act as agents for foreigners, to protest loudly be-

---

142 Poitiers, Bib. mun., MS 548, pp. 178-184. Pottier's view may be
contrasted with the following lines from Fénelon: "Tout ce qui est
corporel ne se détermine en rien soi-meme, et est au contraire
déterminé en tout par des lois qu'on nomme physiques, qui sont
nécessaires, invincibles, et contraires à ce que j'appelle liberté"
(*Traité de l'existence de Dieu*, pp. 79-80).

143 *Ibid.*, p. 184.

cause they would be compelled to cease their so-
called trade. . . . It is in this way that the Court
will discover to what extent foreigners are masters
of the kingdom's trade, and how important it is
to put things in order promptly. What reason
could merchants have to complain about an establishment which concerns only foreigners, if
they themselves were not bound by the same
interests and did not trade exclusively on their
account? Could this prejudice . . . their commerce in any way? No! But it would deprive
them of the profit they share with the foreigner.
. . . You must agree that it is not just to ruin
the State for private interests and to deprive
other subjects of the profits reaped by foreigners
with whom they have an agreement. Let them
[the merchants] trade on their own account,
seeking profit in those things which are useful to
the State and which prejudice no one.[144]

Only toward the end of the treatise did Pottier
make clear that his frequent diatribes against merchants were part of an argument against the proposal
that merchants elect deputies to a Council of Commerce. This section reveals that Pottier had one overriding concern: to preserve and assure the crown's
continued effective direction over all areas of economic activity. Alarmed by merchant ascendancy and
aware that institutional reforms in areas relating to
trade were imminent, Pottier outlined in considerable detail a plan for elaborate administrative reorganization which would establish immediate and continual supervision over even the most local levels of
the economy. Moreover, an unmistakable sense of
urgency emerges from the last quarter of this treatise.

[144] *Ibid.*, pp. 309-311.

Pottier was no leisurely memorialist. As an experienced administrator, he believed merchants were becoming powerful at the expense of royal authority, and unless their activities were brought under prompt control, France would enter a period of political decline.

Introducing his plan for reorganization, Pottier again reminded the reader how "private interests are contrary to the more general [interest] of the state." There were "almost no merchants in France, and those whom we regard as such are only commercial agents employed by foreigners." These men made great profits, but by placing French trade in alien hands "they ruin the state." Here Pottier exclaimed: "It is necessary to pay particular attention: what use will all these handsome commercial enterprises serve if foreigners profit from the very activity of the French who lend them their names?" Advice from such businessmen was pernicious. The late Monsieur Colbert, for example, thought it wise to consult "the cleverest merchants in the realm":

> Toward this end he caused the Royal Council to issue an edict on 5 December 1664 . . . ordering leading merchants in the towns of Dunkirk, Calais, Abbeville, La Rochelle, Bordeaux, Bayonne, Tours, Narbonne, Arles, Marseille, Toulon, and Lyon to be assembled by the Mayors, Aldermen and Consuls . . . in order to name the two most experienced merchants from each town. . . . They [the merchants] would then present themselves to the Court where they would reside for a year [a new group was to be subsequently named for another year], and correspond with merchants in the towns of each department, informing His

Majesty about everything which could serve to reestablish and increase trade. . . .

According to Pottier, this procedure failed to "produce the promised results" because it was not possible for true merchants, as distinguished from commercial agents in foreign employ, to answer Colbert's call. A "real" merchant could not leave his profession for a full year. Anyone with an intimate knowledge of commerce would know that

> merchants do not choose occasions for profit at their will . . . they often arise when least expected. In order to profit merchants must have an exact correspondence with all countries. The advice they receive about the value of merchandise everywhere, which increases or diminishes from one moment to the next and differently in one place and in another, obliges them to make decisions on the moment. Minutes are precious when buying and selling, and great profits depend always on diligence in making transactions. They must pay careful attention to foreign exchange whose [fluctuating rates] can procure great losses or great profits. . . . The exchange varies in each country according to the volume of commerce, the value of the merchandise, the scarcity or abundance and the [ratio of the intrinsic] to the extrinsic value of different species of money. All of this the merchant must know precisely. . . . Merchants do not trade only with the capital they possess, . . . it all revolves on credit which each gives to the other; they therefore must be attentive to dispose of their money and letters of exchange in such a way as to make payments precisely when they are due. . . . All this creates a chain of actions and incidents re-

quiring continual application; we must see it as the movements of wheels in a clock which must follow each other continually; we cannot interrupt without risk of overturning both the commerce and the merchant.[145]

Thus even on an individual basis, commerce, like the cosmos and society, was a machine whose parts should be organized so as to assure perpetual and synchronous operation. It was no wonder that "the best merchants sought every means to avoid nomination."[146] The unfortunate Colbert found only traitors at his side, men in the pay of foreigners. They deceived him at every turn. It was certain, warned Pottier, that if

merchants are called from the Provinces to the Court, the cleverest and most experienced [among them] will avoid nomination whenever possible. Only the least able . . . , commercial agents in foreign employ, will be named. And they will act according to their private interests.[147]

Instead of resorting to so dangerous an expedient, Pottier proposed the creation of a Council of Commerce which would not be staffed by merchants at all, but by royal officials. The establishment of this body was part of a program for much wider institutional reorganization, the purpose of which was to strengthen government control over all sectors of the economy. In the provinces, traveling inspectors would enter into a periodic detailed examination of the local economy, and they would submit extensive reports to the Royal Council of Commerce "composed of eight or ten persons appointed from the Council of State."[148] Moreover, Pottier proposed that intendants

145 *Ibid.*, pp. 330-339.   146 *Ibid.*, p. 343.
147 *Ibid.*, pp. 348-349.   148 *Ibid.*, p. 353.

general of commerce be appointed in each province and placed under the jurisdiction of the traditional intendant. Residing in the principal town of the province or in the same place as the intendant, the intendants general would examine local economic activity in even greater detail than traveling inspectors who were assigned a wider jurisdiction. For page after page, Pottier specified the investigatory tasks of intendants general; no area of economic life, agriculture, industry or business, in even the smallest hamlet, was to escape their expert attention. Further, every intendant general would draft an annual quantitative report on the state of each category of economic activity in his local jurisdiction. And from this mass of individual reports the central government would draw up a national economic chart. Also, the intendant general would make a table naming each merchant along with a precise description of his business activities. He would convene local assemblies of merchants once every six months where they would state their grievances, give advice and present petitions; royal officials would in turn give them an account of the general state of commerce both in the generality and in the kingdom. And with respect to foreign trade, customs officials would submit their records to the intendants general once a year so that an exact commercial balance on both local and national levels could be calculated. Moreover, checking local customs registers against data compiled independently by intendants general would considerably reduce the fraud traditionally connected with import and export. Elsewhere, intendants general would supervise closely all areas of commercial litigation, assuring the business community efficient and impartial justice; in this regard, these officials would serve also as arbitrators in business affairs. Finally, the

processing of the immense amount of data coming to Paris from every locality would be undertaken by the office of a national intendant of commerce, an agency to be responsible for presenting to the Council of Commerce a precise picture of every sector of the economy and furnishing the Council or the King's ministers with any information it might desire. By these means "His Majesty, who is the greatest King in the world, will become the most powerful, most cherished and most loved."[149]

Pottier was no isolated figure. At almost exactly the same time, other administrators who had started their careers in the service of Colbert or Seignelay, men like Bonrepaus and De Lagny, wrote extensively in the same vein.[150] While they had not drawn up re-

[149] *Ibid.*, p. 386.

[150] The title of De Lagny's memoir alone (A.N. Archives de la Marine, B7 497, ff. 406-466) reveals both the tone and the burden of his argument: "Mémoire par lequel on justiffie que la police établie et les reglemens donnés pour le commerce de france depuis la paix des Pyrénées ont produit l'abondance de l'or et de l'argent dans le Royaume, et que l'on n'y peut faire de changement sans remettre l'Etat dans l'esclavage des Estrangers 1696." As for Bonrepaus, his writings are more voluminous: the series of "Mémoires sur la marine" (A.N., K 1360), were written at different times from 20 June 1691 to a date subsequent to the Peace of Ryswick. These present a point of view identical to that of Pottier and De Lagny. Bonrepaus also wrote a more extended treatise in 1699. The document, entitled "Mémoire concernant le commerce des Hollandois, depuis leur establissement jusqu'en la présente année 1699" (*ibid.*, K 1349, no 132) is a copy and not entirely complete.

That these writings, like those of Pottier, were directed above all against merchant demands and arguments for free trade may be seen, for example, in the following passages from De Lagny:

"Il n'est pas aisé de comprendre ce qu'on entend par liberté dans le commerce pour le rendre plus avantageux, car ordinairement ce mot de liberté signiffie une scituation naturelle dans laquelle on exerce les mouvemens de sa volonté, et si on ne supose une volonté éclairée, Et soumise aux regles prescrites, cette liberté est un libertinage. . . .

"En effet c'est le sens que donnent ceux qui demandent cette Liberté, laisser nous faire, disent ils, notre commerce comme nous

organizational plans either so precise or so vast as those of Pottier, the letters and treatises of Bonrepaus and De Lagny reveal the same militant desire for effective government control over France's economic life. They believed not only that the clause in the Treaty of Ryswick granting the Dutch exemption from Foucquet's tax of 50 sous per ton was disastrous for France's national interests, but also that merchant influence had pressured the crown into accepting so pernicious a provision. They were alarmed both by the treaty and by the precipitous decline in effective government control over the business community.

Indeed, administrators like Pottier, Bonrepaus, and De Lagny had much to be alarmed about. We have seen how the merchant-privateers' invaluable wartime services, along with the quasi-public character which prolonged and open debate had given to questions about political economy, made it difficult for ministers to ignore merchant opinions. The crown could not silence merchant criticism in the same manner that it had dealt with the shadow government growing up around the Duke of Burgundy. Ministerial uncertainty, government consultation with businessmen about the most fundamental principles of trade, the parceling out of economic regulation among different agencies, and, finally, the establishment of the Council of Commerce, unleashing a torrent of pent-up

---

le jugerons à propos, si nous perdons sur l'achapt ou sur la vente d'une telle ou telle marchandise, nous avons pas besoin de deffences, nous n'en commercerons plus.

"Mais les sujets d'un Estat sont à cet estat, ce que les Enfants sont à leurs familles, les premiers sont obligés par les loix divines Et humaines de concourir au bien de l'Estat pour lequel bien les loix sont Establies. . . .

"Tous ces gens qui demandent cette liberté se regardent seuls, sans Examiner qu'en leur accordant ce qu'ils demandent on ruineroit Insensiblement par degrés tous les sujets de l'Estat" (ff. 430-431).

criticism, were signs pointing toward a serious failure of authority. Moreover, the decline of royal power had become even more general. By 1693, the year of the great famine and two years before the first Capitation, it was apparent to even the most obtuse observer that purely traditional sources of taxation could no longer support the full burden of expanding administrative and military structures. There was no choice but to tax the nobles. Their profound antagonism, however, caused the monarchy to repeal the Capitation with exceptional, indeed, almost unseemly haste, and in the absence of alternative sources of revenue, such an act was a confession of weakness. Royal fiscal policies were as disastrous for France's rural populations as they were for the crown itself which, living from day to day on uncertain income and forced loans, was financially incapable of carrying out long-term policies in any domain.[151]

Finally, beyond the area of political opposition and the failure of authority, there is evidence suggesting that merchants began to espouse the wider philosophical doctrines elaborated by aristocratic reformers simply as testimony of their social acceptability. When the businessman joined with the aristocracy in public attacks against the government, the ideological differences among reformers, especially over issues raised by luxury trade, were probably obscure matters for him. Unity of political action may have suggested a common philosophy; and the merchant, for whom restrictions on the luxury trade would be indistinguishable in principle from other troublesome government restrictions, may well have understood this

[151] Some idea of the progress of the disintegration of government authority during the Spanish Succession War is given in the interesting article by Marcel Giraud "Crise de conscience et d'autorité à la fin du règne de Louis XIV," *Annales, économies, sociétés, civilisations* (April-September 1952), pp. 172-190, 293-302.

philosophy as utilitarianism. Indeed, it is difficult to imagine an intellectual tradition which could have proved more congenial to both his activities and his aspirations.

To become an aristocrat was among the merchant's most cherished ambitions. Traditionally rich *roturiers* acquired a more distinguished status commensurate with their wealth by purchasing nobility, but this practice had reached such proportions by Louis XIV's reign that it seriously alarmed the nobility. The popularity of the *Bourgeois Gentilhomme*, Saint-Simon's almost pathological attention to the minutiae of an elaborate court etiquette and his bitterness toward Louis XIV's "bourgeois" reign were part of a general stiffening of class lines. And as scholars have shown, another aspect of the nobility's heightened class consciousness, particularly in the provinces, was a more strict observance of the custom of derogation. In the words of one historian, R. B. Grassby, "the voluntary rejection of business was expected to separate the sheep from the goats, and by renouncing the only means of restoring their economic position, the rural families hoped to avert their annihilation as a class."[152] But as Grassby points out, far from slowing *roturier* penetration into the aristocracy, the more rigid observance of derogation only encouraged the process. The aristocracy's efforts to sharpen class lines made the businessman feel more acutely the distance separating him from his "social superiors," and he now redoubled his efforts to achieve noble status. The widening chasm between the business community and polite society not only directed disproportionate amounts of capital investment into land, honorific

[152] R. B. Grassby, "Social Status and Commercial Enterprise under Louis XIV," *The Economic History Review*, 2d series, XIII (1960), 19.

offices, and government annuities (a phenomenon already observable under Louis XIII), much of which would otherwise have gone into commerce and industry; but the merchant, newly ennobled, was understandably eager to acquire aristocratic culture. Perhaps commentators have not sufficiently emphasized that, however ridiculous Molière made Monsieur Jourdain appear, no sensitive spectator could be unaware of the former merchant's pathetic determination to become a "cultured" gentleman.

The "culture" toward which a bourgeois gentleman might be attracted around 1700 included the new currents of thought popular in the fashionable *salons* of Paris. Indeed, he might even seek acceptance in polite society via the *salon* by championing the most recent and the most daring ideas. This may have been true, for example, in the case of young Nicolas Baudôt de Juilly, son of a receiver of *tailles* in Vendôme, who later became a payer of *rentes* in Paris. Trying his hand at literature, he expressed the social climber's preoccupation with manners, and his delight in being accepted by circles for which *politesse* was so important. As he wrote in *Dialogues entre Messieurs Patru et d'Ablancourt sur les plaisirs*:

> There has always been a circle of select people at the *Hotel de Condé* and *de Conti*; it has also been the same at Madame la Marquise de Sablé's, at Madame de Sevigné's, and above all at the *Hotel de Rambouillet*. The endless conversations so agreeable to all those who have been accepted have also been useful to the Court and to the Town; because from these sources have come that politeness and gallantry, up to now unknown, which we have seen in a certain number of persons who subsequently have given an en-

tirely different taste to our nation, and [taught them] manners which they previously did not have.[153]

Manners were not the only key to social advancement, however; it was also necessary to be familiar with ideas current in fashionable circles. In Baudôt's garbled version of these topics, we see the distortion of sophisticated reform doctrines. The careful reasoning of earlier thinkers and aristocratic critics emerged in this young man's eyes as an apology for pure hedonism.

After setting up Patru, a spokesman for tradition, as a straw man, the author had Ablancourt, representing the modern view, lay down as first principles that "we are permitted to live according to nature," and that nature "is nothing else than God Himself." Moreover, all men agreed by universal consent that "no sentiment is more natural to man than the desire for pleasure." Thus the cradle was a virtual "mirror for nature";[154] as men grew older their senses required more complex satisfaction. The drive for pleasure and the wish to avoid pain were weak reflections of the fundamental human instinct for self-preservation and the fear of death. Thus sexual satisfaction, emanating from man's drive to preserve and perpetuate his kind, was "the most vivid, the most sweet and the most touching of which he is capable."[155]

Here Baudôt becomes, so to speak, naïvely anti-Christian. God in His infinite wisdom had so disposed things that there was nothing necessary which was not at the same time pleasurable: "All nature is . . . a great feast where in His inexhaustible good-

[153] *Dialogue*, 2 vols., Paris, 1701, II, 107.
[154] *Ibid.*, I, 179-182.   [155] *Ibid.*, I, 185.

ness God has convened us."[156] Even in the Garden of Paradise, Adam lived in sensual pleasure; the Fall clouded men's minds and original sin caused them to mistake the proper objects of pleasure. Jesus came down on earth, however, to guide men toward the true enjoyment of pleasure: "Properly speaking, religion is established only in order to return us to our [original] felicity."[157] It was a gross error to believe that "austere people" alone lead a Christian life.

Indeed, such a view was not only mistaken, but positively uncharitable and anti-social. "France, for example, has ten times more men than are needed to cultivate the soil; . . . other employment is necessary so that the remainder may subsist. We turn to Painting, Music, Architecture, a few apply themselves to Manufactures, and others to Arts which, although not necessary and contributing only to cleanliness, agreement, convenience and pleasure, do not cease thereby to provide a living for an infinity of people who would otherwise die of hunger."[158] Certainly men must consume the products of these arts. Thus an incalculable number of things purely pleasurable were also vitally necessary. In place of the charitable instinct, God had "purposely permitted us to multiply our needs in order to cause money to circulate among all men, passing from the purses of the rich to those of the poor."[159] Finally, Ablan-

---

[156] *Ibid.*, II, 73.   [157] *Ibid.*, II, 222-223.   [158] *Ibid.*, II, 302.

[159] *Ibid.*, II, 304-305. An unusual application of the social utility theory of luxury consumption was made by Pierre Bayle in 1697 in a letter to the Abbé Du Bos:

Après tout le public en France a beaucoup d'obligation au sexe, car que ferait-on du vin et de l'eau-de-vie, depuis que les Anglois et les Hollandois n'en vont point charger des flottes entières à Bordaux, à La Rochelle, à Nantes . . . , si les femmes, devenues grandes buveuses, n'en faisoient une terrible consommation? Par ce moyen ceux qui ont des vignes, vendent bien leurs vins, et sont en état de payer la taille et les autres charges

court explained to Patru that by observing the relations between the different regions of the earth and
the pattern of trade

> you will see the inconveniences and even the
> absurdities which follow from too extreme a
> morality. But God who is much wiser is not
> rigorous; He purposely endowed countries with
> different qualities so that we can find at our
> neighbors' what we do not have ourselves, so
> those who have only things which are agreeable
> may also buy those which are necessary and
> useful.

In order that this trade should be conducted

---

de L'Etat (quoted from Bayle's *Oeuvres* by A. Lombard, *L'Abbé
du Bos un initiateur de la pensée moderne, 1670-1742*, Paris,
1913, p. 67).

An indication of how widespread this attitude became during
the subsequent decade is provided by a provincial ecclesiastic,
Jean Artur de la Gibonais, who wrote a treatise on the hoary problems of interest and usury: *De l'usure, intérest et profit qu'on tire
du Prest: ou l'ancienne doctrine sur le Prest usuraire opposée aux
nouvelles opinions*, Paris, 1710, pp. 464-465.

> Les partisans des interests usuraires font grand bruit sur la
> nécessité du commerce d'argent entre les négocians, Banquiers
> et gens d'affaires. Vous les entendez dire tous les jours, que
> l'Etat ne peut subsister sans cela, parce que si vous ostez l'in-
> térest ou profit de l'argent, vous détruisez le commerce qui ne
> se fait que pour gagner; et en détruisant le commerce, vous
> ruinez l'Etat dans lequel cet argent qui roule et qui passe de
> main en main, est comme le sang qui circule dans les veines du
> corps humain. Ils prétendent que cette raison est décisive pour
> justifier les intérêts qu'on prend ordinairement dans le négoce
> de Billets, de Lettres de Change et d'argent; comme si l'homme
> n'avoit d'autre affaire en ce monde que de s'enrichir à quelque
> prix que ce soit, et comme si la premiere de toutes les nécessités
> ou plutost l'unique n'étoit pas le soin du salut éternel.

True, Gibonais said nothing explicit about luxury, but he is clearly attacking the argument which he "hears everyday," that private
vice is justified when it proves to be in the public interest. This
was the real issue.

easily, He has caused great rivers to flow everywhere, and He has disposed the oceans so that after surrounding all parts of the earth they cut across it with a thousand different arms to serve as communication for all the countries in the world.

All this has been so admirably accomplished in order to bind men to one another, who in effect should form only one single family *so that the need they would have for one another would accomplish among them what charity alone ought to do.* It is for this reason that men . . . , however different in mores, language and Religion . . . are becoming united from one end of the world to the other by reciprocal trade. It is also for this reason that they exchange equally things which are agreeable and those which are necessary, so that they can not only sustain life as in a pasture like beasts, but also to render it sweeter, more humane and more polished by pleasures.[160]

By defining free trade as the golden rule in action, indeed, as a substitute for charity, Baudôt reveals unmistakably the influence of anti-mercantilist and anti-Christian utilitarianism. Moreover, his explanation of trade as an exchange of things agreeable for those which were necessary so that men of different mores, language, and religion could unite in mutual interdependence, ushering in the age of the golden rule, displays a confused but recognizable effort to integrate Epicurean and international themes into the moral structure of the universe. Baudôt also believed that progressively freer interaction of interests and the reasonable pursuit of pleasure would lead man-

[160] Baudôt de Juilly, *Dialogues*, II, 309-311.

kind down the path of refinement toward the good and, above all, the happy life. This is a distorted reflection of Saint-Evremond's concept that advancement toward a social rather than a religious morality, based on man's search for the intelligent experience of pleasure, was the only sure foundation for a happy society. Finally, by an awkward, almost simple-minded equation of pleasure with interest, Baudôt revealed how speculative currents had become an integral part of a political program for even superficial and shallow minds. It seems most probable that this garbled elementary version of aristocratic ideological opposition is the expression of a bourgeois who, wishing to become an accepted member of polite society, felt compelled to exhibit his understanding of the latest developments in the intellectual world. And in this way the most abstruse considerations became matters of immediate political and social importance for people who scarcely knew what they meant.[161]

[161] Another instance of this phenomenon may be seen in the case of Jean Le Pelletier, merchant at Salines and Rouen, "Ancien Juge et Consul." According to Father Léonard, Le Pelletier

> par son seul travail . . . a apris les langues Latine, Grecque, Hebraique, Espagnole, Italiene, Angloise. Il fait toutes sortes de microscopes et de lunettes. On attend de luy des nouvelles du Commerce . . . (A.N. M 760, no. 1).

This same Le Pelletier published in 1701 a book entitled *Mémoires pour le rétablissement du commerce en France . . . pour être presentez à Nos Seigneurs du Conseil du Commerce.* Curiously enough, the copy at Rouen is bound with Boisguilbert's *Détail de la France.* A passage from the very beginning of the otherwise unexceptional book is most revealing:

> L'intelligence a été donnée aux hommes pour apercevoir leur bonheur, qui consiste dans le Monde, en la possession de l'abondance des biens qui regardent l'esprit et le corps. Tous aspirent à ce bonheur; c'est l'unique but ou ils tendent, du moment de leur naissance jusques à celui de leur mort: mais comme c'est l'ouvrage de plusieurs d'entre eux, et qu'il est de telle

It was the aristocracy who first made speculative themes the foundation for programs of political action; the merchants entered late onto the scene. Although presenting a common front to the central government in 1700, the two classes soon became rivals for control of a state apparatus which was growing progressively incapable of imposing authority in any area of society. By the end of Louis XIV's reign the aristocracy appeared for an instant victorious: the *Polysynodie* of 1715-1718 was nothing less than the aristocratic answer to the Council of Commerce. But the sorry spectacle of its brief and inglorious existence only further emphasizes the ironic and tragic role played by nobility throughout the Sun King's reign: they made triumphant a philosophy which most powerfully supported the cause of reform, a movement undermining their existence as a social class.

---

nature, qu'on y contribue de son propre travail; il faut que ceux-la travaillent pour les autres, qui veulent que les autres travaillent pour eux. Ces travaux réciproques, qui sont les fruits des différentes occupations des hommes, chacun dans sa vocation, sont les secours mutuels dont ces memes hommes se soulagent les uns les autres dans leur nécessités et les moyens par lesquels ils se communiquent les choses nécessaires à leur bonheur, ne cédant celles qu'ils possèdent et qu'ils ont acquises par leur travail et leur industrie, que pour d'autres qui valent mieux. Ce mieux est ce que nous apellons profit, et ce profit est ce qui augmente nos possessions, dont l'abondance fait le bonheur dont nous parlons.

La Profession étant l'unique moyen pour arriver à ce bonheur, ou qui le peut produire, tous les hommes ont intérêt de veiller à la conservation de leurs différentes Professions. . . . Mais parce qu'entre ces Professions, il s'en trouve une qui est la liaison des autres . . . elle est l'unique canal de ces communications réciproques.

Cette profession si utile et si nécessaire au bonheur des hommes est celle de Négotiant (pp. 3-4).

CONCLUSION

THE HISTORY of critics and reformers during Louis XIV's reign is in part an analysis of the political origins of the French Enlightenment. It is the story of how conditions external to the history of ideas helped to transform speculative currents of one period into the political doctrines of another, thus preparing for the rise of the purely secular ideologies which characterized the eighteenth century. During the Wars of Religion, increased attention to both theology and philosophy caused writers to relate their views about government and trade more closely to abstruse notions about the nature of the soul and the structure of the cosmos. The two generations separating Bodin from Richelieu saw the most remote considerations become more and more part of political theory. In the subsequent period ending with Colbert's death, axioms of political economy extended even further into spheres of abstract thought. At the same time, however, political principles became increasingly expressions of agreement or opposition to royal policies. And concepts about God, man, or the universe acquired in this way the most immediate partisan implications—even the most routine exercise of authority came to be judged according to its conformity to abstract principles. Between 1683 and 1700, conflict between government and the forces of opposition finally assumed a new order of magnitude: France was shaken by a vast ideological struggle.

The tendency to politicize thought, to ignore tradition, and to analyze society in terms of pure theory was related to the progressive depersonalization of authority in a country ruled by a huge, rapidly expanding bureaucracy. Traditional concepts of justice, which were inseparable from the central mysteries of faith, became dimmed or even disappeared as "reason of state," the "general interest," or some other abstract political principle was systematically invoked for administrative convenience. In fact, immoral acts were even termed virtuous at this time, if they were judged to be in the public interest. Yet, despite the fact that administrative growth accelerated the secularization of thought among writers principally concerned with imposing order on society, it was these very people who most insisted that the state was a consequence of original sin. Their motives, however, often seemed more political than spiritual. Indeed, in order to reinforce even further their negative principles of government, some mercantilists also espoused skeptical doctrines which seemed to undercut Christianity by suggesting that man's rational faculties were so feeble as to constitute no proof that he was created in the image of God. Only the coercive power of the state, they said, not reason, could restrain man's virtually ungovernable passions.

Contrary to mercantilist spokesmen, writers who decried increased political centralization were hostile not only toward theories which schematized human relations, but secular and religious critics, attacking the mercantilist depersonalization of authority, gradually formulated positive views of government which were based on optimistic and anti-skeptical judgments of human nature. Thus Jean de Lartigue, an early secular critic and the first to expound a fully developed theory of opposition, insisted that philosophy can instruct the crown to exercise authority so as to lead Frenchmen, indeed, ultimately all mankind, toward the good life. Moreover, Lartigue's arguments in the secular field were in important respects analogous to those of Fleury and Fénelon in the religious domain. As an aristocrat, Lartigue objected to statist doctrines which transformed all human relationships into an inanimate power system of interchangeable and anonymous interests. Similarly aristocrats like Fleury and Fénelon were alarmed by theories like those of Pierre Nicole, which made both religion and political philosophy not only more impersonal, but also dangerously compatible with the mercantilist ethic: Nicole's conviction that men behave in the same manner as atoms in space gave added support to doctrines which would transform human beings into interchangeable parts of a political machine. And, like the skeptics before him, Nicole also pointed to the incomprehensible character of an infinite universe in order to justify negative or "Machiavellian" views of government. Thus the earliest expression of religiously inspired opposition, Christian agrarianism, first appeared in Fleury's answers to Machiavelli, whose doctrines he associated with mercantilism on one hand and with skepticism on the other. Also, along with his attacks on skepticism, Fleury's description of big cities as friendless amalgams of the best and the worst, his idealization of the happy independent *Laboureur,* reflect a strong antagonism to the administrative habit of treating men as if they were easily combinable parts of some larger machine. Thus by 1670-1675 the ideological foundations had been laid for both secular and religiously inspired reformers: they all represented one side in the growing controversy between those who viewed the state primarily in terms of impersonal and repressive functions and others who, insisting on the King's love for his people, believed government was obliged to help man achieve the good life.

In 1693, the year of Fénelon's letter to the King, it was not at all evident that within a decade the reform movement would become predominantly anti-Christian. The reasons were complex. The famine, substantially diminishing royal revenues at the height of France's immense war effort, caused most aristocrats to realize they would have to be taxed. But because problems of fiscal reform, no longer isolated, were made an integral part of the general philosophy of opposition, the aristocracy for the first time had a strong theoretical base from which it could refuse to consider fiscal matters outside the wider context of institutional, political, and social reform. Moreover, the very ideas which permitted fiscal thought to become part of expanded anti-mercantilist arguments also transformed agrarian doctrine and utilitarian ethics into a comprehensive system which, substituting the golden rule for Redemption and "utility" for "justice," attacked directly the intellectual and spiritual foundations of the old regime.

The dramatic development and elaboration of anti-Christian themes in the years 1693-1700 cannot be understood, however, outside the more general context of Church-State relations. Indeed, the roots of militant secularism at the end of the century go back to the intense hostility which existed between the crown and large areas of the clergy since the days of the *Ligue*. The Concordat of Bologna (1516) had at an early date seriously impeded efforts to raise the level of spiritual life in the Church. Internal reform became most difficult when ecclesiastical offices were transformed into political appointments; indeed, such an arrangement seemed to institutionalize pluralism and a host of related abuses which had long been the object of righteous complaint. Moreover, the legal corollary to the Concordat appeared in 1539 when legislation promulgated at Villers-Cotterets established a procedure, called *appel comme d'abus*, which transformed ecclesiastical courts into tribunals of lower instance. Subsequently, one year later, even heresy was placed under the jurisdiction of the *Parlements*. Thus when the full amplitude of the French Protestant movement first became clear (1555-1561), Catholic reformers, who thought heresy largely a consequence of clerical worldliness and corruption, insisted that Protestantism could be fought effectively only when the Church was liberated from royal subjugation. It was this issue above all others which divided the ultramontanes, *La Ligue*, from the *Politiques* during the Wars of Religion. The conflict, remaining unresolved, injected a political dimension into early seventeenth century religious life.

Ecclesiastical insistence that a greater measure of autonomy was essential to their spiritual mission was frequently associated in the seventeenth century with a conviction that divine law could effectively limit royal power only if the Church enjoyed a degree of independence sufficient to criticize the immoral exercise of political authority. The two related ecclesiastical demands were contrary to the monarchy's historical claims on the Gallican Church; and, while they explain of course much about Richelieu's struggles with both the *dévots* and the founders of Jansenism— the disgrace of Marillac, Richelieu's isolation of Bérulle, and his imprisonment of Saint-Cyran—these principles, remaining important throughout the century, also lay at the very heart of Fénelon's impassioned attacks against the Sun King's regime. The Archbishop's disgrace was only one among many incidents in the crown's century-long endeavor first to regain and finally to reassert its undisputed dominion over French religious life. Moreover, the progressive establishment of the mercantilist state, keeping pace with increasing political control over the Church, caused ecclesiastical protest to merge gradually with purely secular resistance to Louis XIV's vast program for commercial and industrial expansion. Thus it was only after Colbert's ministry was well established that anti-mercantilist themes became a central part of religiously inspired criticism; the *dévots* of Marillac's day inveighed against venality and unjust taxation, but they said little about trade.

Devout and secular critics became engaged in a common struggle against mercantilist programs, and the similarity of their arguments helped to transform hitherto disparate protests into a more widely based movement of opposition. But religious themes did not immediately give way to secular theories. It was above all Fénelon's disgrace which intensified the secular character of political dissent, for the exile of this great protagonist deprived opposition movements of religious leadership at the time of their greatest *élan*. The fact that Fénelon's retreat to Cambrai coincided with an immense outpouring of criticism, flowing from the breakdown of royal authority and the dramatic failure of the administration, among other things, either to placate or to control the merchant, made the Archbishop's cause appear as part of a more general movement for reform. Fénelon's opinions became indistinguishable from the spate of demands, protests, and theories which appeared on all sides in the years immediately before and after the Peace of Ryswick. It was in this context that the most anti-Christian arguments received a new aura of respectability, and for the first time secular theories tended to play a dominant role in opposition literature. In short, the crown's long series of victories over its clerical critics finally destroyed the traditional restraints which ecclesiastical institutions had hitherto imposed on the great body of European political theory. And the disappearance of theological limits to the exercise of political authority, accompanied as it was by the monarchy's rapid political decline and a new florescence of purely secular theories, explains more than any other phenomena the transition from the concept of Divine Right of kings to eighteenth century views of Enlightened Despotism.

The monarchy's continued feebleness throughout the eighteenth century and the more intense secular theories expounded by later *philosophes* are rooted in this peculiar combination of ecclesiastical defeat and political inadequacy which characterized Louis XIV's reign after 1697. A crisis of confidence, existing in the highest circles of government and paralyzing the exercise of political authority, provided the background against which the *philosophes* adopted and elaborated the doctrines of seventeenth century reformers. The death of the Sun King in 1715 removed the last restraint to a public avowal of the ideological as well as the financial bankruptcy of the old regime. As early as 1710, high-ranking administrators admitted openly that principles to which the government had held firm for over a half century were mistaken.[1] The most dramatic event, however, occurring two months after Louis XIV's death, was the founding of the *Polysynodie* (1715-1718), the aristocratic answer to the Council of Commerce and a form of government dear to the hearts of Belesbat, the Duke of

[1] See Chapter V, above, n. 29.

Saint-Simon, and the Abbé of Saint-Pierre. Established at the time of John Law's "System" and when Vauban's *Dixme Royale* (a scheme adopted by reformers such as Saint-Pierre after its publication in 1707 had provoked intense government disapproval) was actually imposed on a trial basis in two provinces, the *Polysynodie* marks the first aristocratic attempt to govern France according to agrarian precepts and a most optimistic interpretation of utilitarian principles.

The Abbé of Saint-Pierre, traditionally seen as an early Enlightenment figure and perhaps remembered most for his stubborn defense of the *Polysynodie,* is the spokesman who by reason of his enormous life-span (1658-1743) illustrates how *philosophes,* familiar with seventeenth century reform doctrines, employed them early to explain the agrarian and utilitarian bases of civilization. His *Projet de paix perpetuelle,* first published in 1712, and the *Discours sur la polysynodie* (1718), apart from demanding free trade, developed an optimistic utilitarianism which carried the themes contained in the manuscript abridgments at the Bibliothèque Sainte-Geneviève (discussed above in Chapter VI) to their logical conclusion. The Marquis de Lassay's *Relation de Félice* is an agrarian utopia where "they are busily trying to make everybody happy" and the manufacture of luxury products permits the poor to share the "magnificence of the rich."[2] Among more well-known figures, like Montesquieu, we read that the earth "always yields [harvests] in proportion to what is demanded of it . . . flocks grow in numbers with

[2] Armand Léon de Madaillan de Lesparre, Marquis de Lassay, born in 1652, elected *president de la noblesse aux etats de Bourgogne* in 1700, wrote a number of works, including the *Relation de Felice* in 1715, all of which were published under the title *Recueil de différentes choses,* 4 vols., Lausanne, 1756.

those who rear them."[3] And as for luxury, Montesquieu calculated its utility, along with its tendency to encourage sociability, according to an exact table of proportions.[4] Moreover, Montesquieu's conviction that climate determined the "spirit of the laws" in each country was a view with almost as long a history as his belief that the "natural effect of commerce is to bring peace" and to create "in men a certain sentiment of exact justice."[5] It remained only, on the one hand, for Helvétius in *De l'esprit* (1758) to derive the most elaborate theory of morals and legislation from association psychology and the pleasure-pain principle, and, on the other, for the physiocrats, equally convinced that pleasure and pain are the "two springs" of human behavior, to draw the full economic implications from agrarian doctrines and utilitarian ethics.

Historians writing about the eighteenth century have frequently observed that the concept of a wise

[3] Montesquieu, "Dossier de l'Esprit des Lois," *Oeuvres Complètes*, 2 vols., Paris; 1949-1951, II, 1093.

[4] "Le luxe est toujours en proportion avec l'inégalité des fortunes. Si dans un Etat, les richesses sont également partagées, il n'y aura point de luxe; car il n'est fondé que sur les commodités qu'on se donne par le travail des autres. . . .

"Supposant le nécessaire physique égal à une somme donnée, le luxe de ceux qui n'auront que le nécessaire sera égal à zéro; celui qui aura le double aura un luxe égal à un; celui qui aura le double du bien de ce dernier aura un luxe égal à trois; quand on aura encore le double on aura un luxe égal à sept; de sorte que le bien du particulier qui suit, étant toujours supposé double de celui du précédent, le luxe croîtra du double plus une unité dans cette progression o, 1, 3, 7, 15, 31, 6̣3̣ 127. . . .

"Le luxe est encore en proportion avec la grandeur des villes, et surtout de la capitale; en sorte qu'il est en raison composé des richesses de l'Etat, de l'inégalité des fortunes des particuliers et du nombre d'hommes qu'on assemble dans de certains lieux. . . . On a plus de desires, plus de besoins, plus de fantaisies quand on est ensemble" (*Esprit des Lois*, ed. Gonzague Truc, 2 vols., Paris, 1956, I, Bk. VII, chap. I, 102-104).

[5] *Ibid.*, II, Bk. XX, chap. II, 8-9.

legislator creating a perfect society through the proper calculation of pleasure and pain is a concept inconsistent with the idea of men who act properly because nature rather than government regulates their behavior. The point is well taken if one ignores history and invokes only the rules of logic. Utilitarianism and its empirical context were above all the product of intellectual currents which attempted to substitute the golden rule, or the principle of reciprocity, for the mystery of the Redemption, denying the transcendental character of good and evil. The use of principles of natural law in expounding these arguments was connected with the dissociation of aristocratic nationalism from the general context of centralization of government, allowing men to propose reform of purely French institutions in the name of nature and all humanity. To call the joining of these ideas illogical, while technically correct, is misleading unless the scholar also emphasizes their profoundly political character. Indeed, the intellectual currents of the French Enlightenment all reflect, to some degree, the influence of opposition movements which developed during Louis XIV's reign.

More fundamental than the similarity of particular arguments, however, is an underlying attitude toward the concept of nature which seventeenth century reformers shared with eighteenth century *philosophes*. In opposing the centralizing policies of the crown, men like Lartigue, Fleury, Fénelon, and Belesbat expanded the authority of nature at the expense of government jurisdiction. They asserted that the power of the state was measured by the ability of the sovereign to permit the free play of natural laws. But in expounding this view, they subtly changed the concept of nature. Lartigue and Belesbat especially emphasized that nature was an infallible guide to ethical and political conduct. What was natural was necessarily moral. Belesbat further insisted that religion was nothing more than a series of ethical precepts. Religion became "natural" in a new sense: the world did not lead man to God; instead God was made part of the physical order. The Creator's personal and transcendental character was destroyed. Cosmic regularities were at once a proof and a description of God. Transformed into an abstract and purely natural force, God was identified with the principle of universality. To Belesbat and to the *philosophes*, universality, the very essence of that which was "natural," served both as an epistemological and a normative criterion: it described the character of knowledge everywhere and, at the same time, it guided humanity toward the good life. In this way, Belesbat's conviction that "the entire science of Religion" consisted in treating others as we would have them treat us, his belief that the golden rule was an axiom operative both in heaven and on earth, proceeded directly from his attempt to substitute natural laws for mercantilist codes. How closely these themes are reflected in the views of the *philosophes*! Voltaire, for example, who said that religion is a belief which nature imparts to human beings throughout the earth and Condorçet, who thought that nature infused morality into men everywhere, were both convinced that the state would flourish when natural law was permitted to supplant government legislation in economic activity.[6] In sum, the attempt to have nature play the role of government

[6] Statements by Voltaire and Condorçet praising Turgot's efforts in this direction, for instance, may be seen in *Oeuvres de Turgot*, ed. Gustave Schelle, 5 vols., Paris, 1913-1923, IV, 78-79.

was a piece with the tendency to make God part of nature: both views represent the culmination of efforts of men like Postel, Campanella, and Lartigue to reaffirm the solidarity of mankind in the face of political and religious forces which divided it.

CONCLUSION

BIBLIOGRAPHY

PRIMARY SOURCES

MANUSCRIPT

1. *Archives*

ARCHIVES NATIONALES

Série F^{12} Volume: 641.

Série G^7 Cartons: 1-22; 71-76; 84-89; 104-117; 131-162; 178-182; 214-239; 295-296; 337-357; 390; 405-458; 494-497; 510-518; 552; 694-696; 1143-1154; 1158-1178; 1614-1619; 1630; 1685-1686.

Série K Cartons: 1349; 1360.

Série M Cartons: 757; 760; 768.

Minutier Central

Etude IX, paquets: 470; 472; 490; 506; 511; 535; 538; 564.

Etude XLIV, paquet: 162.

Etude LII, 22 février 1696.

Etude LXV, paquet: 156.

Etude XC, paquet: 267.

Etude XCIV, 18 juin 1693.

Etude XCV, paquet: 45.

Etude XCVI, 29 mars 1697.

Etude XCIX, paquets: 283; 333; 337; 344; 346; 347; 348; 352; 377.

Etude CXII, paquet: 420 A.

Etude CXV, paquet: 294.

ARCHIVES DE LA MARINE

Série B^2 Volumes: 57; 64; 65-84; 88-105; 107; 109-145.

Série B^7 Volumes: 58; 60; 62; 64; 219; 492-499.

Série G^{40}.

ARCHIVES DES COLONIES

Série C^2 Volume: 5.

471

BIBLIOGRAPHY

ARCHIVES DE LA GUERRE
  Série A¹ Volume: 795.
  Volume 2469 (papiers de Chamlay).
ARCHIVES DES AFFAIRES ETRANGERES
  Série mémoires et documents:
    France: Volumes: 93; 302; 991 (papiers Colbert de
      Croissy). Supplément, manuscrit 1999.
    Hollande: Volumes: 49; 90.
ARCHIVES PROVINCIALES
  Loire-Atlantique: Série E, supplément: dossier Desca-
    zeaux et famille.
    Série B (Amirauté): B 4672; B 4741; B 4886; B 4897.
    Série C Cartons: 694; 695.
  Seine-Maritime: Tabellionage (minutes Cavé):
    3 avril 1692;
    10 juillet 1692.
ARCHIVES PRIVEES
  Château de Saint-Aignan (Fonds Beauvillier), manu-
    scrits: 255; 278; 282; 283; 304.

2. Bibliothèques

BIBLIOTHEQUE NATIONALE
  Série Fonds Français, MSS 646; 807; 1205; 1735; 1736;
    1946; 1947; 4156; 4164; 4165; 4826; 7009; 7732;
    10629-10639; 11149; 13585; 14294; 16736; 17461;
    18591-18597; 19050; 23022; 23484; 23504.
  Série Fonds Français, nouvelle acquisition, MSS 507;
    5247; 9505; 21261.
  Série Fonds Clairambault, MSS 216; 286; 709; 869;
    873; 881; 1064; 1066; 1073; 1103; 1174.
  Cinq Cents Colbert, MSS 203; 497.
  Mélanges de Colbert, MSS 64; 66; 142 bis.
  Joly de Fleury, MS 2510.
BIBLIOTHEQUE DE L'ARSENAL
  MSS 3186; 4069; 4496; 4561.

BIBLIOTHEQUE SAINTE-GENEVIEVE
  MSS 2012; 2015; 2997; 3082; 3085.
BIBLIOTHEQUE THIERS
  MS 30.
BIBLIOTHEQUES PROVINCIALES
  Nantes, MS 1154.
  Poitiers, MSS 259; 329; 548; 964.
  Reims, MS 955.
  Rennes, MS 155.
  Rouen, MSS 225; 3450; 5804.

Printed Works

ANONYMOUS. De la vertu de Noblesse. No place of publication, 1553.

ANONYMOUS. Avis au roi des moyens de bannir le luxe du royaume, d'établir un grand nombre de manufactures en icelui, d'empecher le transport de l'argent et faire demeurer par chacun an dans le royaume pres cinq millions d'or de sept millions ou environ qui en sont transportés, et en affaiblir d'autant aucuns étrangers. De faire par chacun an un fonds assuré, qui pourra etre destiné en des armemens de mer, afin de pouvoir employer beaucoup de noblesse et de gens courageux. Eviter les guerres civiles et faire de grands progres et conquetes. Enfin rendre la France l'une des plus grandes et redoubtables monarchies qui fut oncques. Le tout à la gloire de Dieu, à la grandeur du roi sans diminution ni charge de ses finances, au bien commun de tous ses sujets sans aucunement les charger, mais au contraire les décharger de beaucoup. No place of publication: 1614.

ANONYMOUS. Discours des Princes et Estats de la Chrétienté plus considérables à la France selon leurs diverses qualitez et conditions, pub. in Recueil de quelques discours politiques, escrits sur diverses occurrences des affaires et Guerres Estrangeres depuis quinze ans. . . . 1632.

ANONYMOUS. Renonciation non valable que la reine de France a faite de la succession à la couronne d'Espagne et des pays qui en dépendent. Paris: 1667.

ANONYMOUS. Mémoires pour servir à l'histoire D.M.R. avec quelques réflexions politiques sur les mémoires. No place of publication: 1668.

ANONYMOUS. Histoire de la décadence de la France procurée par sa conduite. Cologne: 1687.

ANONYMOUS. Etat présent de la France et de ses finances; ou l'on prouve qu'il lui est impossible de se maintenir si la guerre que les alliez lui font continue. Geneva: 1692.

ANONYMOUS. Lettres d'un gentilhomme François sur l'établissement d'une Capitation générale en France. Liège: 1695.

AGRIPPA, Henricus Cornelius. Déclamation sur l'incertitude, vanité et abus des sciences. Paris: 1582.

AGUESSEAU, Henri-François de. Discours sur la vie et la mort, le caractère et les moeurs de M. d'Aguesseau, conseiller d'état. Paris: 1812.

AQUINAS, Thomas. Basic Writings. Ed. Anton C. Pegis. 2 vols.; New York: 1945.

ARNAULD, Antoine. Oeuvres. 42 vols.; Lausanne: 1775-1783.

BARRILLON, Jean. Journal . . . 1515-1521. Ed. Pierre de Vaissière. 2 vols.; Paris: 1897.

BAUDOT DE JUILLY. Dialogues entre Monsieur Patru et D'Ablancourt. 2 vols.; Paris: 1701.

BAYLE, Pierre. Continuation des Pensées diverses. 4 vols., Rotterdam: 1721.

———. Dictionnaire historique et critique. 3d ed. 3 vols., Rotterdam: 1715.

———. Oeuvres diverses. 4 vols.; La Haye et Rotterdam: 1727-1731.

BEAUREPAIRE, Ch. de Robillard de, ed. Cahiers des Etats de Normandie sous les règnes de Louis XIII et Louis XIV. 3 vols.; Paris: 1876-1878.

BETHUNE, Philippe de. Le Conseiller d'Estat ou recueil des plus générales considérations servant au maniement des affaires publiques. 1645.

BODIN, Jean. Response aux paradoxes de M. de Malestroit, ed. Henri Hauser. Paris: 1932.

———. Méthode pour faciliter la connaissance d'Histoire. "Oeuvre philosophique de J. Bodin," ed. P. Mesnard. Paris: 1566.

———. Le paradoxe moral . . . Qu'il n'y a pas une seule vertu en médiocrité, ny au milieu de deux vices. Paris: 1604.

———. Les six livres de la république. Paris: 1608.

BOISGUILBERT, Pierre le Pesant de. Le Détail de la France, Factum, Traité des Grains, Dissertation sur la nature des richesses. "Economistes-financiers du XVIIIe siècle," ed. E. Daire. Paris: 1843, Vol. I.

BOISLISLE, A. M. de. Correspondance des contrôleurs-Généraux des finances avec les intendants des provinces 1683-1715. 3 vols.; Paris: 1874-1897.

———. Mémoire de la généralité de Paris. Paris: 1881.

BONNASSIEUX, P. and LELONG, E. Conseil de commerce et bureau de commerce, 1700-1791, inventaire analytique des procès-verbaux. Paris: 1900.

BOSSUET, J. B. Oeuvres complètes. Ed. F. Lachat. 31 vols.; Paris: 1862-1866.

———. Correspondance. Ed. C. Urbain and E. Levesque. 15 vols.; Paris: 1909-1925.

BOULAINVILLIER, Henri de. Etat de la France. Extrait des mémoires dressés par les intendants du royaume, par ordre du roi Louis XIV. 6 vols.; London: 1737.

———. Lettres sur les anciens parlements de France que l'on nomme Etats-Généraux. 3 vols.; London: 1753.

BURNET, Gilbert. Voyage de Suisse, d'Italie et quelques endroits d'Allemagne et de France. 2d ed. Rotterdam: 1688.

CAMPANELLA, Tommasio. La Cité du Soleil. Edition translated from Latin by Villegardelle. "Abonnement Germinal," No. 10, Vol. VII; Gand: 1911.

CHALLE, A. Documents statistiques. "Annuaire historique du département de l'Yonne." Auxerre: 1853.

CHALLES, Robert de. Mémoires. Ed. A. Augustin-Thierry. Paris: 1931.

CHAMILLART, Michel. Correspondance et papiers inédits. Ed. G. Esnault. 2 vols.; Le Mans: 1884.

CHARRON, Pierre. De La Sagesse, Trois Livres. Paris: 1886.

HAY DU CHASTELLET, Paul. Traité de la politique de la France. Paris: 1669.

COLBERT de CROISSY, Charles, marquis. Etat du Poitou sous Louis XIV. Rapport au roi et mémoire sur le clergé, la noblesse, la justice et les finances. Ed. Charles Du Gast-Matifeux. Fontenay-le-Comte: 1865.

COLBERT, Jean-Baptiste. Lettres, instructions et mémoires de Colbert. Ed. P. Clément. 7 vols.; Paris: 1861-1882.

COMBES, Jehan. Traicté des tailles et aultres charges et subsides tant ordinaires qu'extraordinaires. Paris: 1576.

CORDEMOY, Gérard. Divers traitez de métaphysique, d'histoire et de politique. Paris: 1691.

COURTILZ de SANDRAS, Gatien. L'Alcoran de Louis XIV ou le testament politique du cardinal Jules Mazarin, traduit de l'italien. Roma (Hollande?): 1691.

————. Nouveaux intérests des princes de l'Europe, où l'on traite des maximes qu'ils doivent observer pour se maintenir dans leurs états et pour empecher qu'il ne se forme une monarchie universelle. La Haye: 1685.

————. Testament politique du marquis de Louvois. Cologne: 1695.

————. Testament politique de messire Jean Baptiste Colbert, ministre et secrétaire d'état, où l'on voit tout ce qui s'est passé sous le règne de Louis le Grand jusqu'en l'année 1684, avec des remarques sur le gouvernement du royaume. La Haye: 1693.

————. Vie de J. B. Colbert, ministre d'état sous Louis XIV, roi de France. Cologne: 1695.

CRUCE, Emeric. Nouveau Cynée ou Discours d'Estat représentant les occasions et moyens d'establir une paix générale et la liberté du commerce par tout le monde. Paris: 1623.

CTESIPHON, A. Le labyrinthe de l'estat, ou les véritables causes des malheurs de la France. Paris: 1652.

DANGEAU, Philippe de Courcillon, marquis de. Mémoires, Eds. Soulié, Dussieux, Mantz, Montaiglon, de Chennevières, Feuillet de Conches. 19 vols.; Paris: 1854-1860.

DEPPING, B. Correspondance Administrative sous le règne de Louis XIV. 4 vols.; Paris: 1850-1855.

DESCARTES, René. Oeuvres. Ed. C. Adam and P. Tannery. 10 vols.; Paris: 1897-1910.

DESMAISONS, François. Traité des aydes, tailles et gabelles. Paris: 1666.

DOMAT, Jean. Les lois civiles dans leur ordre naturel, le droit public. . . . 5 vols.; Paris: 1692.

DUCROT, Lazare. Le nouveau traité des aides, tailles et gabelles. Paris: 1636.

DU VAIR, Guillaume. Oeuvres. Paris: 1625.

EON, Jean. Le commerce honorable. Nantes: 1646.

ERASMUS, Desiderius. The Education of a Christian Prince. Trans. L. K. Born. New York: 1936.

FENELON, François de Salignac de la Motte. Oeuvres. 10 vols.; Paris: 1851-1852.

————. Les Aventures de Télémaque. Ed. A. Cahen. 2 vols.; Paris: 1927.

FENELON, Ecrits et lettres politiques de Fénelon. Ed. Charles Urbain. Paris: 1920.

————. Traité de l'existence et des Attributs de Dieu. Ed. A. Aulard. Paris: 1874.

FLEURY, Claude. Opuscules. Ed. L. E. Rondet. 5 vols.; Nismes: 1780-1783.

————. Oeuvres. Ed. M. Aimée-Martin, Paris: 1837.

FONTENELLE, B. le Bovier de. Oeuvres. Ed. J.B.J. Champagne. 5 vols.; Paris: 1825.

FORBONNAIS, Véron de. Recherches et considérations sur les finances de France depuis l'année 1595 jusqu'à l'année 1721. 2 vols.; Bâle: 1758.

FORTIN DE LA HOGUETTE, Philippe. Eléments de la politique selon les principes de la nature. Paris: 1663.

FOUCQUET. Les oeuvres de M. Foucquet ministre d'Estat contenant son accusation, son proces et ses défenses, contre Louis XIV Roy de France. 16 vols.; Paris: 1696.

FOURNIER, George. Hydrographe contenant la théorie et la practique de toutes les parties de la navigation. Paris: 1643.

FRANKLIN, Alfred. Mémoire confidentiel adressé à Mazarin après la mort de Richelieu. Paris: 1870.

GARASSE, François. Somme théologique des véritez capitales de la religion chrestienne. Paris: 1625.

GIBONAIS, Jean Artur de la. De l'usure, intérest et profit qu'on tire du Prest; ou l'ancienne doctrine sur le Prest usuraire opposée aux nouvelles opinions. Paris: 1710.

GROTIUS, Hugo. Three Books on the Law of War and Peace. Ed. James Brown Scott, The Classics of International Law, Vol. III. Oxford: 1925.

HAYEM, J., Ed. Mémoires et documents pour servir à l'histoire du commerce et de l'industrie en France. 12 séries. Paris: 1911-1929.

HOBBES, Thomas. English Works. Ed. Molesworth. 11 vols.; London: 1839.

———. Leviathan. Ed. M. Oakeshott. Oxford: 1955.

HOTMAN, Antoine. "Deux paradoxes de l'amitié et de l'avarice," Opuscules françoises des Hotmans. Paris: 1616, pp. 113-183.

HUET, Pierre Daniel. Le grand trésor historique et politique du florissant commerce des Hollandois dans tous les états et empires du monde. Rouen: 1712.

ISAMBERT, JOURDAN, DECRUSY, ARMET and GAILLANDIER. Recueil général des anciennes lois françaises . . . jusqu'à la révolution de 1789. 29 vols.; Paris: 1821-1833.

LAFFEMAS, B. de. Les trésors et richesses pour mettre l'estat en splendeur et monstrer au vray la ruine des françois par le trafic et négoce des estrangers: et empescher facilement les petits procez en toute vacation; voir comme la justice des consuls doit etre supprimée, et autres belles raisons. Le Tout pour le bien de ce royaume. Paris: 1598.

———. L'incrédulité ou l'ignorance de ceux qui ne veulent cognoistre le bien & repos de l'estat & veoir renaistre la vie heureuse des françois. Paris: 1600.

———. Advis et remonstrance à MM. les commissaires députez du roy au faict du commerce avec les moyens de soulager le peuple des tailles et autre bien nécessaire pour la police du royaume. Paris: 1600.

———. Les Discours d'une liberté générale et vie heureuse pour le bien du peuple. Paris: 1601.

———. Comme l'on doibt permettre la liberté du transport de l'or et de l'argent hors du royaume: et par tel moyen conserver le nostre et attirer celuy des estrangers. Paris: 1602.

———. La Commission, édit et partie des mémoires de l'ordre et establissement du commerce général des manufactures en ce royaume. Paris: 1601. Also in Collection de documents inédits sur l'histoire de France, Mélanges historiques, IV, xiii-lxvi. Ed. M. Champollion-Figeac.

————. La Façon de faire et semer la graine des meuriers, les eslever en pépinieres, et les replanter aux champs: gouverner et nourrir les vers à soye au climat de la France, plus facilement que par les mémoires de tous ceux qui en ont escript. Paris: 1604. Also in Mémoires et documents sur la sériculture. Montpellier: 1877.

————. Le Plaisir de la noblesse et autres qui ont des éritages aux champs, sur la preuve certaine et profict des estouffes et soyes qui se font à Paris, Orléans, Tours, et Lyon pour l'année 1603. Paris: 1603.

————. Discours sur la figure du roy eslevée à la porte de la maison de ville. 2d ed. Paris: 1607.

————. Advertissement et responce aux marchands et autres, ou il est touché des changes, banquiers, et banqueroutiers. Paris: 1609.

————. Advertissement sur les divers crimes des banqueroutiers, suivant les édicts et ordonnances des roys de France. Paris: 1609.

————. Advis sur l'usage des passements d'or et d'argent. Paris: 1610.

LAMY, Bernard. Entretiens sur les Sciences dans lesquelles outre la méthode d'étudier on apprend comme l'on doit se servir des sciences pour se faire l'esprit juste et le coeur droit et pour se rendre utile à l'Eglise. . . . Grenoble: 1683.

LA NOUE, François de. Discours politiques et militaires. Basle: 1587.

LA ROCHEFOUCAULD. Oeuvres. Ed. L. Gilbert. 3 vols.; Paris: 1868.

LARTIGUE, Jean de. La politique des conquérans. Paris: 1661.

LAW, John. Oeuvres complètes. Ed. P. Harsin. 3 vols.; Paris: 1934.

LE BLANC, François. Traité historique des monnoies depuis le commencement de la monarchie jusqu'à présent. Paris: 1690.

LE DIEU, François, abbé. Mémoire sur le Quiétisme. Ed. E. Levesque. "Revue Bossuet," VIII, supplément 7, 1909, pp. 19-56.

LEFEVRE d'ORMESSON, Olivier. Journal. Ed. A. Chéruel. 2 vols.; Paris: 1860.

LELONG, Jacques. Bibliothèque historique de la France. 5 vols.; Paris: 1769, new edition.

LE MOYNE, Pierre. Les peintures morales. 2d edn. 2 vols.; Paris: 1654.

————. L'Art de Régner. Paris: 1665.

LE PELLETIER, Jean. Mémoires pour le rétablissement du commerce en France . . . pour etre presentez à Nos Seigneurs du Conseil du Commerce. Rouen: 1701.

[LE VASSOR], Michel. Les soupirs de la France esclave qui aspire apres la liberté. 1689.

LIPSIUS, Justus. Two Bookes of Constancie. Ed. Rudolf Kirk, New Brunswick, 1939.

LOPPIN, Isaac. Advis tres juste et légitime au Roy tres Chrestien pour le repos et soulagement des trois ordres de son estat et le moyen de dresser une milice de cinquante mil hommes pour la décharge de toutes Tailles, Taillons, Aydes, Gabelles, et générallement tous subsides et impots tant anciens que nouveaux. No date nor place of publication.

LOUIS XIV. Mémoires de Louis XIV pour l'instruction du dauphin. Ed. J. Longnon. Paris: 1927.

LOYSEAU, Charles. Cinq Livres du Droit des Offices. Paris: 1610.

————. Traicté des Seigneuries. Paris: 1613.

————. Traicté des Ordres et simples Dignitez. Paris: 1613.

MACHIAVELLI, Niccolo. The Discourses. Trans. Leslie J. Walker. 2 vols.; London: 1950.

MAINTENON, Madame de. Lettres. Ed. M. Langlois. 5 vols.; Paris: 1935-1939.

MALEBRANCHE, N. de. De la recherche de la Vérité. Ed. G. Lewis. Paris: 1946.

―――. Traité de la Nature et de la Grâce. "Oeuvres complètes de Malebranche," Vol. V; Paris: 1958.

MALLET, J. R. Comptes rendus de l'administration des finances du royaume de France, pendant les onze dernières années du règne de Henri IV, le règne de Louis XIII, et soixante cinq années de celui de Louis XIV. . . . London and Paris: 1789.

MARIOTTE, Edmé. Essai de Logique. Paris: 1678.

MARSILIUS OF PADUA. Defensor pacis. Trans. A. Gewirth. 2 vols., New York: 1951, 1956.

MAYER, Charles Joseph, ed. Des Etats Généraux et Autres Assemblées Nationales. 18 vols.; La Haye: 1789.

MAYERNE, Turquet de la. La monarchie aristodémocratique. Paris: 1611.

MAZARIN, Jules, Cardinal. Lettres du Cardinal Mazarin pendant son ministere, recueillies et publiées par M. A. Chéruel. In "Collection de documents inédits sur l'histoire de France," I⁰ Série, Histoire politique, 9 vols.

MERCURE FRANCOIS. Paris: 1611-1648. Published under official auspices. Vols. XII, XIII, and XIV especially reflect the views of Richelieu's government.

MOLE, Mathieu. Mémoires. In "Société de l'histoire de France," ed. Aimé Champollion-Figeac. 4 vols.; Paris: 1855-1857.

MONTAIGNE, Michel de. Essays. Trans. Donald Frame, Stanford, 1957.

MONTCHRETIEN, Antoyne de. Traicté de l'oéconomie politique. Ed. Funck-Brentano. Paris: 1889.

MORE, Thomas. Utopia and a Dialogue of Comfort. Edn. Everyman's Library. London and New York: 1946.

MORERI, L. Le grand dictionnaire historique. Paris: 1759.

MOTHE LE VAYER, François de la. Quatre dialogues faits à l'imitation des Anciens. Paris: 1930.

NAUDE, Gabriel. Considérations politiques sur les coups d'Estat. Rome: 1639.

——. Mémoire confidentiel adressé à Mazarin après la mort de Richelieu. Ed. Alfred Franklin. Paris: 1870.

NICOLE, Pierre. Essais de morale contenus en divers traittés sur plusieurs devoirs importans. 13 vols.; Paris: 1714-1715.

NOIRAYE, Voysin de la. Mémoire sur la généralité de Rouen. Ed. E. Esmonin. Paris: 1913.

PALATINE, Charlotte-Elisabeth de Bavierre, Princesse. Correspondance de Madame la Duchesse d'Orléans. Ed. E. Jaeglé. 3 vols.; Paris: 1890.

PASCAL, Blaise. Pensées et Opuscules. Ed. L. Brunschvicg. Paris: 1945.

PERRIERE, Guillaume de la. The Mirrour of Policie: A Worke no lesse profitable than necessarie, for all Magistrates, and Gouvernours of Estates and Commonweales. London: 1958.

PERWICH, William. The Despatches of William Perwich, English Agent in Paris 1669-1677. Ed. Beryl Curran. London: 1903.

PHELIPEAUX, Jean, abbé. Relation de l'origine, du progrès et de la condamnation du Quiétisme répandu en France. 2 vols.; no place of publication: 1732.

POMPONNE, Arnauld de. Relation de mon ambassade en Hollande. Ed. H. Rowen. Utrecht: 1955.

POTTIER DE LA HESTROYE, J. Réflexions sur le traité de la Dixme de M. le Maréchal de Vauban. Paris: 1716.

PRIMAUDAYE, Pierre de la. Troisieme tome de l'Académie Françoise. Lyon: 1599.

——. L'Académie Françoise. Saumur: 1613.

RICHELIEU, A. J. du Plessis, Cardinal de. Testament

politique d'Armand du Plessis Cardinal duc de Richelieu. Amsterdam: 1688.

————. Lettres, instructions diplomatiques, et papiers d'état du cardinal de Richelieu, recueillies et publiées par M. d'Avenel. In "Collection de documents inédits sur l'histoire de France," Ie Série, Histoire politique, 9 vols.

————. Maximes d'état et fragments politiques du cardinal de Richelieu. Pub. by M. Gabriel Hanotaux. In "Collection de documents inédits sur l'histoire de France, Melanges historiques, choix de documents," Vol. III.

————. Succincte Narration des grandes actions du roi. In "Nouvelle Collection des Mémoires relatifs à l'histoire de France depuis le XIIIe siècle jusqu'à la fin du XVIIIe siècle, Vol. XXIII. Ed. Michaud and Poujoulat. Paris: 1854. This work is often printed as an introduction to the *Testament Politique*.

————. Mémoires sur le règne de Louis XIII, depuis 1610 jusqu'à 1638. In "Nouvelle Collection des mémoires relatifs à l'histoire de France depuis le XIIIe siècle jusqu'à la fin du XVIIIe siècle," Vols. XXI, XXII, XXIII. Ed. Michaud and Poujoulat. Paris: 1857. These memoirs are generally accepted as authentic, that is, as compiled by Richelieu's secretaries under his supervision.

————. Instruction que le roi a commandé etre mise entre les mains des commissaires envoyes aux provinces pour l'exécution de ses lettres de déclaration en forme d'Edit. . . . Pub. in Lazare Du Crot, "Traité des aides, tailles et gabelles." Paris: 1636.

SAINT-EVREMOND. Oeuvres de Monsieur de Saint-Evremond, avec la vie de l'auteur. Par Monsieur Des Maizeaux, Membre de la Société Royale. Nouvelle édition, ornée de Figures et Vignettes en taille-douce. 5 vols.; Paris: 1740.

SAINT-SIMON. Mémoires. Ed. A. de Boislisle. 41 vols.; Paris: 1879-1928.

SAVARY, Jacques. Le Parfait Négociant ou instruction générale pour ce qui regarde le commerce de toute sorte de marchandises, tant de France que des pays estrangers. Paris: 1675. In two books paged separately but bound as one volume.

SAVARY des BRUSLONS, Jacques and SAVARY, Philémon Louis. Dictionnaire universel de commerce, d'histoire naturelle et des arts et métiers. 5 vols.; Copenhagen: 1759.

SENAULT, J. Le monarque ou les devoirs du souverain. Paris: 1661.

SEYSSEL, Claude de. La grande monarchie de France et deux autres fragments politiques. Ed. Jacques Poujol. Paris: 1961.

SILHON, Jean. Le Ministre d'Estat avec le véritable usage de la politique moderne. Paris: 1665.

————. De la certitude des connoissances humaines ou sont particulièrement expliquez les principes et les fondemens de la Morale et de la Politique. . . . Paris: 1661.

SORBIERE, Samuel. Relations, Lettres et Discours de M. de Sorbière sur diverses matieres curieuses. Paris: 1660.

————. Discours sceptique. Pub. in Les mémoires de Michel de Marolles, abbé de Villeloin. Paris: 1656.

SOURCHES, L. F. du Bouchet, marquis de. Mémoires secrets et inédits de la cour de France sur la fin du règne de Louis XIV. Ed. de Cosnac, Bertrand and Pontal. 13 vols.; Paris: 1882-1883.

SPANHEIM, E. Relation de la Cour de France en 1690. Ed. E. Bourgeois. Lyon: 1900.

SULLY, Maximillien de Béthune, Duc de. Mémoires des sages et royalles oeconomies d'estat, domestiques, politiques, et militaires de Henry le Grand . . . et des servitudes utiles, obéissances convenables et administrations loyales de Maximillien de Béthune, l'un des plus confidens, familiers et utiles soldats et serviteurs du grand Mars des françois. In "Nouvelle Collection des mémoires relatifs à l'histoire de France depuis le XIIIe siècle jusqu'à la fin du XVIIIe siècle." Vols. II and III, ed. Michaud and Poujoulat. 32 vols.; Paris: 1854.

THIMOLEON, François, abbé de Choisy. Mémoires. Ed. M. de Lescure. Paris: 1888.

QUINCY, le Chevalier de. Mémoires. Ed. L. Lecestre. 3 vols.; Paris: 1898.

VAUBAN, Sébastien le Prestre de Vauban, sa famille et ses écrits. Ses oisivetés et sa correspondance. Ed. R. D'Aiglun. 2 vols.; Paris: 1910.

————. Dixme royale, suivie de deux écrits financiers. Ed. E. Coornaert. Paris: 1933.

VIVES, Juan Luis. L'Aumonerie. Lyon: 1583.

————. Introduction à la Sagesse. Paris: 1670.

Secondary Works

ADAM, Antoine. Histoire de la littérature française au XVIIe siècle. 5 vols.; Paris: 1949-1956.

————. Sur le problème religieux dans la premièie moitié du XVIIe siècle. Oxford: 1959.

ANDRE, Louis. Michel Le Tellier et l'organisation de l'armée monarchique. Paris: 1906.

————. Michel Le Tellier et Louvois. Paris: 1943.

————. Louis XIV et l'Europe. Paris: 1950.

ASCOLI, George. La Grande-Bretagne devant l'opinion Française au XVIIe siècle. 2 vols.; Paris: 1930.

ASHER, E. L., The Resistance to the Maritime Classes: the Survival of Feudalism in the France of Colbert. Berkeley and Los Angeles: 1960.

ASHLEY, M. P. Financial and Commercial Policy under the Cromwellian Protectorate. London: 1934.

ATKINSON, G. The Extraordinary Voyage in French Literature before 1700. New York: 1900.

AVENEL, le vicomte G. de. Richelieu et la monarchie absolue. 4 vols.; Paris: 1887.

——. Etude d'histoire sociale. La noblesse française sous Richelieu. Paris: 1901.

BAMFORD, Paul. Forests and French Sea Power 1600-1789. Toronto: 1956.

BARBOUR, Violet. Capitalism in Amsterdam in the Seventeenth Century. "The Johns Hopkins University Studies in Historical and Political Science," Series LXVII, Vol. I, Baltimore: 1950.

BARNWELL, H. T. Les idées morales et critiques de Saint-Evremond. Paris: 1957.

BARON, Hans. The Crisis of the Early Italian Renaissance: Civic Humanism and Republican Liberty in an Age of Classicism and Tyranny. Princeton: 1955.

BATTIFOL, L. Richelieu et le roi Louis XIII. Paris: 1934.

BAUDRILLART, H. J. Bodin et son temps. Paris: 1853.

BAULANT, M. and MEUVRET, J. Prix des céréales extraits de la Mercuriale de Paris (1520-1698). 2 vols.; Paris: 1960-1962.

BECKER, A. Henri. Un humaniste du XVIe siècle: Loys Le Roy de Coutances. Paris: 1896.

BENICHOU, P. Morales du Grand Siècle. Paris: 1948.

BLANCHET, Léon. Les antécédents historiques du "je pense, donc je suis." Paris: 1920.

——. Campanella. Paris: 1920.

BLET, P. Le clergé de France et la monarchie. 2 vols.; Rome: 1959.

BODIN DE SAINT-LAURENT, Jean de. Les Idées monétaires et commerciales de Jean Bodin. Bordeaux: 1907.

BOISSONNADE, P. Colbert, le triomphe de l'étatisme,

la fondation de la suprématie industrielle de la France, la dictature de travail 1661-1683. Paris: 1932.

―――. Essai sur l'organization du travail en Poitou depuis le XIe siècle jusqu'à la Révolution. 2 vols.; Paris: 1900.

―――. Le socialisme d'état, l'industrie et les classes industrielles en France pendant les deux premiers siècles de l'ère moderne, 1453-1661. Paris: 1927.

――― and CHARLIAT, P. Colbert et la compagnie de commerce du Nord 1661-1689. Paris: 1930.

BOITEUX, L. A. Richelieu, grand maître de la navigation et du commerce de France. Paris-Caen: 1955.

BONNASSIEUX, P. Les Grandes Compagnies de Commerce. Paris: 1892.

BOURELLY, Jules. Le Maréchal de Fabert 1599-1662. 2 vols.; Paris: 1880-1881.

BOURGEOIS, E. Manuel historique de politique étrangère, I. Paris: 1892.

―――― and L. ANDRÉ. Les sources de l'histoire de France au XVIIe siècle 1610-1715. 8 vols.; Paris: 1913-1935.

BOUWSMA, William J. Concordia Mundi: the Career and Thought of Guillaume Postel, 1510-1581. Cambridge, Mass.: 1957.

BRAUDEL, Fernand. La Méditerranée et le monde méditerranéen à l'époque de Philippe II. Paris: 1949.

BREMOND, Henri. Histoire littéraire du sentiment religieux en France. 12 vols.; Paris: 1929-1933.

――――. La querelle du Pur Amour au temps de Louis XIII. Paris: 1932.

BUSSON, H. La Pensée religieuse française de Charron à Pascal. Paris: 1933.

CAILLET, J. L'administration en France sous le ministère du cardinal de Richelieu. 2 vols.; Paris: 1863.

CANS, A. L'organisation financière du Clergé de France. Paris: 1911.

————. La contribution du clergé de France à l'impôt pendant la deuxième moitié du règne de Louis XIV, 1689-1715. Paris: 1911.

CARCASSONE, E. Montesquieu et le problème de la Constitution Française au XVIIIe siècle. Paris: 1927.

————. Etat présent des travaux sur Fénelon. Paris: 1939.

CELESTE, Raymond. Louis Machon, apologiste de Machiavel, et de la politique du cardinal de Richelieu: Recherches sur sa vie et ses oeuvres. Bordeaux: 1882.

————. Louis Machon, apologiste de Machiavel . . . nouvelles recherches sur sa vie et ses oeuvres 1600-1672. Bordeaux: 1883.

CHARBONNEL, J. R. La Pensée italienne et le courant libertin. Paris: 1917.

CHAUVIRE, Roger. Jean Bodin, auteur de la "République." Paris: 1914.

CHEREL, Albert. La pensée de Machiavel en France. Paris: 1935.

————. Fénelon ou la religion du pur amour. Paris: 1934.

————. De Télémaque à Candide. Paris: 1933.

CHERUEL, A. De l'administration de Louis XIV (1661-1672) d'après les Mémoires inédits d'Olivier d'Ormesson. Paris: 1850.

————. Histoire de France pendant la minorité de Louis XIV. 4 vols.; Paris: 1879-1880.

————. Mémoires sur la vie publique et privée de Fouquet, surintendant des finances. 2 vols.; Paris: 1862.

CHESNEAU, Charles (Julien-Eymard d'Angers). Le Père Yves de Paris et son temps (1590-1678). 2 vols.; Paris: 1946.

CHINARD, G. En lisant Pascal. Geneva: 1948.

CILLEULS, A. des. Histoire et régime de la grande industrie aux XVIIe et XVIIIe siècles. Paris: 1898.

CLAMAGERAN, Jean-Jules. Histoire de l'impôt en France. 3 vols.; Paris: 1867-1876.

CLARK, G. N. The Dutch Alliance and the War Against French Trade. Manchester: 1923.

———. The Seventeenth Century. 2d ed. London: 1947.

CLEMENT, Pierre. Le Gouvernement de Louis XIV, ou la cour, l'administration, et le commerce de 1683 à 1689. Paris: 1848.

———. Histoire de la vie et de l'administration de Colbert—précédée d'une étude historique sur Nicolas Fouquet—suivie de pièces justificatives. Paris: 1846.

———. Histoire du système protectioniste en France, depuis le ministère de Colbert jusqu'à la révolution de 1848-1854. Paris: 1854.

———. La police sous Louis XIV. Paris: 1866.

———. Histoire de Colbert. 2 vols.; Paris: 1874.

COGNET, Louis. Les origines de la spiritualité française au XVIIe siècle. Paris: 1949.

———. Crépuscule des Mystiques: le conflit Fénelon-Bossuet. Tournai: 1958.

———. Le Jansénisme. Paris: 1964.

COLE, C. W. Colbert and a Century of French Mercantilism. 2 vols.; New York: 1939.

———. French Mercantilism 1683-1700. New York: 1943.

———. French Mercantilist Doctrines before Colbert. New York: 1931.

COORNAERT, E. Les Corporations en France avant 1789. Paris: 1941.

DAHLGREN, M. E. W. Les relations commerciales maritimes entre la France et les côtes de l'Océan Pacifique. Paris: 1909.

DARESTE DE LA CHAVANNE, M. C. Histoire de l'administration en France. 2 vols.; Paris: 1848.

DEDIEU, J. Le Rôle politique des protestants français, 1685-1715. Paris: 1925.

DEPITRE, Edgar. La toile peinte en France au XVIIe et XVIIIe siècles. Paris: 1912.

DERBLAY, Claude. Un drame sous Louis XIV: l'affaire du Chevalier Rohan. Paris: 1945.

DESAUTELS, Alfred R. Les mémoires de Trévoux et le mouvement des idées au XVIIIe siècle, 1701-1734. Rome: 1956.

DREYFUS, Ginette. La Volonté selon Malebranche. Paris: 1958.

DRUON, H. Histoire de l'éducation des princes dans la maison des Bourbons de France. 2 vols.; Paris: 1897.

DUBOIS, A. Précis de l'histoire des doctrines économiques. Paris: 1903.

DUCASSE, R. L'Amiral Ducasse. Paris: 1876.

DUGAST-MATIFEUX, C. Le Commerce honorable, et son auteur. Nantes: 1854.

DUMAS, René. La Politique financière de Nicolas Desmaretz. Paris: 1927.

DUPRONT, H. Pierre Daniel Huet et l'exégèse comparatiste au XVIIe siècle. Paris: 1930.

ESMONIN, E. La taille en Normandie au temps de Colbert 1661-1683. Paris: 1913.

FEBVRE, Lucien. Le problème de l'incroyance au XVIe siècle: La religion de Rabelais. Paris: 1962.

FIGGIS, J. N. Political Thought from Gerson to Grotius 1414-1625. London: 1907.

GABORY, Emile. La marine et le commerce de Nantes au XVIIIe siècle. Rennes: 1901.

GAQUERE, François. La vie et les Oeuvres de Claude Fleury 1640-1723. Paris: 1925.

GIRARD, Albert. Le commerce français à Séville et Cadix au temps des Habsbourgs. Paris: 1932.

GAZIER, A. Histoire générale du mouvement janséniste. 2 vols.; Paris: 1922.

GILSON, E. Introduction à l'étude de St. Augustin. Paris: 1943.

GIRBAL, François. Bernard Lamy: étude biographique et bibliographique. Paris: 1964.

GLASSON, E. D. Histoire du droit et des institutions de la France. 8 vols.; Paris: 1887-1903.

GOLDMANN, Lucien. Le Dieu caché: étude sur la vision tragique dans les "Pensées" de Pascal et dans le théâtre de Racine. Paris: 1955.

GORE, J.-L. L'Itinéraire de Fénelon: Humanisme et Spiritualité. Paris: 1957.

GOUBERT, Pierre. Beauvais et le Beauvaisis de 1600 à 1730: contribution à l'histoire sociale de la France du XVIIe siècle. Paris: 1960.

————. Familles marchandes sous l'ancien régime: les Motte et les Danses de Beauvais. Paris: 1961.

GOUHIER, Henri. La philosophie de Malebranche et son expérience religieuse. Paris: 1948.

GROETHUYSEN, Bernard. Origines de l'esprit bourgeois en France. Paris: 1927.

HARSIN, Paul. Les doctrines monétaires et financières en France du XVIe au XVIIIe siècle. Paris: 1928.

————. Crédit public et banque d'état en France du XVIe au XVIIIe siècles. Paris: 1933.

HAUSER, Henri. Travailleurs et marchands dans l'ancienne France. Paris: 1929.

————. La pensée et l'action économiques du Cardinal de Richelieu. Paris: 1944.

————. François de la Noue (1531-1591). Paris: 1892.

HAUSSONVILLE, Le comte d'. La duchesse de Bourgogne et l'alliance Savoyarde sous Louis XIV. 4 vols.; Paris: 1909.

HAZARD, Paul. La crise de la conscience européenne. 2 vols.; Paris: 1935.

HECKSCHER, E. F. Mercantilism. Trans. Mendel Shapiro. 2 vols.; London: 1935.

HEXTER, J. H. More's Utopia: the Biography of an Idea. Princeton: 1952.

JOPPIN, Gabriel. Une querelle autour de l'Amour pur, Jean-Pierre Camus, évêque de Belley. Paris: 1938.

JOURDAN, Emile. Ephémérides de La Rochelle. 2 vols.; La Rochelle: 1871.

JOUVENCEL, H. de. Le contrôleur général des finances sous l'ancien régime. Paris: 1901.

KAEPPELIN, Paul. La Compagnie des Indes Orientales et François Martin. Paris: 1908.

KING, James E. Science and Rationalism in the Government of Louis XIV 1661-1683. "The Johns Hopkins University Studies in Historical and Political Science," Series LXVI, Vol. II, Baltimore: 1949.

KIRKENEN, Heikki. Les origines de la conception moderne de l'homme-machine: le problème de l'âme en France à la fin du règne de Louis XIV (1670-1715). Helsinki: 1960.

KRAILSHEIMER, A. J. Studies in Self-Interest from Descartes to La Bruyère. Oxford: 1962.

KUHN, T. S. The Copernical Revolution, Planetary Astronomy in the Development of Western Thought. Cambridge, Mass.: 1957.

LABROUSSE, C. E. Esquisse du mouvement des prix et des revenus en France au XVIIIe siècle. Paris: 1932.

LACHEVRE, A. Les oeuvres libertines de Cyrano de Bergerac. 2 vols.; Paris: 1921.

LACOUR-GAYET, Georges. L'Education politique de Louis XIV. Paris: 1898.

LAIR, Jules. Nicolas Foucquet. 2 vols.; Paris: 1890.

LARDE, G. La Capitation dans les pays de taille personnelle. Paris: 1906.

LA RONCIERE, Charles de. Histoire de la marine française. 6 vols.; Paris: 1899-1932.

LAVISSE, E. Louis XIV de 1643 à 1685. "Histoire de France." Vols. IV, V, VI, VII, VIII. Paris: 1911.

LECLERQ, Henri. Dom Mabillon. 2 vols.; Paris: 1953-1957.

LEGRELLE, G. La diplomatie française et la succession d'Espagne. 4 vols.; Paris: 1888-1892.

LEVASSEUR, Emile. Histoire des classes ouvrières en France avant 1789. 2 vols.; Paris: 1900-1901.

———. Histoire du commerce de la France. 2 vols.; Paris: 1911.

LIVET, Georges. L'Intendance d'Alsace sous Louis XIV. Strasbourg: 1956.

LIZERAND, G. Le duc de Beauvillier, 1648-1714. Paris: 1933.

LOMBARD, A. L'abbé du Bos, un initiateur de la pensée moderne, 1670-1742. Paris: 1913.

LUCAY, le comte de. Les secrétaires d'Etat depuis leur institution jusqu'à la mort de Louis XV. Paris: 1881.

LUTHY, H. La Banque protestante en France de la Révocation de l'Edit de Nantes à la Révolution. 2 vols.; Paris: 1959-1962.

LY, Abdoulaye. La compagnie du Sénégal. Paris: 1958.

MACPHERSON, C. B. The Political Theory of Possessive Individualism. Oxford: 1962.

MAJOR, J. R. Representative Institutions in Renaissance France 1421-1559. Madison: 1960.

MALO, Henri. Les corsaires dunkerquois et Jean-Bart. Paris: 1913.

MARION, Marcel. Dictionnaire des institutions de la France aux XVIIe et XVIIIe siècles. Paris: 1923.

MARTIMORT, A. G. Le Gallicaniame de Bossuet. Paris: 1953.

MARTIN, Gaston. Nantes et la compagnie des indes orientales, 1664-1679. Paris: n.d.

MARTIN, Germain and M. Bezançon. Histoire du crédit en France sous le règne de Louis XIV. Paris: 1913.

———. La grande industrie sous le règne de Louis XIV. Paris: 1898.

MARTIN, Victor. Le gallicanisme politique et le clergé de France. Paris: 1929.

————. Les origines du gallicanisme. 2 vols.; Paris: 1939.

MASSON, Paul. Histoire du commerce français dans le Levant au XVIIe siècle. Paris: 1896.

MATHOREZ, J. Les Etrangers en France sous l'ancien régime. 2 vols.; Paris: 1919-1921.

MATTHEWS, George T. The Royal General Farms in Eighteenth Century France. New York: 1958.

MEINECKE, F. Machiavellism. Trans. from the German by W. Stark. New Haven: 1957.

MIMS, S. L. Colbert's West India Policy. New Haven: 1912.

MITARD, Stanislas. La crise financière en France à la fin du XVIIe siècle: la première capitation, 1695-1698. Rennes: 1934.

MONGREDIEN, Georges. L'Affaire Foucquet. Paris: 1956.

————. Le bourreau du cardinal de Richelieu; Isaac de Laffemas. Paris: 1929.

MOREAU, A. de Jonnès. Etat économique et social de la France depuis Henri IV jusqu'à Louis XIV. Paris: 1867.

MORINI-COMBY, J. Mercantilisme et protectionisme. Paris: 1930.

MORIZE, André. L'Apologie du luxe au XVIIIe siècle et "Le Mondain" de Voltaire: étude critique sur le mondain et ses sources. Paris: 1909.

MORNET, Daniel. Les Origines intellectuelles de la révolution française. Paris: 1933.

MOUSNIER, Roland. La vénalité des offices sous Henri IV et Louis XIII. Rouen: 1949.

————. Les XVIe et XVIIIe siècles. Paris: 1956.

NICOLLIERE-TEIJEIRO, S. de La. La course et les corsaires du port de Nantes. Paris: 1896.

ORCIBAL, Jean. Les origines du Jansénisme. 5 vols.; Paris: 1947-1962.

————. Louis XIV contre Innnocent XI. Paris: 1949.

ORCIBAL, Jean. Louis XIV et les protestants, la cabale des accomodeurs de religion, la caisse des conversions, la révocation de l'Edit de Nantes. Paris: 1951.

―――. Le premier Port Royal: réforme ou contre-réforme? Paris: Centre de documentation universitaire, 1956.

PAGES, Georges. La Monarchie d'ancien régime. 5th edn. Paris: 1952.

―――. Louis XIV et le Grand Electeur. Paris: 1905.

PALMER, R. R. Catholics and Unbelievers in Eighteenth Century France. Princeton: 1939.

PICAVET, C. G. La diplomatie française au temps de Louis XIV, 1661-1715. Paris: 1930.

―――. Les dernières années de Turin. Lille: 1914.

PICCIONI, Camille. Les premiers commis des affaires aux XVIIe et XVIIIe siècles. Paris: 1928.

PINOT, V. La Chine et la formation de l'esprit philosophique en France. Paris: 1932.

PINTARD, René. Le libertinage érudit dans la première moitié du XVIIe siècle. 2 vols.; Paris: 1943.

POPKIN, Richard H. The History of Scepticism from Erasmus to Descartes. Assen, the Netherlands: 1960.

PORCHNEV, Boris. Les soulèvements populaires en France de 1623 à 1648. Paris: 1963.

PRECLIN, Edmond. Les Jansénistes du XVIIIe siècle et la constitution civile du Clergé. Paris: 1928.

PROYART, abbé. Vie du Dauphin, père de Louis XIV. 2 vols.; Paris: 1782.

PRZYREMBEL, A. La controverse théologique et morale entre Saint-Cyran et le P. Garasse. Paris: 1917.

PUYOL, Edouard. Edmond Richer, étude historique et critique sur la rénovation du gallicanisme au commencement du XVIIe siècle. 2 vols.; Paris: 1876.

RANUM, Orest A. Richelieu and the Councillors of Louis XIII. Oxford: 1963.

REYNOLDS, Beatrice. Proponents of Limited Monarchy

in Sixteenth Century France: Francis Hotman and Jean Bodin. New York: 1931.

ROBERTS, Hazel Van Dyke. Boisguilbert: Economist of the Reign of Louis XIV. New York: 1935.

ROSENFIELD, L. C. From Beast-Machine to Man-Machine. New York: 1941.

ROUPNEL, G. Les populations de la ville et de la campagne dijonnaise au XVIIe siècle. Paris: 1922.

ROUSSET, C. Histoire de Louvois et de son administration politique et militaire. 4 vols.; Paris: 1862-1864.

ROWEN, Herbert H. The Ambassador Prepares for War, the Dutch Embassy of Arnauld de Pomponne, 1669-1671. The Hague: 1957.

RUYSSEN, Théodore. Les sources doctrinales de l'internationalisme. 2 vols.; Paris: 1951, 1958.

SAGNAC, Philippe. La formation de la société française moderne. 2 vols.; Paris: 1946.

SAINTE-BEUVE, Denys Eugène de. Port-Royal. 7 vols.; Paris: 1878.

SAINT-GERMAIN, Jacques. Samuel Bernard le banquier des rois. Paris: 1960.

SCELLE, Georges. La traite négrière aux Indes de Castille. 2 vols.; Paris: 1906.

SCHMITTLEIN, M. R. L'aspect politique du différend Bossuet-Fénelon. Baden: 1954.

SCHMOLLER, Gustav. The Mercantile System and Its Historical Significance. New York: 1910.

SCOVILLE, Warren C. The Persecution of the Huguenots and French Economic Development 1680-1720. Berkeley and Los Angeles: 1960.

SEE, Henri. Les idées politiques en France au XVIIe siècle. Paris: 1923.

————. Histoire économique de la France. 2 vols.; Paris: 1939-1942.

SEGUR-DUPEYRON, P. de. Histoire des négotiations

commerciales et maritimes de la France au XVIIe et XVIIIe siècles. 3 vols.; Paris: 1872-1873.

SILBERNER, E. La guerre dans la pensée économique du XVIe au XVIIIe siècle. Paris: 1939.

SIMON, R. Henri de Boulainvillier 1658-1722. Paris: 1951.

SPOONER, Frank C. L'économie mondiale et les frappes monétaires en France 1493-1680. Paris: 1956.

SPINK, J. S. French Free-Thought from Gassendi to Voltaire. London: 1960.

STOURM, R. Finances de l'ancien régime: les systèmes généraux d'impôts. 2 vols.; Paris: 1885.

STROWSKI, Fortunat. Histoire du sentiment religieux en France au XVIIe siècle: Pascal et son temps. 3 vols.; Paris: 1921-1922.

TALBOT, A. Les théories de Boisguilbert et leur place dans l'histoire des doctrines économiques. Paris: 1903.

TAPIE, V. L. La France de Louis XIII et de Richelieu. Paris: 1952.

THOMAS, A. Une Province sous Louis XIV, situation politique et administrative de la Bourgogne. Paris: 1844.

TOCQUEVILLE, Alexis de. The Old Regime and the French Revolution. Trans. Stuart Gilbert, Anchor Book. New York: 1955.

TRECA, G. Les doctrines et les réformes de droit public en réaction contre l'absolutisme de Louis XIV dans l'entourage du duc de Bourgogne. Lille: 1909.

USHER, A. P. The History of the Grain Trade in France, 1400-1710. Cambridge: 1913.

VENE, André. Montchrétien et le nationalisme économique. Paris: 1923.

VIGNES, J. B. Maurice. Histoire des doctrines sur l'impôt en France: les origines et les destinées de la Dixme Royale de Vauban. Paris: 1909.

VIOLLET, Paul. Le Roi et ses ministres pendant les trois derniers siècles de la monarchie. Paris: 1912.

VOELTZEL, R. F. Jean Domat, 1625-1696: Essais de reconstruction de sa philosophie juridique précédés de la biographie du jurisconsulte. Paris: 1936.

VOLTAIRE, F. M. A. de. Le Siècle de Louis XIV. New edn., 2 vols.; Paris: 1929-1930.

VUITRY, A. Le désordre des finances et les excès de la spéculation dans les quinze dernières années du règne de Louis XIV. Paris: 1885.

WADE, Ira. The Clandestine Organization and Diffusion of Philosophic Ideas in France from 1700 to 1750. Princeton: 1938.

WILLEY, Basil. The Seventeenth Century Background. London: 1934.

WOODBRIDGE, B. M. Gatien de Courtilz sieur du Verger: étude sur un précurseur de roman réaliste en France. "The Johns Hopkins Studies in Romance Literature and Languages," Vol. V, Paris and Baltimore: 1925.

WOODBRIDGE, Homer E. Sir William Temple: the Man and his Work. New York and Oxford: 1940.

WYBO, Bernard. Le Conseil de commerce et le commerce intérieur de la France au XVIIIe siècle. Paris: 1936.

ZANTA, Léontine. La Renaissance du stoicisme au XVIe siècle. Paris: 1914.

Articles

ASHLEY, W. J. "Traicté de l'oeconomie politique" (Review), English Historical Review (October 1891).

BOISSONNADE, P. "Colbert, son système et les entreprises industrielles d'état en Languedoc, 1661-1683," reprint from Annales du Midi, XIV (1902).

————. "Colbert et la souscription aux actions de la compagnie des Indes, spécialement en Poitou, 1664-1668," reprinted from the Bulletin de la Société des Antiquaires de l'Ouest (1908).

BOITEUX, L. A. "Un économiste méconnu: Du Noyer de Saint-Martin 1608-1639," Revue d'histoire des colonies, XLIV (1957), 5-68.

BONDOIS, P. M. "La Misère sous Louis XIV, la disette de 1662." Revue d'histoire économique et sociale, XII (1924), 53-118.

BRAUER, Walter. "Quelques remarques sur l'oeuvre économique de Vauban," Revue d'histoire économique et sociale, XXIX (1951), 8-25.

BROMLEY, J. S. "Le Commerce de la France de l'Ouest et la Guerre Maritime," Annales du Midi (1953), pp. 49-66.

——. "The French Privateering War, 1702-1713," Historical Essays 1600-1750 Presented to David Ogg (London, 1963), pp. 203-231.

BUTLER, K. T. "Louis Machon's 'Apologie Pour Machiavelle'—1643 and 1668," Journal of The Warburg and Courtauld Institutes, III (1939-1940), 208-227.

CAIN, Julien, "Les mémoires des députés au conseil de commerce de 1700," Revue d'histoire moderne et contemporaine, XVIII (1913), 5-20.

CARDASCIA, G. "Machiavel et Jean Bodin," Bibliothèque d'humanisme et renaissance. III (1943) 129-167.

CHALLE, A. "Documents statistiques," Annuaire historique du département de l'Yonne (Auxerre, 1853).

CHEMIN-DUPONTES, P. "Les Compagnies de colonisation de l'Afrique occidentale sous Colbert," Revue coloniale, (1902-1903), pp. 339-372, 451-494, 600-619, 717-739; (1903-1904), pp. 99-124. Also published in book form (Paris: 1903).

CHILL, Emanuel Stanley, "The Company of the Holy Sacrament (1630-1666): Social Aspects of the French

Counter Reformation." Doctoral Dissertation, Columbia University, 1960.

DELAFOSSE, M. "La Rochelle et les Isles au XVIIe siècle," Revue d'histoire des colonies, XXXVI (1949), 238-281.

DELUMEAU, Jean. "Le commerce Malouin à la fin du XVIIe siècle," Annales de Bretagne, LVI (1959), 263-286.

DEXTER, G. "Guillaume de la Perrière," Bibliothèque d'humanisme et renaissance, XVII (1955) 56-73.

DEYON, Pierre. "A propos des rapports entre la noblesse française et la monarchie absolue pendant la première moitié du XVIIe siècle," Revue historique, CCXXXI (1964), 341-356.

DUCROQ, Théodore. "Le mémoire de Boulainvillier sur le droit d'amortissement des gabelles et la conversion du revenu des aides, antérieurs au Détail de Bois-guilbert et à la Dîme Royale de Vauban," Etudes d'histoire financière et monétaire (Poitiers: 1887), pp. 3-32.

ESMONIN, E. "Les mémoires des intendants pour l'instruction du duc de Bourgogne," Bulletin de la société d'histoire moderne (8 January 1956).

ESPINAS, Alfred. "La troisième phase et la dissolution du mercantilisme," Revue internationale de sociologie, X (1902), 161-180.

GIRAUD, Marcel. "Crise de conscience et d'autorité à la fin du règne de Louis XIV," Annales, économies, sociétés, civilisations (April-September 1952), pp. 172-190; 293-302.

GIRBAL, François. "La formation Augustinienne du P. S. Lamy, de l'Oratoire (1660-1680)," Société des amis de Port Royal, VIII (1957), 48-85.

GRASSBY, R. B. "Social Status and Commercial Enterprise under Louis XIV," The Economic History Review, 2d series, XIII (1960), 19-38.

HARSIN, Paul. "Vauban ou Boulainviller?" Bulletin de

la société d'histoire moderne (October 1936), p. 183.

HARTUNG, Franz, and MOUSNIER, R. "Quelques problèmes concernant la monarchie absolue," Relazioni del X congresso internazionale di scienze storiche, IV (1955), 1-55.

HAUSER, Henri. "The Characteristic Features of French Economic History from the Middle of the Sixteenth to the Middle of the Eighteenth Century," Economic History Review, IV (1933), 257-272.

———. "Le Colbertisme avant Colbert et la liberté du travail sous Henri IV, Lyon et Tours, 1596-1601," Revue bourguignonne de l'enseignement supérieur, VIII, 3-69.

———. "Le Système social de Barthélemy de Laffemas," Revue bourguignonne de l'enseignement supérieur, XII, 113-131.

HERLAUT, Colonel. "Projets de création d'une banque royale en France à la fin du règne de Louis XIV, 1702-1712," Revue d'histoire moderne (1933), pp. 143-160.

JANNET, Claudio. "Le monde de la finance au XVIIe siècle," Journal des économistes, X (1892), 68-86.

KANTOROWICZ, Ernst A. *"Pro patria mori* in Medieval Political Thought," American Historical Review. LVI (April 1951), 472-492.

LAFFITTE. "Notice sur Barthélemy de Laffemas," Journal des économistes (May 1876), pp. 181-218.

LANDES, David S. "The Statistical Study of French Crises," Journal of Economic History, X (1950), 195-211.

LANE, Frederic C. "The Economic Meaning of War and Protection," Journal of Social Philosophy and Jurisprudence, VII (April 1942) 254-270.

LANGLOIS, Marcel. "Le journal du ministre Chamillart ou les mémoires attribués au marquis de Sourches," reprint from Comptes-rendus de l'Académie des Sciences Morales et Politiques (Paris: 1925).

LANSON, Gustave. "Questions diverses sur l'histoire de l'esprit philosophique en France avant 1750," Revue d'histoire littéraire de la France (1912).

———. "Origines et premières manifestations de l'esprit philosophique dans la littérature française de 1675 à 1748," Revue des cours et conférences (1907-1909).

———. "Le rôle de l'expérience dans la formation de la philosophie du XVIIIe siècle en France, Revue du mois, IV.

LEONARD, Emile-G. "Le Protestantisme français au XVIIe siècle," Revue Historique, CC (1948), 153-179.

LEVY-BRUHL, Henri. "Les différentes espèces de sociétés de commerce en France aux XVIIe et XVIIIe siècles," Revue historique de droit français et étranger, 4th series, XVI (1937), 294-332.

LORSON, P. "Guerre et paix chez Fénelon," Le XVIIe siècle, nos. 12-14, Numéro Spécial, Fénelon et le tricentenaire de sa naissance 1651-1951 (1951-1952), 207-214.

MAJOR, J. Russell. "The French Renaissance Monarchy as Seen through the Estates General," Studies in the Renaissance, IX (1962), 113-125.

MAURY, Alfred. "Une conspiration républicaine sous Louis XIV," Revue des Deux Mondes, LXXVI (July-August 1886), 376-406, 756-784.

MEUVRET, Jean. "Comment les Français voyaient l'impôt au XVIIe siècle?" Le XVIIe siècle, XXV-XXVI (1955), 59-82.

———. "Les mouvements des prix de 1661 à 1715 et leurs répercussions," Journal de la Société de Statistique de Paris (May 1944).

———. "Circulation monétaire et utilisation économique de la monnaie dans la France du XVIe et du XVIIe siècles," Etudes d'histoire moderne et contemporaine, I (1947), 15-28.

MONGREDIEN, G. "Isaac de Laffemas d'après des documents inédits," Revue des questions historiques (January 1928), pp. 5-114; (April 1928), pp. 257-299.

MOUSNIER, Roland. "Sully et le conseil d'état et des finances: la lutte entre Bellieure et Sully," Revue historique, CXCII (1941), 68-86.

————. "Le Conseil du Roi, de la mort de Henri IV au gouvernement personnel de Louis XIV," Etudes d'histoire moderne et contemporaine, I (1947), 29-67.

————. "L'Opposition politique bourgeoise à la fin du XVIe siècle et au début du XVIIe siècle: L'oeuvre de Louis Turquet de Mayerne," Revue historique, CCXIII (1955), 1-20.

————. "Monarchie contre Aristocratie dans la France du XVIIe siècle," Le XVIIe siècle, no. 31 (April 1956), pp. 377-381.

————. "Recherches sur les soulèvements populaires en France avant la Fronde," Revue d'histoire moderne et contemporaine, V (1958), 81-113.

PAGES, Georges. "L'Evolution des institutions administratives en France du commencement du XVIe siècle à la fin du XVIIe," Revue d'histoire moderne, VII (1932), 8-57.

————. "La vénalité des offices dans l'ancienne France," Revue historique, CLXIX (1932), 477-495.

————. "Autour du grand orage. Richelieu et Marillac: deux politiques," Revue historique, CLXXIX (1937), 63-97.

PITHON, R. "A propos du testament politique de Richelieu," Revue Suisse d'histoire, VI (1956), 177-214.

POPKIN, Richard H. "Skepticism and the Counter-Reformation in France," Archive für Reformationgeschichte, LI (1960), 58-86.

PRECLIN, Edmond. "Edmond Richer (1559-1631), sa vie, son oeuvre, le Richérisme," Revue d'histoire moderne, V (1930), 241-269, 321-336.

REBELLIAU, A. "Bossuet et les débuts de Louis XIV,"

Revue des Deux Mondes, XLI (1927), 826-859; XLII (1928), 117-141, 306-328.

ROCHOT, Bernard. "Pierre Gassendi: la vie, le caractère et la formation intellectuelle," Centre international de Synthèse, Pierre Gassendi, sa vie et son oeuvre 1592-1655 (Paris: 1955), 48-54.

ROTHKRUG, Lionel. "Critiques de la politique commerciale et projets de réforme de la fiscalité au temps de Colbert," Revue d'histoire moderne et contemporaine, VIII (April-June 1961), 83-102.

SAGNAC, Philippe. "L'histoire économique de la France de 1683 à 1714," Revue d'histoire moderne et contemporaine, IV (1902-1903) 5-15, 89-97.

―――. "La politique commerciale de la France avec l'étranger de la paix de Ryswick à la paix d'Utrecht," Revue historique, CIV (1910), 265-285.

―――. "Le crédit d'Etat et les banquiers en France à la fin du XVIIe siècle et au commencement du XVIIIe," Revue d'histoire moderne, X (1908) 257-272.

SCHATZ, Albert, and CAILLEMER, Robert. "Le mercantilisme libéral à la fin du XVIIe siècle en France. Les idées économiques et politiques de M. de Belesbat," Revue économique et politique, XX (1906), 29-70; 387-396; 559-574; 630-642; 791-816.

SEE, Henri. "Le commerce des étrangers et notamment des Hollandais à Nantes pendant la minorité de Louis XIV," Tijdschrift voor Geschiedenis (1926), pp. 246-260.

―――. "L'activité commerciale de la Hollande à la fin du XVIIe siècle," Revue d'histoire économique et sociale, XIV (1926), 200-253.

―――. "Le Commerce Français à Cadix et dans l'Amérique espagnole au XVIIIe siècle," Revue d'histoire moderne (1928), pp. 13-31.

―――. "Quelques aperçus sur le capitalisme commercial en France au XVIIe siècle," Revue d'histoire économique et sociale, XII (1924), 161-176.

―――. "Que faut-il penser de l'oeuvre économique de Colbert?" Revue historique, CLII (May-August 1926), 181-194.

SOMMER, L. "Mercantilisme et théorie de la valeur," Revue d'histoire économique et sociale, XIV (No. 1, 1927), 5ff.

SONNINO, Paul. "The Dating and Authorship of Louis XIV's *Mémoires*," French Historical Studies, III (Spring 1964), 303-337.

STROWSKI, Fortunat. "Etudes critiques et morales sur Bossuet," Annales de Philosophie chrétienne, XLIII (1900-1901), 257-269; 579-594.

TENTLER, Thomas N. "The Meaning of Prudence in Bodin," *Traditio*, XV (1959), 365-384.

THUILLIER, Guy. "Economie et administration au grand siècle," La Revue Administrative, LVIII (1957), 348-357.

―――. "Manuscrits inédits du XVIIe siècle: les 'maximes politiques' du Duc de Montausier," La revue administrative (May 1962), pp. 262-272.

VANIER, Georges. "Une famille de grands marchands Rouennais aux XVIe et XVIIe siècles: les Le Gendre," Société libre d'émulation du commerce et de l'industrie de la Seine-Inférieure (Dieppe: 1950).

VIARD, Pierre-Paul. "La dime en France au XVIIe siècle," Revue historique, CLVI (1927), 241-268.

VIGNOLS, Léon. "Le commerce maritime et les aspects du capitalisme commercial à Saint-Malo de 1680 à 1792," Revue d'histoire économique et sociale, XXX (1931), 9-27.

WILSON, C. H. "The Other Face of Mercantilism," Transactions of the Royal Historical Society, 5th series, 9 (1959), 81-101.

WOLF, John B. "The Reign of Louis XIV: A Selected

Bibliography of Writings since the War of 1914-1918," Journal of Modern History, XXXVI (June 1964), 127-144.

ZELLER, Gaston. "Le commerce international en temps de guerre sous l'Ancien Régime," Revue d'histoire moderne et contemporaine, IV (1957), 112-120.

INDEX